RENDERING
THINGS
VISIBLE

RENDERING THINGS VISIBLE

Essays
on South African Literary Culture

Edited by
Martin Trump

Ohio University Press • Athens

First published by Ravan Press, Johannesburg, 1990

Ohio University Press edition published with permission from Ravan Press

Printed in the United States of America
97 96 95 94 93 92 91   5 4 3 2 1

Ohio University Press books are printed on acid-free paper

Library of Congress Cataloging-in-Publication Data
Rendering things visible : essays on South African literary culture /
  edited by Martin Trump. -- Ohio University Press ed.
      p.   cm.
    Reprint. Originally published: Johannesburg : Ravan Press, 1990.
        Includes bibliographical references
    ISBN 0-8214-0988-3. -- ISBN 0-8214-0993-X (pbk.)
    1. South African literature (English)--History and criticism.
    2. Literature and society--South Africa. 3. South Africa-
    -Intellectual life. 4. South Africa in literature.   I. Trump,
    Martin.
    PR9355.2.R46 1991
    820.9'968--dc20   90-25740
                                                          CIP

Contents

The Contributors

David Attwell lectures in English at the University of the Western Cape. As a fellow of the University of Texas at Austin he has been associated with the journal *Research in African Literatures*. He is currently completing a doctoral dissertation on J.M. Coetzee, concentrating on the relationship between the structuralisms and history.

Stephen Clingman has degrees from the Universities of the Witwatersrand and Oxford. He has been a visiting and research fellow at Yale, Witwatersrand and Cornell Universities. He is the author of *The Novels of Nadine Gordimer: History from the Inside* (Ravan: 1986) and has edited and introduced a collection of Nadine Gordimer's essays, *The Essential Gesture* (Taurus/David Philip: 1988). He lectures in the English Department at the University of Massachusetts, Amherst.

Ampie Coetzee studied at the University of the Witwatersrand and did graduate work at the University of Ghent, Belgium. He has lectured on Afrikaans and Dutch literatures at the Universities of Natal and the Witwatersrand. He is presently professor of South African literature in the Afrikaans Department at the University of the Western Cape. His publications include *Poësie en Politiek* (1976) and *Marxisme en die Afrikaanse Letterkunde* (1988).

Brenda Cooper has a doctoral degree from the University of Sussex, and teaches African literature at the Centre for African Studies, University of Cape Town.

Jeremy Cronin is a poet and activist. His publications include *Inside*, a collection of poems written while he was serving a prison sentence for his political work, and *Thirty Years of the Freedom Charter*.

Dorothy Driver is a senior lecturer in the English Department at the University of Cape Town, and has published various essays on writing by South African women. She is also the South African correspondent to *Journal of Commonwealth Literature* (London), where she publishes an annual bibliography and survey of the year's work in South African literature and literary criticism. Her book, *Pauline Smith and the Crisis of Daughterhood*, is due from David Philip Publishers early in 1990.

Dirk Klopper teaches in the Department of English at Vista University: Mamelodi campus. He has published in the field of literary theory and is currently doing research on South African English poetry.

Eddie Koch has degrees from the University of the Witwatersrand. His M.A. examined popular culture in Johannesburg of the 1920s and 1930s. At present he is labour reporter for the *Weekly Mail*.

David Maughan-Brown is professor of English at the University of Natal in Pietermaritzburg. He is the author of *Land Freedom and Fiction: History and Ideology in Kenya* (Zed: 1985), which examines the literature, including popular fiction, written about 'Mau Mau'.

Karen Press completed an honours degree in African Studies at the University of Cape Town in 1987. Her article in this collection is a reworking of sections of the dissertation: 'Towards a Revolutionary Artistic Practice in South Africa'. She has published a collection of poetry, *This Winter Coming*, and a book of children's stories, *Children of Africa*.

Rory Ryan teaches in the English Department at the University of South Africa. He has published in literary theory.

Kelwyn Sole holds degrees from the Universities of the Witwatersrand and London. He lectures in the English Department at the University of Cape Town.

Ian Steadman is head of the School of Dramatic Art at the University of the Witwatersrand. He is co-editor of the *South African Theatre Journal* and associate editor of *Critical Arts*.

Martin Trump is a lecturer in the English Department at the University of South Africa. He co-edited with Kofi Buenor Hadjor a thematic issue of *Third World Book Review* (1986) on Writers and Artists Against Apartheid. He has edited *Armed Vision: Afrikaans Writers in English* (Donker: 1987).

Michael Vaughan works in the English Department at the University of Natal, Durban. He has published widely in the field of South African literature.

Nicholas Visser lectures in the English Department at the University of Cape Town. For several years he edited the journal *English* *in Africa* and he has co-edited with Tim Couzens *H.I.E. Dhlomo: Complete Works* (Ravan: 1985). He has published widely on literary theory, English fiction, and South African writing.

Hein Willemse is a senior lecturer in South African literature in the Afrikaans Department, University of the Western Cape. He has published academic articles, a book of poetry, *Angsland,* and co-edited *Die Trojaanse Perd* and *Swart Afrikaanse Skrywers.*

Introduction

The 1970s and 1980s have been particularly turbulent decades for South Africa. The country has been torn apart, to an extent not evident earlier in the century, by discordant ideologies. The ethnic mobilization of Afrikaners to secure economic and political mastery for themselves has achieved spectacular success, but has also found itself challenged both within and beyond Afrikanerdom and the South African ruling class. The period is characterized by repression, revolt and the spectre of an increasingly disabled South African economy.[1] All this has led to an overwhelming politicization of consciousness in South Africa.

In a situation as inexorably politicized as that of South Africa today, why should the study of the country's literature compel our interest? What special claims can one make for literary studies in such a fraught context?

Let us attempt to answer these questions by posing another. In what ways do literary works and their study add to our knowledge of society? Literary works and their study offer particularly complex ways of describing society. Literature occupies terrain which it shares with a large number of social discourses. What one perceives in literary works is an opening up of a broad discursive area: what one critic has called literature's 'fundamental entanglement with all discourses' (Lentricchia, 1980: 351).[2] The hybrid, polysemic discourse of literature includes and might even be said to enlarge the epistemological realm of other discourses.

It is through this understanding of literature that I think one can offer some affirmative answers to the questions posed earlier. There is an interplay of discourses in literature — an intertextuality — not usually apparent in the discourses of politics, history and the social sciences. A number of contributors to this book have noted, moreover, certain distinguishing features of literary discourse which tend to set it apart from other discursive forms. The polysemic rather

Warm thanks to Michael Green and Rory Ryan for their comments on the first draft of this introduction.

than univocal character of literary works; the subjective reference; the subjective address; and the particular prescience of literary works are features that receive detailed examination in this book. Taken together, all of this suggests the importance of being attentive to the forms of address and reference within South African literary discourse.

The discussion above, however, also points to a potential con-. tradiction: namely, that while there is an interplay of different discourses in literature, literature appears to be distinguishable as a discourse having its own particular characteristics. This is an area for intense debate within materialist criticism. The kind of questions that have been raised take the form of: does one admit to the existence of 'literariness' (a set of distinguishing codes within literature)? That is, is there such a discipline as *literary* studies — separate and legitimate?

The responses to these questions are numerous. Yet most materialist critics agree about literature's complex insertion within a broad socio-cultural terrain, rather than regarding it as an apparently autonomous practice. Materialist criticism clearly rejects what Dirk Klopper calls in his essay the 'ultimately idealist binary system' which opposes the socio-historical with the literary, where the former is viewed as 'the material exteriority of a mystifying interiority'. Critical disaffection with this opposition is most clearly revealed in the following two ways in this book. Stephen Clingman, David Attwell and Brenda Cooper refer in their essays to the opposition J.M. Coetzee perceives between the discourses of literature and history (Coetzee, 1988: 3). In their own way, each rejects Coetzee's proposal that the relationship between these discourses is one of 'rivalry, even enmity' (1988:3), and suggests the relationship is best understood in terms of the interpenetration of these discourses and their complementarity. Secondly, and possibly with more far-reaching consequences, a number of contributors develop a critical methodology which bases itself on a semiological understanding of material processes. Here the disjunction between the real or material world and the linguistically formed constructs of literature is opened up to radical questioning by an understanding of the *discursive* means by which society constructs reality. In his book *Marxism and Literary History*, John Frow argues that precisely because it is not possible to appeal to a form of reality outside the discursive, 'the decisive criterion of analysis can thus no longer be the relation between discourse and a reality which is external to it . . . . Instead, the relevant criterion is that of the relations between discourse and *power*, the intrication of power in discourse.' (1986: 57)[3]

Rendering Things Visible, the title of this book, is derived from two sources: a statement of Paul Klee's — 'Art does not reproduce the visible, art makes visible' — quoted by Karen Press in her essay, and a set of comments made by Brenda Cooper in hers. Aware that I am deflecting wind from Cooper's sails I would, nonetheless, like to quote her conclusion, in which certain crucial aspects of the notion of 'rendering things visible' are made explicit:

> The critical battle is not to colonize, but to cultivate, a new territory. This new ground could be fertilized with enlightened and appropriate priorities, and, perhaps even more importantly, visible and overt debates around those priorities. Tolerance and flexibility remain essential ingredients and should not be placed in false opposition to the commitment to a better life for people. This is said knowing that the foregoing has run the risk of accusations of prescriptiveness. I would contend that all serious critics, readers and writers bring values, priorities and hierarchies to bear on what they read and write. Prescription lies only in the concealment of these, thereby rendering them authoritative without question.

These comments have relevance vis-à-vis two sites of social power that are of central concern in this book: the political government of South Africa; and South African universities (and, more particularly, literature departments within them). Let us consider with reference to these two sites of power several consequences that flow from a critical practice that bases itself on principles of rendering things visible, of laying structures bare.

The process antithetical to rendering things visible is one of distortion, repression and concealment. It is not insignificant that the current political government of South Africa is based to a very large extent precisely on forms of repression and concealment. Processes and practices which set out to expose areas of state repression are, by implication, termed revolutionary.[4] They form part of a culture of resistance.

Similar processes of repressive concealment characterize, at less brutal and extreme levels, most literature departments in the country.[5] Rory Ryan speaks of institutionalized literary studies in South Africa as being dominated by a humanist agenda which 'dovetails with the ideals and activities of a civilized and civilizing colonial patriarchy'. He goes on to suggest that 'the institutionalization of an imperialist discursive form under the guise of a neutral (objective, truth-serving, self-evident, ideologically disinterested) rationality is the source of current cultural-social power in the South African academy'.

What are the implications of this, particularly for the kind of critical practice displayed in this book? In the first place, oppositional critical voices are subjected to a complex process of disablement by the South African literary academy. Ryan is eloquent in his account of this:

> First, oppositional discourses are ignored. Secondly, they are recuperated and marginalized; shoved into a corner or put to use by the hegemony. Thirdly, if these blatantly dismissive strategies fail, a polarization or strategic opposition is created . . . . All oppositional forces are reduced to a set of bad-mannered activities.

As a result, the force of oppositional critical thinking is marvellously dispersed and its impact diminished by the literary academy. Power remains locked within a discursive terrain defined and maintained by a colonial hegemony.

A further consequence of this institutional repression — the maintenance of a lily-white South African literary academy — is clearly and sadly evident in this book. Affirmative action programmes, while in practice at a small number of South African universities and often only in certain of their departments, have scarcely been promoted, and in most cases have been rejected in literature departments. Tertiary-level literature teaching and criticism is, like most sites of power in South Africa, by and large a white preserve.[6]

This repressive context suggests a gloomy outlook for socially responsible and self-questioning criticism in South Africa. However, one needs to recall that criticism is responsive and answerable mercifully not only to the academy as site of power, but to people (students) in society and to forces of change in society. Criticism does not operate in an entirely closed circuit.

Processes of socio-political democratization in South Africa are beginning to be reflected in a democratization of critical concerns and practices. This is most clearly displayed in the essays by David Maughan-Brown, Jeremy Cronin and Ian Steadman, which extend our notions of literature with their consideration of populist forms, but a responsiveness to democratic processes is apparent throughout the book. One sees here how criticism is consciously linked to those processes of democracy that are slowly transforming the dynamics of social structuring and interaction in South Africa. This is responsible criticism in the fullest sense of the word.

Martin Trump
Johannesburg
July 1989

Notes

1. I shall not be offering a detailed characterization of this period in South Africa. Such a formidable task is beyond the scope of this book. I suspect, moreover, that many readers will have more than a passing familiarity with the politico-socio-economic history of South Africa during the 1970s and 1980s. All the essays in this book refer in greater or lesser detail to this history. The concluding section of David Attwell's essay offers a lucid account of key elements in the history of this period and — apart from consulting authoritative monographs — readers may also wish to refer specifically to Ampie Coetzee's essay which traverses the terrain in a fascinating way.
2. In her essay in this volume, Brenda Cooper refers in similar fashion to 'the huge space of fiction'.
3. Shortly afterwards, Frow goes on to argue that:

   The distinction between the real and symbolic realms is not ontologically given but is a social and historical result. The discursive is a socially constructed reality which constructs the categories of the real and the symbolic and this distinction between them. It assigns structures to the real at the same time as it is a product and a moment of real structures. It therefore covers a spectrum of semiotic systems from both realms. Thus 'material' structures — for example specific work processes — are also immediately symbolic structures (structures of power — that is, the meaningful position of individuals within these processes). (1986: 58)

4. For a penetrating analysis of this kind of critical practice, which suggests some of its inherent complexities and contradictions, see Paul Ricoeur's *Lectures on Ideology and Utopia* (1986).
5. The term 'repressive concealment' is drawn from Rory Ryan's characterization of South African literature departments.
6. This dismal state of affairs is reflected in this book, where 16 of the 17 contributors are white. There are very few black critics in South Africa, of whom only a tiny group are working in the field of materialist criticism. My editorial range was thus severely curtailed as a result of educational imbalances in the country.

References

Coetzee, J.M. 1988. 'The Novel Today'. *Upstream*, 6(1), 1-4.
Frow, John. 1986. *Marxism and Literary History*. Cambridge, Mass.: Harvard University Press.
Lentricchia, Frank. 1980. *After the New Criticism*. Chicago: University of Chicago Press.
Ricoeur, Paul. 1986. *Lectures on Ideology and Utopia*. (ed.) George Taylor. New York: Columbia University Press.

Literary-Intellectual Behaviour in South Africa[1]

Rory Ryan

There is no document of civilization which is not at the same time a document of barbarism. And just as such a document is not free of barbarism, barbarism taints also the manner in which it was transmitted. A historical materialist therefore dissociates himself from it as far as possible. He regards it as his task to brush history against the grain.

> — *Walter Benjamin*

Critique from the point of view of endlessly revisionist imagining must become critical practice carried out in the historically specific, situated locale of the critic's work. Without such a return to history, oppositional criticism remains little more than yet another variation of the self-empowering, transcendent, ironic practice of practical and New Critics alike.

> — *Paul Bové*

For what is critical consciousness at bottom but an unstoppable predilection for alternatives?

> — *Edward Said*

In South Africa, institutionalized literary studies have been, and continue to be, dominated by the humanist agenda insofar as humanism dovetails with the ideals and activities of a civilized and civilizing colonial patriarchy. This humanist-colonial agenda has overshadowed, and used, the New Critical programme for its own ends. The apparent quarrel between the colonial-humanist belief in the direct and immediate grasp of truth within texts and the New Critical insistence on formal methods, universal keys and literariness is dwarfed by the persistence of the humanist ontotheological tradi-

---

This essay first appeared in *boundary 2*, 15(3), Spring 1988.

tion. New Criticism might still insist that it has the key for unlocking texts, but the treasured prize nevertheless remains humanist truth.

One of the most seriously hegemonic and repressive gestures produced by humanism has been to offer up its social-cultural goals as 'truth', and its methods (of self-perpetuation and glorification) as 'truth-seeking'. The recoverability of transhistorical truth is thus at once demonstrated and subordinated to humanist authority, so creating the idea of real knowledge beyond time and ensuring that no unauthorized personnel ever 'find' this knowledge. The idea of truth, in South African literary studies (as in its English and American antecedents), acts as a supremely justifying technique for all dominant cultural-intellectual practice, by removing such practice from struggles of power, legitimation and authority. One must applaud the cleverness of this operational device, while expressing dismay at the massive shut-down of intellectual argument and investigation which it causes. It is necessary that humanist truth is seen as no more or less than the act of venerating and protecting imperialistic group interest. Hegemonic discursive practice represses, marginalizes and recuperates all rival practices in order to present itself as crucial; its existence is a sign of limitation and closure masquerading as freedom, invigoration and necessity. The widespread use of the term 'truth' is always the signal that, temporarily, one from a number of competing interest groups (in this case, the colonial-humanist tradition) has successfully suppressed all oppositional voices, so that not one of these oppositional voices is strong enough to expose the ridiculously self-congratulatory nature of the claim to truth/objective knowledge.

The South African College (later the University of Cape Town) was founded in 1929, although the B.A. degree with English was first offered in 1873.[2,3] Professor James Cameron (Cape Town) made the following pronouncements in an essay in 1869:

> We wish to *educate* the higher nature — to bring out its powers, to make its ear delicately keen to all the deep harmonies of Truth, and its eye quick to discern the spiritual beauties which other eyes have not seen and duller ears have never heard. And whatever helps to do this is an element in true education — *useful* in the large and noble sense of the word — a living stone in the walls of an Eternal Temple.
>
> It is not memory alone and the reasoning faculties that need culture, — the judgment, the taste, the imagination, the sense of beauty must be cared for.

The end of all literary studies is to expand the mind by familiarity with the noblest products of the human intellect.

It is a rich inheritance that we have received, and if we would hand it down not impoverished, but strengthened, it must be by duly appreciating the relations that we bear to it. They who have no past can have no future. It is as wise for races as for individuals to wish their 'days to be bound each to each in natural piety;' and an indispensable condition to our contributing anything to other generations, either in science, literature, or politics, is that we forbear to look on what we have as the fruit of our own toil, but reverently and gratefully own our debts to other and earlier nations.[4]

Neither the rhetoric nor the humanist-colonial agenda has altered significantly since then: ninety-nine years after the publication of this polemical outburst, Trevor Whittock (another university teacher of English literature) makes the following statement of group interest:

We are expatriates, and the literature we teach is expatriate too. This can be over-emphasized: our students are emerging into a world-wide English culture, and will have to come to terms with many people from places far away. Undoubtedly there is a case for providing them with terms of reference they can share with these others, including the common experience of a shared literary heritage. The twentieth century has given us a new sense in which Shakespeare is for the world and for all time. But the English literary heritage, even as seen in small groups of selected works, not to mention the European literary heritage, is overwhelming in power. Africa has nothing, as yet, in the way of literature to compare with it. Classics bear in their wake the full weight of English, of European, culture and civilization. The effect of this upon our students who become enthralled with the works they study could be to totally alienate them from their own culture and their own environment. I think we should guard against this if we can. Our aim is not to produce, if I may use a phrase of Dr Verwoerd's, 'black Englishmen'. But how do we guard against this? (1968: 91)

Here, the smugness, self-righteousness, paternalism, dismissive gesturing, and ontotheological posturing of humanist colonialism are most evident. English culture is given the 'centric' position — it is 'world-wide' — and all other cultures become eccentric.[5] The local student, whether English or Afrikaans, white or black, Indian or so-called 'coloured' must come to terms with English culture, rather than vice versa. Whittock then celebrates the continuation of humanist value-structures, by affirming the canonicity of Shakespeare for 'the world and for all time'. Africa can only kneel in the face of such 'overwhelming . . . power'. Civilization (the humanist-colonial-patriarchal agenda) will bear down inexorably.

Finally, Whittock does not forget the manners appropriate to an English gentleman by suggesting that 'we' must guard against alienating local students 'from their own culture and their own environment'.

Paul Bové, in his study of critical humanism, makes the following general statement, so applicable to the above passage:

> This humanistic project is politically and intellectually inappropriate. Its political liberalism is divisive, disciplinary, often oppressive and imperialistic; intellectually, it is self-contradictory, at best tragically belated, at most comically self-betraying. What is significant about it is its *power*. (1986: 303)

The institutionalization of an imperialist discursive form under the guise of a neutral (objective, truth-serving, self-evident, ideologically disinterested) rationality is the source of current cultural-social power in the South African academy. The situational, historical and ideological basis of the controlling voices in literary studies is effectively concealed. The so-called 'common-sensical' nature of Leavisite textual operations is no more than an indication that the hegemonic discursive practice has become firmly lodged, naturalized, and taken for granted as the site of literary studies rather than as a temporary invasion of that site. William Spanos reveals the repressive concealment of the humanist enterprise in this way:

> Despite its liberal and humane pretensions, disinterested or objective inquiry becomes, in fact, a theoretical mechanism of *super-vision*, domestication, and mastery — 'reformation' — grounded in an anthropological Norm or, more historically precise, an anthropological Norm established in the image of the dominant bourgeois/capitalistic culture: the *proper* self. (1984: 178)

All opposition is trivialized — literally. Consider the following pronouncement:

> . . . our civilization is not 'South African', except in trivial details; it is Western European, and more specifically as far as poetry written in English is concerned, English. Such poetry will therefore inevitably form a part of the general body and tradition of English literature. (Harvey, 1955: 93)

This humanist-colonial 'civilization' is the 'formidable library'[6] penetrating and controlling the production of cultural value. The social-cultural task of the colonialist is one of 'educating, liberalizing and salvaging from irreligious backwardness, a vast proletariat of both colours' (Partridge, 1958: 49). The humanist-colonial literary-intellectual enterprise has been sinister in its arrogance and complacency, in its seizure and indiscriminate use of cultural-social power, and in its swift and cynical marginalization of all oppositional critiques. That is not to say these critiques have been feeble.[7] Roy Campbell, one of the editors of *Voorslag* (a literary journal, begun in 1926, whose Afrikaans title translates as 'whiplash'), makes the following remark concerning hegemonic habits of mind:

> We are so afraid of liberty ourselves that we absolutely rely on discipline and live it better than anything on earth: this makes us suspicious of others who do not need the same amount of outward discipline. We forget that we are probably the most rapacious savages on the face of the globe, and that what we are pleased to call culture is little more than a vast array of instruments of destruction which we have had to invent for keeping each other in order. (1926a: 14)

And N.W. Visser, more than half a century later, continues the appeal to reject an ideology of repression and exclusion:

> Purporting to prepare people to read sensitively any literary work, practical criticism enables them to read only a drastically circumscribed set of texts and leaves them mute before all else. In a move that the clothiers to the emperor would relish, it then tells them the fault lies not in themselves but in all those other texts. Instead of encouraging our students to attempt to come to terms with the cultural products of classes and cultures other than our own, we have trained them in a rhetoric of contempt. (1984: 4)

It is, of course, possible to expose irrationality in the humanist-colonial literary-intellectual enterprise, and thus subject it to the cruelty of its own inaugurating oppositions of truth and falsity (reason/unreason). C. van Heyningen, in 1963, unwittingly reveals the epistemologically tangled consequences (for literary studies) of being at once civilized and civilizing. First, there is a clear appeal for textual autonomy and the recoverability of intact meaning, in the rhetoric of excited discovery:

> It is never enough to say of a passage, 'It is impressive', 'it is effective', 'it moves me', 'it is beautiful'. If he [the student] wants to make anyone believe him, to make anyone see what he sees in it, he must show exactly *what* impresses him, *what* the effect is, *how* he is moved and by *what*, and if possible *what* the beauty is. (And, of course, if he doesn't like the passage he ought to be able to demonstrate why not.) (1963: 55)

This is the grammar of civilized literary study. However, prominent in the figure of the gentleman-scholar is the gentleness of his
touch.[8] His voraciously imperialistic/exclusionary programme of
civilizing the world must be disguised by a 'deep concern' for the
preservation of native culture (evidenced as an afterthought in the
passage by Whittock, quoted above) and the 'rights' of the individual
response. Van Heyningen proceeds, immediately after the above
endorsement of objectivity in literary studies, to cherish the inaliena-
ble right of 'personal freedom' and subjective response to the literary work:

> At this point may we say that the sole value of a passage to each reader
> consists in its effect upon him personally. As far as he is concerned,
> it does not matter in the least what other people think and feel about
> it. (1963: 55)

It is gratifying to expose the dark spots, slippages and vacancies
in the humanist enterprise by employing its own founding oppositional structures of value (in this case, those of objectivity/subjectivi-
ty, truth/conjecture, etc.). However, the act of finding epistemological inconsistencies can be mean-minded, forcing the humanist to
eat his own words in order only to point to methodological inadequacy when, in fact, it is the cynical repressive-coercive strategies
of humanism, and not simply a methodological infelicity, one wants
to expose and condemn. It is so much simpler, more direct (and less
contaminated by the mechanisms of humanism) to expose the hegemony in literary studies as a gentleman's club, a back-patting society, a *laager* of good manners and mutual protection. All the talk
of truth, greatness and beauty can be seen as the jig performed by
a self-perpetuating bureaucracy of knowledge. Once again I turn
to William Spanos for an articulation of this phenomenon:

> . . . the professional ethics authorized by the humanistic discourse,
> essentially the polite ethics of the 'gentleman,' inhibits by colonizing
> radical dissent as ungentlemanly interestedness or partiality. More
> fundamentally, however, such evidence is not immediately available
> because, no less than the hard sciences, the work of selection is car-
> ried on inside the humanistic problematic — i.e., 'disinterested' evalu-
> ative action — and the decision and rationale for them transmitted
> in the 'disinterested' rhetoric of the humanistic discourse. . . . Because
> the professional ethics of civility — of 'Decorum' — has made the rela-
> tionship between the institutions of knowledge transmission and the
> individual contributor a highly private or clandestine affair — a con-
> spiracy of polite silence, as it were, grounded in the propriety of the
> proper self — the documents of which rarely enter the public domain,

one is compelled to rely on his or her own transactions with the cer-
tifying institution if he or she wishes to publicly interrogate or
challenge the philology of its discourse. And this breaking of the code,
of course, risks the accusation of pettiness or arrogance or resentment,
i.e., a failure of manners. (1984: 193)

There have been many failures of manners in the last fifty years,
as hegemonic discourse in South African literary studies has come
to be seen as temporally arrested, hypostatized, excessively curatorial and unmindful of its socio-political situation. Increasing numbers
of voices, from a variety of interest groups, have come to articulate
a sense of (at least) unease at the inappropriately dehistoricized
literary-critical academy, that which Michael Vaughan calls 'a sha-
dy spot for the refreshment of the harassed (white, petty bourgeois) . . .' (1984: 36).

However, the hegemony responds by way of three superbly successful manoeuvres. First, oppositional discourses are ignored.[9] Secondly, they are recuperated and marginalized; shoved into a corner or put to use by the hegemony. Thirdly, if these blatantly dismissive strategies fail, a polarization or strategic opposition is created, a very common manoeuvre in the history of the maintenance
of knowledge formations. All oppositional forces are reduced to a
set of bad-mannered activities. They are seen to display, among
other faults, excessive zeal, blatant bias, no 'real' interest in literature, crude Marxism, an unhealthy fascination for theory (far removed from the practicalities of unlocking transcendental literariness from *Hamlet* yet again), hysteria, subjectivism and brattish rebellion. The hegemony thus controls the way in which the oppositional programme will be perceived. The challenger becomes the
champion of 'un-': unnatural, illogical, irrational, unmannerly and
so on. By being cast into this dependence-opposition, the oppositional thinker is always portrayed as simply destructive, while the
idealism, courage and clear-thinking which often prompt opposition are ignored and parodied. Any epistemological-intellectual infe-
licities (discussed above) in the humanist-colonial programme pale
in comparison with the basic immorality of some of its practices.

A canon of hallowed literary texts is the word made flesh: the ideological structure which dominates the site of literary studies at any
given time nominates texts to be blessed in its name. The canon is
the holy icon which stands for (and stands in for) pure transcendental literariness. In South African literary studies, the transhistor-

ical configuration of exemplary texts reveals a great deal concerning the forces which maintain its glossy, healthy appearance. It must
be stressed that canons are culturally-specific monuments, and that
value is created and not discovered — all canons function in the
realm of cultural politics. South African departments of English
preserve and protect a broadly Leavisite set of texts. Chaucer,
Shakespeare, Milton, Pope, Wordsworth, Yeats and Eliot constitute
the measure of greatness. The dominant function of these departments is assumed to be the teaching of English literature, that is,
literature from England, with a few gentlemanly gestures to the 'colonies' (the USA, South Africa and Australia). There have always been
protests against this gross imperialism — R.K. Cope, for example,
asks in 1947 for the 'literature of England' to be held at arm's length:

> As a starting point, it appears to me necessary that the modern liter-
> ature of England should be treated with French, Spanish, Russian
> or other work as something *foreign*. The fact that contemporary Eng-
> lish writers are readily understood should not deceive us into the be-
> lief that their work is of the same significance to us as it is to them.
> (1947: 12)

The South African academy is principally responsible for canon
maintenance: it creates curricula, commissions works to be published, awards prizes, compiles anthologies and edits journals. But
there are numerous other participants directly involved in canon
maintenance: publishers (there is more than one instance of mutual back-scratching between specific publishers and sections of the
academy), journalists, reviewers, librarians — the entire white society is indirectly involved. Attempts to reveal the ideological basis
of canon-formation and to displace the tired myth of innate value
are seen as mannerless, unscholarly and simply wrong-headed.

It would be unfair to pretend that, in the last twenty years, no
concessions had been made by the hegemony concerning the teaching of 'S.A. lit.'. A number of zealous (largely white, humanist)
university teachers have undertaken the task of assembling a South
African canon. Already a local canon has stabilized, consisting largely of texts which satisfy (or which can be forced to satisfy) the demands of the humanist-colonial and Leavisite/New Critical agendas. Canonicity, transhistoricism, universality and the preservation
of dominant cultural habits and ideals thus prevail. A. JanMohamed
is persuasive in his abhorrence of this recuperative phenomenon:

> Thus we must insist that criticism, whether we like it or not, is a field
> marked by constant struggle over definitions of individual and social

formation. Until recently, minority literatures were effectively excluded from adequate critical consideration; however, now that they have been admitted into the margins of the canon, minority criticism must resist the hegemonic pressures which seek to neutralize them by repressing their political nature. In fact a viable counter-hegemonic discourse must consist of minority literary texts and a criticism that can further articulate the challenge of the texts; if apolitical humanistic definitions are allowed to emasculate minority critical discourse, then the challenge of minority literature can be easily neutralized or ignored. If minority literature repeatedly explores the political, collective, and marginal aspects of human experience, then minority criticism must also systematically avoid the temptation of a seductively inclusive, apolitical humanism: it must articulate and help to bring to consciousness those elements of minority literature that oppose, subvert, or negate the power of hegemonic culture, and it must learn to celebrate marginality in its specific manifestations without fetishizing or reifying it. (1984: 297-298)

However, South African writing has to contend with more than neutralization. Perhaps of far greater urgency is the series of problems surrounding literary production in South Africa. There are often massive obstacles to be overcome before one has the luxury of worrying about neutralization/recuperation by the hegemony. Michael Vaughan sums up this category of problems in the following way:

Here, many texts cannot reach the hands of the critic. It may well be that the author is banned/harassed/frightened/in jail/in exile: that the text is banned for possession/for distribution: that the publishers are unwilling/unable to publish: that the critic is afraid of being raided, etc., etc. In other words, an extensive and repressive 'security' apparatus is levelled against literary production. (1984: 48)

Moreover, one must bear in mind that not all 'minority' interest groups have the same goals. The hegemony is opposed by the 'left' and the 'right', and the creation of a so-called 'South African literature' cannot be seen as the product of a counterhegemonic group characterized by fair disinterestedness, unanimity, and super-ideological evaluative criteria and procedures. The existence of various interest groups, or of oppositional canon-formers *opposed* to each other is, moreover, not a recent phenomenon. An exchange within the first volume of *Voorslag* might serve as an example. Erich Mayer expresses 'utter disappointment' at finding 'the virile spirit of our young South African culture . . . supplanted by the disillusioned spirit of the aged and overcivilized countries of Central and Western Europe' (1926: 67).[10] Roy Campbell replies:

Yet even a world-wide aesthetic reputation is less ignominious than the local anaesthetic oblivion which envelops most of the artistic efforts of Mr. Mayer's young and 'virile' culture. God forbid that art should ever express the 'soul' of such a small, rancidly-racial nation as ours. The soul of our nation is always being expressed in Eisteddfods, exhibitions or paintings by South African artists, and anthologies of bad poetry. If this is art, then the soul it expresses must be suffering from senile decrepitude. Let us rather believe that art is the conscience of a nation, troublesome perhaps, but like most consciences allowed no say in daily affairs. (1926b: 59)

Mayer and Campbell desire the creation of a distinctively South African literature for opposed reasons and so have in mind presumably very different works when they envisage a South African canon. If Mayer is correct in suggesting that inordinate attention has been given (in *Voorslag*) to European works, it is because (according to Campbell) so far, local works have ignored their true function as the 'conscience of a nation'. If one has come to expect all those who are scornful of South African literary productions (and who continue to uphold the humanist-colonial canon) to be as culturally reactionary, then one's categories must be overhauled in order to cope with the apparent role reversal enacted by Mayer and Campbell. Campbell was (in the pages of *Voorslag*) a fierce opponent of habitual practice, colonial paternalism, prejudice and hypocrisy, and can be seen here as attempting to prevent South African literature from embodying the worst diseases introduced by the white humanist-colonial invasion of South Africa.

It is at the point, in this essay, when the narrative begins to accrue credibility and weight — the weight of 'true representation' — that its problematization is a necessity, lest the critique of humanist-colonial dogma take on the proportions of a dogma itself, replete with authority, presence and transhistorical disinterestedness. Any authoritative critique must set up (albeit implicitly) its own constituting oppositions (true/false, reason/unreason, hegemonic/oppositional and so on) which become reified, embedded and 'objective' − once again, interest masquerades as disinterest. The term 'humanist-colonial' becomes a strategically employed straw man, and various individuals and practices are conflated into expressions of a single and unified ideology.

Moreover, even if one avoids reducing the figure of the humanist-colonial to one obedient term in a strategic opposition of good versus bad, one is still prey to the levelling effects of generalizations. An historical examination of curricula, departmental policy statements, corporate expressions concerning the value of literature and the function of criticism in South Africa leads one to (at best) an accurate reconstruction of block proposals or ideological consensus on what literary intellectuals held to be true in the 1920s, 1970s or whatever. While this information would be telling — and there is pitifully little research being undertaken into the sociology of knowledge in literary studies in South Africa — it tends to blur differences within the hegemony.

The humanist agenda allows, within obvious limits, for the existence of non-consensual individual articulations of method, value and function, which can amount to a questioning of that agenda. If the growth of humanism involved a denial of divine authority, making man the measure of all things, then the flip-side of this new boldness in human knowledge is an awareness that caution is required in the creation of human knowledge programmes precisely because of the absence of any objective, transcendental, immovable pillar of knowledge. At its best, humanism has always stuttered and faltered; at its worst it is smoothly confident and self-righteous. The South African academy has retained the vestiges of a built-in escape clause, thereby allowing its best (but not its most praised) thinkers to question the master narratives. In its most ideal form, humanism has been marked by contrary impulses. First, the humanist academy has, ideally speaking, attempted to create a space for uncluttered thinking concerning culture and its products, past and future, beyond the vice-like grip of its current and controlling structures of thought. Secondly, the humanist programme (once again, ideally speaking) remains responsible to the society within which it functions. Sadly, it is easier to venerate the old vessels of thought and to ignore one's social-historical juncture; it is easier to locate oneself between these two ideals, avoiding both generative thought and social-historical responsibility by steeping oneself in repetitive, habitual interpretive actions as a kind of autism to shut out all else. This surely dominates most humanist institutions, but its exceptions provide interest here.

Two South African heads of departments of English can be singled out, not for the purposes of unqualified praise, but to illustrate that autism can be avoided, albeit only partially, in order to pursue the contrary impulses of the ideal humanist programme. Anthony Woodward, head of English at the University of the Witwatersrand, undoubtedly derives from the humanist-colonial consensual hegemony, yet an examination of three essays published within two years

12 *Rory Ryan*

(1962; 1963a; 1963b) reveals a rigorous interrogation of the humanist declarations concerning truth, value, English studies and the role of the intellectual in society. And Colin Gardner, head of English at the University of Natal (Pietermaritzburg), also of good standing within the hegemony, has retained a strong sense of social-historical responsibility and is a fierce critic of repression and discrimination. Of course, there are many others within the South African academy who undertake perhaps more valuable projects, but both of these men are to be located at the very centre of the humanist-colonial system of power-relations, and so, both reveal the need for the problematization of potentially reductive/dismissive strategies employed by over-enthusiastic critiques of humanist-colonial practice in South Africa.

However, a shrewd hegemony, mindful of its future endurance, is one which accommodates opposition and even encourages dissent within its sheltering domain, thereby ensuring that opposition occurs within authorized territory, with official blessing (and official control). One might conclude that by monitoring such apparent dissent, the humanist-colonial power structure effectively prevents real change. And a rather bleak inference may follow: the present essay can be seen as part of the unfolding of the humanist story-line, feebly resistant to humanist-colonialism and unrealistically confident of its own oppositional power. Master narratives tend to remain unscathed in the face of attempted opposition because of an excess of zeal and an insufficiency of cunning. By crudely homogenizing hegemonic voices, ignoring differences within its ranks and dismissing all of its practices and practitioners equally, the arrows of oppositional discourse are deflected from the centre of hegemonic practice and pierce instead a pathetic scarecrow, that oversimplified parody of humanist-colonial practice. Deference to the most laudable aspects of the humanist agenda does not imply a veiled desire for the massive recuperation of the most repressive power-seeking and self-serving strategies employed by the academy — instead, it more accurately situates the humanist event.

The humanist ideals of self-questioning and social responsibility deserve a different kind of treatment to the rigidly curatorial, escapist and intellectually autistic activities which are so prevalent in the South African literary academy, if one is to formulate an effectively oppositional voice. Oppositional voices which employ a rhetoric of indiscriminate hate for past practice remain blind to historical complexity, and to the mechanism of power which inscribes and monitors such voices by chaining all opposition to feeble versions and images of the oppressor and the oppressed. Humanist-colonialism in the academy will give way only when its history is rigorously re-written and not righteously berated. It is only in this way that the mechanisms of humanist-colonial power-preservation are exposed. A detailed and differentiating critique will reveal

> how resistant most traditional humanistic and belletristic forms of literary critical or theoretical activity are to admitting any involvement of criticism or theory with specific forms of power, politics, desire, or interest. (Bové, 1986: ix)

In the preceding discussion, I have attempted to problematize the first term in the oversimplified old/new, bad/good, hegemonic/oppositional conceptual pairs currently employed in oppositional discourse, by pointing to the ways in which an homogenized, crudely dismissive characterization of humanism can fail in its oppositional objective and even reinforce the hegemony by perpetuating scarecrow accounts of its mechanisms and internal differences. It is similarly judicious to problematize the second term of these strategically employed pairs. A common cause, one is told, creates strange bedfellows and, one might add, under the covers differences are trivialized in the face of a common enemy. But one can be antihumanistic in different ways. The residual intention of the present essay is to assist in, and to motivate, the exposure of mechanisms whereby the programmes/ideologies of a particular interest group are given the status of enduring truth, objective knowledge, common-sensical usefulness, or obvious and supreme value. Such mechanisms enable the historical to masquerade as the transhistorical, and all manner of repressive/coercive operations are sanctioned in the name of truth: the 'one' is glorified, and the 'many' are silenced in its name. This totalization and reification of the humanist-colonial programme in literary studies can be seen as the primary strategic manoeuvre which enables all of the other self-glorifying repressive practices to continue, practices such as the canonization of humanist monumental texts, the institutionalization of Leavisite/New Critical habits of mind, the perpetuation of objectivist epistemologies, the marginalization of non-hegemonic habits and texts, and so on. Frequently, oppositional discourses in literary studies are as fixated as the hegemony on transcendental meaning and ultimate significance. This inclination to leave the authoritarian epistemology intact is often all too explicable and depressing; the marginalized voice opposes *this* particular knowledge hegemony, and seeks the displacement of the prevailing monuments in order to erect others and to codify a new totalization of knowledge, one as potentially repressive as that which it seeks to displace. Replacing old fascisms with new ones might serve the democratic purpose of giving everyone a chance at being undemocratic, but change under these conditions may not be attractive.

However, a general satisfaction (among oppositional voices in South African literary studies) with the prevailing objectivist mode of epistemological foundation can be traced to the Marxist basis of much oppositional practice. Although some notable exceptions exist, the tradition of Marxist 'theories' of literature has a strong vested interest in the existence and the recoverability of knowledge. Philip Goldstein makes the following observation:

> Like the other humanists, the Marxists accept the mimetic text of the classical tradition and the liberal emphasis on the individual author. They believe, as the liberals and conservatives do, that the literary text mirrors an independent, external world . . . . In other words, they assume that texts possess intentions representing the acts of individual authors, not the patterns of an archetype, the inspired voice of a divinity, or the common fund of our knowledge. (1984: 237)

Goldstein continues:

> . . . to Fredric Jameson, who voices this as well as other currents of Marxist thought, entrenched social structures firmly constrain generic types like realism or romance so they can no longer express social criticism; however, the artist who rebels against established forms and structures can produce an enticing utopian world. In sum, the Marxist text reveals an individual intention but the intention expresses an objective social insight or a rebellious utopian vision, not an individual outlook. (1984: 238)

And Goldstein concludes:

> In sum, Marxist and non-Marxist humanists consider literature a genuine source of knowledge, not a kind of 'pseudo-statement' or a 'dramatic' form of unity. Literature does not play with words; it asserts substantial wisdom. (1984: 239)

My aim here is not to attempt a disabling of Marxism, for it has provided a powerful locus around which much oppositional practice in literary studies has occurred. Nevertheless, it is compelling for Marxist-inspired discourse to overlook the powerfully coercive-repressive functions of an authorized ideology which exercises control by stressing its 'neutrality', 'obviousness', 'objectivity' — in short, by claiming to be knowledge. Njabulo Ndebele, one of the most articulate and persuasive opponents of the hegemony in the South African literary academy, ends an excellent paper with the following wish:

I can hope that the persistent and fearless pursuit of truth will be the key guiding principle behind our intellectual work, to enrich the theoretical content of our struggle wherever that struggle is taking place. (1984: 32)

History demonstrates that if the 'persistent and fearless pursuit of truth' is successful, the intellectual adventurer is swiftly replaced by the conservative bureaucrat, jealously guarding the new dogma as the 'higher truth' or trans-ideological knowledge which has ousted false consciousness. But it is only by perceiving the instability, humanness, regionality and the *interested* nature of knowledge (as opposed to the fiction of disinterested, universal and enduring knowledge) that the realm of cultural production can remain free of imperialistic epistemologies.

Stanley Fish makes the following resigned comment:

. . . even if one is convinced (as I am) that the world he sees and the values he espouses are constructions, or, as some say, 'effects of discourse,' that conviction will in no way render that world any less perspicuous or those values any less compelling. It is thus a condition of human life always to be operating as an extension of beliefs and assumptions that are historically contingent, and yet to be holding those beliefs and assumptions with an absoluteness that is the necessary consequence of the absoluteness with which they hold — inform, shape, constitute — us. (1985: 107)

It is necessary to explore just what 'a condition of human life' entails, constrains and enables, and whether the interest/disinterest pair can be resolved or dissolved in some way.

If the recurrent refrain of this essay has been to expose the repressive-coercive effects of authorized and authorizing knowledge programmes by way of paying close attention to a particularly choice example of hegemony in South African literary studies, then the essay itself is not aloof from the contradictions engendered by the phrase 'interested knowledge'. Perhaps the pursuit of aloofness (or disinterested knowledge) is entrenched in Western intellectual behaviour, as Fish suggests, but that does not prevent one from trying to kick the habit, or problematize the programme. The present essay is not a free-floating, objectively investigative overview. Despite its attempts at generality (the 'fair' account, the 'accurate' detail), the piece is historically positioned. Like so many oppositional voices in South African literary studies, mine was trained to sing by humanist-colonial choristers in South African universities, and continues to sing with those choirs, if a little discordantly. This essay is marked by a strong schizophrenia, one which attempts to achieve a balance between the impulse to cajole, whine, reproach and scorn (all in an effort to release literary studies from the humanist-colonial stranglehold) and the need to suppress polemical utterances in the search for the 'true account'. If all writing can be likened to a dog lifting its leg to demonstrate interest in this or that territory, then successful writing masks the mechanics of persuasion behind apparently 'plain and neutral, historically accurate statements', all of which terms owe their existence to precisely this need for disguise. Oppositional discourse aims at trapping the hegemonic within the realm of interest (the grubby politics of truth) while releasing one's own discourse into the unimpeachable realm of disinterest. Faced with this fact, one can resolve constantly to problematize so-called disinterest, to give the problem of interest/disinterest a permanent address, by incorporating within each discursive site a fallibility clause, a rejection of gross transcendentalism, and a pursuit of problematized, discredited and distinctly human knowledge. At the very least, one cannot remain silent. Edward Said declares:

> I take criticism so seriously as to believe that, even in the very midst of a battle in which one is unmistakably on one side against another, there should be criticism, because there must be critical consciousness if there are to be issues, problems, values, even lives to be fought for. (1983: 28)

The remainder of this essay will concern itself with the future of literary studies.

If the defining features of discursive practice are self-totalization and the exclusion of all other practices, then those opposed to the exclusionary and regulatory powers of any hegemony in literary studies should conscientiously and doggedly undermine intellectual imperialisms. The temptation to totalize and to perpetuate the fantasy of objective and transhistorical knowledge must actively be opposed. Edward Said condemns a criticism 'most unlike itself':

> In its suspicion of totalizing concepts, in its discontent with reified objects, in its impatience with guilds, special interests, imperialized

fiefdoms, and orthodox habits of mind, criticism is most itself and, if the paradox can be tolerated, most unlike itself at the moment it starts turning into organized dogma. (1983: 29)

Iconoclastic intellectual behaviour acts as a powerful safeguard against the imperialistic desires of any interest group and so acts not only as a check against yet another round of transcendental truth, but also as a check against the women and men who wish to monopolize knowledge-production. William Spanos describes such a detotalized site:

> To put it positively, criticism is the essential activity of intellectual life in the always already 'fallen' realm of difference, of temporality, of history, or what is the same thing, of crisis. It is the practice, not of angels or divinely inspired exegetes in the service of an Inscrutable Deity nor of members of a board of directors in the service of the Inscrutable Corporation, but of mortal men in the service of be-ing — the open-ing in being which teleological modes of inquiry close off and forget, which is to say, of always already being in the midst, *interesse*, of freedom, of the difference that makes a critical difference all along the continuum of being from language through conscious-ness to law, gender, class, culture, and the *polis*. (1984: 200)

Conscientious opposition to the creation of master narratives and to the monopolistic urges of certain individuals and groups amounts to the same thing. The academy is created within society and to deny that context seems to be neither good academic practice nor good human practice. In South Africa, the exclusionary and self-aggrandizing powers of the literary academy have created a mons-trously detached site, strongly curatorial and preservatory, as terri-fied of the so-called darkly destructive oppositional forces as it is of confronting its own historical-political origins. Michael Vaughan calls for new vigour in South African literary studies in this way:

> Freed of these shackles, we need to determine new literary concepts and practices, by means of which we can engage — as a new priority — with the material reality in which our academic structures are en-closed (enclaved), and, in particular, with the real state of all literary practices in the Southern Africa of our own time, with regard to the economic, social, political and cultural aspects of this 'real state'. Only on the basis of such a re-orientation can the academic business of research into and teaching of literature regain some vitality and relevance, in a wider context than the self-perpetuation of academic rituals. (1984: 49)

While it is crucially important to work towards a more socially responsible and self-problematized site of literary studies, one must not naively believe that its practitioners decide fundamentally on its future. All sites of discourse, it is true, aim first at creating their own inviolable present with projections into the past (a narrative history, with fathers and forefathers) and the future (a beacon of sheer explicability to aim for). Consequent on this, all sites of discourse like to believe they are masters of their own fate. The site of literary studies is substantially dependent on the larger discursive sites which inscribe it. In a society as potentially explosive as the present South African one, traditional institutions and practices can swiftly be effaced or transformed, obliterating all arguments and practices with frightening neutrality, and revealing how dependent the academy must be on its own social-political context. Nevertheless, fatalistic acceptance of one's sheer powerlessness can begin to look ominously like covert support for the current hegemony. Such passive fatalism is as extreme and unwarranted as the belief that the site of literary studies is an island, governed and governable only from within. Literary studies currently forms part of a wider humanist programme and is subject to the control of the university. And, if 'liberal humanistic institutions have a way of turning marginalized opposition to their advantage' (Bové, 1986: 298) then the conscientious intellectual must expand his/her careful scrutiny of all imperialist knowledge programmes to include the wider institutional realm, or postulate an extra-institutional site. Batsleer *et al.* (1985) offer their book *Rewriting English: Cultural Politics of Gender and Class* as

> a contribution, not, certainly, to literary criticism, nor even to cultural studies in the academic sense, but rather to a still undeveloped but possible and very necessary cultural politics of reading and writing. (1985: 6)

Nevertheless, the authors are not so cavalier as to overestimate their ability to remain free of institutional discourses:

> If the book's aim is to contribute to the analysis and, thereby, to the transformation of the institutions of cultural power, it must also be acknowledged, as one of its many contradictions, that in this respect it speaks from and serves to reinforce those very institutions. (1985: 10)

However difficult an effective exposure of monopoly and exclusion might be, and however hesitant one might be to clear the site only to permit the inauguration of new monopolies, the intellectual's role is strenuously to resist closure and the deadening effects of repetitive rituals. Despite the particularities of the history of the South

African academy, it reveals depressing parallels with the history of most major Western knowledge-productive institutions. If I may, in conclusion, be permitted to sloganize phrases from two of Paul Bové's essays, one must promote, and continue to promote, a 'radically active skepticism' (1986: 297) as an alternative to the habitual practices of 'culturally comfortable critics' (1985: 97).

Notes

1. I wish to thank Paul A. Bové for his long-distance friendship and kindness. Thanks also to Pam Ryan and Ken Saycell for comments on the draft of this essay.
2. See Partridge, 1958: 5 for details.
3. While the majority of the following comments, examples and analyses pertain to the role of the English-speaking literary intellectual in South Africa, they have bearing upon the Afrikaans situation as well. The Afrikaans counterpart has inherited, and continues in the main to support, a predominantly humanist-colonial formalism with an inscribed materialist opposition. Differences in the two roles (English and Afrikaans) may be traced to the fact that while the English tradition in South Africa looks to England and the USA for paternity, the Afrikaans tradition looks to Holland and Germany (and minimally, to France) although it has, by virtue of close proximity, absorbed some of the literary critical habits of the Leavisite tradition.
4. Quoted in Partridge, 1958: 7.
5. Whittock's claim that 'we are expatriates' cannot be meant literally, for now (as in the late 1960s) the majority of university teachers of English are South African by birth.
6. This phrase is borrowed from Edward Said, 1978: 156.
7. It is unusual for commentary on humanist-colonial literary-intellectual patterns of behaviour in South Africa to venture beyond statements of condemnation: often, declarations of ideological alignment with the 'new' against the 'old' (or with the 'right' against the 'wrong') are sufficient for the audiences for which they are written. Detailed, historically accurate and carefully argued critiques which deserve attention and praise are Kirkwood (1976) and Vaughan (1984). Kirkwood uses a prominent person in the academy of English studies, Guy Butler, to flesh out the figure of the colonizer in South Africa, and Vaughan's dismantling of 'dominant ideologies' is sophisticated and scholarly in the 'best modern way'. The degree of scholarship in these studies underlines, by contrast, that very little historical-critical research exists concerning the features and development of the literary-intellectual academy in South Africa from a post-colonial perspective.
8. I do not wish to mislead the reader: Van Heyningen is not a gentleman but a gentlewoman, although she promotes the cause of the gentleman-scholar and uses the term 'he' to represent the figure of the student.
9. The most explosive critiques of humanist-colonialism, such as those by Vaughan and Kirkwood (footnote 7), created no more than minor ripples — perhaps *not even* minor ripples.

10. It may be interesting to note that Mayer speaks, in the same letter, of the 'ascending South African nation', and of the 'numerous black races' as being in a state of 'healthful adolescence', as if there were a united white voice in South Africa in 1926 constituting a nation, and as if blacks in Africa had been culturally inert for thousands of years, pristine and asleep, awaiting the kiss of the white prince.

References

Batsleer, Janet; Tony Davies; Rebecca O'Rourke and Chris Weedon. 1985. *Rewriting English: Cultural Politics of Gender and Class*. New Accents. London: Methuen.

Bové, Paul A. 1985. 'Closing Up the Ranks: Xerxes Hordes are at the Pass'. *Contemporary Literature*, 26, 91-106.

Bové, Paul A. 1986. *Intellectuals in Power: A Genealogy of Critical Humanism*. New York: Columbia.

Campbell, Roy. 1926a. 'Fetish Worship in South Africa: A Skirmish on the Borders of Popular Opinion'. *Voorslag*, 1(2), 3-19.

Campbell, Roy. 1926b. 'To the Editor of *Voorslag* ...'. *Voorslag*, 1(3), 59-60.

Campbell, Roy; William Plomer and Laurens van der Post (eds). 1985[1926]. *Voorslag: A Magazine of South African Life and Art*. Introduction and Notes by C. Gardner and M. Chapman. Pietermaritzburg: University of Natal Press.

Cope, R.K. 1947. 'Language and Nationality in South Africa'. *Standpunte*, 2(2), 5-20.

Fish, Stanley. 1985. 'Anti-Professionalism'. *New Literary History*, 17 (1985), 89-108.

Goldstein, Philip. 1984. 'Humanism and the Politics of Truth'. *boundary 2*, 12 + 13, 235-257.

Harvey, C.J.D. 1955. '"Local Colour" in South African Poetry'. *Theoria*, 7, 93-100.

JanMohamed, Abdul R. 1984. 'Humanism and Minority Literature: Toward a Definition of Counter-hegemonic Discourse'. *boundary 2*, 12 + 13, 281-299.

Kirkwood, Mike. 1976. 'The Colonizer: A Critique of the English South African Culture Theory'. In Wilhelm, P. and J. Polley (eds). *Poetry South Africa*. Johannesburg: Ad. Donker, 102-133.

Mayer, Erich. 1926. 'To the Editor of *Voorslag* ...'. *Voorslag*, 1(2), 67-68.

Ndebele, Njabulo S. 1984. 'Actors and Interpreters: Popular Culture and Progressive Formalism'. Sol Plaatje Memorial Lecture delivered at the University of Bophuthatswana.

Partridge, A.C. 1958. 'English Scholarship: A Transmutation of Species'. *English Studies in Africa*, 1, 1-9.

Said, Edward S. 1978. *Orientalism*. New York: Pantheon Books.

Said, Edward S. 1983. *The World, the Text, and the Critic*. Cambridge, Mass.: Harvard University Press.

Spanos, William. 1984. '*Boundary 2* and the Polity of Interest: Humanism, the "Centre Elsewhere", and Power'. *Boundary 2*, 12 + 13, 173-213.

Van Heyningen, C. 1963. 'Manifesto for a Group of English Literature Teachers'. *Theoria*, 21, 52-57.

Vaughan, Michael. 1984. 'A Critique of Dominant Ideas in Departments of English in the English-Speaking Universities of South Africa'. *Critical Arts*, 3, 35-51.

Visser, N.W. 1984. 'The Critical Situation and the Situation of Criticism'. *Critical Arts*, 3, 2-9.

Whittock, T. 1968. 'The Function of an English Faculty in an African University'. *English Studies in Africa*, 11, 81-94.

Woodward, A.G. 1962. 'Society and the Intellectual'. *Standpunte*, 16(2), 8-17.

Woodward, A.G. 1963a. 'The English Course in the Modern University'. *English Studies in Africa*, 6, 27-43.

Woodward, A.G. 1963b. 'Literature and Truth'. *English Studies in Africa*, 6, 121-136.

Building a National Culture in South Africa

Karen Press

The call to build a national culture in South Africa has become an important element of the political programmes of most organizations within the liberation movement. The Azanian Manifesto, the political programme of those organizations who work together under the umbrella of the National Forum, includes a pledge to work for 'the development of one national culture, inspired by socialist values'; and the organizations adhering to the Freedom Charter have committed themselves to the 'people's culture' campaign which aims, among other things, to '[build] a national people's culture' (Arts Festival '86 Programme, 1986: 2).

The fact of this call has a dual significance: firstly, it indicates that a particular cultural perspective is seen by the liberation movement as a necessary component of the struggle for revolutionary change in South Africa; and secondly, it provides a clear (if broad) definition of the task facing artists who are committed to this struggle.

However, it is not enough for artists to take this task upon themselves simply because various political organizations believe they should do so. A careful analysis of the notion of a 'national culture', and of its significance in the South African context, is necessary. My aim, here, is to attempt such an analysis. I shall not be concerned with the specificities of organizational policies and practices within the liberation movement; I wish, rather, to take a step back from these, and examine the issue at a more general level. This is because I believe that any consideration by artists of the role that they can play in the process of liberation in South Africa should be based, in the first instance, not on the requests or dictates of particular organizations but on a more fundamental analysis of what it can mean to build a progressive culture in this country.

The idea of creating a national culture must be seen as a political need, arising from a desire on the part of a government or the leadership of a liberation movement, to create an independent, unitary nation out of a diverse range of social groups that were previously seen (and saw themselves) as separate political entities. Lloyd Fallers, in a discussion of Ugandan nationalism, explains the connection thus:

> The new nations, in order to achieve a degree of unity of purpose, need cultures which, first, will provide a measure of consensus among their diverse peoples and, second, will be capable of the constant innovation which existence in the modern world requires. (Fallers quoted in Mazrui, 1972: xiv)

Before analysing the call to build a national culture in South Africa, therefore, we must examine the political strategy underlying it, namely, the call to build a unitary nation.

The building of a nation is not something any political movement can undertake as an act of will, irrespective of the nature of the society in which it exists. Nations come into being as part of an objective historical process. It is not coincidental that the national state should have become the predominant political entity in those regions of the world where capitalism has been most fully developed. Through capitalist economic processes, amongst which industrialization and technological modernization are the most significant, fragmented social groups are brought together in systematic contact. Trading practices forge links between the owners of the means of production across regional political boundaries; and the creation of a proletariat brings together large numbers of people who previously pursued independent economic activities within small agrarian communities.

The history of capitalist development in South Africa (from the time of the discovery of diamonds (1867) and gold (1886)) is the history of a nation coming into being. The migration (forced or voluntary) of black people to the cities over the past century, and their loss of property rights in the rural areas, has disrupted and virtually destroyed the pre-capitalist political structures which governed their lives (except, of course, where the South African government has deliberately perpetuated these, as in the system of bantustan 'tribal authorities') and made them all subjects of one national South African economic and social system. In the same manner, the fragmented colonial and settler communities have become one indigenous fraction of the South African nation, forging among themselves a series of class alliances to keep economic control of the country in the hands of those classified as 'white'.[1]

This objective process, then, is generated by economic factors and the social changes they necessitate. The various political groups contending for power in the country articulate this process in terms of their own interests, and try to create a vision of the nation 'in their own image' — that is, in terms of their own ideological perspective. Thus, for example, the Afrikaners constructed a 'national identity' for themselves, as part of a strategy of forging a class alliance amongst different classes within the Afrikaans-speaking community (see O'Meara, 1983), and when they came to power in 1948 proceeded to establish ideological and institutional mechanisms for creating a society which perpetuated their own ethnic conception of 'the nation'.

At a more fundamental level, the peculiar racial form of capitalist development in South Africa, in which the owners of the means of production were of European descent, and the vast majority of the workers were indigenous Africans and descendants of African and Asian slaves, made it necessary, and possible, for the bourgeoisie to divide the working class at the level of consciousness and culture, so as to prevent any united challenge to the racial basis of this economic exploitation and the political instruments of its perpetuation. The ethnic identities of pre-capitalist Southern African societies were, and continue to be, perpetuated by the bourgeoisie, so that black workers should see themselves as Xhosas, Zulus, Sothos, etc., with separate cultures and group interests (such as access to land), rather than as citizens of one united country who can, together, fight to take control of it.

It is evident, therefore, that any liberation struggle in South Africa which commits itself to the overthrow of the exploitative capitalist system, must include a rejection of this fragmentation of the black working class along ethnic lines, and must actively build on non-racial, national consciousness within the ranks of the black working class and its allies. While the ultimate aim of any struggle for socialism in this regard must be the development within the working class of an international consciousness, which acknowledges the need for international worker unity to combat all forms of economic exploitation, the creation of a united national culture amongst the workers of South Africa is a first vital step in this direction. An abstract theoretical understanding of the struggle for socialism might reject this dimension of national struggle (whether at the cultural or the political level) as contradictory to the international perspective of Marxism, in terms of which the working class must unite internationally against the divisive (nationalist) political strategies of the bourgeoisie. But the inadequacy of such an abstract approach is clear in relation to a concrete historical example such as that of South Africa: in this country, the struggle for national unity is an unavoidable aspect of a struggle for socialism. The task of the liberation movement, in this situation, is to try and overcome the potential contradictions between nationalism and socialism; further on, I shall consider whether this is in fact possible, on the terrain of culture.

The need to build such a national culture is not unique to South Africa. The colonial experience of most African countries has been one of social groups that were separate (geographically and politically, as well as culturally) being united under one colonial regime, and left at the moment of independence to forge for themselves a national identity that corresponds to their now interconnected economic and political situations. Nor is this process necessarily a revolutionary one; it can in effect be a way for the new national bourgeoisie to consolidate its ideological control over the exploited classes, by submerging class differences in a populist nationalism. Ali Mazrui, in an analysis of the process of nation-building in East Africa, offers a 'recipe' for this process which is clearly independent of class consciousness:

> Four guiding principles help to determine the planning behind social engineering when the ideology is nationalistic. The principles can be formulated in terms of four imperatives: first, indigenizing what is foreign; second, idealizing what is indigenous; third, nationalizing what is sectional; and fourth, emphasizing what is African. The four principles are interrelated and often reinforce each other. (Mazrui, 1972: 16)

For an African liberation movement committed to fundamental social and economic change, the key question becomes how to take on the necessary task of building a national culture in such a way that it leads towards, rather than away from, the goal of socialism. This is the question facing the South African liberation movement today.

The question can be posed in another way: what should be the character of the national culture to be built in South Africa, as part of the struggle for socialist values and structures? The various tendencies within the liberation movement are beginning to formulate answers to this question, in ways which reflect their political analyses and goals. These range from a relatively clear socialist perspective on nation-building amongst groups such as the Cape Action League and certain trade unions, to the Africanist populism of organizations working in the tradition of the Black Consciousness movement (such as the Azanian People's Organization), with the national democratic argument of the United Democratic Front lying somewhere in between. An adequate answer to the question must be based on an analysis of three issues:

- the 'anti-colonial', indigenizing aspect of the call for a national culture;
- the necessity for a national culture to be anti-ethnic and anti-racist;
- the extent to which the call for a national culture can intersect with a call for socialism.

An 'Indigenized' National Culture?

A common theme in the current arguments for a national culture in South Africa is a criticism of the American and European cultural styles that predominate within black social and cultural experience — the 'disco' music, television soap operas, glossy permed hair, and so on. Instead of aping imperialist styles, it is argued, black South Africans should be promoting their 'own' indigenous culture, drawing on forms of entertainment and social customs from their past.

This approach to the indigenization of the national culture has been most powerfully argued for elsewhere in Africa by the Kenyan writer Ngugi wa Thiong'o. He has, on many occasions, analysed the role of European culture in implementing the policies of colonial powers in Africa, most specifically by imposing a Eurocentric education system on the population of the colony; and he has insisted on the need to throw off the yoke of this system, and of the alien culture it propagates, before any African country can free itself from colonial and neo-colonial control:

> . . . for the anti-colonial and anti-imperialist (i.e. anti-neocolonial) struggle to be complete, it must also be a cultural struggle since the aim is to restore the African personality to its true human creative potentialities in history, so as to enhance the quality of life and of life-based values.
>
> Indeed most national liberation movements start by rejecting the culture of the colonizer, by repudiating the religion of the oppressing nation and class and the entire education system of the colonizer. People create their own songs, poems, dances, literature, which embody a structure of values dialectically opposed to those of the ruling classes of the oppressing race and nation. (Ngugi, 1981: 26-27)

There is an assumption here that the 'original' indigenous culture of the oppressed people has remained intact throughout the period of colonial domination, and is available to be mobilized by them at the moment of independence. And there is, too, a belief in the necessarily progressive character of this indigenous culture, whose values are 'dialectically opposed to those of the ruling class'; the implication here is that there were no oppressive aspects to the traditional culture and consciousness now being revived. The extreme form of this argument, of course, was the *nègritude* movement of the francophone colonies, which created a myth of an African cultural past of blissful purity and goodness. Ngugi does, in some of his writings, qualify this idealization of indigenous culture, and he strongly endorses Fanon's attack on the African national bourgeoisie for its perpetuation of the oppression of the people (see for example Ngugi, 1981: 78-79). He has linked his call for the revival of an indigenous culture to a socialist commitment (as in Ngugi, 1981: 71-81 *passim*), but in a very problematic manner: in effect, the national bourgeoisie is seen to demonstrate its oppressive role in African societies by its allegiance to European cultural practices and values — which allows Ngugi to argue that indigenous culture is, by definition, in the interests of the oppressed classes. For this reason he insists that, in the creation of a national culture that will lead to the economic and political liberation of the Kenyan people, African literature, music, dance and so on should be prioritized over progressive cultural forms from other parts of the world (Ngugi, 1981: 38).

A different approach to this question of indigenization can be found in Amilcar Cabral's essay, 'National Liberation and Culture' (Cabral, 1980). Like Ngugi, he argues for the building of an indigenous national culture, but his stress is less on the intrinsic value of African culture than on the psychological significance for a people of returning to their cultural traditions, which grow out of their material experience of life:

> A people who free themselves from foreign domination will not be culturally free unless, without underestimating the importance of positive contributions from the oppressor's culture and other cultures, they return to the upwards [sic] paths of their own culture. The latter is nourished by the living reality of the environment and rejects harmful influences as much as any kind of subjection to foreign cultures. (Cabral, 1980: 43)

The important issue raised here by Cabral is that a culture must be created which is *relevant* to the oppressed people, in the sense that it articulates their own experience. To be relevant in this way, it must necessarily draw on the tangible manifestations of that experience — the geography, the social traditions, the history of the people.

But this indigenization is not an end in itself. Though Cabral and Ngugi both argue for the rejection of the colonial oppressor's culture, they differ in their views on the significance of this rejection. For Ngugi, it is a return to an innately valuable African culture; for Cabral, it is a means for reviving the creative initiative of the oppressed people.

In South Africa today, these arguments cannot be applied without modification. To begin with, the political context is clearly different; the South African ruling class is an indigenous one which will not, at the moment of victory of the liberation movement, pack up and return to its 'mother country', taking its cultural institutions and values with it. The cultural practices brought into South Africa by successive waves of people from abroad (and here one must include not only English and Dutch invaders/settlers, but also Indonesian slaves, Indian labourers, Portuguese traders and refugees, and others) have taken root here, changing and being changed by their new social and geographical environment. And, most importantly, all political decisions about the cultural and educational practices that should predominate in South Africa are taken by the ruling parties *inside* the country, not by an external metropolitan power, although the cultural models of the ruling classes remain fundamentally European in origin.

Furthermore, South Africa's integration into an international economy in the twentieth century has also connected it to an international consumer culture — shaped largely by American and British marketing forces — which permeates every aspect of social life. It would be a quixotic aim, and one going against the grain of history, for any liberation movement to want to uproot this cultural 'invasion' in the name of a pre-colonial 'original' culture.

At the same time, it must be recognized that cultural practices which originated in Britain, the USA and Europe have, in South Africa, been perpetuated and controlled by the institutions of the dominant classes, and have been brought into service by them to perpetuate a system of economic and political oppression. A Eurocentric education system, and institutionalized 'high art' practices rooted in bourgeois European artistic traditions, are both ways of denying the majority of the population access to, and control over, cultural experience.[2] The cultural traditions of the black population in South Africa have been subjected to a host of disruptive and destructive forces, as part of the strategies of successive governments to limit the extent of black social autonomy.

It is not surprising, therefore, that there has consistently been an Africanist element in liberatory ideology in South Africa; the Pan

Africanist Congress and the Black Consciousness movement, as well as the African National Congress, have in different ways called for the 're-Africanization' of South Africa, culturally and politically. But such a call, although it has sometimes tended to invoke a nationalist chauvinism (and even a racist argument about who constitute 'true Africans'), and has given rise at times to the specific invocation of 'traditional' cultural practices, has never pushed Africanization as far as did the proponents of *nègritude* and the 'African Personality' ideology elsewhere in Africa.

The reasons for this are clear. Firstly, the extent of industrialization in South Africa is such that it is no longer possible to imagine a liberated society reviving the peasant economy and lifestyle of the past. The proletarianization of the vast majority of blacks, and the growth of major urban centres throughout the country, have given rise to new forms of cultural activity in the black community directed more towards the present reality of social and commercial possibilities than towards the preservation or revival of past traditions.

Secondly, any attempt to retrieve a typically African set of cultural practices in South Africa would be highly problematic, given the fact that the ruling National Party has built the entire structure of the apartheid system with the help of precisely such a retrieval. The National Party's insistence on ethnic 'own cultures' for sections of the population has been the basis for a fostering of 'traditional' cultural activities which is intended to maintain the present, racial form of political oppression. One of the greatest challenges facing progressive activists and artists is how to bring about a necessary 'Africanization' of South African social life — in the sense of freeing it from the economic and ideological dictates of imperialism — without invoking the same tribal ideology as the present government.

I shall return shortly to this question of mobilizing traditions in a progressive way. At this point, I want to focus on the necessity for any efforts to create an 'indigenous' national culture to distinguish between the approaches of Ngugi and Cabral. The value of the indigenous must be assessed in terms of its relevance to the lives of the oppressed population. It *is* important that people should see their own world depicted in the art produced for and by them: a people which does not have access to an aesthetic vocabulary for expressing its own material experience is deprived of a tool for examining that experience. And it is important, equally, that the lifestyle and cultural habits of a society should grow out of its own history and present needs, rather than aping an inappropriate model imported from elsewhere. The indigenous, insofar as it serves the social and cultural needs of society, should be incorporated into a progressive national culture; it should not, however, find its place there simply because it is indigenous.

A National Culture That Is Anti-ethnic

The argument for an anti-ethnic culture may appear a very simple one, and it is the clearest logical consequence of my analysis of the need for a national culture in South Africa, but we have to consider carefully how it is possible to achieve this goal.

To begin with, it must be made clear that a new, politically acceptable national culture cannot be imposed upon people. Just as the political education of the oppressed and exploited classes must begin with an understanding of their present level of political awareness, so any efforts to create a new culture must take as their starting point the cultural practices at present valued by those classes. Unless this is done, the liberation movement will be doing nothing different from those colonial powers which denied people the right to participate actively in the shaping of their own culture. This point is made clearly by Cabral:

> . . . the liberation movement must, on the cultural level, base its action on popular culture, whatever the diversity of cultural levels in the country. The cultural challenge . . . can be effectively envisaged only on the basis of the culture of the mass of workers in the countryside and the towns, including the (revolutionary) nationalist petty-bourgeoisie . . . . (Cabral, 1980: 146)

A new national culture, in other words, must begin with the raw materials of existing 'popular culture' amongst the masses. This culture is composed of a host of traditions, indigenous and imported; in South Africa one could name anything ranging from traditional marriage and funeral ceremonies amongst the various religious communities, be they Muslim, 'red' Xhosa, Zionist Christian, Jewish, Hindu, etc., to the many social customs focussed on the home brewing of beer (from the rural beer-drink with its accompaniment of African songs, to the urban shebeen, with its similarities to American jazz subculture), to the Michael Jackson-lookalike competitions amongst urban teenagers. Cabral argues for the need to draw on the positive aspects of these traditions in the process of building a national culture — positive in the sense that the traditions do not perpetuate values of inequality (gender or racial), individualism, greed, etc.

A similar argument to Cabral's has been put forward in the South African context by Neville Alexander:

The economic, material, language, religious and other differences between colour groups are *real*. They influence and determine the ways
in which people live and experience their lives. Reactionary ethnic
organizations would not have been so successful in this country had
these differences not been of a certain order of reality. However, these
differences are neither permanent nor necessarily divisive if they are
restructured and redirected for the purpose of national liberation and
thus in order to build the nation. (Alexander, 1985a: 52-53)

Alexander goes on to give an example of the way in which elements
of the various indigenous cultural traditions in South Africa can be
drawn into one national culture:

The songs, stories, poems, dances of one group should become the
common property of all even if their content has to be conveyed by
means of different language media. In this way, and in many other
ways, by means of class struggle on the political and on the cultural
front, the cultural achievements of the people will be woven together
into one Azanian fabric. In this way, we shall eliminate divisive ethnic consciousness and separatist lines of division without eliminat-
ing our cultural achievements and cultural variety. But it will be experienced by all as different aspects of one national culture accessible to all. (Alexander, 1985a: 54-55)

The mention of 'class struggle on the political and on the cultural
front' in this passage is a reminder that this 'blending' of cultural
traditions cannot take place at the expense of a class analysis of such
traditions. Those traditions, for example, which perpetuate and
celebrate elitist social structures (such as the ceremonies confirm-
ing the power of individual leaders over communities) need to be
rejected by a liberation movement committed to the principle of
democracy. There is a vital need to analyse the culture 'of the people' critically, and not to assume that it is automatically progressive. This critical perspective is a necessary component of any strategy aimed at building a national culture of a genuinely progressive
character.

This is a complex, difficult process. On the one hand, such a strategy cannot aim for a national culture 'purged' of all the idiosyncra-
sies present in cultural communities which derive from regional, religious, language, and inherited 'ethnic' identity differences. In their
concrete manifestations, these are the essence of people's lived cultural experience, and they cannot be wrenched away regardless of
the value people place upon them. On the other hand, if these various cultural traditions are reified and celebrated as the most significant markers of the identity of the communities who practise them,
it becomes impossible to develop a genuinely national cultural iden-

tity amongst the people as a whole. Such an identity can only be forged over a long period in which the various ethnically-defined traditions are infused with, and ultimately transformed by, values and practices consistent with the goal of a socialist society.

The Socialist Dimension of a National Culture

There are those who would argue that the creation of a national culture is a goal fundamentally incompatible with socialism. But, as I hope I have made clear in my initial argument about the need to build a progressive national culture in South Africa, the two concepts are not at all incompatible in the South African context. However, this remains true only if the progressive dimension of this national culture is present from the start, and comes to predominate over all other aspects in the course of time.

In practice, this means promoting values and practices that contribute towards the achievement of a socialist society. This process has already begun: organizations within the liberation movement are, increasingly, defining their cultural and education projects in terms of a socialist as well as a national perspective. In the many local and regional educational initiatives of recent years, for example, students and teachers have begun demanding resources that examine the class nature of the South African conflict and present the history of other worker struggles around the world. Projects such as co-operatives, which consciously attempt to promote democracy and the sharing of resources, are being initiated in many parts of the country. And, on the more specifically artistic front, certain organizations are trying to create new art forms, and new ways of producing them, which challenge the capitalist ethos. A most significant initiative here comes from the progressive trade union movement, which is in a better position than most to perceive the need for connecting national and class issues in the cultural arena. The members of the Durban Workers Cultural Local, in answering the question 'Why do we believe cultural work has an important role to play in the workers' struggle?', make the connection simply and eloquently:

> . . . we have been culturally exploited time and time again: we have been singing, parading, boxing, acting and writing within a system we did not control. So far, black workers have been feeding all their creativity into a culture machine to make profit for others ... it is time to begin controlling our creativity: we must create space in our struggle — through our own songs, our own slogans, our own poems, our own artwork, our own plays and dances. At the same time, in our

struggle we must also fight against the cultural profit machines. (Sitas, 1986: 69)

It is not possible to start off with a 'ready-made' socialist culture
which must somehow be injected into the developing national culture of the oppressed people. Rather, it is a matter of starting with
people's actual experiences of exploitation — as, in the above example, the Cultural Local begins with the real situation in which
black artists find themselves — and creating new, non-exploitative
practices that can be taken up and become part of a national culture. Thus, it could become possible for the trade unions and community organizations to develop a network of structures for organizing events such as plays, concerts and exhibitions, so that artists
are no longer subject to the control of capitalist institutions. And,
looking more at the content of work produced by artists, the possibilities of creating a socialist society need to be 'indigenized' through
stories, paintings, plays, and so on, so that people do not imagine
such a society only in terms of the imagery of China, Russia or Cuba.
By working to create such an indigenous socialist culture, rooted
in the languages and landscapes of South African society, artists
and activists within the liberation movement can help to prevent
the national culture which will inevitably develop in South Africa
from becoming a reactionary, exclusivist and *nationalist* culture.

So far in this essay, I have approached the question of a progressive cultural strategy largely from the angle of what is desirable in
the context of the South African liberation struggle. I have not
focussed on the ways in which this (in my view) politically desirable cultural strategy can be integrated with what is aesthetically and
psychologically desirable for those who must labour to produce such
culture — the artists who commit themselves to working for liberation. I should like now to redress the balance somewhat.

There does not yet seem to be a discourse available to progressive artists in South Africa which can adequately connect the complexities of artistic production to a revolutionary political perspective. Yet such a discourse is necessary, if artists are to be able to
respond critically to the demands made on them by political organizations. In sketching out some of the lines of argument which I think
should be developed to become the skeleton of an appropriate discourse, I shall draw on the analyses of Leon Trotsky and Mao Tse-
Tung concerning the relationship between artistic practice and
revolutionary struggle.

The aspects of Trotsky's analysis that I wish to draw on are, firstly, his discussion of the psychological complexity of artistic produc-

tion, and secondly, his argument that artists explore vital aspects of human experience in a way not possible within the framework of purely political (i.e. theoretical and organizational) activity. Both these ideas are nicely connected in the following passage from his essay 'Class and Art':

> One cannot approach art as one can politics, not because artistic creation is a religious rite or something mystical . . . but because it has its own laws of development, and above all because in artistic creation an enormous role is played by subconscious processes — slower, more idle and less subjected to management and guidance, just because they are subconscious. (Siegel, 1970: 76-77)

Trotsky's insistence on the effect of subconscious processes in shaping the work of the artist is, I believe, of exceptional importance for an understanding of the way in which artists can define their role in the South African liberation struggle. This definition must be able to contain within it an acknowledgement — if not a clear articulation — of such subconscious processes. I don't know if a single artist would deny the fact that his or her creative work is influenced by these processes; but the acceptable political understanding of artistic production within the liberation movement often refuses to see this influence as an inevitable and *valid* phenomenon. I am not talking here of a Romantic notion of 'inspiration', traceable to no earthly source, but emanating rather from a combination of individual artistic genius and the benevolence of some extra-terrestrial muse. I am talking of such phenomena as 'imagination', the sudden insight into the possibilities of aesthetic forms, the ability to identify ways of depicting social experience that offer new images, new meanings for that experience, which characterize the creative skills of the artist. Perhaps these activities should not be seen as purely subconscious, since the process of producing comprehensible artworks requires that they be shaped by the artist's rational consciousness. The mechanism of artistic creation is one which few artists can articulate clearly, and I freely admit that I do not have an adequate language for doing so. What I am trying to grasp, here, is the necessary dimension of unpredictability in the work of any artist: the fact that artistic production is not a matter of turning out poems, plays, songs, images, according to a pre-given 'recipe', but an *exploration*, an experiment in understanding, using a combination of aesthetic, intellectual and subconscious raw materials. Trotsky's acknowledgement of this dimension is the basis of his refusal to see the work of the artist as controllable by the political structures of the revolutionary movement:

We believe that the supreme task of art in our epoch is to take part actively and consciously in the preparation of the revolution. But the artist cannot serve the struggle for freedom unless he subjectively assimilates its social content, unless he feels in his very nerves its meaning and drama and freely seeks to give his own inner world incarnation in his art. (Siegel, 1970: 120)

The effect of defining the artist's work in terms of the agenda of a political organization is to amputate his or her 'nerves' and 'inner world'. And the result of this, I would argue, is that artists are no longer able to create the polysemic meanings possible within aesthetic vocabulary, but become instead reproducers of univocal meanings created elsewhere.

The second aspect of Trotsky's analysis that needs to be woven into a discourse of revolutionary artistic practice is contained in the following passage:

[Art] finds the necessary rhythm of words for dark and vague moods, it brings thought and feeling closer or contrasts them with one another, it enriches the spiritual experience of the individual and of the community, it refines feeling, makes it more flexible, more responsive, it enlarges the volume of thought in advance and not through the personal method of accumulated experience, it educates the individual, the social group, the class and the nation. (Siegel, 1970: 30)

The knowledge that art offers to a society, in other words, is not coterminous with the knowledge produced by other practices, such as theoretical analysis, political organization and mobilization, and so on. To concretize this in the South African context: one needs to reject the demand made by so many political activists that artists depict only certain of the experiences of the oppressed community, and these only in a language that is identical to the language of political analysis. This rejection is not a retreat from 'the political' in people's lives; it is an attack on the fallacious argument that only certain aspects of human experience are political, and therefore worth depicting. To take perhaps the archetypal example: the ways in which people respond to nature (their love of its 'beauty', their thoughtless destruction of it, etc.) are not peripheral matters, distractions from 'real' social issues, but significant aspects of their political relationship with the world. To say to the artist, 'Don't write about the sea, write about detention' is to refuse to explore the meanings which people give to nature, and to refuse to allow these meanings to exist. Artists who believe, with Trotsky, that the 'dark and vague moods' of the people are worth understanding, must begin to make a space for them within a revolutionary perspective, instead of leaving them trapped within the aesthetic language of a bourgeois world-view.

This is one of the implications of the demand made on artists by Mao Tse-Tung, that they learn ways of depicting *every aspect* of human life through the prism of class consciousness. Mao's argument, in the Yenan Forum Talks, that all art is constructed in terms of class ideologies, and that artists committed to the revolution must commit themselves fully to its class perspective, is one which I believe progressive artists in South Africa must accept as an essential part of their understanding of their role. That is to say, if they wish to commit themselves to the liberatory process, they must subject their artistic aims to the discipline of a radical political analysis, and must consciously attempt to develop aesthetic forms that are consistent with this analysis. In Mao's words:

> It is right for writers and artists to study literary and artistic creation, but the science of Marxism-Leninism must be studied by all revolutionaries, writers and artists not excepted. Writers and artists should study society, that is to say, should study the various classes in society, their mutual relations and respective conditions, their physiognomy and their psychology. Only when we grasp all this clearly can we have a literature and art that is rich in content and correct in orientation. (Mao, 1971: 256)

One might want to add to 'Marxism-Leninism' a study of Trotsky, Gramsci, Mao himself and other revolutionary theorists; the basic point remains. The '[correctness] in orientation' that the progressive artist must aim to achieve is not the following of orders issued by an organization, but the creation of artworks informed by both a historical materialist understanding of society and a radical analysis of the nature of the struggle for liberation. Artists cannot renounce the responsibility of developing a political perspective on the liberation struggle, through careful study and debate, unless they are content to subject their sense of judgement to the analyses of organizations that do have such a perspective. And such subjection would be nothing other than a perpetuation of the bourgeois notion that art is incapable of producing political meanings on its own terms, but must instead confine itself to relating political perspectives created elsewhere to the minutiae of individual experience. The desire of artists to work 'on their own terms' is a perfectly valid one, consistent with the democratic principle that workers should control their own labour power. But these terms are, willy-nilly, political ones, and artists must acknowledge the fact.

Trotsky's belief in the necessary creative freedom of the artist and

Mao's demand that artists submit to the discipline of revolutionary political theory need to be synthesized, via an understanding of the dialectical relationship between the psychological and the social. This relationship is significant both for the individual artist and for the political organizations involved in the liberation struggle.

By the psychological, here, I mean the subjectivity of individuals within a society, a subjectivity shaped by social processes and in its turn engaging with and affecting these processes. For the artist, this social-psychological dialectic necessitates an examination, in aesthetic forms, of the subjective implications of social processes, based on a radical political analysis. For political organizations, it becomes necessary to infuse the analysis of social processes with an understanding of the psychological experiences of the people caught up in them, so that they are better able to analyse the effects of oppression and exploitation on people, and to find methods of mobilizing them psychologically to resist these effects.

The role of art in this process is a valuable one. Art is one — though not the only — site of examination of the relationship between the psychological and social; it offers a type of knowledge that is necessary to an understanding (and thus to the changing) of society, and this knowledge cannot be collapsed into some other type of knowledge, some body of theory of which art is only an illustration. Artistic activity should therefore be seen as a form of laboratory research, not as a production-line for ideas moulded elsewhere. In the words of Paul Klee, 'Art does not reproduce the visible, art makes visible' (Fischer, 1969: 138).

This is *not* an argument for artistic 'licence', free of responsibility. I must anticipate, and rebut, this charge, since it is still so difficult for people of a radical political persuasion to conceive of artistic freedom in any other form than a reactionary bourgeois one. There can be no guarantee that what artists create during the course of their explorations will be of value for the liberation struggle, or for any audience at all; and what is of no value will be rejected, or quickly discarded. In this respect the relationship between progressive artists and their audience must remain one based on a 'free market economy' of supply and demand. What I am arguing for is a situation in which artists have the right to produce what *they* believe to be of use to the liberation struggle, and to take their work to the widest possible audience within that struggle for assessment — in other words, a democratization of the relationship between artists and their audiences.

The answer is not to have each political organization within the liberation movement developing its own cultural programme, with artists having the 'freedom' to align themselves with any programme on offer. Just as the knowledge produced by the artist is different from, but interacts with, the knowledge produced by political theory and practice, so the dynamics of cultural activism (the work of individual artists, cultural organizations, drama and music projects, etc.) need to be seen as different from those of political activism, though influencing and being influenced by them at every turn.

The fostering of a diversity of cultural initiatives is a prerequisite for the development of a culture of democracy and of liberatory power in South Africa. Radical change is about the generating of new social energies, new possibilities for knowledge and experience; it is predicated on an interrogation of social processes that refuses to stop questioning and exploring. No artistic activity which is straitjacketed by the control of a political organization can fulfil these requirements.

In South Africa at present the pressure on artists to don straitjackets is very strong. But it is not irresistible. If this pressure is to be countered, it will be up to artists themselves to do so, by adding their own conceptions of the role they can play to the debate on culture within the liberation movement.

My argument in this essay has been that the task of building a progressive national culture in South Africa is a necessary one. I have also indicated the nature of the contribution that artists can make to the creation of such a culture. In concluding my discussion, it is interesting to consider the different implications that the 'people's culture' campaign and the call to build a 'national culture' have for the role of the artist in the liberation struggle.

The call for a 'people's culture' has been made in the mid-1980s by organizations operating under the umbrella of the United Democratic Front, and the strategy of building a 'people's culture' has become an integral part of a broader UDF strategy for achieving 'people's power' in South Africa. The impetus for 'people's culture' can be traced to two sources: firstly, a growing concern among certain progressive artists to connect their activities more closely to the work of community and political organizations; and secondly, a developing desire within the UDF to establish cultural projects and a cultural ethos that would reinforce its political perspective and strategies.

Perhaps the most significant characteristic of 'people's culture' is its insistence that the task of progressive artists should be defined in terms of the political analysis and strategies of the ANC and the UDF. Johnny Issel, in a keynote speech delivered at a 'People's Culture Symposium' held at the University of the Western Cape on 24

October 1987, made this clear: he stated that the 'true cultural worker' refused to be a 'weirdo' or a 'gypsy', but worked instead in a 'disciplined way' within the broad democratic movement (a standard circumlocution for those organizations which have adopted the Freedom Charter as their political programme). This demand is an inevitable consequence of the desire on the part of the UDF and the ANC to shape and control the work of artists in both practical and ideological ways — a desire consonant with their insistence that they are the only authentic voices of the oppressed people of South Africa.[3]

The 'people's culture' campaign, like the call for a 'national culture', therefore, has been generated by political organizations within the liberation movement. But whereas 'people's culture' is a notion tied to the principles and strategies of one specific political tendency, the idea of a 'national culture' remains open to debate and to varying interpretations by a range of tendencies within the movement. The artist who participates in the 'people's culture' campaign must be prepared to accept the UDF's perspective on the role of art in changing South Africa, and its vision of the form that change should take. The artist who responds to the call to create a 'national culture', on the other hand, can do so in terms of his or her own assessment of this call, without necessarily adopting the approach of any one political organization to the idea.

The point of this comparison is that it indicates the variety of ways in which political and artistic perspectives can be combined. Artists can analyse the work they are doing in relation to the call for a 'national culture' without losing either their critical perspective on that call, or their freedom to decide what they want to produce; whereas the 'people's culture' campaign allows them no such critical independence, either politically or artistically. If the controlling mechanisms of 'people's culture' have the potential to undermine the democratic rights and creative role of artists in the liberation struggle, the argument for a progressive 'national culture' shows the possibility of fruitful interaction between artistic and political concerns in the process of bringing about a new, liberated South African society.

Notes

1. There is one perspective within the liberation movement which holds that the 'white' ruling class and its 'white' allies cannot be seen as part of the same nation as the 'black' oppressed classes, but rather constitute

40   *Karen Press*

'internal colonial power'. (See Alexander, 1985b: 19-20, and No Sizwe, 1979: 105-111, for a discussion of this position.) Following Alexander's critique of this perspective, I do not regard it as a valid explanation of the nature of the South African nation. Nor, it must be noted, have recent analyses by advocates of this position based their call for a national culture on any reference to the 'internal colonialism' thesis. (See for example Suttner and Cronin, n.d.: 136-137)

2. Although we are focussing on the question of indigenization here, it must also be borne in mind that there is a class dimension to the cultural oppression of South African blacks. There has always been a small proportion of the black population which embraced the Anglocentric culture of the missionaries and the liberal white community, hoping in this way to attain the 'civilized' status of whites, and thereby gain access to political power. Today, there is a growing black middle class which embraces whole-heartedly the values and lifestyle of American corporate culture (the Soweto yuppies . . .), as a brief perusal of any issue of *Tribute* magazine will confirm. It remains the working class (rural and urban) which suffers most severely under the cultural imperialism of the ruling class.

3. A more detailed analysis of the 'people's culture' campaign can be found in the dissertation from which this article has been extracted, 'Towards a Revolutionary Artistic Practice in South Africa' (Press, 1987).

References

Alexander, Neville. 1985a. *Sow the Wind*. Johannesburg: Skotaville.
Alexander, Neville. 1985b. 'For a Socialist Azania: an Approach to the National Question in South Africa'. Unpublished mimeo.
Arts Festival '86. 1986. *Festival Programme*. Cape Town.
Cabral, Amilcar. 1980. *Unity and Struggle*. London: Heinemann.
Fischer, Ernst. 1969. *Art Against Ideology*. London: Penguin.
Issel, Johnny. 1987. 'Keynote speech at People's Culture Symposium'. University of the Western Cape, 24 October 1987. Unpublished speech.
Mao Tse-Tung. 1971. 'Talks at the Yenan Forum on Literature and Art'. *Selected Readings from the Works of Mao Tse-Tung*. Peking: Foreign Languages Press.
Mazrui, Ali A. 1972. *Cultural Engineering and Nation-Building in East Africa*. Illinois: Northwestern University Press.
Ngugi wa Thiong'o. 1981. *Writers in Politics*. London: Heinemann.
No Sizwe. 1979. *One Azania, One Nation*. London: Zed Press.
O'Meara, Dan. 1983. *Volkskapitalisme: Class, capital and ideology in the development of Afrikaner nationalism, 1934-1948*. Johannesburg: Ravan Press.
Press, Karen. 1987. 'Towards a Revolutionary Artistic Practice in South Africa'. University of Cape Town: unpublished Honours dissertation.
Siegel, Paul (ed.). 1970. *Leon Trotsky on Literature and Art*. New York: Pathfinder Press.
Sitas, Ari (ed.). 1986. *Black Mamba Rising*. Natal: Worker Resistance and Culture Publications, Dept of Industrial Sociology, University of Natal for COSATU Workers' Cultural Local.
Suttner, Raymond and Jeremy Cronin. n.d.. *30 Years of the Freedom Charter*. Johannesburg: Ravan Press.

Revolution and Reality: South African Fiction in the 1980s

Stephen Clingman

One should speak of a struggle for a 'new culture' and not for a 'new art'.

— *Antonio Gramsci*

1

In writing of Olive Schreiner's *The Story of an African Farm* — widely credited as being the book which originated modern white South African fiction[1] — Dan Jacobson remarks that a colonial culture 'is one which has no memory' (1971: 7). In this sense he is correct, that a colonial culture must needs repress the real history of violent aggrandizement that underlies its claim to the colonized land as of natural right. He is especially acute in introducing this topic in relation to Schreiner, for her novel is the embodiment of an essential paradox: claiming to be the story of an *African* farm, what it reveals in part is its alienation from the African environment. Unsure of how it got there, it is not very sure it belongs.[2] For the originator of modern black South African fiction, on the other hand, the past exists not so much as the implicit source of an unease, but as the locus of a specific claim. In Sol Plaatje's path-breaking novel *Mhudi*, he looks explicitly to the historical past (of the 1830s) in order to establish an entitlement in the present: of at least an equal share in the land with a colonizing order (see Plaatje: 1978). Here the *recovery* of memory is an essential part of his project.

This introduces a theme of some importance in the history of South

I should like to thank Derek Spitz for his comments on this essay.

African literature over the past one hundred years, in which we are able to discern certain phases identifiable as a sequence of shifts in temporal preoccupation. Thus, Schreiner's novel, though firmly rooted in its own times (for instance in its almost prescient feminism) implicitly revolves around a disappeared and disappearing past (Pechey, 1983: 75-76). In Plaatje's novel it is the *present* which is implicit, as the novel sets up a dialogue with the past in order to illuminate its author's deep perturbations about his contemporary social and political situation. A novel such as Sarah Gertrude Millin's *God's Stepchildren* (1924), on the other hand, written not much later than Plaatje's, works religiously from a past set in the early 1820s to the period just after the First World War — almost the time in which the novel first appeared. And perhaps it is this movement which is symbolic, representing the slip away from concerns with the past as such in South African literature towards an increasing engagement with the present from then on. David Rabkin (1978) has pointed out that both *God's Stepchildren* and William Plomer's *Turbott Wolfe*, in their overwhelming absorption in issues of race, came to light in a period of more widely manifested racial obsession in the 1920s, evinced in part in legislation dealing with everything from labour relations on the mines and in industry to what was considered to be sexual 'morality'. Thus both novels are deeply immersed in their times.

Thereafter the trend continued, though obvious layerings occurred. In Modikwe Dikobe's *The Marabi Dance* (1973)[3] the past is still embedded in the present — like a deeper textual stratum, as it were, in the mind of Martha's father Mabongo and in the traditional cultural practices with which he retains some link — but the novel is more directly concerned with the transformation of that past, as it confronts issues of identity, culture, class and ideology in circumstances of mass urbanization for blacks between the wars. This is true, too, of Peter Abrahams and Alan Paton, both writing in the 1940s, who (albeit in rather different ways) manifest their preoccupation with these same questions against the backdrop of a segregationism already evolving into apartheid. In the 1950s the writers of the *Drum* generation took this one stage further, vividly evoking the world of Sophiatown as a tempestuous battleground and cradle of an urban identity and culture in which ties with the past had disappeared even further. In the 1960s other pressing issues defined the present: authors such as Richard Rive, Jack Cope, C.J. Driver, Nadine Gordimer and Alex La Guma immediately took to the changed circumstances of that period, writing of sabotage and the underground organizations, and the suppression of the latter by the state. As for the period from the early to mid-1970s, the Black Consciousness movement and the Soweto Revolt are almost inconceivable without thinking too of the new wave of poetry and poets borne by but also bearing the historic currents of resistance of that time. In the 1980s, however, there is a new topic. If there has been this shift over the course of the century away from concerns with the past and towards successive engagements with the present, now it seems South African literature has a new obsession: it is preoccupied with issues of the *future*. Again, this development has not been sudden, but graded. The tendency began as early as Karel Schoeman's *Promised Land* (1972) and Gordimer's *The Conservationist* (1974),[4] in which questions concerning the future are (respectively) explicitly and more implicitly addressed. But in the following decade it became clear as a specific phenomenon: in South African fiction, as in South African culture and politics more generally, the future is *the* presiding question of the 1980s.

One may say then that over the past hundred years South African fiction has acted as a kind of crucial historical signposting of deeper transformations of consciousness in society. It also appears that the fiction delineates successive phases in the modern history of a framework of reality which has helped constitute that consciousness: its early construction (as obliquely suggested in Schreiner) and resistance to this (as in Plaatje); its consolidation and elaboration through various supremacist forms, and complex forms of resistance to these (from the 1920s to the 1970s); and the current phase, in which the framework is crumbling, and very different visions are emerging. As far as the 1980s are concerned, three questions arise from these observations. First, why is this current shift taking place? Second, what exactly is contemporary South African fiction signalling in its address to the future? And third, what happens to fiction — and to social consciousness more generally — when one framework of reality is about to be replaced by another?

This essay represents a modest attempt to address these three questions. After a brief consideration of the first, it will deal with the second and third by differentiating between the responses of South African writers in the current period, but also in seeing what unites them. To these ends the central focus of the essay will be on three related, but equally opposing texts — as if they were the three corners of a triangle representing different, but connected, options in this period: Nadine Gordimer's *July's People*, J.M. Coetzee's *Life & Times of Michael K*, and Mongane Serote's *To Every Birth its Blood*.

44   *Stephen Clingman*

2

A complete answer as to why there is such a dramatic shift in South
African fiction in the 1980s would be a complex and detailed one;
its outlines can only be suggested here. To some extent it goes back
to transitions over the last thirty to forty years in South Africa. Thus,
in the 1950s, the movements opposed to apartheid were nonetheless active *within* the framework of what already existed.[5] Fully be-
lieving in the potential of South African democracy, what the opposition movements of the time wanted primarily was its *extension*,
to include blacks and everyone else within it. Though employing
extra-parliamentary methods — as in the Defiance Campaign and
the Congress of the People — the Congress Alliance found no lack
of credit or credibility in the inherent promise of the parliamentary
system as such, and in a sense wanted only its actual improvement.
In its moral positivism, its almost-binary opposition to apartheid in
the form of multiracialism, its belief in the rational superiority of
its case and the way in which it presented the latter in various symbolic demonstrations designed in part as a kind of logical argument
in favour of that superiority, the Alliance in the 1950s explored to
the utmost the limits of an existing framework, but did not really
go beyond it. Similarly the social and cultural world of the period
explored all the options available to it within the apartheid framework, and embodied in its own way the code of 'multiracialism',
but this ultimately proved subject to the legislative, administrative
and police power of the state — that is, to power exerted within and
by existing structures.

This happened at the turn of the decade. After the Sharpeville
massacre the opposition movements were outlawed, driven underground and into exile. Symbolically as well as literally now they were
outside the framework of existing South African reality (Clingman,
1986: 167-168). It was from this position that they began to think
not so much in terms of the *perfection* of this framework, but of its
wholesale *replacement*: that is, of revolution. This was also manifested
in new methods, now no longer peaceful but exploring — at least
on the part of the African National Congress (ANC) and its allies
— sabotage as a preface to more heightened forms of violent
resistance. Amongst other things, what the transition from a non-
violent to violent struggle expressed was the *illegitimacy* of what existed and the need for its overturn. As for the South African writers
of the time, in taking to themes of sabotage and the underground
resistance, they were no doubt also concerned — albeit at deeper
levels and in sometimes tentative fashion — with questions of

illegitimacy and the need for systematic social change. It is this agenda which has intensified since then. Through the strikes of 1973-74, the Black Consciousness movement of the early 1970s and the Soweto Revolt of 1976, and, in the present phase, a deepening struggle throughout the country, the overall stakes have become increasingly clear, though precise battle-lines and prospects often seem confused and in flux. In time of economic recession, of two States of Emergency, of the Botha government's alternating 'reformism' and ruthless repression, of the growth of a multitude of nationalist, working-class, regional and local organizations — and, on the other side, of a neo-fascist far right — South Africa's framework of reality is shifting. Indeed from questions of 'reformism', to competing socialist and nationalist agendas, to transformations in everyday political culture, the issue which dominates everything is that of the nature and shape of a future South Africa. In its own shifting framework and concerted address to the future, then, the response of South African fiction in the 1980s is a layered one. In part it is reworking transitions from the 1950s through to the 1970s; but in part it is enacting and anticipating developments in the current phase as well. Indeed, one should lay some stress on the anticipatory function of the fiction, since all three novels under consideration were written before the heightening of the political struggle in the mid-1980s. This suggests the depth to which issues such as those specified here were already present in South Africa before their explicit realization and elaboration.

3

Nadine Gordimer's *July's People* (1981) approaches the future by being situated in the future itself (I have discussed this novel elsewhere, and so shall simply emphasize certain thematic considerations here) (Clingman, 1986: 193-204). It is at the posited moment of actual revolution that Maureen Smales, her husband Bam, and their children find themselves in the care of their servant July in his rural home. In this context, as I have argued, the setting allows for complex negotiations between present and future; writing from the *perspective* of the future enables Gordimer to undertake a devastating critique of the present. Thus, in perhaps the most crucial perception of the novel, Maureen comes to understand that revolution also means 'an explosion of roles' (1981: 117), and this is exactly what we see as her previous framework of reality breaks down completely. As the patriarchal identity of her husband is shattered in a context which allows him no authority, so, consequently, is Maureen's role as wife to him; she and Bam simply become 'her' and 'he' in one another's minds, in a movement of radical sexual clarification. Maureen's status as 'mother' also shifts, as her children become independent of her in a different set of child-parent relationships in the village, and she of them in her growing autonomy. As for her ironic position as 'mistress' of a white South African household,[6] this is devastated by July; he too reveals how far language has broken down between them, insisting that the realities of a master-servant relationship not be covered over by the facade of a linguistic equality. Eventually he reviles Maureen in his own language, which she literally cannot comprehend. As Rowland Smith has perceptively remarked, 'only when the black man refuses to talk the white woman's language is she able to understand "everything" ' (1984: 107). If we understand by 'language' here that set of codes and linguistic positionings which, in her purportedly empathetic humanism, Maureen had always imposed upon July, that is an accurate statement.

It is then as the only resolution of a total breakdown in, and evident inadequacy of, all the structural supports of Maureen's existence, that there is at the end of the novel the figuration of a 'crossing'. Abandoning husband and children, but running 'with all the suppressed trust of a lifetime' (160), Maureen heads across a river to where an unidentified helicopter has been heard. This ending is sufficiently ambiguous, and has aroused enough critical debate, to warrant some discussion here. Rowland Smith finds in it the expression of an insoluble impasse: Maureen is leaving the emptiness of her old life, but has no future in terms of the only identity with which her historical and social situation has provided her; hence the ending is 'inconclusive' and 'unpredictable' (1984: 96). Perhaps representing another strand of opinion, Nancy Bailey deduces that the helicopter is more likely a symbol of 'death rather than life' since it is more probable that it is 'manned by black revolutionaries . . . than that it represents an American *deus ex machina*' (1984: 221). Besides the fact that an American presence in that geographical zone and at that stage in the novel is hardly worth thinking about, why should one assume that it would represent something 'positive' and the guerillas a 'negative' resolution?

The point is worth raising because it has been Maureen's experience in the novel to smash such identifications utterly. The central issue is that Maureen *has seen through her old life*, in both senses of the phrase; an American 'rescue' in this context would simply

immerse her yet again in the bourgeois set of images and power
relations which have already come to seem to her like a living death.
Instead she is prepared to risk a real death (both the guerillas and
the South African army might kill her because she is herself as yet
objectively 'unidentified') for the sake of at least *the possibility* of a
new life, an alternative future, which the helicopter undoubtedly
represents. It should be noted that as she runs Maureen is herself
no longer a repressed or suppressed individual, and that it is this
liberatory revolution in her *own* identity that leads her on in her commitment towards this risk.[7] The fact that the idea of death and that
of such a transformation are, by force of symbolic compression and
association, so closely associated in this way in the novel may be
indicative of an apocalyptic element in Gordimer's own consciousness regarding revolution. But there is at least the notion of the
necessity of embracing the future, whatever it may bring, of the possibility of historical salvation, and of the need for a transformed kind
of participation.

The innermost gesture of J.M. Coetzee's *Life & Times of Michael
K* (1983), by contrast, is one of *refusal* of any such possibility. Also
set in a future moment of breakdown — in the case of this novel
one hesitates to use the word 'revolution' — Coetzee's depiction
of that moment is already more drawn-out than Gordimer's rather
dramatic presentation. Where she has strikes, fighting in the streets,
and bombs exploding in Johannesburg, Coetzee shows instead the
slow running-down of an increasingly militarized state bureaucracy, an apperception which has enough purchase in the present to
represent a compelling, atmospheric image of the future. In this setting it is the sense of an ending which prevails: the almost elegiac,
but just about humorous way in which the Medical Officer records
the prospect of a return cricket match in the late summer with a team
from the Quartermaster-General's 'if we are all still around' (210)
is enough to convey the feeling of a terminal historical condition.
Other phenomena are more ominous. As Michael K passes from
the labour-camp in which he is interned to the convalescent/rehabili-
tation camp in which the Medical Officer works, both equally institutions of social and political control (Foucault is surely the analytical presence here),[8] one understands the potential for totalitarian
degeneracy which systems such as apartheid engender, albeit, as
in this case, in a clumsy and somewhat inefficient form.

It is across this particular landscape of possibility that Michael K
travels. Originally he carts his mother in a home-made barrow away
from the embattled environs of Cape Town towards her birthplace,
where the idea is that they might live in peace, but after she dies

along the way his objective becomes more strictly one of survival. In the course of this quest Michael K comes to conform to the typology of the 'holy fool' or 'idiot'; physically disfigured and possibly mentally retarded, through his innocent certitudes he exposes the corrupt nature of the system which attempts to contain him, and develops his own philosophy of meaning — which in his case is very nearly one of its total rejection. For in many ways it is clear that Michael K is to be regarded as a 'resistant signifier' in the novel — one who will not be subject to any order of meaning other than his own individual and resolutely indeterminate one. It is no accident then that like Maureen in *July's People* he abandons the old order, but that, unlike her, he equally will not entertain any idea of a salvationary future. For him, on the contrary, the future is connected only obscurely with a 'sense of pain' (82).

Indeed, Michael K's whole being becomes directed against incorporation into any system, whether of the present or posited for the future. Surveying the ruined house of a family of white farmers he considers that the worst mistake would be 'to try to found ... a rival line' (143). Despite slight pangs of nostalgia for the idea of positive resistance, he rejects participation of any kind — 'I am not in the war', he declares (189) — and is described as being a soul 'untouched by history' (207). Instead, incarcerated in various settings, but also contemplating the claims various parties have made on him, Michael K's deepest consolation is 'to be out of the camps, out of all the camps at the same time' (248); in a novel in which no *double entendre* is accidental, evidently for Coetzee there is a sense in which political camps and prison camps are indistinguishable. For him, it becomes clear, any form of systematization — including *political* systematization — is a form of *control*; and it is this, fundamentally, that Michael K refuses. Thus he is described as a 'stone' passing 'through the intestines of a war' (185); resolute and hardy, he will be unabsorbed, unincorporated into *any* body politic. On the contrary, as Michael K's aim becomes to be again what he was in the beginning, a gardener, a 'tender of the soil' (156), the novel seems to be directed to issues of resistance as *total* — to *any* form of politics — and to clarifications of a physical, but also almost spiritual nature in this setting.

Il faut cultiver notre jardin: is Coetzee simply returning us to this Voltairean dictum without any sense of irony?[9] In the heightening political circumstances of South Africa in the current phase, what are we to make of these outright rejections? Are they not fundamentally evasive and conservative? Certainly if Coetzee sees his work as connected with history, it is not in the usual way. In a recent discussion he saw the link between literature and history as one not of complementarity, but rather of 'rivalry, even enmity' (Coetzee, 1987: 19). On the other hand, as Stephen Watson has pointed out, all Coetzee's novels are deeply related to the history of colonialism (1986: 370); and it might be said that his real topic — as expressed in one form most directly in *Waiting for the Barbarians* (1980) — is the end of empire, mental and conceptual as well as political. Indeed, if one wished to fashion a defence for Coetzee against allegations of conservatism (if he wanted or needed such a thing) this is the only way of establishing that objective link which he himself denies: his novels have to do with the *longue durèe* of a history of frames of consciousness.[10] That is why there is no 'rival line' which Coetzee is prepared to see constructed. For him, because of his evident belief in the long-term and all-enveloping determinations of 'discourse' as against history (which he sees as yet another *kind* of 'discourse') (Coetzee, 1987), the sway of imperial control is not yet over. Any resistance to it is always open to the liability of merely duplicating in alternative form the dominant terms of power.

That is why, instead of resistance, he offers us refusal. Watson speaks of a 'failed dialectic' (1986: 382) in Coetzee's work, but perhaps it is more accurate to talk of a more principled 'negative' dialectic in which Coetzee's fiction stands as the ostensible second term. Rather than constructing an antithesis to colonial or imperial power, it rejects that temptation at the same time as it does the dominant term, and this becomes a different kind of antithesis (hence in Coetzee's latest novel, *Foe* (1986), it is Friday's *silence* which is his ultimate resistance). In this scheme of things perhaps it would be the refusal in turn of that negative antithesis at some future stage which would introduce a synthesis of yet again a very different kind: a history which at present is literally unthinkable. As to the future, however, Coetzee averts his eyes from any hoped-for eventuality as well, contenting himself with what he perhaps sees as the more authentic present act of abnegation. Hence the ascetic minimalism which underlies *Life & Times*: for Coetzee, one senses, the future could be a matter only of a Pascalian wager, and should not be presumed upon. Instead it is clear that for the present he is satisfied to be defined as what the Medical Officer calls Michael K: 'a great escape artist' (1983: 228). Not a writer of escap*ist* fiction, Coetzee is nonetheless determined to make his work escape the ordinary determinations of politics and history. In *Life & Times* there is the refusal of anything we would normally count as political. Certainly untempted by the past, Coetzee will not be tempted by any notions of partisanship, participation or salvation in the future.

Mongane Serote's *To Every Birth its Blood* (1981), by contrast, is whole-heartedly committed to the idea of a necessary alternative future, and the fact that it must be constructed through collective political agency and organization. It does this not only through its content, but also through a series of formal and structural 'dialogues' in the text. Thus, it begins not with political agency, but with the lack of it, in the nightmare world of Tsi Molope, who, in his active immersion in the conditions of his degradation under apartheid, reinforces his own victimization. In a setting now far worse than anything described by the writers of the 1950s in their frequent moments of anguish, Tsi lives in a world of apparent chaos and anarchy. Walking through the streets of Alexandra Township with a friend, he remarks with grim dispassion and despair: 'We saw someone get killed. We watched silently.' (1981: 7) It is a world of physical and emotional violence against women: Tsi's brother, Ndo, and he himself participate in different ways in this syndrome. As for Tsi, in his state of mental extremity, the external world has become sickeningly internalized: 'The smell of the dirty water in the streets — the water, full of shit and all imaginable rubbish — felt as though it had become my saliva . . . . My stomach felt hard, like a stone . . . .' (32) Elsewhere it is the all-encompassing futility of his situation that becomes apparent:

> What's all this shit? Heaven knows. What is going to happen to us?
> The men. The women. The children. What is going to happen to us?
> What shit is this? Does it not feel like mud, mud we have to wade
> through, mud we have to sink into? What are we going to
> do? . . . Everything had become so futile. (53)

Against the visionary displacements of Gordimer and the consummate intellectuality of Coetzee, this has an inescapable, direct force. The nature of this sort of representation, mediated entirely through Tsi's mind in Part I of the book, conveys all too well a life lived on the edge of political as well as personal dissolution.

On one occasion this condition is given a specific cause: it is after a devastating physical, sexual assault by the police — exercised on the body, which means that its effects are also felt in the mind — that Tsi's worst instability and feelings of alienation set in. Yet it also galvanizes him into action: realizing, as his photographer cohort Boykie puts it, that 'we are at war' (126), Tsi leaves his job as a journalist and takes up work in community education. Neither then nor by the end of the novel is it clear, however, that any hope for the future lies in Tsi; indeed, something very different happens in Part II of the book. In this the novel seems like a gloss on Lukács's differentiation between modernism and realism: Tsi's stream of consciousness *is* his entrapment within the world of *durèe*, of pure subjectivity; but the second part of the book puts this in what Lukács would call *perspective* (Lukács: 1963).[11] Here Tsi disappears almost entirely, and a different set of protagonists takes over: as the narrative is brought under control, these characters work for liberation, and they do so *collectively*.

At the same time a number of interesting shifts occur. Whereas Part I of the novel manifests some of the characteristic moods, methods and insights of the Black Consciousness movement (Serote was one of the key Black Consciousness poets, and this book was begun in 1975) in Part II this is meshed with what can only be taken as an affiliation to the ANC: the 'core group' of characters — John, Dikeledi, Onalenna, Tuki, Themba, Jully, Mandla and Oupa — belong to what they term 'the Movement'.[12] Where the Black Consciousness generation rejected its parents because of their political failures — and where Tsi, for instance, sees only defeat in his — in Part II there is a renewed respect for an older and continuing struggle. The trial of Mike Ramono, an older ANC man and Dikeledi's father, is a case in point, while the very name of 'Oupa', the youngest member of the group and the one who pays the most terrible price for his commitment, signifies a reconnection with earlier traditions at the same time as it reflects the reality of an urban 'post-ethnic' identity.

What characterizes the group chiefly, however, is its moral ascendancy. Where in Tsi's world women are victimized, in this movement they play a central role, liberating themselves as well as others at the same time.[13] As for the mania of Tsi's existence, it is entirely overcome in the collective support, mutuality and political dedication of the group. The choice seems to be clear: either one lives in the crazed world of Tsi's individualism — which it appears can only be a dead-end — or one works rationally and purposively together with others towards a new order. As if in support of this the book in itself embodies a new kind of fictional and political *presence*: when Oupa announces, just before he dies under torture at the hands of the Security Police, 'Yes, I am a member of the Movement' (313), it reads like a particular culmination in the history of identity among the oppressed in South Africa. This new presence is evident also in the candid inspection — with devastating imagery — of the need for retaliatory violence against the agents of apartheid. As Captain Mpando, a black policeman, lies shot in the toilets of a shebeen, what was internalized for Tsi is externalized again:

'His [Mpando's] brain had spilled and was mixed with the shit and urine. Joe [his colleague], looking at all this, tasting the Shevas [sic] Regal on his tongue, felt bilious.' (263) It is not as if the novel all too easily foresees certain victory: some of the characters have much to overcome in their personal lives, and the end of the novel, structurally reformulating that choice between Tsi's dissolution and a difficult struggle, indicates that everything is still to be done. Yet it has shown triumphs of a kind: the novel places itself as exhortatory and *inspirational*,[14] firmly aligned with the liberation movement whose social and psychological impulses it describes.

4

In many ways then the three novels we have been discussing could not be more different in terms of their approach to the future, varying from the guarded welcome of Gordimer, to the political refusals of Coetzee, to the whole-hearted embrace and affirmations of Serote. This indicates the degree of ideological range there can be in fictional works emerging from and responding to the same historical moment. The complexities and honesties of fiction also allow us to see here what might normally be more concealed: the degree of underlying difference and even conflict there is between three writers who in general terms would probably insist they were on the 'same side'; such conflict is no doubt more broadly dispersed in South African society as well. In addition there is another significant difference in the novels, in this case one which divides the white writers from Serote: where the work of the former is essentially *reactive* to a future being made beyond the control of their characters, Serote's protagonists are centrally concerned with *constructing* the future for themselves. Although there have been significant shifts, for instance, within Gordimer's position over the last forty years, this probably suggests the residual social and political marginality of the white writer in South Africa in comparison with the black. (On the other hand this is not a distinction one would wish to make too much of: the poetry of Jeremy Cronin, for instance, has shown its own impulse towards the 'inspirational', as his work becomes part of a common identification in active struggle.)[15]

Over and above these different approaches to the future, however, we still need to know what all this means for the replacement of a framework of reality in these works: here we should discuss what divides and unites the novels at hand in other formal, generic and thematic terms. From this point of view, initially, it is clear that while all three works approach the future, they are still barred from its realization. Thus, the sense of an ending is realized as the sense of a *limit*. This is represented variously in formal, internal terms by *symbolism* in the texts; and structurally and generically as a whole by the use of *allegory*.[16]

For the beginnings of the use of symbolism by white writers in the current phase one should go back at least as far as Gordimer's *The Conservationist* (1974) and Coetzee's *In the Heart of the Country* (1978). Here one might suggest as a general proposition what I argued at some length in relation to *The Conservationist*: that symbolism represents in these works what is unavailable, or else not yet fully present in society realistically or historically (1986: ch. 5). (*In the Heart of the Country* connects with that implied absence in exploring in symbolic form what appears to be the ending point of a whole history and culture; the future is what waits 'on the other side' of the novel, as it were.) In different ways this kind of prolepsis applies in *July's People* and *Life & Times*. In *July's People* Maureen's crossing of the river is presented in symbolic baptismal terms; it is almost like a rebirth, while the landed helicopter, unseen yet felt by Maureen, is as nearly symbolic as real. What awaits *her* on the other side of this boundary to the future is clearly something quite profoundly different from her previous existence; hence also the analogy of the crossing from 'life' to 'death', in which the symbolic significance inverts the realistic order of meaning through an act of political translation. Indeed, in a novel in which 'mistranslation' is central to the relationships between Maureen and July, Maureen and Bam, and to Maureen's past understanding of her own existence, the symbolic dimension extends powerfully to the domain of language itself. In this the word 'translation' is apposite: coming from the Latin *transferre*, to carry across, we can see how Maureen is 'carried across' the symbolic river boundary and simultaneously finds a new mode of seeing and comprehending her world, in which old understandings are stripped away and everyday language emerges transformed. On one level in the novel the symbolic dimension is made to coincide with revolutionary meaning.

In *Life & Times* virtually the entire setting is symbolic — a symbolic landscape as much as a real one traversed by Michael K. Here the function of the symbolism is also specific, having to do with the confrontation of various choices in the landscape of the future. In Serote's *To Every Birth*, however, the pattern of the two other works is reversed. In this novel the shift in the text is not from the realistic to the symbolic, but from the symbolic to the 'real' — from the chaos and disorder of Tsi's nightmare world in Part I to the ordered, purposive and controlled world of 'the Movement' in Part II. Despite the fact that the novel returns to its central symbol at the end — that of a woman in the process of giving birth, the 'birth' of its title — to negotiate its way into the future, a different point seems to be emerging: that what is or used to be 'reality' for the white writer is or used to be chaos for the black, and that at some level the replacement of a framework of reality means the reversal of these states. White writing is somewhat fearfully or apocalyptically entering the 'unknown', usually represented in symbolic terms, while black writing attempts to move beyond the chaotic 'unknown' of the present in creating the reality of the future.

This again differentiates between white and black writers, but we may also — now drawing in other works as well — see what unites them. For overall in South Africa it seems one might speak of 'allegory for the eighties': it appears that allegory, by and large, is the genre which communicates with the future. In both *July's People* and *Life & Times* the allegory works both ways, as the future acts as a vehicle for commenting on the present, while the 'present' of the novels is a way of engaging with choices and meanings felt to be emerging from the future. In these terms *Life & Times* is perhaps the most explicit of the works we are considering, as it follows the almost entirely allegorical life of Michael K, but in *July's People* Maureen's experience, too, is allegorical, of the transformations that will occur under conditions of revolution. In *To Every Birth* it is more complex. Here the difficulty is that insofar as the group which forms the core of 'the Movement' represents anything, it is only an extension of itself: that is, the wider 'Movement' for liberation at large. However, when that wider movement is described, this is always done in symbolic, organic terms as a 'river', 'the sea' or 'the wind',[17] and it is clear that in portraying the growing pace, organization and effectiveness of the core group the novel is to some extent going beyond realism. The novel becomes an allegory of how the future is to be made.

Elsewhere in current South African literature we see similar usages. Thus, of the black writers, Njabulo Ndebele is perhaps the one most committed to exploring social realities and individual interiorities in the quotidian life of the townships; yet his most triumphal story, 'Uncle' (1983), may once again be read allegorically, as, culminating in a glorious, impromptu musical extravaganza, it celebrates community strengths and perhaps heralds a different future to come. Similarly the play *Woza Albert* (Mtwa, *et al.*, 1983), first and most prominent in the 'new wave' of black drama in the 1980s, is, explicitly, an allegory. Utilizing the story of the Second Coming for its basic impulses and structure, it engages deep desires for the future. This is all of some significance then, for it seems in current South African literature that allegory is the formal limit across which the future is approached. For Walter Benjamin allegory was associated with a lost past: 'allegories are in the realm of thoughts what ruins are in the realm of things.'[18] But in South Africa allegory is, amidst the ruin of things, a way of constructing thoughts about the future.

Even within this, however, one might still ask the question: *how* is the future being approached? Here I should like to draw attention to one phenomenon only, which is a shift from the representation of mental conditions to a focus on physical realities or resistance; that is, a shift from *mind* to *body* in the fiction. This of course has a genealogy. In white writing since Schreiner encapsulation within a subjectivized 'mental' world has always been the sign of social and historical alienation and marginality; it was only in that short period in the elaboration of white control from the 1920s to the 1950s that white writing did not necessarily feel itself alienated and marginal in this way. Indeed, as a previous framework of reality began to crumble dramatically in the 1970s, an older theme re-entered in a new form: that of *madness* within the white mental world.[19] Black writing has always been more secure in its social identity, but at times of stress — such as in the writing of Can Themba in the 1950s, or Black Consciousness poetry of the 1970s — mental conditions were evoked with some intensity.

In the 1980s, however, a resolute physicality reappears. In *July's People* Maureen — having rediscovered the forgotten realities of her body in the bush — escapes the breakdown of her framework of reality by finding a *physical* solution: running towards the future. In Gordimer's latest novel, *A Sport of Nature* (1987), its central character, Hillela, lives and finds the future entirely — and in part allegorically — through her body. In *Life & Times* Michael K is described in irreducibly bodily terms — he is after all the 'stone' passing through the intestines of the war — while in *Foe* Coetzee presents the resolute 'otherness' of the body, especially of the black body, and perhaps extends the allegory: it is this body which will make its own liberation, out of its own impenetrable meanings (that hidden future to which Coetzee's fiction can only defer). In white fiction in the 1980s it is only Menán du Plessis's *A State of Fear* (1983) that remains trapped within a world of oppressive self-consciousness for its protagonist; but here the external setting is described with such unmitigating physical attention that one senses the hidden need physically to come to grips with it. As far as black fiction is concerned, the same general shift towards 'bodily' representations is apparent. In *To Every Birth* the mental extremity of Tsi is overcome in the collective social body of 'the Movement'. In Ndebele's collection of short stories, *Fools*, the body of the black community is seen both as a resource and strength. In black theatre over the last decade we have seen the transition from depictions of 'consciousness' to enactions of 'presence'. Here — prototypically again in *Woza Albert* — the 'carnival' of black theatre celebrates the body as it overthrows oppressive hierarchies which had reduced it within a certain mental as well as physical framework.[20]

What, we may ask, is the significance of all of this? We may begin again with a question of difference. Thus, for Gordimer, the physicality of *July's People* and *A Sport of Nature* marks something of a turning point, clarifying the need of whites *themselves* for revolutionary change, and the turn away from marginality to a rejoining of society, but on very different terms; this is what underlies the separate transformations of Maureen and Hillela. Cronin's poetry explicitly announces his own move, while Du Plessis's *A State of Fear* reads almost as the preface to such a shift. At the same time it must be said that the dominant focus of white writing is still on the individual — expressed in extreme form in Michael K's 'minimal' body — while black writing is concerned with elaborating, primarily, a sense of *social* identity, of the regenerative, expansive *social* body. This is what we see in the work of Serote and Ndebele.

Above and beyond this, however, there is a larger significance; here we may take Gordimer and Serote as representative. Where a framework of reality is crumbling, consciousness *per se* loses its 'rationale', so to speak. Thus, in *July's People* Maureen faces a problem which can no longer be solved mentally, since the limits of a framework have been reached; rather, something must be *done*, as the only way out of 'madness'. For Serote, what exists in the first part of his novel is very nearly madness; again, it is in physically making a new world that this condition is overcome. Even Coetzee's work — though it shows no impulse towards the future — attempts to find a different way out of a framework of consciousness which has apparently reached its limits.

These patterns are not confined simply to the world of fiction in South Africa. Here in the 1980s forms of community, trade-union and street culture resist the onslaught of state power driven seemingly insane on the one hand, and ever stricter in its thought-control on the other, by fashioning new ways of life, internal organization, symbolic value.[21] The political propensities and prospects of street and area committees, and of the plethora of alternative organizations which exist are not yet clear, but it is evident that they are attempting to fashion, amongst other things, a new 'order' as a way out of the broken framework of the present. This is the significance too of South African fiction in the 1980s: at a level far deeper than that of slogan or propaganda it tells us it is time for a new reality to be made.

Notes

1. See Gray, 1979, ch. 6, 'Schreiner and the novel tradition'.
2. For further discussion see Clingman, 1986: 135-136. For an article which analyses Schreiner's text by taking the idea of 'discontinuity' implied in Jacobson's comment much further, see Pechey, 1983: 65-78.
3. Though published later, the novel derives from and relates to the 1930s and '40s in Johannesburg.
4. For an extended analysis of *The Conservationist* in its engagement with the present and the future, see Clingman, 1986: ch. 5.
5. For a fuller analysis of the 1950s in the terms suggested in this discussion, see Clingman, 1986: ch. 2. Also see Lodge, 1983: ch. 3 & 202; Gerhart, 1978: ch.4, especially 94; Robertson, 1971: 145.
6. For a short story which explores similar ironies, see Nadine Gordimer, 'Blinder', in *Something Out There* (Johannesburg: Ravan Press/Taurus, 1984; London: Cape).
7. This transition is prefaced in Gordimer's *Burger's Daughter* — the novel which preceded *July's People* — where Rosa Burger finds her own reasons for continuing her family heritage of struggle, and where this is also precipitated by a moment of physical and mental stress.
8. See, for example, Michel Foucault, *Discipline and Punish: The Birth of the Prison*, 1979.
9. 'We must tend our garden' — the climactic line of Voltaire's *Candide*. It is possible that Coetzee would see in the history of the French Revolution — taking into account the demise of the *philosophes*, the Terror, and the Napoleonic supercession — some justification for the refusal of an obvious political role in South Africa, on the grounds that the dominant terms of power were not overthrown by resistance but simply transformed; see further discussion below.
10. See Braudel, 1980. One might suggest that Coetzee's work enacts without stepping outside of or beyond the kind of moment suggested by Braudel: 'even more significant than the deep-rooted structures of life are their points of rupture, their swift or slow deterioration under the effects of contradictory pressures' (1980: 45). For an article using Braudel's concept in a different way, see Rich, 1984.
11. I remember a conversation with Nick Visser on this point.
12. In this respect *To Every Birth* appears to be a displaced autobiography — not only personal, but ideological, since Serote is now an ANC cultural representative in London. For the recurrent appearance of 'core groups' in leadership roles in South African novels dealing with the period of the Soweto Revolt and after, see Sole, 1988: 76-78.

13. In this their function is different from the symbolic role assigned to women in European nationalist movements of the 19th and 20th centuries: See Mosse, 1985: ch. 5. Yet for some of the ambiguities of a possible idealization of the role of women which remain in the novel, see Sole, 1988: 79.

14. For the distinction between black writing in South Africa as 'inspirational' and white writing as essentially 'protestant' in mood, see Gordimer, 'Censorship and Unconfessed History': 1988.

15. See Jeremy Cronin, *Inside*. Johannesburg: Ravan Press, 1983.

16. The distinction between symbolism and allegory is not always an easy one to make. Northrop Frye (1957: 89) comments that any reading which searches for the meaning of a text will always be allegorical. Yet it is clear that some works themselves foreground or urge an allegorical method. The working position for the present essay is that texts which are allegorical in their overall tendency will, to a greater or lesser extent, use forms of symbolism internally in order to carry their meaning.

17. In the novel's transitions from descriptions of the core group to symbolic representations of the wider 'Movement' at large, *To Every Birth* appears to exemplify quite remarkably Elias Canetti's presentation of the relationship between what he calls 'crowd crystals' and 'crowd symbols' in *Crowds and Power* (1973: 85ff); at the same time Canetti provides a basic repertoire of organicist symbols used in the formation of what we may think of as nationalist movements.

18. Quoted by Fredric Jameson, 1971: 71. Benjamin's argument is also taken up in a strong form by Lukács in 'The Ideology of Modernism', 1963: 40-45.

19. This is a phenomenon which I have begun to explore more broadly elsewhere: see Clingman (forthcoming). For an analysis of the mental breakdown of Mehring, the central character of Gordimer's *The Conservationist*, see Clingman, 1986: ch. 5.

20. For the founding exposition of the idea of 'carnival' in this sense, see Mikhail Bakhtin, *Rabelais and his World* (1984). For the applicability of this idea more generally, see Stallybrass and White, 1986.

21. For the way in which this has been embodied in current South African poetry, see Cronin, 1988: 12-23. This essay appears later in this book.

References

Bailey, Nancy. 1984. 'Living without the Future: Nadine Gordimer's *July's People*'. *World Literature Written in English*, 24(2).

Bakhtin, Mikhail. 1984. *Rabelais and his World*. Translated by Helene Iswolsky. Bloomington: Indiana University Press.

Braudel, Fernand. 1980. 'History and the Social Sciences: the *Longue Durèe*'. In Braudel's *On History*. Translated by Sarah Matthews. Chicago: University of Chicago Press.

Canetti, Elias. 1973. *Crowds and Power*. Translated by Carol Stewart. Harmondsworth: Penguin.

Clingman, Stephen. 1986. *The Novels of Nadine Gordimer: History from the Inside*. Johannesburg: Ravan Press; London & Boston: Allen & Unwin.

Clingman, Stephen. Forthcoming. 'Beyond the Limit: The Social Relations of Madness in Southern African fiction'. In *The Bounds of Race: Colonial Relations in Culture and History*. Edited and introduced by Dominick la Capra. Ithaca: Cornell University Press.

Coetzee, J.M. 1978. *In the Heart of the Country*. Johannesburg: Ravan Press; London: Secker.

Coetzee, J.M. 1980. *Waiting for the Barbarians*. London: Secker; Harmondsworth: Penguin (1982).

Coetzee, J.M. 1983. *Life & Times of Michael K*. Harmondsworth: Penguin.

Coetzee, J.M. 1986. *Foe*. Johannesburg: Ravan Press; London: Secker.

Coetzee, J.M. 1987. 'Coetzee and the Cockroach which Can't be Killed': Account of an address by J.M. Coetzee at the *Weekly Mail* Book Week, Cape Town — November. *Weekly Mail* (Johannesburg) 13-19 November 1987.

Cronin, Jeremy. 1983. *Inside*. Johannesburg: Ravan Press.

Cronin, Jeremy. 1988. ' "Even under the Rine of Terror . . . ." ': Insurgent South African Poetry'. *Research in African Literatures*, 19(1), 12-23. The essay is reprinted in this book.

Dikobe, Modikwe. 1973. *The Marabi Dance*. London: Heinemann.

Du Plessis, Menán. 1983. *A State of Fear*. Cape Town: David Philip.

Foucault, Michel. 1979. *Discipline and Punish: The Birth of the Prison*. Translated by Alan Sheridan. New York: Vintage Books.

Frye, Northrop. 1957. *Anatomy of Criticism*. Princeton: Princeton University Press.

Gerhart, Gail. 1978. *Black Power in South Africa: The Evolution of an Ideology*. Berkeley: University of California Press.

Gordimer, Nadine. 1974. *The Conservationist*. London: Cape.

Gordimer, Nadine. 1981. *July's People*. London: Cape.

Gordimer, Nadine. 1987. *A Sport of Nature*. Cape Town/Johannesburg: David Philip/Taurus; London: Cape; New York: Knopf.

Gordimer, Nadine. 1988. 'Censorship and Unconfessed History'. In *The Essential Gesture: Writing Politics and Places*. Edited and introduced by Stephen Clingman. Johannesburg/Cape Town: Taurus/David Philip; London: Cape; New York: Knopf.

Gramsci, Antonio. 1985. *Selections From Cultural Writings*. Edited by David Forgacs and Geoffrey Nowell-Smith; translated by William Boellhower. London: Lawrence & Wishart.

Gray, Stephen. 1979. *Southern African Literature. An Introduction*. Cape Town: David Philip.

Jacobson, Dan. 1971. Introduction to Olive Schreiner's *The Story of an African Farm* (1883). Harmondsworth: Penguin.

Jameson, Fredric. 1971. *Marxism and Form: Twentieth Century Dialectical Theories of Literature*. Princeton: Princeton University Press.

Lodge, Tom. 1983. *Black Politics in South Africa since 1945*. Johannesburg: Ravan; London & New York: Longman.

Lukács, Georg. 1963. 'The Ideology of Modernism'. In *The Meaning of Contemporary Realism*. Translated by John and Necker Mander. London: Merlin.

Millin, Sarah Gertrude. 1924. *God's Stepchildren*. London: Constable. With an introduction by Tony Voss, Johannesburg: Ad. Donker, 1980.

Mosse, George L. 1985. *Nationalism and Sexuality*. New York: Howard Fertig.

Mtwa, Percy; Mbongeni Ngema and Barney Simon. 1983. *Woza Albert!* London: Methuen.

Ndebele, Njabulo. 1983. *Fools and Other Stories*. Johannesburg: Ravan Press.

Pechey, Graham. 1983. '*The Story of an African Farm*: Colonial History and the Discontinuous Text'. *Critical Arts*, 3(1), 65-78.

Plaatje, Sol T. 1978. (original composition c. 1920). *Mhudi*. Introduction by Tim Couzens. London: Heinemann.

Rabkin, David. 1978. 'Race and Fiction: *God's Stepchildren* and *Turbott Wolfe*'. In *The South African Novel in English*. Edited by Kenneth Parker. London: Macmillan.

Rich, Paul. 1984. 'The Decline of the Civilization Idea: An Essay on Nadine Gordimer's *July's People* and J.M. Coetzee's *Waiting for the Barbarians*'. *Research in African Literatures*, 15(3).

Robertson, Janet. 1971. *Liberalism in South Africa, 1948-1963*. Oxford: Clarendon Press.

Schoeman, Karel, 1978. *Promised Land* (Afrikaans original *Na die Geliefde Land* appeared in 1972). London: Julian Friedmann.

Serote, Mongane. 1981. *To Every Birth its Blood*. Johannesburg: Ravan Press.

Smith, Rowland. 1984. 'Masters and Servants: Nadine Gordimer's *July's People* and the Themes of her Fiction'. *Salmagundi*, 62.

Sole, Kelwyn. 1988. 'The Days of Power: Depictions of Politics and Community in Four Recent South African Novels'. *Research in African Literatures*, 19(1).

Stallybrass, Peter and Allon White. 1986. *The Politics and Poetics of Transgression*. Ithaca: Cornell University Press.

Watson, Stephen. 1986. 'Colonialism and the Novels of J.M. Coetzee'. *Research in African Literatures*, 17(3).

Beyond the Interregnum: A Note on the Ending of July's People

Nicholas Visser

It is hardly surprising that the ending of Nadine Gordimer's *July's People* should have occasioned a fair amount of puzzlement. As Maureen Smales runs towards the helicopter, neither she nor the reader has any way of knowing 'whether it holds saviours or murderers; and — even if she were to have identified the markings — for whom' (Gordimer, 1981: 158). And not knowing that, we are left uncertain what to make of the conclusion.

One impression readers may gain from the final pages of the novel is that they constitute what Russian Formalists called a 'zero ending', an ending in which the conclusion is left hanging in the air. Certainly, given Gordimer's guiding conception of the historical moment in which she was engaged in writing the novel, a zero ending would make sense. She chose as an epigraph for *July's People* a well-known formulation by Gramsci that was to become particularly significant for her: 'The old is dying and the new cannot be born; in this interregnum there arises a great diversity of morbid symptoms.'[1] A notion of interregnum — a moment *between* two states of affairs, in which outcomes are not only unclear but cannot yet come into being — is necessarily going to make closure problematic. Nevertheless, I hope to show that, however perplexing the ending of *July's People* may be, it is not simply left hanging.

What we might think of as the polarities in interpretative responses to the ending of the novel have been outlined by Stephen Clingman and Margaret Lenta.[2] Clingman is so far the only critic to opt for what might be thought of as the positive interpretation:

at the end of the novel Maureen is running. The circumstances in which this occurs are ambiguous, but their significance surely is not.

An unmarked helicopter has flown over near July's village and is coming down to land. No one knows whether it is manned by freedom
fighters or by the South African army. But Maureen knows she must
run. She is running from old structures and relationships, which have
led her to this cul-de-sac; but she is also running towards her revolutionary destiny. She does not know what that destiny may be, whether
it will bring death or life. All she knows is that it is the only authentic
future awaiting her. (1986: 203)

The confidence of Clingman's second sentence ('their significance
surely is not') is belied by what follows.[3] At precisely the moment
we are to be informed of the significance, we are told 'she is running . . . towards her revolutionary destiny'. The phrase is rhetor-
ically impressive, but it is more of an evasion than an explanation.
Linking it to a generalized notion of authenticity only further ob-
scures whatever significance the ending might be thought to have.
Clingman sets out to address the problem of the ending; he ends
up writing his way out of the interpretative dilemma the ending
creates.

Clingman's account of the novel nowhere suggests why Gordimer
would want to provide Maureen with a positive ending. Everything
the novel discloses about Maureen's life 'back there', before South
Africa boiled over into full-scale civil war, renders her as the very
type of the white suburban liberal. Clingman himself (145-146, 245n)
recounts Gordimer's public break with South African liberalism in
1974, some seven years before the publication of *July's People*. To
suggest, in light of that break, that such a figure moves at the conclusion of the novel towards a positive resolution of her dilemma
would have to entail that Maureen has undergone some sort of con-
version experience, a moment of Aristotelian anagnorisis or self-
recognition. No such experience is rendered at the conclusion of the
novel. Indeed, in linking her final action to her confrontation with
July, Clingman has to supply Maureen with thoughts that are nowhere expressed: 'she *realizes* that this too [the reversal of roles
whereby July is now dominant] is a circle she must break out of'
(203).

Lenta takes issue with Clingman's account of the ending, discount-
ing not only his positive interpretation but also the view, perhaps
set out most clearly by Rowland Smith (1984: 96), that the ending
is ambiguous and inconclusive. For Lenta,

The fact that the nationality and loyalties of the crew of the plane are
unknown to [Maureen], and that there has been earlier reference to
several opposing South African and foreign contenders for power sug-

gests strongly to me that Gordimer intends us to reflect on the negative meaning of her act: she is leaving, not joining. Our verdict is to be passed on the education and social conditioning of a white woman of our own day. (1988: 135).

At first glance Lenta's suggestion that the novel prompts a critique of the social conditioning of Maureen in particular and, by extension, liberal values in general is persuasive. Such a view would certainly seem more in accord with Gordimer's reassessment of South African liberalism than Clingman's view. Somewhat less certain is what connection that might have with the ending. The critique is woven into the entire fabric of the novel; it does not have to wait for the ending to be initiated. Moreover, a critique does not imply a comprehensively negative judgement. After all, the Smaleses are not the villains of the piece, and certainly in the context of South African politics and history, not villains in any more general way either. Gordimer's critique of South African liberalism does not include the facile premise that liberals are fully the partners of white racists. The Smaleses are, to be sure, limited, and those limitations are explored at length; nevertheless, the novel does not in any straightforward way condemn the Smaleses. What it does, and does unrelentingly, is expose the intractable contradictions inherent in the lives of such people. In this respect, the novel does not seek to incriminate the Smaleses, but to lay bare the conditions of their social existence.

Clingman and Lenta are unable to provide convincing grounds for their views of the ending. Clingman assures us that its significance is obvious, but cannot say with sufficient clarity just what it is. Lenta says that Maureen's running 'suggests strongly' to her that the ending is to be construed negatively, but it is not immediately clear why the uncertainty about the helicopter's occupants or the fact of contending military forces should suggest *anything* in particular. Their claims to the contrary, within the framework of interpretation they share, the conclusion to the novel is undecidable.

That framework centres the significance of the ending on the particular action of an individual character — Maureen's running. The meaning of the ending, then, hinges on its significance within the fate of the individual. Given Gordimer's break with liberalism and commitment to an avowedly radical position, which must at the very least imply a shift from the privileging of the individual over the collectivity to a position directly contrary to that, it becomes open to question whether any interpretation which does not shift its gaze beyond Maureen can hope to account for the ending.

One feature of the ending, unremarked by either critic, may provide a clue to what Gordimer is about. The helicopter's approach is represented in a language of aggressive sexuality. We read of the village 'cringing beneath the hoverer'; Maureen is 'invaded by a force pumping, jigging in its monstrous orgasm'; the helicopter descends with 'its landing gear like spread legs', making a 'rutting racket' (1981: 158-159).[4] The helicopter is the figure of a rapist; Maureen moves spontaneously towards it. That might appear to lend itself to a negative interpretation of the ending, but something quite different is in fact implied, or so I believe.

What I want to suggest about the ending will doubtless seem, at least initially, unlikely to the point of being bizarre. All I can ask is that readers bear with me for a moment. My suggestion is that behind the ending of *July's People* is another text — Yeats's 'Leda and the Swan'. Copyright statutes preclude quoting the poem in full, which is unfortunate since a direct comparison would make it easier to argue my case.

What initially prompted my impression that Gordimer is invoking Yeats's poem is a series of parallel expressions embedded in the sexually charged language. Some of the parallels are fairly strongly marked; others are subtle echoes. There are at least four of the more direct parallels: Gordimer has 'A racket of blows', Yeats opens the poem with 'A sudden blow'; Gordimer has the 'shuddering of air', Yeats 'A shudder in the loins'; Gordimer has 'terrifying thing', Yeats 'terrified vague fingers'. The most persuasive parallel is Gordimer's 'the beating wings of its noise' and Yeats's 'the great wings beating still'. Since helicopters do not have wings, it would appear that the reference is retained to preserve the connection between the two texts, and to reproduce the excited atmosphere of the moment.

If the more obvious echoes and parallels led me to wonder about the possible connection between the two works, other features reinforced the case. The ending of *July's People* has some curious stylistic features. There is, for instance, an unusual use of the passive: 'A high ringing is produced in her ears, her body . . . is thudded with deafening vibration, invaded by a force'; and 'She is righted'. Related to this are such expressions as 'she must have screwed up her eyes: she could not have said what colour it was'. And finally, there is the shift in the final chapter to the present tense. Such stylistic devices may be seen as transformations of some of the linguistic forms and effects of 'Leda and the Swan', notably the mixing of present and past tenses, and the questions of the second quatrain and the conclusion of the poem.

What is involved in these stylistic devices is the relation established between Maureen and the helicopter on the one hand and Leda and Zeus in the form of a swan on the other. In both works, the violently possessed woman is overwhelmed by the violator. Not just physically — the very will to resist is obliterated. The stylistic features in both texts also operate to blur perspective so that descriptions made ostensibly in the voice of the speaker or narrator are given from the standpoint of, or filtered through the numbed, barely registering consciousness of, the woman.[5] The 'racket of blows' is not just stated; it is experienced by Maureen: it 'comes down at her head', just as the 'sudden blow' and 'the great wings beating' are registered, if only dimly, by the consciousness of Leda. The passives in *July's People* reproduce stylistically the submission of Maureen to the 'force' of the helicopter, just as Leda is 'mastered by the brute blood of the air'.

It is never easy to demonstrate that one text functions as a source for another. The moment one attempts to set out the traces of the one work in the other, the relations between the two, for all that they seemed so obvious, suddenly seem quite tenuous. Nevertheless, I think a careful reading of the two works will persuade readers that 'Leda and the Swan' underlies Gordimer's conclusion. What is more, I think the relation between the two is crucial for our understanding of the ending of *July's People*.[6]

The standard interpretation of Yeats's poem situates it within his reworking of Viconian notions of historical cycles. Following her rape by Zeus, Leda gives birth to Helen of Troy, whose abduction by Paris gives rise to the Trojan War. The editors of *The Norton Anthology of Poetry* provide a gloss that sets out the conventional understanding of the poem: 'Yeats saw Leda as the recipient of an annunciation that would found Greek civilization, as the Annunciation to Mary would found Christianity' (Allison, *et al.*, 1983: 888).

Such an 'annunciation' is what I believe is suggested in Maureen's final action. It is not a question of deciding whether she is running 'towards' or running 'away from'. In any event, there is no clear support in the text for either view. She is *drawn to* the helicopter, by a power she does not understand, does not even reflect on. On her way, she crosses the river, undergoing what is explicitly figured as a 'baptismal' experience — a ritual cleansing — in which she is 'born again', and passes over the 'landmark of the bank she has never crossed to before'.

The imminent convergence of Maureen and the helicopter, like the convergence of Leda and the god-swan, heralds a new civilization, a new epoch for South Africa that cannot, particularly from within a moment of interregnum, be described but can only be symbolically prefigured in a prophetic gesture of revolutionary optimism. If in the interregnum, as Gramsci puts it, 'the new cannot be born', the convergence, taking the metaphor a vital step further, is a moment of insemination, from which new possibilities will emerge. The significance of Gordimer's conclusion lies not, then, in the particular fate of Maureen: it does not really matter whether we see her opened up to negative judgement or going to seek her revolutionary destiny (though the latter, in its very vagueness, comes closer to capturing what is going on at the end of the novel). Maureen has been overtaken by something far larger than herself, than her self. The ending is neither positive (in any narrow sense focussed on the vicissitudes of Maureen) nor negative; it is not even undecidable or inconclusive. At this moment of closure, *July's People* moves from a mode of future projection concerned, as Clingman notes, with 'seeing the present through the eyes of the future' to a mode of revolutionary, Utopian vision — a future projection intimating a realm of possibilities beyond interregnum.

Notes

1. Gordimer used Gramsci's concept of the interregnum in an important article published two years after *July's People*, 'Living in the Interregnum' (1983), in which she described South Africa as a pre-revolutionary society. It seems clear that the notion came to represent for Gordimer the historical conjuncture within which she was living and writing.
2. The ending has also been discussed by Nancy Bailey (1984), Rowland Smith (1984), and Richard I. Smyer (1985). Clingman challenges the interpretations the first two place on the ending in his essay in this volume, which expands on, but does not materially alter, his earlier discussion. I confine my remarks to Clingman's earlier discussion since that is the one that has been available to critics.
3. Our confidence in Clingman is momentarily shaken as well: the helicopter is not unmarked; Maureen 'could not have said . . . what marking it had . . . and — even if she were to have identified the markings . . .' (1981: 158). My comments are fairly minor disagreements with a book that has made a significant contribution to South African literary studies.
4. All further references are to the final three pages of the novel (158-160).
5. Leo Spitzer's philological analysis of the poem focusses on the significance of the stylistic devices and their relation to perspective (1962, see especially his remarks on 12).
6. It is usually assumed that a work cannot legitimately depend for its meaning on a source. I would argue that the sexually charged language of the final pages of the novel is sufficient to establish the necessary linkage with notions of birth and insemination, which in turn would suggest a shift from what 'cannot be born' (Gramsci) to an impending birth of the 'new'. Recognition of the reference to 'Leda and the Swan' enriches the meaning of the novel's ending; it does not create it.

References

Allison, A.W. *et al.* (eds). 1983. *Norton Anthology of Poetry*, 3rd edn. New York: Norton.
Bailey, N. 1984. 'Living Without a Future: Nadine Gordimer's *July's People*'. *World Literature Written in English*, 24(2), 215-224.
Clingman, S.R. 1986. *The Novels of Nadine Gordimer: History from the Inside*. Johannesburg: Ravan.
Gordimer, N. 1981. *July's People*, repr. 1982. Harmondsworth: Penguin.
Gordimer, N. 1983. 'Living in the Interregnum'. *New York Review of Books*, 20 January, 21-22, 24-29.
Lenta, M. 1988. 'Fictions of the Future'. *English Academy Review*, 5, 133-145.
Smith, R. 1984. 'Masters and Servants: Nadine Gordimer's *July's People* and the Themes of Her Fiction'. *Salmagundi*, 62, 93-107.
Smyer, R.I. 1985. 'Risk, Frontier, and Interregnum in the Fiction of Nadine Gordimer'. *Journal of Commonwealth Literature*, 20 (1), 68-80.
Spitzer, L. 1962. *Essays on English and American Literature*. Princeton: Princeton University Press.

New Criteria for an 'Abnormal Mutation'? An Evaluation of Gordimer's A Sport of Nature

Brenda Cooper

The question of the nature of appropriate critical criteria for evaluating literary texts has greatly preoccupied the field of African writing. Without entering that old war zone, I would like to examine Gordimer's latest novel in the light of a central question: what are the appropriate criteria, arising out of the distinctive political and historical South African realities, with which to assess this novel?

Two fundamentals underlie this essay and that question. Firstly, evaluative criteria are not set in cement and, once established, applicable universally in all political, social and literary contexts. Nor, however, are they entirely relative, free-wheeling and buffeted about by time and place. Secondly, there is an urgent need for the critic's criteria to be made overt so that debate and discussion can be facilitated.

The three categories to be considered here are *the politics* to which *A Sport of Nature* is committed; related to this, the nature of *the knowledge* imparted by that novel; and finally, *the fictional forms and devices* therein. These are categories of value, in that I will be assessing the novel's achievement in terms of them. This should become clear as we go along.

Breaking Out of the Pauline Syndrome: The New White Politics

A Sport of Nature is perhaps Gordimer's most optimistic novel to date. Coming from a generation of writers many of whom chose exile, she is, notably, the one who 'stuck it out', who, through her example, helped establish the importance of an enlightened white participation in South African culture and politics. Paradoxically, however, her fiction has, up until now, enacted the 'inner exile' of many liberal whites and could be called an exile literature written from within the country. Her novels have reflected the deep burden of white guilt and impotence; they have embodied ambivalence regarding the possibility of a political role or a deep, rooted home in Africa for whites. They have set Tests of courage and Trials of strength for beleaguered protagonists gasping beneath the burden of privilege and humiliations of self-justification.

These themes of past novels are most obviously present in *A Sport of Nature* as the character Pauline. The novel is an interesting and powerful attempt to break out of this Syndrome — powerful and brave and interesting, but ultimately, I think, falling short of both its own aspirations and the criteria that I as critic will be bringing to bear.

Firstly then, what are the politics symbolized by Pauline and how and why is she challenged, both by Sasha, her son, and Hillela, the sport of nature herself, Gordimer's fresh and new protagonist?

> She's jealous. Saturday classes for kids. Reformers are (take pride in being) totally rational, but the dynamic of real change is always utopian. The original impetus may get modified — even messed up — in the result, but it has to be there no matter how far from utopia that result may be.
>
> Utopia is unattainable; without aiming for it — taking a chance! — you can never hope even to fall far short of it.
>
> Instinct is utopian. Emotion is utopian. But reformers can't imagine any other way. They want to adapt what is. You move around, don't you, bumping up against — brought up short every time! — by the same old walls. If you reform the laws, the economy defeats the reforms . . . If you reform the economy, the laws defeat the reforms . . . Don't you see? It's all got to come down, mother. Without utopia — the idea of utopia — there's a failure of the imagination — and that's a failure to know how to go on living. It will take another kind of being to stay on, here. A new white person. Not us. The chance is a wild chance — like falling in love. (Gordimer, 1987: 187)

The novel in a nutshell. The 'she' who is jealous is Pauline. Pauline is Gordimer's albatross. She is a politically aware, middle-class, middle-aged white South African. She is the archetypal Gordimer protagonist — she is, with some variations, Elizabeth of *The Late Bourgeois World* or Maureen of *July's People*. Her dilemmas, her anguish, her choices — these have become the monumental, liberal intellectual white South African condition, and what a ghastly dead-ended terminal condition it continues to be! In her latest novel, Gordimer attempts a cure.

Pauline is the question (and I hesitate to pose it, so monotonous has even the wording of it become): what is the role of a politically aware white South African? Or, how can such a being overcome the crippling ambivalence to political commitment that her privileged position inculcates? How will she cope with the inevitable *Test* — if she is asked to take a terrible risk like hiding someone, or blowing something up? Will she meet the challenge and earn the credentials, the place, the dignity that will thereby legitimate her existence?

> . . . We're right on the street, it's not a big property. There's nowhere anyone like that would be safe. — It wouldn't be for long. Haven't you somewhere in the house; anything — (1987: 27)

Later:

> I should have told her. Not lawyers' houses. I should have said, if you were to be accused of being involved in any way other than professionally, you'd never be able to take on such cases again . . . would you? They ought to understand they also need people like you. —
> — You acted correctly. That's the end of it. —
> The boy and girl saw Pauline's hands falter on knife and fork. She put them down and her hands sought each other, each stiff finger pushed through the interstices between those of the other hand. —
> 'People are expected to put their actions where their mouths have been.' You can imagine how the word will get around. (1987: 29)

Gordimer despises the sincere, hard-working, humourless and fervent Pauline with all the force of self-hatred.

Sasha is, literally, Pauline's offspring, a new generation of whites of the eighties. These whites have a political role in the non-racial politics of unity, in the UDF, in the trade-union movement. Sasha is the fictional author of the words in the first quotation above, and in many important ways is Gordimer's spokesman — Gordimer's critique of Pauline's mode of being and brand of politics.

Sasha has this to say in a very important letter:

> What the young really were doing was beginning to put their small or half-formed bodies under the centuries' millstone. And they have lifted it as no adult was able to do, by the process of growing under the weight, something so elemental that it can no more be stopped than time can be turned back. They have lifted it by the measure of more than ten years of continuous revolt — pausing to take breath in one part of the country, heaving with a surge of energy in another

— and by showing their parents how it can be done, making room
through the '80s for new adult liberation organizations — you've heard
about the UDF — for militancy in the trade unions and churches.
That's where I come in — came in. If you couldn't wait, I suppose
you had to go: Pauline went. There was nothing for whites to do but
wait to see what blacks might want them to do. There was a lot of
shit to take from them — blacks. Why should I be called whitey? I
didn't ever say 'kaffir' in my life. Not being needed at all is the big-
gest shit of the lot. But everything was changing — . . . (1987: 319)

Sasha, then, is the potential answer to Pauline's/Gordimer's ago-
nies and self-doubts. He is Gordimer's new-found hope of a politics and a place for white activists.

However, the cerebral, rational, guilt-stricken and ultimately im-
potent Pauline is swept away even more definitively not by her direct
line of descent, but by her niece, daughter of her renegade sister
— the sensuous, poised, fresh and lovely Hillela, the true, the new,
protagonist. Hillela it is who takes a chance, who relies on instinct
and emotion, whose imagination does not fail her, who is 'another
kind of being', a 'new white person'. Hillela, however, does not
represent Gordimer's own history, path or future. She is a 'sport
of nature', an 'abnormal variation', a fundamental biological mutation, a mode of fantasy:

Lusus naturae — Sport of nature.
    A plant, animal, etc., which exhibits abnormal variation or a depar-
ture from the parent stock or type . . . a spontaneous mutation; a new
variety produced in this way.
                                                    Oxford English Dictionary
(Quoted by Gordimer before the title page)

Hillela's politics are physical, her decisions instinctual, her training
experiential. Her sexuality, far greater than mere sexiness, is a huge
and awe-inspiring kind of radical passion. She merges and flows
with her environment, her daughter, her friends, her lovers. She
is the polar opposite of the incapacitated and alienated white
consciousness:

It was just then that she experienced a surge of something, a falling
into place of people passing that came from the unfamiliar moments
of standing still while all flowed, as if one belonged there like the
shoemaker, instead of being in passage. And the Africans, the Arabs,
the Lebanese, and the Europeans from embassies, economic missions
and multinational companies wearing tropical-weight trousers wrin-
kled at buttocks and knees by sweat, no longer were a spectacle but

motes in a kind of suspension, a fluid in which she was sustained. (1987: 132)

Her sexuality is 'the bread of her being':

> Everyone has some cache of trust, while everything else — family love, love of fellow man — takes on suspect interpretations. In her, it seemed to be sexuality. However devious she might have to be . . . and however she had to accept deviousness in others, in himself — she drew upon the surety of her sexuality as the bread of her being. (1987: 283)

To come back to earth for a moment. Hillela is Gordimer's fantasy of the resolution of the racial issue that is so central to South Africa's politics and to its fiction. *Race is the pivot of the novel, of its politics, of its view of South African realities.* In this Sasha and Hillela are soul mates. They have had a brief childhood love affair which, significantly and symbolically, results in a rift with Pauline and Hillela's departure from Pauline's home. They work towards the same goal from different dimensions. If Sasha breaks through the barriers of race in his work and in his politics, Hillela does so in her relationships, her dreams of a 'rainbow family', her husbands, her black child, her sexuality.

I think that, paradoxically, by focussing so emphatically on race Gordimer reaffirms its paralysing hold on perceptions of South African political priorities and historical realities. She reaffirms not its resolution, but its stranglehold. By privileging race, she underplays the realities of *social class* and compromises on issues of *gender*. I am critical of this both in terms of the politics of which it forms a part and also the knowledge of South Africa that it stands for. Before providing examples to back up this sweeping criticism I would like to enlarge upon the demands regarding content being made here and the implied distinction between politics and knowledge.

Fiction as 'Truth in the Round'?

What kinds of demands on fiction, regarding the veracity of its content, are appropriate and justified? What, in other words, is the possible nature of the historical knowledge embedded within creative art and literature, as opposed to that of history books or political monographs?

Norman Geras, in a wonderfully stimulating paper, questions the nature of the contribution of the 'literary' to the political and historical insights of Trotsky:

Trotsky was no stranger to the necessities and the demands of theory, but he brought also to his writing a power of historical synthesis and a keen faculty of perception which added another dimension to it. Thereby he tried to capture for the worker's movement the many-sided reality of its history, to hold before it the experiences of victory and defeat, the emotions and the deeds of individuals and of masses. He gave these a literary as well as theoretical expression. When so many have been prepared to play fast and loose with the same history, the importance of his effort, for a picture of the truth in the round, should not be undervalued. (Geras, 1986: 267)

Geras's interests are not identical to my own — we are, in fact, coming from different directions. While intentionally smudging the definitions of Literature, his interest is in the 'political writer', the historian, who employs techniques traditionally associated with creative literature. My focus, on the other hand, is on Gordimer as novelist, and the nature and status of the history and the politics embedded in her fiction. However, Geras's penetrating questions, problematizing definitions of 'literature and art in the strict sense', and exploring the territory 'beyond a boundary', have been invaluable in helping me to clarify my own project. If we refuse 'the strict sense' and venture 'beyond the boundary', where shall we peg the new signposts? Fictional discourse is not historical discourse although there are overlaps. Where do commonalities end and specificities begin?

Already we can see the danger of questions lining up to be begged. How are these issues to be posed in the first place, without ascribing traditional roles to the disciplines, whose cumbersome and rooted boundaries we are attempting to re-situate? This dilemma expresses itself as a tension in Geras's article — a tension between ascribing old definitions to the literary, and, simultaneously, breaking new ground.

For example, Geras emphasizes the 'strictly circumscribed' nature of his own focus as being 'only a particular aspect of [Trotsky's] politics . . .namely, the quality of his writing' (1986: 221). In this, Geras is in danger of relegating Literature to the old sidelines, of regarding it primarily as a set of techniques, a particular form, and separable from knowledge in the more 'scientific', or as I prefer to call it, 'objective' sense of the term. In other words:

I am not now speaking about the strictly scientific value of these writings, about their strengths and deficiencies as political theory or historical analysis (or, for that matter, literary criticism) . . . (1986: 218)

Is Geras suggesting, then, that it is only in political theory or historical analysis that this objective knowledge may be discovered?

> The language of Marxist objectivity (not, of course, the same thing
> as neutrality) is doubled by the vivid recreation of some lived ex-
> perience, the subjectivity, so to speak, of that objectivity. Global histor-
> ical forces in movement are set off against a small detail of individual
> humour or tragedy. A personal portrait is given depth by the invoca-
> tion of impersonal structures. . . . One result, in particular, is that
> the book of 1905, as well as being a political text of capital importance,
> is a great book of the revolutionary experience of that year . . . proffer-
> ing, to be sure, a theory of the unfolding events, sketching the out-
> lines of a history of them but, over and above this communicating
> an acute *sense* of them. (1986: 218)

I would refuse the polarization here between the portrayal of the
'global historical forces', the 'impersonal structures', on the one
hand, and on the other hand, 'the subjectivity', 'a personal portrait'. The literary should not be characterized as either a kind of
micro-knowledge — a small detail, a personal portrait — or a set of
devices — metaphors and images which enable a 'vivid recreation
of the climate and atmosphere of upheaval' (1986: 242), but say little about the cause, nature or outcome of that upheaval itself. The
dichotomy between 'the scientific' as verifiable knowledge and the
artistic as intuition, the emotional, the subjective, is a false one, as
Della Volpe categorically asserts:

> . . . only if we acknowledge the *intellectual* nature of poetry . . .can
> we demonstrate its power to 'reflect' a society and hence its ideolo-
> gy. It is a flagrant contradiction to emphasize this power and still be-
> lieve in art . . . as intuitive knowledge or knowledge 'through im-
> ages', in abstract antithesis to science, understood as knowledge
> 'through concepts.' (1978: 183)

Della Volpe insists equally on this intellectual nature of poetry and
on its specificity, in terms of *both* the kind of knowledge *and* the kind
of language distinctive to it. Fundamental to him is the distinction
between what he terms the *univocal* language of history, as opposed
to the *polysemic* language of poetry (1978: 175).

Clearly both kinds of language are available to, and used by, poets
and novelists, on the one hand, *and* historians on the other. But there
is an important difference in the degree of such usage. The language
of poetry, and to some significant degree, of fiction, is characterized by its multiplicity of signs, its playfulness, its sensuality, its
images and diverse linguistic gymnastics, that render it multi-
dimensional, polysemic. Univocal language, then, tends to be more
one-dimensional, prosaic, directed and explanatory.

I will be touching on the question of form later. However, this stylistic dichotomy points also to the difference in the nature of the knowledge produced. I would like to suggest that *knowledge embedded within great creative writing is also polysemic, exemplifying the relationship between and interconnectedness of the many different and complex dimensions of life*. This deceptively simple point is fundamental. It is what Geras means by 'the literariness' of Trotsky's writing — his attempts at capturing the 'many-sided reality', 'the truth in the round'.

I take full responsibility, moreover, for the use of the term 'great', which sets many a tooth on edge. However sophisticated our theories become, or however much our priorities change, we retain a hierarchy of value. It may not be the one of the dominant ideology, but that is no reason for it to go into hiding.

I am also emphatically not dispensing with the whole valuable Marxist tradition which identifies literature as ideological. I am simply refusing the *definition* of the ideological as necessarily false. I am suggesting thereby that in a minority of memorable texts, or even of parts of such texts, the authorial ideology has found access to an aspect of knowledge, of reality. I am, in other words, here suggesting a criterion, an ultimate goal. The extent to which texts in general, and, for our purposes, *A Sport of Nature* in particular, reach or fail to reach this goal, has to be assessed in practice.

Having said all this, is it not possible that polysemic knowledge may come into conflict with political strategy? Might 'truth in the round' be regarded as a luxury in the urgencies of our current situation? Is it not divisive to depict class struggle among blacks themselves; to depict women as doubly oppressed — by the Apartheid state as well as by their own men? Is it not demoralizing to portray change as involving the long slog of organization and efficient filing of letters? Is depicting the overthrow of Apartheid as not necessarily synonymous with the dismantling of Capitalism, losing sight of the main enemy?

I have heard *A Sport of Nature* highly praised in discussions relating to the necessity of non-racial politics of unity. It is commended as an inspirational component of the progressive national culture struggling to be born. The point here is not whether Gordimer herself strategized in this highly aware political way. The important issue is that the text has spoken to sectors of the politically active, progressive readership in ways that answer to their current needs and demands; in ways that lead them to assess the text favourably.

This is a very fundamental and interesting issue for which there are no easy answers. I tend, however, to disagree with this favourable assessment. Is there not something patronizing in intellectuals as critics or as writers, censoring complexities so as to inspire ordinary people, who, it is assumed, would otherwise become depressed and inactive. If there are, as undoubtedly there must be, problems, difficulties and pitfalls along the road to liberation, why should there be selective access to them?

I am not here going to fall into that treacherous quagmire where politics' gain signifies aesthetics' loss. What I am suggesting is that a different kind of politics seems to me to be appropriate to the realm of creative literature. 'Truth in the round' is *highly political*. If the debates and struggles, victories as well as defeats, cannot be rehearsed in the huge space of fiction, then a progressive culture truly has little chance of emerging anywhere else.

These comments are only tentative, as warranted by the importance of the issues involved and what is at stake. I will be returning to the question of politics and the novel in my conclusion.

In the meantime there is another question. Where is the very necessary space for the relative autonomy of individual uniqueness? On what grounds am I about to make a critique of a fictional creature such as Hillela? Art, surely, encompasses the creative imagination running riot, inventing new beings, rainbows, utopias? Great progressive art, surely, along with the perception of social forces and political realities, the predictable and the possible, must be able to incorporate the aberrant and abnormal, the impossible and the strange? Why not Hillela? Where does the crunch come?

In my view, writers have enormous freedom in their choice of subject. Gordimer was certainly free to create a fictional fantasy of a new being unscarred by the disfigurements of guilt and placed in the important space of dreams. She was not free, however, in the name of art, to simplify and rearrange the ordering of social and political forces and their varying determining strengths. Gordimer is *not* free to present biological and mysteriously sensual solutions to the vast range of social and political problems and difficult emotional choices faced by whites in South Africa today, and in the future. She, moreover, is not choosing ultimately to focus on the aberrant and unreal. These are for her tools in the task of depicting South African truths and pains and problems and possible paths forward. She has pointedly linked the life of Hillela to the historical times in which she lives. As Stephen Clingman puts it, she attempts to write 'history from the inside'.

This point must be further clarified. What I am *not* doing is infringing upon the writer's freedom to choose a focus. I am not prescribing a particular content. Novels can, and indeed must, be written about the whole range of possibilities ever imagined — about the personal, or the political, the idiosyncratic or the social. The expectation is, however, that the reader has a sense of where the chosen focus falls in the wider scheme of things. Polysemic knowledge does not mean dealing with multi-dimensions in the novel itself. It means that the text is informed by complex understanding, whatever it ultimately focusses upon. A degree of contextualization (which can only be specified in relation to concrete texts) *is* desirable.

What I am suggesting is that there needs to be *a certain weighting of forces*, but that this does not dictate the writer's focus. In the greatest fiction an understanding of such forces and their weighting provides a crucial pivot to the text. In other words, economic structures and the class relationships arising out of them, are unquestionably more powerful determinants of history, society and culture, than individuals, their dreams, aspirations and consciousness. These economic structures and those class relationships should, then, carry more explanatory weight, whether the bulk of the novel happens to be about those dreams and aspirations or not. And, to go back to a key passage quoted above, failure of the imagination should not even be hinted at as *the main cause* of the political impasse; it is just not good enough to create a false cycle where reforms are defeated by economic forces, which are overcome once again by laws, with only a sport of nature to break the tedious cycle!

Having established a basis for evaluating fictional content, I would like to examine in more detail the nature of the history and politics in the novel under discussion.

The Orgasmic Revolutionary Moment, and the Gods Who Consummate It

Clingman in his stimulating study of Gordimer focusses quite specifically on this question of the relationship between her fiction and historical reality (1986). His book, completed before the publication of *A Sport of Nature*, suggests that Gordimer, over her long career, has made fundamental advances in her understanding of history and politics (see, for example, 1986: 215). I would agree that real changes in Gordimer's choice of plots can be perceived, and that these changes are indeed indicative of her ear being tuned quite finely to political developments. Nonetheless, I feel that her deepest preoccupations have not, in fact, moved as far or as fast as her choice of subject matter. This I think continues to be the case in her latest novel. I come here to the illustrative substance of my critique of its contents.

In *A Sport of Nature*, Gordimer's view of *the historical* is grounded in the big names and great heroes; of *the political* it is almost exclusively of sabotage, underground cells and guerilla movements. Sasha, as the representative of *trade unionism*, has almost nothing to say about organization and the struggle between different social classes. When it comes to *gender* the novel seems only to suggest the possibility of one serving one's man in new ways.

For example, the famous figures surrounding Hillela sufficiently dominate the novel as to form an historical framework for it — 'Agostinho Neto was another friend of the General' (1987: 288). Later Hillela and the President have many important visitors at State House:

> Tambo came but did not swim; neither did Thabo Mbeki. . . . The year he was the Nobel Laureate, Bishop Tutu and his wife Leah were guests and walked in the garden with her. (1987: 333)

There seems to be little hint of the view that ordinary people might have a hand in the great sweep of events. If Gordimer admires the famous, however, she pays ultimate homage to the guerilla activists.

It is, therefore, not surprising that the novel enters the realm of Myth, an appropriate dimension for a mutated goddess. Both Hillela's first and second husbands are deified in one way or the other. They are both black guerilla fighters and fantastic lovers. They are entirely romanticized and worshipped by Hillela, and, by extension, her creator, in the absence of any significant authorial distancing.

Hillela's first 'encounter' with Whaila occurs when she is swimming in the sea with a man and Whaila swims to them, in order to tell the man that one of their comrades has been killed in a car bomb. 'The man's urgency did not acknowledge the girl' and 'neither man noticed her go' (1987: 140). Later, however, he becomes 'the disguised god from the sea' (1987: 198), and

> Whaila had for her, beyond sensuality, a concentration within himself that kept her steadily magnetized. The presence of a power. . . . The concentration was like that a woman must feel when a general comes to her on the nights before a great offensive begins. (1987: 201)

This anticipates the General, who will come to Hillela as her second husband after Whaila is cruelly assassinated — 'The obsidian god from the waves, the comrade was buried in the gold, green and black flag he died for' (1987: 216).

His death is mythologized, and thereby de-historicized, becoming a tragedy as defined by the ancient Greeks and coming 'from the gods'.

> A tragedy, Hillela, is when a human being is destroyed engaging him-self with events greater than personal relationships. Tragedy is an idea from the ancient Greeks; from the gods. A tragic death results from the struggle between good and evil. And it has results that out-last grief. Grief is a rot, it belongs with the dead, but tragedy is a sign that the struggle must go on. . . .
> Whaila is dead. There have been others. There will be others. (1987: 215)

There is nothing wrong with the depiction of a special kind of death — a life given for a cause greater than an individual. The problem comes in, firstly, when political activity is conceptualized almost en-tirely in these highly covert, conspiratorial and extreme terms, a pit-fall in Gordimer probably exacerbated by the susceptibility of art to succumb to the melodramatic, to the heroic, to the secretive.

Secondly, it is highly problematic to couch the complexities of po-litical struggle in the universal and simplistic paradigm of 'the strug-gle between good and evil'. Look, for example, at the ramifications — there is the General, who is a 'good god'. The general, ousted African leader, who wages a guerilla war, regains his country, and becomes the President. He is able to negotiate billion dollar loans from the USA and the World Bank. He is also 'a professed Socialist with a mixed economy in his own country' (1987: 337). No problems, no compromises, no multi-dimensionality — but then gods can suc-ceed where ordinary mortals fail:

> . . . the President successfully negotiated a $3 billion loan from the United States for the rehabilitation of war-devastated areas in his coun-try. It was all as he had said: he had to win his war with arms from the East, and to win his peace with money from the West. The world press was amazed to report that only a rainy season after his troops still had been monitoring the physical surrender of arms in the South-West, his Ministry of Agriculture held an agricultural show in the region and the President was rapturously received when he addressed rallies there. His pithy style of comment on the event made a good quote: My popularity comes from the full stomachs of my people. (1987: 307-308)

The repressive laws, the bannings, the bombings, the torture, un-derground activity and guerilla warfare, encompass Gordimer's South African history entirely, rather than constituting one aspect of it. What can this be other than some kind of archetypal battle between good and evil in the absence of a hint of social and economic structures, or of class interests with historically traceable and even rational foundations?

> . . . he carried a forged passbook with a false name, and that persona was under orders to see what could be done to revive the internal structure of the movement and accelerate recruitment of men for military training outside. (1987: 188)

And then there are always the explosives:

> It was long before the Underground organizations were to have limpet mines, SAM missiles and AK47s; these bombs were homemade, with petrol bought in cans from the service station. Letter boxes, electrical installations, beerhalls owned by the white administration boards in the black townships and railway carriages owned by the State monopoly — explosions attacked what represented the white man's power where blacks could get at it: in the places where blacks themselves lived. (1987: 107)

The racial framework ensures that State House with its lavishness has nothing to do with the growth of a ruling class in the General's country, and Socialism is not compromised as Hillela ensures that the swimming pool is placed at the disposal of black South African freedom fighters!

Gordimer, realizing that working for a trade union is an important activity for a politically aware young man like Sasha to engage in, tells us very little about his work beyond the vague UDF reference and 'What I do: I'm helping to organize workers' (1987: 300). In fact, the major advantage of this job appears to be not the organization of workers, but, once again, the *racial* challenge and individual, uniquely South African triumph of working with blacks and *even* having black seniors:

> It's wonderful to be with blacks. Working with blacks. Already there are some who are senior to me, one or two who have been, for training, to England and West Germany. I take orders from them. (1987: 301)

Maybe a touch of irony *here*? I doubt it. With all his new-found social and political insertion, Sasha remains Gordimer's/Pauline's offspring. But yet, note Gordimer's apparently helpless awareness of getting bogged down in the suffocating, old familiar bog: 'I'm like Pauline, really. Where I get my thrills.' (1987: 302)

Sasha sneers at 'Pauline's Great Search for Meaning' as 'a pain in the arse' (1987: 317). His search doesn't appear much less of a Search, however muted the tone of it all, at least partly as a result of the letter format within which we receive it (more about that later). He suggests in this same letter that his own adjustment problems stem from the wonderful multiracial, utopian school he attended in Swaziland:

> At Kamhlaba blacks were just other boys in the same class, in the dormitory beds, you could fight with them or confide in them, masturbate with them, they were friends or schoolboy enemies. At the house, my mother's blacks were like Aunt Olga's whatnots, they were handled with such care not to say or do anything that might chip the friendship they allowed her to claim — and she had some awful layabouts and spivs among them. I smelt them out, because where I was at 'home', that sort of relationship, carrying its own death, didn't have to exist. Poor Pauline. I hated South Africa so much. (1987: 317)

Certainly a non-racial education is desirable. But there is no hint that it would have been mainly very upper-class black children with whom he mixed there, perhaps accounting for some of the ease of the interaction. The black workers he helps to organize in the trade union are from quite a different social stratum. Blacks continue to be presented by Gordimer as homogeneous; politics remain apocalyptic, and it comes as no surprise that the pinnacle of Sasha's union career is his placing of the bomb, resulting in no less than Pauline's own exit from South Africa, the hopes and possibilities of UDF notwithstanding:

> One day he telephoned Pauline from Amsterdam. Sasha had no passport, she knew he must have come out the way she had helped a black family escape when he was a schoolboy — not by the same route, for a long time there had been no safe houses in Botswana that the South African army hadn't destroyed — but with the help of someone like herself. She had seen on television the bombed walls of police headquarters in two cities. A limpet mine had been placed in the women's lavatory, in one, and in the men's lavatory in the other. Pauline thought how obvious it was that the first must have been placed by a woman, and the other by a man; an error on the part of the saboteurs to give away this clue. Then she read that a young woman had, indeed, been arrested, a white woman. When her son called from Amsterdam she believed she knew the identity of the man. (1987: 336)

Gordimer seems to be doing some running on the spot here. The novel remains firmly situated within the drama and secrecy of safe houses and limpet mines. UDF and Trade Unionism notwithstanding, there appears to be little sense of the slow undramatic, unromantic slog of building up organization. After all that seems to have happened, Sasha follows obediently in the exiled footsteps of the mother whose route he had, apparently, so firmly rejected. He may have taken things further than her, but merely by travelling a greater distance along the same road. Gordimer cannot supersede her Pauline, her history, herself, despite the enormous effort to do so expended in the novel.

As for Hillela, new heroine, she will find greatness only through the gods, with whom she makes love, and whom she inspires, so that *they* may have the strength to participate in the great offensives out there. When out of bed, moreover, she must be correctly dressed for the occasion, in order to do her famous second husband justice:

> Quite soon after their alliance began the President had made it clear that his companion could not go about with him in cotton shifts, jeans, and sandals made by street cobblers. Fortunately, she knew fine fabric and good cut . . . (1987: 307)

It is interesting that it is still possible in the 1980s for a woman writer to create such a 'heroine', or, perhaps, it is only still possible in a situation like South Africa, where the priority issue that Gordimer is handling is that of race, and her primary concern is to illustrate the ways in which her new breed of white South African can love, serve and physically worship *black* men. She is not alone in this. It is also, by now, an old African tale, as women's issues are sacrificed to the prior claims of national liberation. Hillela is happy — is honoured — to feed, nurture, give physical and intellectual support to her black freedom fighter husbands. She wants to be 'a real African woman' to Whaila, which means bearing him many children. She manages 'somehow [to] produce enough food to go round whomever Whaila brought home' (1987: 205). She cooks and cleans, looks after her baby, and all this is categorized unproblematically as 'the marvel of daily life' — Hillela's perception as she hangs up the washing!

Again, in Gordimer's lastest novel we probably have one of the least critical portraits of polygamy yet painted by a woman writer of Africa. The President's first wife, conveniently, dies and he, magnanimously, it is implied, 'gave her a funeral in keeping with her status' (1987: 309). The second wife 'does not live in State House but has a large house of her own, in town, and maybe the President still visits her occasionally' (1987: 309). (That is, presumably, if he has the energy, what with Hillela and a Scotch 'passing fancy' (1987: 333), but no one seems too put out by all this.) In fact, he has more children by this second wife, children who are perfectly brought up by Hillela and who are often seen at State House. Everyone seems contented enough:

> The charming children, who have the composure and good manners of black and the precocity of white upper-class children, dressed by Hillela and educated at schools chosen by her, probably have been born to the President since his third marriage, by the second wife. Anyway, that one will never lose her position as mother of the best of them. That is something between the President and her no other woman will ever have. It would not trouble Hillela. (1987: 310)

I have looked for the irony here — the passage is bordering on, begging to be, ironic. However, the whole drift of the novel rests on the positive attributes of Hillela and her General and their ideal marriage, heralding a new South Africa in a triumphal, unqualified and unambiguous conclusion.

What must be emphasized is that the critic who accepts that raising issues of gender at this political moment in time is divisive, that the most urgent task is that of national liberation, will assess this aspect of the novel very differently from the foregoing. This is a very clear-cut example of the way in which one's criteria and priorities affect one's assessments.

Would it be overly critical, I wonder, to suggest that Hillela, that free and untrammelled fantasy figure, is, in all her mutated strangeness, a signpost 'rendering visible' *not* Gordimer's solution to the South African White Liberal Syndrome, but its opposite, her paralysis within its confines? She is, in other words, an extraordinarily powerful example of an attempt to resolve fictionally and through fantasy issues that are irresolvable in authorial reality. The biological wonder, in all her strangeness and abnormality, draws attention to, and acts as a signal for, Gordimer's dilemmas, her frustrated inability to throw off her albatrosses. In fulfilling this function, Hillela compels the critic to place limits on the 'boundless imagination', on Gordimer's 'poetic licence' to create figments and utopias.

I do, however, think that there is evidence that Gordimer attempted to control her fatal attraction to old and worn-out paths. And in her awareness of the Pauline cul-de-sac, the novel can be assessed as having made progress. She tries to free Sasha from his mother, and to focus on Hillela as something entirely new. Sasha acts in the wings of the novel, so to speak, while Hillela occupies the centre-stage. There is his illicit, incestuous and, for him definitive, love affair with Hillela. This affair serves to place him more firmly with Hillela and assists in the attempt to free him from his mother. That is, the text attempts to drive a silent wedge between Pauline and her son — a silence shocking in the ambit of that cerebral, wordy family. The most concrete and visible distancing device becomes the increasingly refracted access we have to Sasha through his letters to Hillela, which she does not receive and which we read in her place. We are informed about Sasha's trade union activities via his own reading of his own letter — words within the words of the novel.

'Words within words' — is this not the very polysemeity for which Della Volpe called in describing poetic language? This brings me to a brief examination of the language and fictional techniques of the novel, as a criterion for assessing it.

Letters, Voices and Viewpoints: The Language of Fiction

There are many voices, points of view and styles in *A Sport of Nature*. Do these fulfil the demand for literary polysemeity, or do they smudge and obscure the novel's content? Or both?

Sasha's letters form part of a jigsaw of fictional points of view — a fragmentation of viewpoint. Gordimer attempts, as mentioned, to muffle Sasha's voice and thereby his choice of direction. She also tries to free Hillela from her own (Gordimer's) long-standing obsessions, at the same time as being the omniscient author of her text. This results in a contradictory authorial voice — both know-nothing and all-knowing. Let us take some examples and consider their effects.

There is, in the first place, a strongly controlling narrative voice. The tone is set by the chapter titles which range from the slightly amusing ('DON'T LEAN YOUR SMELLY ARM OVER MY FACE' (1987: 18)), to the somewhat ironic ('A FACE FOR A POSTAGE STAMP' (1987: 264)) towards the end. These establish clearly that the author knows what is coming each time. In addition, Gordimer sometimes stands above the scene and presents an overview of what different characters in different places are doing, information accessible only to an omniscient narrator:

> The father of Ruthie's grandchild moved in the streets of South African cities within passing distance of Olga (in Cape Town at the tail-end of her summer holiday), Pauline and Joe (on their way to a lecture at the Institute of Race Relations in Johannesburg) and Sasha (leaving the city's reference library and taking a detour into the black end of town to buy an African jazz record for a girl-friend's birthday). (1987: 188)

The author's authority is further established by the constant indication of her knowledge of her character's future fame, especially earlier on in the novel when we, the readers, can see little likelihood of it. We are told that people who knew her at various times of her life will be interviewed. She will appear in press photographs and articles, she will feature in 'a series of mini-biographies of outstanding women' (1987: 140). What is the purpose of all these tantalizing hints about the future fame of the protagonist?

The authorial predictions reinforce Gordimer's superior knowledge over the other biographers, and, ultimately, over the reader:

> A series of mini-biographies of outstanding women cites the news of the assassination of an important West African leader as the turning-point in her political development. Why should it ever have been contradicted?
> But in that hour she was gliding and turning through water as perfectly tempered to the body as amniotic fluid, she heard no commotion but the sound of water getting into her ears and air breaking free in them through bubbles; the dead leader was a name. (1987: 140)

Here the author contradicts the biographer and gives the reader the more accurate information that Hillela was, in fact, quite unconcerned with the assassination.

Finally, the omniscient viewpoint assists the author in her role as historian. Gordimer intersperses her tale with lengthy univocal accounts of what was actually occurring historically at the time. I will come back to this a bit later. Here I only wish to stress the many techniques deployed by the text to amplify the author's voice. This amplification is simultaneously undermined in various ways.

Firstly, the author shares the authoritative point of view with both Sasha and Hillela and there is ample evidence that she identifies with the perceptions of both characters. Note this ironic comment approvingly distinguishing Sasha from the rest:

> I, me.
> Time, now. They had always, they went on fitting that self into their conjugations, leaving out the first person singular. Except one of the cousins, poor boy; he didn't. (1987: 124)

Sasha's letters carry weight, notwithstanding that our knowledge of him as a person is refracted through them. At times Hillela provides italicized commentary, relieving the author of the responsibility of being the sole source and ultimate wisdom of the text. But notice also how reluctantly the author lets Hillela speak, even the confusion of their voices. In this example Hillela is about to break off her engagement with the sweet and kind Brad (the 'you' in the following), her liaison with the General having begun:

> With all the intelligence and willingness and understanding shining the golden-brown lantern so steadily from the dark side of your gaze, you would not be able to follow. Because of that, he could never have told *you* what he told *me*. And because he could tell *me*, and *I* could follow — no, *you'll* never follow, it can't be done in this old house full of heirlooms, . . . and although you'll never follow what he's like, what *she's* like, the one who is going, you did know, oh you did know — no-one can draw a proxy signature beneath a life. (1987: 280-281) (my emphasis)

The 'I' and the 'you' give way to the authorial 'she', a result, I think, of Gordimer's confusion here as to whose perceptions are being portrayed, whose authority it is, whose point of view.

The authorial voice is qualified most strongly, however, by a deliberate vagueness, by statements of ignorance on the part of the author. These occur throughout the novel and appear to be at variance with the above evidence of authorial omniscience: 'It must have been in June 1963, exact date unknown, she left South Africa' (1987: 118) and

> She does appear to have left the ambassadorial employ at some point before or not long after she began to be seen with the black South African revolutionary envoy; and she must have had to earn a living somehow (1987: 171).

I am emphatically not implying that a unified viewpoint or an unambiguously omniscient narrator are desirable or obligatory. Playing around with the point of view in this way is certainly a standard and accepted modern literary-poetic practice. However, experimentation with point of view can either be complex and illuminating or can act as something of a smokescreen concealing authorial uncertainties. And, of course, there is much greater opportunity for language to enlighten or to confuse and conceal when it is polysemic — poetic, emotional and many-faceted. In the case of *A Sport of Nature*, the fragmented viewpoint is *a further rendering visible* of its vulnerabilities.

A Sport of Nature contains some strong and striking poetic language:

> Acronyms the language of love. United States Institute for African-American Cooperation, USIFACO; Third World Committee for Afri-

ca, TWOCA; Operation Africa Education, OPAD; Coordination Committee for Africa, COCA; Commission for Research into Under-
development, CORUD; Foundation for Free People, FOFREP. The
child plays with alphabetical blocks on the floor, builds houses with
them. A career can be built out of acronyms; everyone here must have
a career, you fulfil yourself with a career. . . .
  No need ever to run out of acronyms. There is a career of continued
useful service ahead; there is the example, of Leonie, loverless lover
of all those she is entitled to call by their first names, fulfilment (as
they sum up here) shining out of every group photograph in which
she appears. But no need to emulate entirely. The documentation will
be read in bed beside a young man advancing well in his own career,
ready to help with the dishes and to perform — woman, man, and
the little black daughter he regards as his own — the safe and pleasant
rituals of a family, here; parent-teacher co-operation, playing games,
going to the lake shack and Cape Cod house.
  The real family, how they smell. The real rainbow family. The real
rainbow family stinks. The dried liquid of dysentery streaks the legs
of babies and old men and the women smell of their monthly blood.
They smell of lack of water. They smell of lack of food. They smell
of bodies blown up by the expanding gases of their corpses' innards,
lying in the bush in the sun. Find the acronym for her real family.
(1987: 250-251)

Here Gordimer cleverly builds up a critique of the plasticity of affluent American politics and culture. She does so partly through
the derogatory connotations of the acronym — so neat, so pat, so
clinical — as against the harsh, and yet simultaneously far more
earthy and compelling realities of Africa, for which no acronyms
can be found, according to this description.
  The images are powerful. Hillela's shattered dream of a 'rainbow
family', a dream destroyed by the terrible assassination of Whaila,
becomes a sad and evocative thread in the novel. The repetition of
the phrase in this passage forms a deeper, more moving rhythm,
by contrast with the mindless round of clever acronyms.
  If this passage looks backwards, with its connotations of the old
rainbow family fantasy, it looks forward too to Hillela's relationship
with Brad, the American, and even further to the unlikelihood that
the relationship will survive.
  The passage is quite a bit longer than I have had the space to quote.
Each word is chosen for maximum effect, in order to contrast this
American phase of Hillela's life with her African origins. The American world is one in which 'everything remains in place for them',
the same trees line the same avenues and the cycle of the seasons
regulates an ordered world. The smell is that of spring. The final
paragraph of the passage, on the other hand, spares no detail of
the awful stench of poverty and its accompanying degradation.

The force of the language, its extended images, its play on connotations and memories are products of its status as creative literature. But what does this language tend to conceal?

Although the contrast between America and Africa rings true, it is stereotypical in its extremes. It denies poverty in America and affluence in Africa. It refuses the real implications of State House and its swimming pool. It is further evidence of Gordimer's ignorance of the realities of foreign aid, with the new African middle-class family rituals it enables. Have not the General and Hillela, in reality, by the end of the novel, built themselves fine careers too?

And again, sadly, what is obvious, is Gordimer's abandonment of gender in her desire to portray what she sees as the hard African realities. The white middle-class male, 'ready to help with the dishes' and the 'safe and pleasant rituals of a family', seems thereby unmanned, certainly unable to hold a candle to the virile and brave guerillas, far too busy in the real world of bush war to be concerned with dish washing and child care. As for the smell of 'monthly blood' . . .!

Poetry nonetheless. Look at the conclusion of that passage in which Gordimer's point of view mingles with that of Hillela's as she prepares to leave Brad and go to her General:

> The other will not die. Not even a herd of elephant will trample him out. He is not beautiful, he carries his Parabellum, he knows how to deal with sons, in him the handclasp compresses the pan-pipe bones of the hand with which it makes covenant; it is, on recognition, irresistible. (1987: 281)

Again the handclasp takes us back to Whaila, and beyond to the commitment of comrades together in struggle. The rhythm of 'pan-pipe bones of the hand' is beautiful and requires no paraphrasing. It does, however, reinforce that unhappy and romanticized worship of guerilla fighters.

The pan-pipe poetry coexists with the following heavy, forced and one-dimensional stuff (the quote is rather lengthy, but could have been longer, or many other examples taken in its place):

> — That's the stage we reached after the Defiance Campaign. The realization that we are forced to fight. But it doesn't make a campaign a failure. The campaign simply proved that there is no way but to fight, because the government doesn't know how to respond to anything else. It was a phase we had to complete, to convince ourselves, hey? Over fifty years passed before Umkhonto! Hell — maybe we needed too long for convincing! They were too slow, the old ones . . . .

— . . . We just don't have the manpower to do the job. Too many in prison, or here, outside. Our people are getting arrested and re-arrested all the time. You've got a hundred-and-eighty days' detention, now, not just ninety. And the sentences — they're getting five or ten years for nothing. We don't have the sophisticated weapons to be effective. Have to keep running about . . . we need new sources of supply. The government has all the weapons, all the spies to make the sabotage campaign fail, as things stand now . . . I don't know . . . and maybe we haven't thought enough about the way the enemy will react. We know the reaction to mass action, okay, since Sharpeville — but the type of action the government will take against a sabotage campaign, not only against our Underground but also the people . . . the people! How much more repression can the townships take without expecting more positive results from us? . . . (1987: 184-185)

When the novel uses that kind of language to impart this kind of information, is it overstepping one of the boundaries separating creative literature from other kinds of discourse? Why does one feel manipulated when quite lengthy omniscient authorial analysis is fed into the mouths of fictional characters engaging in fictional conversation? These are important questions, especially given the insistence that literature can, and indeed, most often does, impart knowledge of the world. These issues have also been central in African criticism specifically. African writers have traditionally been deeply preoccupied with their historical pasts. This is reflected in the language and themes of their fiction. Writers like Achebe have articulated the function of writers as teachers, and this attitude is embedded in the style of many novels. This is not to suggest that these novels are necessarily more 'political' or enlightened or 'progressive' than any others. What is true is that the expectations, tastes and preferences of African writers and readers may well allow for a greater degree of univocal description and historical reference than has been acceptable to the dominant Western tradition.

I am convinced, however, that fictional prose can incorporate within the diversity of its language *a degree* of univocality and of abstract analysis. The degree is difficult to quantify and varies from text to text, but there is a cut-off point which is quite different from that of historical discourse. Much politically charged art works against its own effectiveness by its refusal to pay homage to these demands and boundaries.

In considering these boundaries in relation to *A Sport of Nature*, a difficulty is my disagreement, described earlier, with the *content* of much of the univocal, political analysis itself. The boundaries are undoubtedly influenced by the reader's attitude to the argument.

I do, nonetheless, feel that Gordimer relies too heavily on explaining and justifying at the expense of her writing, and that in this she
remains part of an unfortunate South African fictional tradition.

I would like, in conclusion, to return to the question of fictional
content — the politics, the history — as a criterion of value and a
fundamental theme of this essay.

Coetzee and the Cockroach Which CAN Be Killed: Some Conclusions

My subheading has been adapted from the headline of the *Weekly
Mail* review of J.M. Coetzee's contribution to that newspaper's book-
fair, November 1987. In a session entitled 'The Novel Today', Coetzee compared the resilience of storytelling to that of a cockroach and
argued against the 'colonization of creative fiction by the discourse
of history'. What I, on the other hand, have been arguing is that
historical complexity is fundamental to assessing the novel in general
and Gordimer's latest in particular.

What Coetzee objects to is

> . . . what I see as a tendency, a powerful tendency, perhaps even
> dominant tendency, to subsume the novel under history, to read nov-
> els as what I will loosely call imaginative investigations of real histor-
> ical forces and real historical circumstances; and conversely, to treat
> novels that do not perform this investigation of what are deemed to
> be real historical forces and circumstances as lacking in seriousness.
> (1988: 2)

Who is treating novels in this way? Who is Coetzee's adversary?
Why does he have to insist that 'even in South Africa of the 1980's,
I see absolutely no reason why we should agree to agree'? What
or who is the menace threatening a 'moratorium on the kind of reser-
vations I am expressing'? (1988: 4,5) What is the ghost text to which
Coetzee is responding?

Coetzee's adversary is very real. It is not, in my view, the discourse of history. It is, I think, a certain political stratum which, in
the name of returning culture to 'the people', dictates a particular
political role, strategy, content, and even appropriate form to writers.
I think that it is this *political* prescriptiveness that Coetzee is coura-
geously rejecting, albeit confusingly referring to it as 'the discourse
of history'. He is resisting — and I think absolutely correctly — the
prescriptiveness that has dogged the cultural scene in South Africa
in the past and perhaps especially in the eighties. With the massive

suppression of more conventional political forms of organization, culture has become an arena of struggle and an outlet for political commitment. At the heart of Coetzee's outspokenness, however, lies a flaw. This is the no less prescriptive idealism of his total relativism — a rejection not only of literary, but also of historical and political realities:

> I reiterate the elementary and rather obvious point I am making: that history is not reality; that history is a kind of discourse; that a novel is a kind of discourse too, but a different kind of discourse; that, inevitably, in our culture, history will, with varying degrees of forcefulness, try to claim primacy, claim to be a master-form of discourse, just as, inevitably, people like myself will defend themselves by saying that history is nothing but a certain kind of story that people agree to tell each other. (1988: 4)

Coetzee is merely aligning himself with a different set of dictates — a school with its own demands — for the labyrinth, the illusion, the lie. The apple with its tangible core has been replaced by the onion with its elusive layers of skin. Peeling back the skins, moreover, is a deconstructive game of de-mythologizing, exposing, ultimately uncovering the final layer, which reveals only an absence. The game is in the peeling, and at the end of it all the onion is inedible:

> There is a game going on between the covers of the book, but it is not always the game you think it is. No matter what it may appear to be doing, the story may not really be playing the game you call Class Conflict or the game called Male Dominations or any of the other games in the games handbook. While it may certainly be possible to read the book as playing one of those games, in reading it in that way you may have missed something. You may have missed not just something, you may have missed everything. (1988: 3-4)

In equating history with a monolithic prescriptive politics, Coetzee paints himself, however magnificently he is able to paint, into the corner of commitment to artistic autonomy, to the entirely singular paradigms and myths of the novel, to the rivalry, and even enmity, between history and fiction. He presents only two options — rivalry or 'supplementarity' — and justifies his choice with his refusal to see 'why the novel should consent to be anyone's handmaiden'. I am convinced that this is a false, unnecessary and destructive war.

If the ghost text to which Coetzee is responding is a politico-cultural programme of prescriptiveness, then the ghost writer is the critic. And it is with criticism too that Coetzee takes issue. Here the pressure Coetzee obviously feels under manifests itself, ('renders itself visible'?) as a contradiction in his argument. On the one hand there is the assertion that 'censors' (another word for 'critics') have been 'ineffectual, century after century . . .':

> They are ineffectual because, in laying down rules that stories may not transgress, and enforcing these rules, they fail to recognise that the offensiveness of stories lies not in their transgressing particular rules but in their faculty of making and changing their own rules. (1988: 3)

On the other hand, they are obviously quite effective in the here and now:

> Why should a novelist — myself — be speaking here — the Baxter Theatre — in terms of enmity with the discourse of history? Because, as I suggested earlier, in South Africa the colonisation of the novel by the discourse of history is proceeding with alarming rapidity. I speak therefore — to use a figure — as a member of a tribe threatened with colonisation, *a tribe some of whose members have been only too happy* — as is their right — to embrace modernity, to relinquish their bows and arrows and their huts in the wilds and move in under the spacious roof of the great historical myths. (1988: 3) (my emphasis)

Storytelling, then, cannot always 'take care of itself' in the face of the advancing colonizers. (Is Gordimer, I wonder, one of the happy tribe members embracing 'modernity' with her Sasha and his UDF?)

Coetzee insists 'I do not even speak my own language'. His critical voice is 'a fragile metalanguage', at any moment liable to be 'flattened and translated back and down into the discourse of politics, a sub-discourse of the discourse of history' (1988: 3). I have to take issue with him here. Coetzee is writer, critic and teacher of literature. His fiction, perhaps more than that of any other South African writer that I have encountered, is powerfully and even self-consciously fired in the kiln of his chosen body of literary theory. Autonomy is illusory. The language of his criticism is highly poetic (the writer in him latches onto the cockroach), the language of his fiction highly intellectual.

I am the very last one to be calling for the collapse of distinctions. Certainly 'in the end there is still the difference between a cockroach and a story', but what was the point of the extended metaphor if 'the difference remains everything'? (1988: 4) And if, at the end of a long day, it is a capricious symbol, evoked specifically for its obvious and humorous distinction from what it was set up to illuminate, in order to discredit the relationship between history and fiction, then it may have to be killed.

The critical battle is not to colonize, but to cultivate, a new territory. This new ground could be fertilized with enlightened and appropriate priorities, and, perhaps even more importantly, visible and overt debates around those priorities. Tolerance and flexibility remain essential ingredients and should not be placed in false opposition to the commitment to a better life for people. This is said knowing that the foregoing has run the risk of accusations of prescriptiveness. I would contend that all serious critics, readers and writers bring values, priorities and hierarchies to bear on what they read and write. Prescription lies only in the concealment of these, thereby rendering them authoritative without question. This essay has been a tentative attempt at laying open for discussion some of the considerations determining one critic's assessment of Nadine Gordimer's *A Sport of Nature*.

References

Clingman, S. 1986. *The Novels of Nadine Gordimer: History from the Inside.* Johannesburg: Ravan Press.

Coetzee, J.M. 1988. 'The Novel Today'. *Upstream*, 6(1).

Della Volpe, G. 1978. *Critique of Taste*. London: New Left Books.

Geras, N. 1986. *Literature of Revolution*. London: New Left Books.

Gordimer, N. 1987. *A Sport of Nature*. Cape Town: David Philip.

The Problem of History in the Fiction of J.M. Coetzee

David Attwell

J.M. Coetzee completed his Ph.D. at the University of Texas at Austin in 1969 by submitting a stylistic analysis of the English fiction of Samuel Beckett. It is a complex essay, rigorously self-reflective, at times overtly sceptical about its own methods, which tries to negotiate the transition taking place in American linguistics from the structuralism associated with Leonard Bloomfield to generative-transformational grammar. In perhaps the only unequivocal finding of the essay, Coetzee identifies in Beckett's *Watt* two indicators of the writer's dissatisfaction with English, warning signs of his imminent decision to turn to French. They are 'systematic parody', and 'binary patterning at every level of language: words imitating the patterns of other words, and words setting up their own obsessive pattern' (what had earlier been referred to as 'the rhythm of doubt'; 1969: 95, 163). Both patterns have their echoes in Coetzee's own fiction, particularly in his first two novels. Having provided these stylistic observations, however, Coetzee concludes his study with the following extraordinary paragraph:

> There is one further consideration we should not overlook if we wish to explain the nature of *Watt*. *Watt* was begun in 1941 and completed in draft in 1944. It is not entirely strange that during these years, while a statistician in Cambridge was copying *De imitatione Christi* word by word on to cards, while another statistician in a prisoner-of-war camp in Norway was tossing a coin and notating 'H' or 'T' one million times, that an Irishman in France should have been recording for posterity all the permutations which the nouns *door, window, fire,* and *bed* can undergo.[1] (1969: 164)

What Coetzee neglects to mention is that when Beckett wrote out these permutations he was trying to keep one step ahead of the

Gestapo, writing his novel about a distantly remembered Ireland while living in Rousillon in the unoccupied Vaucluse. The reason for his caution — according to Hugh Kenner, whose work on Beckett Coetzee has admired — was his association with the Resistance and the disappearance of his friend Alfred Péron (1961: 22). The omission of such an important detail by Coetzee is significant: his interest falls on the obsessive state of mind, the deliberate and persistent evasion, rather than on its circumstantial causes. This is a characteristic turn in Coetzee, and we can allow it to represent emblematically the difficult, seemingly intractable relationship in all Coetzee's novels between, on the one hand, system, structure, synchrony, acts of apprehension or consciousness, and on the other, events, diachrony, and history. Intractable, because while history is shown here as a final horizon or perhaps a determining frame surrounding and circumscribing human acts, including analytical and methodologically persistent acts, the causal relationships governing this contingency remain opaque. History is more than a referent, it is an almost tyrannical presence, but it is nevertheless elusive and cannot be brought into full consciousness by those who are caught up in it.[2]

The problem touches on the vexed but crucial question of the relationship of the structuralisms, including poststructuralism, to history and historical discourse. To examine the novels of Coetzee contextually, as being both *about* (in sometimes oblique ways) and written *from within* the South African situation, is to engage this larger set of issues. For it is predominantly on a foundation of structure and system that Coetzee erects each of the formidably intellectual constructs that are his novels. Coetzee admits to being a linguist before being a writer.[3] Being a linguist, and then a writer, in the era of structuralism's ascendancy in the West, involves of course far more than simply being unusually self-conscious about the nature of one's medium; it also involves working into one's literary materials the possibility of language serving as a model of thought and culture.

It would be a mistake, however, to try to confine Coetzee to any particular version of structuralism. His linguistic and critical essays reveal a range of philological interests, from historical linguistics, to stylistics, to generative grammar, to continental structuralism and semiotics, to translation. The systemic orientation of the novels is less, I believe, the result of a sectarian adherence to a particular camp than a result of the recognition, which is rooted in all philological studies, that language is constitutive and productive, and that 'making sense of life inside a book is different from making sense of real

life — not more difficult or less difficult, just different'. This conviction would be common to both generative grammar, for example,
with its Cartesian affinities, and to continental structuralism with
its emphasis on signification, these representing two of the more
influential traditions of Coetzee's formative years, from the mid-
sixties to the mid-seventies.[4] In generative grammar, productivity
is the consequence of innate capacities which represent an internalized version of structure; in continental structuralism, it is inherent
in the nature of the linguistic sign.

My purpose in this essay is to begin to examine the relationship
between structural and historical conceptions of discourse as they
are located in Coetzee and in some of the intellectual and cultural
products of his context. In addition to offering a description of Coetzee's fiction in terms of the theory of the political unconscious —
I argue that, implicitly, the novels come close to formally encoding
that theory, although I also try to identify the limits of this description — I shall give an account of Coetzee's oblique position in relation to the various revisionisms of South African literary-intellectual
culture of the early seventies. In the course of discussion I draw
together three strands of narrative theory and semiotics that make
it possible to see the resources of postmodernism as enabling, rather
than undermining, an historical engagement. These are the Witt-
gensteinian account of the relationship between fiction and historical discourse developed by Paul Ricoeur; recent theories of metafiction; and the semiotics of the later Prague School. My implied position in this aspect of the argument is that charges of political evasion in Coetzee have not begun to take account of the specificities
of the fiction: in assuming the moral high ground, and foreclosing
on inquiry in the name of evaluation, they fail to explain the novels
both as encoded history and as historical phenomena in themselves.
If these charges are not re-examined, they will in the end cohere
with and reinforce a stultifying anti-intellectualism and chauvinism
in South African literary culture. They will also serve to establish
a mystified and self-congratulatory conception of the relationship
between historical literary studies and popular struggle. Finally, in
the course of argument it will be necessary to place myself in relation to the two strongest readings of Coetzee thus far in South Africa: Marxism, and Lacanian psychoanalysis.

1 The Debate on Realism

The recognition that meaning in a novel resides in a configuration of elements that are not the same as the elements of real life, a recognition that would be reasonably commonplace were it not being carried through, as we shall see, to a point where it appears uncompromising, has cost Coetzee a great deal in terms of his relationship with other writers in South Africa and with readers whose form of politicization demands a realist documentation of life lived under oppression. As cited, the recognition was made with reference to Sipho Sepamla's *Ride on the Whirlwind* and Mongane Serote's *To Every Birth its Blood*, in both of which Coetzee finds 'a failure, almost a refusal [later a ''programmatic refusal''] to create a structure in which there is some centre of intelligence', a problem which he traces to the continuing influence of European and American Naturalism on the popular novel. If these comments are depreciatory (and rather too literary in their diagnosis of the problem since black prose in South Africa owes more to local traditions of journalism than to the Western popular novel), then it must be recalled that Coetzee is on record at a very early stage as having participated constructively in a debate on the status of realism in black South African fiction, a debate which was started by Lewis Nkosi twenty years ago, and which has been taken up more recently by Njabulo Ndebele. Nkosi argued that black fiction was filled with 'the journalistic fact parading outrageously as imaginative literature', and that seldom were 'social facts' transmuted into 'artistically persuasive works of fiction' (1967: 222). Ndebele's more recent and more sophisticated argument is that structural factors underlie the object of Nkosi's complaint, insofar as black writers have been denied access to an information order through which traditions might have been acquired which would empower a transformative fiction. Without such traditions, the writer produces 'an art of anticipated surfaces rather than one of processes', 'an art that is grounded in social debasement', in which 'little transformation in reader consciousness is to be expected since the only reader faculty engaged is the faculty of recognition. Recognition does not necessarily lead to transformation: it simply confirms.' (1984: 45)

Coetzee's involvement in the debate is by way of his essays on Alex La Guma, the first of which was written in response to Nkosi. He argues that La Guma escapes the limitations of a mundane naturalism by the inclusion of gestures towards a revolutionary transformation of history, encoded in characterization (there is some reference to the Lukácsian theory of typification) and symbolism (1973, 1974b). Although in these essays Coetzee does not show himself to be unsympathetic to the political force of La Guma's position, his interests are formal first, then epistemological, then political. La Guma arrives first at a narrative solution with its own implicit social hermeneutic, which then has political implications which are contrasted, in turn, with the unwittingly conservative implications of Nkosi's position (this is not the order of propositions Coetzee uses, but it reflects the different weight of the analytical emphases). Coetzee's grasp of the difficulties of creating an epistemologically transformative fiction out of the resources of the more pedestrian forms of realism, and his regard for La Guma are, curiously enough, in accordance with his particular attachment to the principle of non-referentiality. One of the reasons for this is that La Guma, in leaning towards social realism, at least acknowledges implicitly a discursive tradition, unlike the 'refusal' that Coetzee finds in more recent black prose which, in assuming an unmediated relationship between the work and the real world, implicitly denies the force of (novelistic) tradition.

What the debate on realism shows, for our purposes, is that the conflict between synchrony and diachrony, structure and history is far from confined to the Western academy, that it spills over and ramifies elsewhere, and takes on unique forms under particular contextual pressures. I do not mean to suggest that the problem is first an *a priori* analytical conflict that emerges in the West and is then exported elsewhere; rather, that in an historical crisis, the dialectic between analysis and process, including the process of social flux in which analysis itself must be located, becomes unusually charged and problematic. It does so *within* Coetzee's oeuvre. For despite its systemic orientation and its obvious familiarity with contemporary Western linguistic and critical theory (although exactly what those correspondences are have never been quite satisfactorily identified), Coetzee's fiction *does* establish a diachronic, historical narrative. For this is what the primary context of colonialism *is* in each of Coetzee's works. He has spoken directly about preferring 'to see the South African situation [today] as only one manifestation of a wider historical situation to do with colonialism, late colonialism, neo-colonialism'; and he adds, 'I'm suspicious of lines of division between a European context and a South African context, because I think our experience remains largely colonial' (Watson interview, 1978b: 23). The sense of a global phenomenon that underlies the South African situation is established with reference to a narrative, one could without too much exaggeration even call it a master narrative, although Coetzee would demur at the term. It is there in the whole corpus of five novels, which collectively and sequentially establish a narrative of aggressive colonial violence in *Dusklands*, followed by settlement (of uncertain standing and duration) in *In the*

Heart of the Country, followed by a defensive imperial phase of anticipated revolution or guerilla insurgency in *Waiting for the Barbarians*, followed by civil war in *Life & Times of Michael K*. The most recent novel, *Foe*, departs from the narrative but is no less concerned with questions of power and authority in a colonial context, appropriately, the power and authority of authorship straddled between the metropolis and the colony, awaiting transformations that are as yet undetermined, perhaps indeterminable. What phase of history could Coetzee reasonably be expected to write, when his anticipation of a pattern of historical inevitability has already pushed beyond the moment delivered up within the context by the historical process itself? *Waiting for the Barbarians* marks a critical point in the development of the whole question of historical meanings in the fiction, for what one finds there is a point at which history, in *failing* to transform the terms of discourse, becomes objectified as myth, which in turn opens up the possibility of partial or qualified forms of freedom being discovered in subsequent novels. It is worth mentioning here, perhaps, that all South African writers face this crisis, of having their teleology, whether liberal, nationalist or radical, continually challenged, and often eroded, by a morbidly protracted historical suspension.[5]

There is more to historicity, obviously, than the construction or projection of a sequential narrative. 'All history,' Paul Ricoeur reminds us, 'may be understood as the advent and progress of a unique meaning and as the emergence of singularities. ... History wavers between a structural type and an "event" type of understanding.' (1975: 73) In the context of Coetzee's fiction, however, as in the socio-historical context itself, the problem comes to us in a unique form. Edward Said's treatment in *The World, the Text, and the Critic* of what he calls 'traveling theory' is relevant here, in the questions it raises concerning the shifts of nuance and allegiance that occur when theories are taken up at some remove from their original source (1983: 230). Since Coetzee's philological background and interests are diverse, even within individual texts, we are not tracing the contextual modification of a single body of theory (as Said does in discussing the uses to which Lukács's theories of totality and reification are put by Lucien Goldmann and Raymond Williams); rather, we are concerned with two cultural 'moments' impacting against one another. On one hand, we have the linguistic moment in the West, represented and partly initiated by the break with historical linguistics in the opening chapters of Ferdinand de Saussure's *Course in General Linguistics*. It is the moment described by Fredric Jameson in terms of 'the spectacle of a world from which

nature as such has been eliminated, a world saturated with messages and information, whose intricate commodity network may be
seen as the very prototype of a system of signs. There is . . . a profound consonance between linguistics as a method and that systema-
tized and disembodied nightmare which is our culture today.' (1972:
ix). On the other hand, we have the thoroughgoing politicization
that defines South African culture in the seventies and eighties, an
absorption into History that allegorizes the smallest acts. It is spectacle too, since everything is seen from the perspective of a cataclys-
mic present, but it is not the spectacle produced by fascination for
the sign. Perhaps one of the most powerful illustrations of this in
contemporary South African literature is the point in Nadine Gordimer's *Burger's Daughter* where Rosa, driving through a peri-urban
wasteland near a Witwatersrand township, sees a donkey being
thrashed by its driver. The image triggers a vision of suffering which,
as suggested, throws all of the past into the present:

> I didn't see the whip. I saw agony. Agony that came from some ter-
> rible centre seized within the group of donkey, cart, driver and peo-
> ple behind him. They made a single object that contracted against
> itself in the desperation of a hideous final energy. Not seeing the whip,
> I saw the infliction of pain broken away from the will that creates it;
> broken loose, a force existing of itself, ravishment without the ravisher,
> torture without the torturer, rampage, pure cruelty gone beyond con-
> trol of the humans who have spent thousands of years devising it.
> The entire ingenuity from thumbscrew and rack to electric shock, the
> infinite variety and gradation of suffering, by lash, by fear, by hun-
> ger, by solitary confinement — the camps, concentration, labour, reset-
> tlement, the Siberias of snow or sun, the lives of Mandela, Sisulu,
> Mbeki, Kathrada, Kgosana, gull-picked on the Island, Lionel propped
> wasting to his skull between two warders, the deaths by question-
> ing, bodies fallen from the height of John Vorster Square, deaths by
> dehydration, the lights beating all night on the faces of those cells
> — Conrad — I conjure you up, I drag you back from wherever you
> are to listen to me — you don't know what I saw, what there is to
> see, you *won't* see, you are becalmed on an empty ocean. (1979: 208)

This History is a hermeneutic pressure that dominates the field,
everywhere establishing its own radical priorities; in the passage,
Conrad's privatized self-affirmations are disavowed and replaced
by the overwhelmingly urgent sense of oppression. Where else but
in an arena of conflict as virulent and exhausting as this — and one
might wish to make the same observation with respect to situations
like those of Nicaragua, Israel, Northern Ireland, or Pakistan — could
one find a politics of signification so evenly and rigorously matched
by a politics of the referent, a politics which appears to crowd out

even the most tentative of epistemological doubts?[6] That a similar pattern of tension emerged in the context of the rebellion in Paris in 1968 is part of the popular history of French structuralism, but the institutionalization of structuralism thereafter shows that if it was doubted, it was doubted from within, and by means of a refinement of a given discourse, rather than by the urgency of political pressure from outside of the discourse, as in the situations I have mentioned. In an address at the *Weekly Mail* Book Week in Cape Town in November 1987, Coetzee demonstrates how sharply he feels these opposing tensions: 'in times of intense ideological pressure like the present, when the space in which the novel and history normally coexist like two cows on the same pasture, each minding its own business, is squeezed to almost nothing, the novel, it seems to me, has only two options: supplementarity or rivalry' (1988a: 3). Supplementarity with the discourse of history would involve novelistic discourse in providing the reader 'with vicarious first-hand experience of living in a certain historical time, embodying contending forces in contending characters and filling our experience with a certain density of observation ...' (1988a: 3). Clearly, this places the novel in a secondary relation to historical discourse. A relation of rivalry, the position Coetzee is defining for himself, would lead to:

. . . a novel that operates in terms of its own procedures and issues in its own conclusions, not one that operates in terms of the procedures of history and eventuates in conclusions that are checkable by history (as a child's schoolwork is checked by a schoolmistress). In particular I mean a novel that evolves its own paradigms and myths, in the process (and here is the point at which true rivalry, even enmity, perhaps enters the picture) perhaps going so far as to show up the mythic status of history — in other words, demythologizing history. Can I be more specific? Yes: for example, a novel that is prepared to work itself out outside the terms of class conflict, race conflict, gender conflict or any of the other oppositions out of which history and the historical disciplines erect themselves. (I need hardly add that to claim the freedom to decline — or better, rethink — such oppositions as propertied/propertyless, colonizer/colonized, masculine/feminine, and so forth, does not mean that one falls back automatically on moral oppositions, open or disguised, like good/bad, life-directed/death-directed, human/mechanical, and so forth.) (1988a: 3)

If I may be allowed to digress briefly, it would be useful to establish the distance that separates Coetzee's work from its polar opposite in South African cultural production: the 'people's culture' campaign spearheaded by the United Democratic Front during the States of Emergency in 1985-1986. This is of course not the first of the populist cultural movements of contemporary resistance in South

Africa; Black Consciousness in the late sixties and seventies had a discursive coherence which was tighter than that of the more recent campaign, in that it produced a central core of myths, an historiography, even a style that was distinctive, all of which turned on the question of black self-affirmation. The 'people's culture' campaign is less a body of doctrine, however, than a set of structural emphases (although it does have an aesthetic); it emerged, moreover, in a quite different political moment. There are four features that distinguish the campaign: the first is its concern with the accessibility of art to underclass audiences and readerships; the second is its aim of building a 'national culture' that would unite different oppressed groups under a common symbolic framework; the third is its emphasis on a concrete, documentary form of realism that depicts the life-experience of the oppressed; and the fourth is its insistence that artists — 'cultural workers', in the coded language — submit themselves to the discipline of a formal alliance with 'the democratic movement' (Press, 1988: 36-37). Each one of these emphases is vulnerable, in an analysis of any rigour. There is an ideological ambiguity about the ethnic and class character of the 'oppressed groups' being referred to, since the position of nationalist mass struggle, although politically ascendant, cannot but be unspecific about the precise meaning of the collectivity being mobilized. The stress on realism runs into the problem raised by Nkosi and Ndebele, the problem of epistemological transformation. The insistence on a formal alliance raises for many artists the spectre of an internal, Stalinist policing. Behind these emphases there also lies the problem of short-term political vision, which easily leads to superficiality and rhetorical endorsements that are continually belied by political realities. The immediate point, however, concerns not the weaknesses of cultural populism but, to return to Coetzee, the distance that separates him from artists at the other end of the spectrum, in terms of the conceived relation between artistic medium and social reality. Coetzee's argument for 'rivalry' with the discourse of history involves a political choice, in the strictest sense, of a refusal of association, affiliation, consensus. The point is made quite explicitly:

> I reiterate the elementary and rather obvious point I am making: that history is not reality; that history is a kind of discourse; that a novel is a kind of discourse, too, but a different kind of discourse; that inevitably, in our culture, history will, with varying degrees of forcefulness, try to claim primacy, claim to be a master-form of discourse, just as, inevitably, people like myself will defend themselves by saying that history is nothing but a certain kind of story that people agree

to tell each other — that, as Don Quixote argued so persuasively but
in the end so vainly, the authority of history lies simply in the consensus it commands. . . . I see absolutely no reason why, even in the
South Africa of the 1980's, we should agree to agree that things are
otherwise. (1988a: 4)

The epistemological and formal stricture is carried through to the
end, to an inevitable and to a certain extent, even bitter conclusion.
The principle of arbitrariness in the relationship between sign and
referent which, among other things, underlies the argument, is enlarged to the point at which writers and (mostly naive) critics and
historians separate off into different camps, never to find, as writers,
critics and historians, common ground. This is not so much a question of ahistoricism, for Coetzee's language is shorn of any reference to what is ordinarily or conventionally called history, that is,
the datum of individual and collectual experience. His emphasis on
discursiveness is not necessarily an indication of the belief that history does not exist, so much as the conviction that since no discourse
has unmediated access to history, any utterance, but the novel in
particular, can claim a qualified freedom from it. But while the position Coetzee adopts might not necessarily deny the reality of historical forces, it is decidedly *anti-political*. And as such, it must be acknowledged, it is as messily involved in historical contingency as
the discourses he accuses of trying to circumvent their discursive
character in order to leap into the Real. Coetzee's very guardedness
and argumentative strength indicates this. To refuse consensus is
to confirm the sense of the 'worldliness' of texts, of which Said
speaks (1983: 31-53). There is even a small admission of this in Coetzee's modifier, 'inevitably': inevitably history will claim primacy,
inevitably novelists will resist; what inevitability is this if not one
that lies beyond the control of those most affected by it, i.e. an historical one?

A general point can be abstracted from all this that is of central
importance to the argument of this essay: that *to decline the politics
of historical discourses does not necessarily involve ahistoricism*. Coetzee's
polemics engage the politics of historical discourses; in order to
preserve their rhetorical force, they are silent about the referents
of these discourses. Elsewhere, he makes no apology when referring to the Real. In the introduction to *White Writing* he states that
he has two concerns, with 'certain of the ideas, the great intellectual schemas, through which South Africa has been thought by Europe; and with the land itself, South Africa as landscape and landed property' (1988b: 10). The fiction itself engages history in the form
of the narrative of colonialism, in ways I shall shortly describe. Be-

fore doing so, I must tease out a theoretical argument relating to the question of postmodernism's historical reference. In his polemics, Coetzee discusses two apparently irreconcilable paths for the relationship between history and fiction: supplementarity, or rivalry. I shall argue that this does not contain the field of possibility. It is perhaps appropriate that via theoretical reflection on the implications of Coetzee's own fiction, we can qualify his polemics.

2 Referentiality and Reflexivity

The question of referentiality is said by Hayden White to be 'the most vexed problem in modern (Western) literary criticism' (1973: 2n). It is not within the power or scope of this essay to try to patch together an artificial solution, or even to survey the literature in the field adequately. White's own treatment of the problem in *Metahistory* is to explain historical discourse in terms of a finite set of tropes and ideological positions which combine in different ways to produce a certain emplotment of history. But in Ricoeur we find a conception of what he calls 'the narrative function' that places White's model within a range of other possibilities and succinctly suggests an approach that relates narrativity to historicity in terms (following Wittgenstein) of their both partaking in the 'language-game' of narrating, which is treated as 'an activity or a form of life' called 'narrative discourse'. The relatedness of the two kinds of discourse, history and narrative, is apparent for Ricoeur both in a unity of structure, and in a unity of sense. The structural unity lies in their both deploying the concept of plot which involves *directedness*, and a creative relationship between *configuration* and *succession*. By definition, narrative must combine these elements. Thus far, the unity of structure; what follows is the unity of sense. Both history and fiction involve a mode of reference 'beyond' the surface of the text. In the case of history this is self-explanatory; in the case of fiction, referentiality is always present, in however qualified a form. Mimesis, he reminds us, brings into play not a reproductive but a *productive imagination*. The referentiality of fictional narrative is characterized 'as *split or cleft reference*, by which I understand a way of relating to things which envelops, as a negative condition, the suspension of the referential claim of ordinary language' (1981: 293).

Contemporary narrative theories of meta- or self-referential fiction are beginning to engage with larger socio-cultural questions. This was not the case in the earlier years of postmodernism, the period of Borges, Barth and Nabokov. In the conclusion to her *Metafiction*, Patricia Waugh asks but leaves open the question of 'the politically "'radical'" status of aesthetically "'radical'" texts', in a gesture which suggests implicitly that self-referential fiction can be placed and examined within larger units of cultural efficacy (1984: 148). Linda Hutcheon's *Narcissistic Narrative* shows that the very reflexivity of metafiction is a gesture outward, specifically toward the reader, whose constitutive role is emphasized in the very act of the narrative turning back on itself and revealing its own fictionality. Finally, Robert Siegle in *The Politics of Reflexivity* argues that all narrative is reflexive to some extent, and that where this function is in evidence its effect is to draw attention to the conditions of meaning in the culture. Understood in these terms, reflexivity is a key element in what Siegle calls a 'constitutive poetics' which is directed at 'the mechanics and assumptions of composing, interpreting, structuring, positing', a poetics which is 'a specialized application of a larger study of how a culture — whether in literature, cultural coding in general, science, or philosophy — composes its identity and that of its individuals and constitutes the "world" within which it takes place' (1986: 11-12).

The dissonance between Coetzee's programmatic statements and his fiction can be discerned more precisely at this point, for in the latter we do find a combination of discursive and structural self-consciousness with a sense of historical inclusiveness, precisely the kind of configuration described by Siegle. Reflexivity for Siegle operates at a point at which 'a thoroughgoing semiotics borders on ideological critique' (1986: 11), surely a description applicable to Coetzee. Siegle's suggestion, to pursue this question further in theoretical terms, of a relationship within narrative reflexivity between semiotics and ideological critique, can be strengthened with reference to the historical themes developed by the Prague School structuralists. Although the Prague School never formulated a totalistic theory of literary history or literature-in-history, F.W. Galan in *Historic Structures* assembles such a theory, or rather shows it as implicitly emerging over a twenty-year period (rather in the manner of De Saussure's followers synthesizing his lectures after his death). The stages in the development of the theory are as follows: (i) there is an attempt to resolve the apparent incompatibility between historical and structural linguistics, diachrony and synchrony, inherited from De Saussure; (ii) having reconciled structural linguistics with the phenomenon of linguistic change, the next step is to extend this approach to the question of literary evolution; (iii) a conceptual and methodological break develops at this point from formalism to semiotics, after which the School looks beyond literary immanence to the relationships between literary and other social structures; (iv) finally, attention is paid to the question of reception.

The stage that concerns us initially is (iii), at which point, having added to the theory of signification descriptions of linguistic functions and the process of norm-violation (key elements of the reinstatement of the diachronic) there was an attempt by the School, largely in the work of Jan Mukařovský, to re-engage the problem of signification but from the point of view of its location *within the aesthetic function*. The orthodox position in Jakobson was that the sign in literature is self-referential; its function is to draw attention to itself, consequently, it obstructs reference to external reality. This position was reformulated, however, to accommodate the insight that in order for the sign to operate as a sign within a communicative context, a referent had to be present in some form or another. The problem was to understand the paradox between the *autonomous* and the *communicative* features of the literary work. Mukařovský resolved this problem, Galan argues, by showing that the literary sign had a special way of pointing to reality which preserves the specificity of the aesthetic function: its reference, quite simply, was oblique and metaphorical. Out of this observation, however, comes a more significant and illuminating paradox: that precisely because the referents of signs in poetic language have no existential value, since the autonomous signs are directed at nothing 'distinctly determinable', the literary work refers to 'the total context of so-called social phenomena' (Galan, 1985: 116). It is because of the global quality of literature's reference to reality that it provides valuable images of the texture of historical epochs. One might add to this the observation that the reference beyond the text is affirmed because of the implicitly *normative* qualities of aesthetic signs.[7]

Galan goes still further, taking the argument into the question of reception, the final stage in the development of the School's literary-historical theory. After an encounter with Husserlian phenomenology, and in an attempt to build into the literary theory the observation that from the point of view of the speaker, the polyfunctionality of language is experienced without difficulty, Mukařovský incorporates the category of the subject into his description of literary signification. Previously he had argued that the reality which is referred to in the literary sign was the social totality, rather than a reality comprising existentially 'real' components; now he modifies that position as follows: 'The reality which as a whole is reflected in the aesthetic sign is also unified in this sign in accordance with the image of the unified subject' (117). Briefly: in the aesthetic function the sign reflects within itself both the whole of social reality and the unified attitude of the subject towards that reality. Thus *intentionality* was added to *functionality*, an intentionality which gives the work a degree of structural coherence and at the same time, positions the reader in a particular relationship with the text. The reader's constitutive role in completing the communicative circuit or 'concretizing' the text is of course variable, providing a further historical locus for the production of meaning.

Coetzee's novels, to complete this excursus, are metafictional and formally reflexive; as such, they establish various forms of discourse — usually, these discourses are projected into the colonial narrative — as *loci* of critical objectification and reflection. Insofar as their reflexivity dramatizes their role as performance, the reader is drawn self-consciously into productivity. The formal possibilities sketched here from the resources of narrative theory and semiotics provide a suitable theoretical description of the path from reflexivity to qualified referentiality that such fiction involves. What remains, at another level of theory and with reference to different traditions, is to connect the formal descriptions validated by these strands of narrative and semiotic theory with a mode of ideological critique.

To return to Ricoeur on 'the narrative function': in the 'split' reference of fiction, and the 'indirect' reference of history (indirect because its reference is through traces, documents and archives), the two discourses share what he calls a point of *crossed reference*, a phenomenon which shows the act of narrating as involving the condition of historicity, now conceived as a form of activity and a form of life: 'It is only insofar as each narrative mode shares in some way the intentionality of the other that their references can cross upon historicity; and it is in the exchange between history and fiction, between their opposed referential modes, that *our historicity is brought to language*' (1981: 294). If it is possible, through Ricoeur, to envisage a third relation to Coetzee's supplementarity and rivalry, namely, a relation of *complementarity*, then it must be asked why Coetzee sets up the relation in terms that are exclusively and unhappily Manichean? The answer will be found in Coetzee's charged relationship with the politics of historical discourses, the grounds for which were prepared by the privileging of the notion of arbitrariness over the notion of convention; a binary conception of genesis in language (the 'oppositions out of which history and the historical disciplines erect themselves'); and a sense of being hemmed in by the inclusiveness of the historical pressures and the discourses that process and produce them. Speaking not as a novelist but in the language of polemic ('I do not even speak my own language' (1988a: 3)), and given these predispositions, Coetzee is bound to point out that 'there is a battlefield' (1988a: 3).

3 *Coetzee, Deconstruction and Lacanian Allegories*

There is a related debate which must be touched on here, although
it has not involved Coetzee directly (in the work of Teresa Dovey,
claims have been made on his behalf), namely, the problem of deconstruction in an historically charged situation like South Africa. It occurs in the pages of *Critical Inquiry* between Jacques Derrida and the
South Africans Anne McClintock and Rob Nixon, the basis of the
dispute being the meaning of the term *apartheid*. In 'Le Dernier Mot
du Racisme', Derrida argues essentially that apartheid is the last
word in racism not only because it is definitive, but also because
it is being consigned to oblivion by a collective investment in its future demise. To McClintock and Nixon, this kind of treatment ignores the term's own contextual history, which involves a degree
of ingenuity on the part of the South African State in revising its
language in accordance with shifts in policy, shifts which have had
the effect of enabling ever more refined, technocratic and legalistic
forms of oppression to replace the more blatant colonial racism of
the early years of white Nationalist rule. The difference in meaning
is crucial to the question of resistance, it is argued, since changes
of language and policy must be opposed by appropriately strategic
counter-measures. The dispute is one of whether the term is unsta-
ble enough to escape the intentions which created it and to become
an instrument in the destruction of those intentions, or whether it
is bound to its original conditions of use in such a way that we are
reminded of their materiality, and by implication, of the distinction
between political and verbal responses (Derrida, 1985; McClintock
and Nixon, 1986).

In Derrida's lengthy reply, in the form of an open letter to the
authors of the critique, he points out, among other things, that his
original text, published in the catalogue of an exhibition, was not
intended as a *descriptive* treatise on the history of the term, but it
was a *prescriptive appeal* with a strategic and pragmatic logic that is
ignored by his interlocutors. Derrida uncovers several instances like
this of what he regards as an expedient disregard for the nature and
purposes of his argument. The point that immediately concerns us,
however, is that throughout the reply, Derrida is quite prepared,
contrary perhaps to popular belief, to talk about apartheid, South
Africa, the Nationalist Party, the functions of capitalism, in terms
of their being quite unproblematically *there* as referents. Not only
is Derrida ostentatiously meticulous about incidentals — as in the
disagreement over where Smuts coined the term *apartheid*: 'I knew
it was in London, but I thought it was the Lord Russel Hotel. Are

you sure about the Savoy? Check it' (1986: 161) — he is strident and insistent on this point:

> Besides (and here I am speaking as an historian, that is in the *indicative*), whatever efforts the ideologues and official representatives of South Africa may have made to efface this embarrassing word from *their* discourse, whatever efforts *you* may make to keep track of their efforts, the failure is not in doubt and historians can attest to it: the word *apartheid* remains and, as I hope or expect, it will remain the 'unique appellation' of this monstrous, unique, and unambiguous *thing* [my emphasis]. You say 'Derrida is repelled by the word' (p.141). No, *what I find repulsive is the thing that history has now linked to the word, which is why I propose keeping the word so that the history will not be forgotten* [my emphasis]. Don't separate word from history! That's what you say to those who apparently have not learned this lesson. It is the South African racists, the National party, the Verwoerds and the Vorsters who ended up being afraid of the word (*their* word!), to whom it began to appear too repulsive because it had become so overseas. . . . But should we, because they wish it, abandon the word *apartheid* and no longer consider it to be the most accurate word in which to designate *this political reality, yesterday's and today's?* [my emphasis] (1986: 159)[8]

Although it might be difficult to say just how much irony there is in this argument, it would certainly be inappropriate to claim, after this, that 'the South African situation' is inevitably in deconstruction merely another transcendental signified dispersed onto the chain of signifiers.

Similarly, in Teresa Dovey's critique of Marxist readings of Coetzee, the 'deconstructive activity' of the novels is emphasized. The Marxist position on Coetzee was initiated by Michael Vaughan and continued by Paul Rich and later, Peter Kohler. Vaughan's argument was that although Coetzee problematizes the aesthetics and ideology of the tradition of liberal realism in South Africa, his treatment of colonialism in *Dusklands* privileges an agonized consciousness over material forces, a reversal which mirrors 'the predicament of a liberal petty bourgeois intelligentsia' (1982: 137). Paul Rich argues similarly that the novels contain a 'disembodied idealism', and that the forces of nationalist resistance leading to decolonization, which are the agents of historical consciousness in colonial situations, are never adequately brought to light (1984: 386-388). Peter Kohler examines *Dusklands* in terms of its reliance on the compromised construct 'frontier', and evaluates it as inaccurate by comparison with the work of revisionist historians led by Martin Legassick (1987: 3-23). Slipping from a debate about referentiality to a debate about politics, Dovey links Gordimer's review of *Michael K* in

The New York Review of Books with the Marxist critique, citing the mis-
giving: 'A revulsion against all political and revolutionary solutions
rises with the insistence of the song of cicadas to the climax of this
novel. I don't think the author would deny that it is his own revulsion.' (from Dovey, 1987: 15)

Defending Coetzee against these charges, she shows that each of
Coetzee's novels positions itself within a particular sub-genre of existing discourses within the culture, and subjects them to a process
of deconstructive disturbance that reveals their blindspots and their
complicity in ideology. The criticism of Coetzee by the Left is included in the critique, insofar as its claims are made on the basis
of an epistemologically naive assumption about the truth-value of
history being greater than that of fiction. It is shown that what has
been read as Coetzee's representation of history is really Coetzee's
representation of the discourses of history, or the discourses of subjects positioned in history, discourses whose purpose is to attempt
to realize the identities of the subjects concerned through their emergence into language, and in relation to an Other. (This observation
touches on the thesis of her subsequent full-length study, *J.M. Coetzee: Lacanian Allegories*. I shall return to this study shortly.) Her final
point is to link the arguments of the critics with what Michel Foucault calls 'the disciplines of surveillance', the twist of the knife being the suggestion that the Marxist critique has been labouring under a meta-myth of Science (not unlike Eugene Dawn's epistemic
megalomania in *Dusklands*). In the light of the discredited but residual claims of Althusserian Marxism to be able to distinguish itself from
ideology by inhabiting the purer air of science, this final point has
the force of a *coup de grâce*.

What Dovey's defence of Coetzee on the grounds of the deconstructive activity of the novels shows, however, together with Derrida's moral seriousness and his willingness to regard *apartheid* as
having a referent, is that deconstruction, in these two powerful instances of its deployment in relation to South Africa, retains an essentially outward or moral or worldly thrust. In Dovey, there is even
an implicit claim that the deconstructive activity of the novels is more
radical — and therefore by implication more responsive to the historical urgency of the situation — than the criticism by the Left. If this
argument is only barely plausible (the radicalism of reflexive discourse is not uncontested), it is clearly because the context itself operates as an unavoidable presence in the most cunning and suspicious
of critical methods. Over against Derrida and Dovey, however, we
must place Coetzee's imperatives, generated from within the situation itself: 'I see absolutely no reason why, even in the South Afri-

ca of the 1980's, we should agree to agree that things are otherwise.' What is remarkable is not that Coetzee is not prepared to equivocate whereas Derrida and Dovey are, but that the competing discourses should be handled by Coetzee in such a way that their internal epistemological orientations are treated as givens, in contrast to the more strictly deconstructive arguments, which seem to treat those givens as *in flux*, in a kind of effective relationship with the context. The conclusion may be drawn that unlike the arguments from deconstruction in these examples, Coetzee's position is more narrowly philological, in that it suggests that the underlying rules establish firm limits as to what language can achieve.

There are other aspects of Dovey's argument that need to be examined more closely. The first has to do with her account of narrative reflexivity; a second concerns the problem of contextualization; and a third involves the Lacanian thesis which is the basis of her longer study. Dovey's treatment of the radicalizing features of the novels poses the question of critical consciousness as if it were operative at an indeterminate number of levels. The novels are Chinese boxes embodying forms of reflexivity that encompass both fiction and the criticism of the fiction — the fiction is called 'fiction-as-criticism' — with the effect that ultimately the authorial agency, or the work that Coetzee as producer of this critique does, is mystified and surrounded with a revered invulnerability. There is a contradiction here, between the value attached to the radicalism of the fiction, and the indeterminacies which are claimed as the means whereby Coetzee's critique is achieved. The argument both preserves and cancels out the very idea of an authorial consciousness, indeed of authorial will, pressure or authority, if 'consciousness' is too essentialist a term; how a non-ideological *intention* can be attributed to the fiction therefore remains obscure.

The argument that each of the novels is positioned within, and deconstructs, a particular sub-genre of discourse within the culture is, I believe, entirely correct. It is an effective reply to the Left. In her essay, however, the analysis of this mode of reference is taken entirely from the text of *Dusklands*; in other words, the representation of the discourses of the culture to which the work refers, directly and indirectly, is extremely thin. This problem is not overcome in the longer study, where the discourses being referred to are almost exclusively literary and scarcely representative of even that (small) terrain within the culture. (For the most part — with the exception of the commentary on *Foe* — the allusions to 'the South African tradition' are dealt with in terms of a set of precise correspondences between each text and a particular work in the tradition; consequently, the allusiveness often becomes severely strained.) This contextual thinness is matched by an entirely honorific regard for Western psychoanalytic and deconstructive theory and its potential role in the context. The sheer weight of textual power in these bodies of theory, in an intellectual relationship with an academic 'third world' that is as determined by the unequal distribution and appropriation of resources under colonialism as is the global production and distribution of wealth, ought to caution one against this kind of reverence. There is a further aspect of the question of contextualization that must be raised, and that is how Coetzee enters, once again as producer and agent, into a certain discursive and social field. There is nominal reference in the opening paragraph to Coetzee's academic position, but this is taken to justify the insertion of Coetzee directly into Western theory and his fiction into fiction-as-criticism; what is circumvented is the extent to which Coetzee both participates and does not participate in the discourses of academic scholarship that immediately surround him.

The introduction of Lacanian theory has a particular contribution to make to Coetzee criticism, which for the most part has been inadequate to the theoretical self-consciousness of the fiction.[9] The thesis — to put it too simply — is that Coetzee's novels constitute a psychoanalytic allegory in which the narrators struggle to represent themselves in language, or to pass successfully from the Imaginary to the Symbolic stage through an encounter with the Other, the task being impossible in every instance because of the very nature of signification which is based on the principle of lack, or the absence of the signified. The desire for self-realization underlies all of the discourses which the novels deconstruct, an exposure which the novels themselves effect through inter-textual relationships that resemble the relationship between the analyst and the analysand of psychoanalysis. The thesis is significant because it attempts to come to terms with the 'failed dialectic' that is so marked a feature of all Coetzee's fiction.

There are limits to the model, however, which are discoverable on several grounds: philosophical, intellectual-biographical, and historical-political. Coetzee's treatment of the failed dialectic owes as much to a philosophical tradition rooted in Cartesianism, and which reaches from Hegelian metaphysics to Sartrean existentialism, as it might to Lacan (on the subject of desire, René Girard has also been influential).[10] If there is a single figure who has influenced Coetzee in the elaboration of these themes more than any other, it is not Lacan, but Beckett. As Kenner puts it, in Beckett's trilogy (*Molloy, Malone Dies,* and *The Unnamable*), the *cogito* devolves into 'a baffling intimacy between discourse and non-existence' (1961: 129). While Dovey does delve into some of Lacan's precursors, her emphasis (and this is the basis of the intellectual-biographical objection as well) involves the reinscription or capture of a developmental eclecticism in Coetzee into a psychoanalytic allegory which is projected across the whole oeuvre from beginning to end. 'There never was a master plan,' says Coetzee (Morphet interview (1983) 460).

The historical-political objection concerns the *cost* of this reinscription. What is not a feature of the various definitions of the Lacanian Other is what we might loosely call the historical Other, the role played in the fiction by the Vietcong, the Nama, the barbarians, and Friday. Dovey attempts at various points to come to terms with this Other via the Lacanian unconscious, but this assimilation is troublesome. One could approach the same question by recalling Hegel's relationship with the Enlightenment. In Dovey, Hegel is the source of the psychoanalytic tradition which is constructed back through Alexandre Kojéve; that Hegel's analysis of the master/slave dialectic is, in its own context, a critique of Enlightenment concepts of rationality, freedom and human progress, a critique which shows that such goals are attainable only *in* community, not outside it, tends to be ignored in the psychoanalytic version of the tradition. Coetzee's fiction incorporates the historical-political aspect. The narrative of colonialism has never allowed us to forget that social distances have a great deal to do with the failure of the colonizing self to enter reciprocal relationships with the new landscape and its people. In Dovey, this failure — Magda's inability to relate to the farm labourers in *In the Heart of the Country* — is primarily, even exclusively, a failure of language (1988: 25), and therefore a universal condition. Surely this is a small peg on which to hang so weighty and damaging a failure?

4 Coetzee and the Political Unconscious

'History is what hurts,' says Fredric Jameson, 'it is what refuses desire and sets inexorable limits to individual as well as collective praxis, which its "ruses" turn into grisly and ironic reversals of their overt intention' (1981: 102). The approach to reflexive fiction that I have outlined from the resources of narrative theory and semiotics can now be developed with reference to the theory of the political unconscious. This approach would try to anchor what Jameson in *The Prison-House of Language* calls deconstruction's 'infinite regress' and 'ontological dispersal' taking place at the level of signification,

with a sense of the force of the contextual pressures that underlie
social discourses and their managed, fictional reproduction. Such
an approach comes close, I believe, to the kind of analysis Jameson
himself envisages in his conclusion to *The Prison-House*, where he
speaks of signification as 'the transposition from one level of language to another, from one language to another language', so that
the availability of meaning is seen as 'nothing but the possibility
of such *transcoding*'. Strictly speaking, although social practices are
not collapsed entirely into verbal discourses, the referent is held in
parenthesis in this model, and both the production of meaning and
its reception are effected by acts of transcoding which are located
in contextually specific ways. As Jameson puts it: 'Indeed, the hermeneutic here foreseen would, by disclosing the presence of pre-
existing codes and models and by reemphasizing the place of the
analyst [reader] himself, reopen text and analytic process alike to
all the winds of history' (1972: 215-216).

Discussing Althusser's antiteleological or 'structural' sense of
causality, in which history is seen as having neither a subject nor
a telos, Jameson shows that Althusser — in taking from Lacan the
notion of the 'Real' as 'that which resists symbolization absolutely', and from Spinoza the concept of 'an absent cause' — avoids
the compromising but fashionable conclusion that 'because history
is a text, the "referent" does not exist' (1981: 35). Jameson then proposes his own influential formulation of the relationship between
history and textuality:

> history is *not* a text, not a narrative, master or otherwise, but . . . as
> an absent cause, it is inaccessible to us except in textual form,
> and . . . our approach to it and to the Real itself necessarily passes
> through its prior textualization, its narrativization in the political un-
> conscious. (35)

While Coetzee's attack on historical discourses in his *Weekly Mail*
Book Week address is almost susceptible — though not quite, as
I have argued — to the charge of turning history into 'one more text
among others', the fiction itself comes close to a formal or an aesthetic encoding of Jameson's proposition regarding the political unconscious: through a masterly control of the *style indirect libre* and
the interior monologue, Coetzee sets in motion the discourses of
the culture, revealing them as ideology, undercutting their attempts
at naturalization, and situating them within an historical narrative.
Consciousness is usually represented in Coetzee as being in a situation of historical flux: this correlates with an interesting affinity discovered by Jameson, again, between Althusser's concept of the

toujours-déjà-donné and Derrida's concept of the trace. In both, there is a recognition of a reality that precedes individual consciousness, of a level of social being which, although acknowledged in both terms, 'never comes to formulation as a concept or signifier in its own right . . . yet which places a floor beneath the infinite regression and flight of the signifier' (1972: 184). I recognize the rhetorical risks involved in suggesting that Coetzee's novels approximate a formal encoding of the theory of the political unconscious: in more orthodox positions, this argument either denies textual instability too freely, or it makes too large a claim for the capacity of aesthetic form to deliver ideological critique. But it seems inescapable in the light of the determination evident in the fiction to set before us not history, nor even interpretations of history (both of which are usually asserted as prerequisites for political accreditation by a more crude historicism which sets out to prove a political apostasy in Coetzee by assessing the truth-value of the fiction) but the forms of consciousness — with all their contradictions, aporias and bad faith — of subjects who are immersed in it. Of course, fiction which participates in the great shift described by Roland Barthes as the movement from *logos* to *lexis* (1966: 114), cannot be said to deliver a hermeneutic, which is what Jameson's analysis of historical interpretation sets out to enable. Anything resembling Jameson's three 'semantic horizons' of historicization will not be found in the fiction. And yet it is possible to take the achronic and depersonalized features of narrative in the classic continental structuralist account (Barthes, 1966: 109-114), and reintegrate them with history at another level. By so doing, one is able to describe in theoretical terms the phenomenon in Coetzee whereby an essentially philological outlook on narrative is pulled into historicity, or projects itself into historicity, because of the force of context.

There are two further, related observations that I will adduce in support of this claim. The first is the radically *provisional* and *methodological* character of Coetzee's novels. The labour involved in textual construction — what I am referring to determines such a term — is on the surface: in the temporal reversals and structural parallelisms of *Dusklands*, in the numbered paragraphs and episodic repetitions of *In the Heart of the Country*, in the elaborate opacity and remoteness of the imperial outpost in *Waiting for the Barbarians*, in the almost ostentatious realism of *Life & Times of Michael K*, and the crafted intertextuality of *Foe*. These things all have local functions within the novels, but my more general point concerns a guarded, formal directedness — to use Ricoeur's term — that drives each of the novels into its particular set of contextual resonances. But this same directedness is paradoxically cleaned of any form of interpolation, so that the narrative voices being set in motion, at some distance from what in a more conventional novelistic discourse would be read as an authorial presence, seem all the more driven by the necessities of their own condition. In other words, the formal strength of Coetzee's representation of subjectivity has the effect of alluding to a source of non-authorial, cultural and by implication, historical conditioning.

My second observation is of another paradoxical implication, found in Coetzee's refusal to 'complete' the historical trajectory of decolonization, of the very palpability of historical forces. Coetzee's scepticism carries an implication of the iron wilfulness of history, of the absolute contingency that belies voluntarist and triumphalist accounts of what we so often and too blithely call 'the historical process'. The refusal that I am referring to is directly related to the moments of apparent political embarrassment in the fiction, not so much in the ending of *Waiting for the Barbarians* but in instances like the enigma of K, who is not really a social being at all, whose ingenuousness is the more remarkable for the minutely detailed realism that creates his world, or perhaps most spectacularly, the mutilation of Friday. The strangeness of such moments, however, lies in their suggestion of the simultaneously inscrutable and irresistible nature of historical forces. The proposition that history is not always writable (and the corollary that I have added, that writing can therefore claim a qualified freedom from it), is a proposition that confirms the very gravity of the forces being alluded to. A fiction that is open to unrealized possibilities is not necessarily evasive; it might also be unwilling to project itself beyond the historically contingent.

While it is possible, however, to argue that Coetzee's fiction comes close to formally encoding the theory of a political unconscious, there must also be a sense in which the account given in the fiction of how subjects are positioned in history is *itself* rooted historically. My argument has effectively ruled out the possibility, however, of a reading which tries to identify symptomatically the operation of a political unconscious on Coetzee. If such a step were possible, it would inevitably involve flattening and denying the historically allusive reflexivity that I have been describing; the fiction, after all, encodes its own symptomatics. But there is a step which is feasible, which preserves the particular characteristics of Coetzee's narrative subtlety, but which simultaneously historicizes the choices that Coetzee makes. If a political unconscious is to be located in Coetzee, it will not be at the level of some ideal content which is built into the novels; it will appear instead in the patterns of association that Coetzee implicitly endorses or rejects. I have stressed, following Said, the authority and agency of Coetzee, and it is necessary to see that authority as having effect in recognizable ways. One might attempt this by asking questions about the kinds of affiliative connections that Coetzee establishes through the novels, the lineages of intellectual, cultural and political heritage that are nurtured, against those that are disclaimed.

Said's essay on 'secular criticism' discusses the process familiar at least since modernism of a transition that individuals undergo or enact — writers and critics especially, since the process is effected within and by culture — from filiation, to affiliation. The process involves moving from 'a failed idea or possibility of filiation to a kind of compensatory order that, whether it is a party, an institution, a culture, a set of beliefs, or even a world-vision, provides men and women with a new form of relationship, which I have been calling affiliation but which is also a new system' (1983: 19). Some of Said's vocabulary is not applicable to so elusive a writer as Coetzee: *party, set of beliefs, compensatory order, world-vision*, etc; but the *process* involving a movement from an initial rejection of filiative relationships to a search within an affiliative culture of intellectual and literary-critical relationships — affiliation that undeniably requires the institutional base provided by scholarship, specifically by universities — is clearly evident in the sequence of novels.[11] The first two novels, *Dusklands* and *In the Heart of the Country*, can be described as delivering a critique of the forms of filiation that must be felt as chains of imprisonment by any critical or reflective white South African. The sheer violence and at times almost oppressive power, as well as the avant-garde features of the prose in these novels, reveal a struggle from within the colonialism, with its attendant discourses, that defines the filiative structure. There is a point — and I refer again to *Waiting for the Barbarians* — at which this struggle seems to pivot, and a tendency in the later fiction towards formal stabilization sets in which is accompanied in thematic terms by what I have described as the search for qualified or partial forms of freedom. In the last two novels, *Life & Times of Michael K* and *Foe*, affiliative patterns appear which, tentatively, I shall call simply the literary system (acknowledging that it is in the nature of this system, when appropriate, to deny its systemic properties). The *inter-textual networks of literature* seem to provide Coetzee with a kind of guarantee of the *possibility* of such freedom, even if this means only the freedom to re-think, as he puts it, the categories of dominance. This large movement through the sequence of novels cannot be discerned, however, without reference to the historical narrative which the fiction itself establishes, not only as a story to be told, but also as a field of authorial endeavour. In *Foe*, this struggle is brought to an extreme point of self-consciousness. Another way of putting this is to say that against the historical narrative, using the materials of structure, Coetzee casts in relief configurations of language — conceived as subjectivity, self-representation, myth, and ideology — which contain different accounts of the limits and possibilities of life lived out in history. While these accounts recognize the moment of narration itself, which is implicitly acknowledged to be an historical act, they must also be read as participating in the affiliative relationships of intellectual, literary-historical and literary-critical culture.

One of the 'grisly and ironic reversals' of history in this instance is that in Coetzee, the inter-textuality that is sought after as a zone of freedom, in a fictional project of great historical strength, is also a form of limitation, because it is axiomatic that the relationships of culture that Coetzee finds to hand, both through personal history and in institutionalized scholarship, are predominantly non-African. On the other hand, were Coetzee to seek non-metropolitan, African forms of affiliation, he would be liable to charges of wanting to manage or appropriate the direction of the revolutionary culture. (What non-racialism means in terms of affective cultural discourse, the defining feature of affiliation — as opposed to, say, political theory — is by no means self-evident in South Africa. The discursive thinness and absence of tradition in the 'people's culture' campaign is perhaps its severest limitation.) It is important to remember that it was before the popularization of Black Consciousness in the mid-seventies that Coetzee published his appreciative essays on La Guma. The fact that Michael K is closer to figures in Beckett or Kafka than to being an activist or revolutionary, or that *Life & Times* offers no ideological investment in a post-revolutionary scenario, ought to be understood in these terms. While there are many white activists who have done so (and at least one white activist-poet, Jeremy Cronin), there are no white South African novelists who have completely and successfully negotiated this transition, not even Nadine Gordimer, despite her magnificent and principled efforts in this direction. Only recently (December, 1987), Lewis Nkosi passed a red-eyed remark about *A Sport of Nature*: 'a great part of the motivating force of this fiction is its fear of exclusion, the fear of loitering without intent in the vicinity of revolution' (1988: 46). This rebuke does no justice to the intelligence and depth of Gordimer's commitment, but at least one half of the process of affiliation involves *acceptance*. Coetzee's choice has been not to test the waters.

5 Coetzee and South African Revisionism

I wish to make good my claim that Coetzee must be read in relation
to the academic discursive context that immediately surrounds him.
Clearly, that context represents a field that is simply too vast to be
adequately surveyed here; what concerns us are those features of
it that most usefully merit comparison with the particular directions
found in Coetzee. We are also attempting to define the moment of
which Coetzee is a part. A suitable point of departure is provided
by comparing Coetzee with Gordimer, through Gordimer's most
authoritative critic, Stephen Clingman. Clingman's concept, 'history from the inside', the subtitle of his *The Novels of Nadine Gordimer*, refers not only to the way Gordimer embodies in her characters the social forces of the historical situation in which she finds
herself, but also to the fact that Gordimer's capacity to characterize
the 'lived' dimensions of her world in this way is necessarily *positioned* within history as well. Given the fact that Gordimer's career
spans virtually the entire period of modern apartheid, from 1948
to the present, Clingman is able to track the various shifts in Gordimer from a liberal humanism of the late forties and early fifties,
to the more dynamic multiracial liberalism of the years of the Defiance Campaign (1952) and the Treason Trial (1956); later, from the
mid-sixties, after the growth of revolutionary politics in South Africa, and by the end of the decade with the rise of Black Consciousness, Gordimer moves unevenly towards a form of post-liberal, radical historicism. In Clingman's account, Gordimer's relationship with
the currents of contemporary South African history comprises in
itself a remarkable narrative.

With Coetzee, the implications of a potentially revolutionary situation, or at least of an end-of-era, dying colonialism, are there from
the start. He enters into a social debate, assisting in defining its
terms, that is already showing signs of being 'post-liberal'. *Dusklands* (1974) announces a break as if it had already happened. I disagree with accounts of Coetzee which claim that along with Gordimer he initiates a break with liberal humanism into something else,
insofar as Coetzee himself undergoes no such break; his entry into
South African intellectual life is angular from the beginning. But
Coetzee is differently placed from Gordimer with respect not only
to historical developments and his relationship with them, but also
to institutional factors, since it is by way of *intellectual scholarship*
that Coetzee enters into fiction-writing. An initial contextualization
of Coetzee can be derived, therefore, from an account of the character of social debates in the country from the early seventies onwards,

and of the ways in which academic discourses helped to define these debates.

The South Africa that emerged from the era of repression following Sharpeville was more riven with insecurity than at any other time since 1948. The early seventies saw a number of developments which either heralded the possibility of major historical transformation, or responded to such a possibility. The most important of these were the rise, during a period of severe recession, of a militant and independent labour movement, culminating in large-scale strikes in the Durban area in 1973; the increasing militancy of black students and the rise of Black Consciousness — exemplified in the schism between SASO and NUSAS — which quickly became popularized in schools and local communities and which played a decisive role in the Soweto Revolt of 1976; finally, from 1977, the development of the strategy of 'reform' by the State, as an attempt to manage the crisis that it seemed to be facing by refining the constitutional, administrative and economic structures on which its hegemony was based. From this period to the present, political culture in South Africa seemed to be locked into an opposing set of categories, either 'revolution' or 'reform', both of which drew their defining features from the large-scale historical momentum with which the decade had begun (Stadler, 1987: 161-184).

In this climate, an academic revisionism that had begun in the late sixties in the field — appropriately — of historiography, acquired a particular urgency. The origins of this revisionism, as its influence and academic purview increased and widened to embrace all the social sciences and humanities, would probably have to be traced to the prominence of radical philosophies in Europe in the sixties, mainly existentialism followed by structuralism, and on a lesser scale, Marxism, and to the anti-war and civil rights movements in the United States. In the local situation, these powerful models of the metropolitan culture seemed to open up new vistas of consciousness and praxis in a South Africa seemingly deadened by apathy, acquiescence and repression. The exemplary book of the period was *The Eye of the Needle* (1972) and the exemplary life was that of its author, Richard Turner, who was assassinated in circumstances which appeared to direct responsibility at the State (a pattern which was later to repeat itself). Turner's exposure to existentialism and Marxism while a student in Paris in the sixties translated into the conviction, expressed in his life and work as an activist (most notably in the labour field) and lecturer in philosophy at the University of Natal in Durban, that objective conditions in South Africa were the consequence of human choices and actions and could therefore be challenged. *The Eye of the Needle* was written specifically as an attempt to popularize this concept, and to project ethical and political alternatives as being thinkable, in a culture which blocked them. Herbert Marcuse's *One Dimensional Man* is a high point of the period, with its resistance to 'the closing of the universe of discourse' and its critique of the associations between Reason, technological rationality, and domination (themes which echo in *Dusklands*). Turner gave currency to Marcuse, writing on 'the power of negative thinking' in the University of Cape Town student journal *Radical* (1970). Turner's most rigorous philosophical project, however, written while under a banning order, was an incomplete and unpublished analysis of the problem of 'the nature and status of the knowing subject in a materialist dialectic' (Morphet, Introduction to *The Eye of the Needle*, 1972: xxix). The problem 'is traced through the idealist/materialist tradition beginning from Kant's criticism of empiricism and proceeding through Hegel to Marx, Engels and Lenin and subsequently to Sartre, Althusser and Habermas' (xxix). Apart from its obvious philosophical importance, the treatise's pertinence lay in its attempt to reconcile the different aspects of Turner's own life, to combine, in other words, a defensible ethical standpoint which was meaningful from the point of view of the subject, with a firm grasp of the material forces underlying the larger, enveloping historical trauma (xxx).[12]

The representative feature of Turner's life and work is this attempt to combine a particular perspective on the self with a larger, historical view. It is a problem towards which South Africa seems prone to drive its more thoughtful citizens, at different levels of its hierarchy, not excluding populism. The prominence of autobiography since the early sixties, in black writing especially, is evidence of this, but it is particularly visible in two major discursive events of the early seventies: Black Consciousness itself, and the Study Project on Christianity in Apartheid Society (SPRO-CAS). The B.C. position was one of self-recovery and self-affirmation in response to the negations of racism. The black world was posited as an organic unity, a trans-individual mode of selfhood, and it was reinforced by a teleology of moral justice. SPRO-CAS was initiated by Beyers Naude in mid-1969 with the following objectives: 'to examine our society in the light of Christian principles; to formulate long-term goals for an acceptable social order; and to consider how change towards such a social order might be accomplished' (SPRO-CAS, 1973: 1). The fields covered by the six commissions established by the Project were economics, education, law, politics, society and the church; the ethical framework underlying the Project was defined in terms of three principles, the 'sanctity of the human person', the need for redemption and reconciliation, and the necessity of working 'with our whole being now towards the maximum of justice and love in all human relationships' (1973: 5-6). The Project combined the efforts of prominent white liberals from a range of backgrounds, but it also won participation from people like Turner, as well as black intellectuals like Steve Biko and Ben Khoapa, spokespersons for B.C., Njabulo Ndebele, the educationist C.M.C. Ndamse, and curiously enough, Gatsha Buthelezi. These two forms of critique, perhaps the most prominent of the period, were really rag-bags of socio-ideological and ethical discourse, articulated by thoughtful people forming, in the case of SPRO-CAS, an unlikely alliance on the basis of a common opposition to apartheid, and more tellingly, a common marginality to the sources of power.

This marginality did not prevent the State from taking seriously the various organizations involved in producing these criticisms. The Schlebusch Commission was set up to investigate NUSAS, The Christian Institute (closely linked to SPRO-CAS) and the Institute of Race Relations. Its report, published in 1974, is a compendious account of the minutiae of the day-to-day affairs of these organizations and their representatives (not excluding their private lives). Its argumentative twists and distortions of logic are usually banal, although its consequences in terms of bannings and restrictions were not. An example is the chapter on 'Polarisation', an account of the formation of SASO, which tries to show that because Black Consciousness incorporated a dialectical account of the progress from racism, to black assertion, to an ultimately non-racial future, its whole method, and its ethnic emphasis, were a veil over a Leninist dialectical materialism (Schlebusch Commission, 1974: 391-463). On the cultural organization within NUSAS called Aquarius, the Commission quotes reams of evidence from student leaders apparently providing their *de facto* guilt by stating that they objected to the environmental conditioning around them (334-352). In these examples and others, the Commission, as in McCarthyism, tries to pin down subversion to particular configurations of thought or consciousness; ironically, in doing so, it participates at a mundane level in one of the powerful cultural currents of the time, which can be conveniently described in terms of the popularization of the concept of paradigm shift well beyond its original relevance in Thomas Kuhn's *The Structure of Scientific Revolutions*.

For the sake of completeness, allow me to refer with rather savage brevity to the historiographical debate being conducted at the time, within a more strictly academic context. Its initial focus was the two-volume *Oxford History of Southern Africa*, edited by Monica Wilson and Leonard Thompson. For a number of younger historians (F.W. Johnstone, Stanley Trapido, Harold Wolpe, Colin Bundy; by the nineteen-eighties, Shula Marks and Charles van Onselen began to feature prominently in a large and varied revisionist movement) the kind of history it represented implied a liberal, positivist conception of racial 'interaction', a top-down sense of agents and actors which underplayed the role of the underclasses and of structural factors in determining events, and a gradualist or reformist perspective on change. Above all, however, the debate centred on how the relationship between capitalism and apartheid was to be examined. In terms of the liberal view, apartheid was irrational and the dynamics of growth in a free market system were bound to undermine steadily the ability of the State to enforce it. In terms of the revisionist perspective, apartheid was intrinsic to the logic of capitalist accumulation because it provided, among other things, for cheap labour by such means as regulating urbanization through the pass laws, and keeping families in the bantustans living on subsistence production and so reducing wage costs. Whereas liberal history implied that capitalism was a progressive force, a modernity that was acting on and transforming pre-capitalist cultures and social structures in preparation for their assimilation into the 'developed' world, revisionism held that capitalism was an invasive force linked internationally to economic imperialism, and that the proper object of study was the capacity of underclass communities to resist this presence or transform it in terms of their own interests (Marks, 1986: 166-169).

From an early stage, a similar re-narrativization of South African history penetrated the literary culture. The conference held at the University of Cape Town Summer School in 1974, whose proceedings were published under the title *Poetry South Africa*, was undoubtedly a watershed event. In particular, in the debate between Guy Butler and Mike Kirkwood one discerns the clash of fundamentally opposed systems, whose purview includes historiography, literary practice and the nature of cultural identity and commitment. What Kirkwood challenged was not Butler himself so much as 'Butlerism', a certain liberal sense of what it meant to be an English-speaking South African (or ESSA, in Butler's account), a liberalism with a considerable history and, until this time, a remarkable consensus in white, English-language circles. This perspective looked back to the arrival of the 1820 settlers in the spirit of mission, in that the particular historical role of the English was thought to be an enlightening, humanizing one in a frontier society of harshly contending

124   *David Attwell*

forces and ideologies. For Butler, the English were 'Athenians', 'traffickers in ideas, and in the arts, transmitters and popularizers of ideas and new ways of feeling' (from Kirkwood, 1976: 103). As the bearers of the English language, the English had a role to play in education and in the literary arts, but the social dimension of Butler's thinking embraced involvement in every sphere, including (constitutional) politics. The historical reality of the settlers' positioning in a 'buffer zone' between warring Xhosas and Afrikaners was rewritten as a cultural and political programme: the English were to be the 'mediators', facilitating the emergence of a more humane national culture and polity. The approach was essentially Arnoldian: *Culture and Anarchy* transposed from the class fractures of nineteenth-century England to the South African 'frontier'.

Kirkwood's challenge was based on a recontextualization of the ESSA identity in terms of imperialism. The historiographical aspect of the argument rejected the thesis that the English occupied a middle group (while this may be true in a simplistic geographical sense, in terms of *social relations* that ground was always occupied by 'coloureds'); the position occupied by the English was one they shared with the Afrikaner, namely that of the ruling class, in an essentially colonial set of relationships where stratification took on a racial colouring. The acknowledgement of class is also an acknowledgement of the extent to which the dynamics of the South African political economy call for a modification of an analysis in terms of classic colonialism. Revisionist historiographers introduced the materialist argument into the terms of debate, and they are taken up by Kirkwood here; but what Kirkwood goes on to do is examine the subject-position of the ESSA-as-colonizer, with reference mainly to Frantz Fanon's *The Wretched of the Earth* and Albert Memmi's *The Colonizer and the Colonized*. In a curious eclecticism characteristic of literary practice, Kirkwood combines the materialist historiographical critique with the psychoanalytic and existentialist extension of the critique of imperialism. The heart of Kirkwood's presentation was to show the three-part process whereby the 'ontology of the colonizer' could be revealed:

In the first [stage] there is an emphasis on cultures rather than on societies, on functional-structuralist anthropology, and on such matters as 'the primitive mind'. The characteristic of this phase is the confidence with which the colonizer makes the collective being of the colonized his object, fails to assert a critical awareness of his own ethnocentric assumptions and projections, and uses the colonized as exotic models for rudimentary raids into the fascinating history of his own psyche.

In the second an awareness of the colonial society as such is dawning but the colonizer retains the role of its interpreter. Mannoni's classic work, *Prospero and Caliban, the Psychology of Colonization*, represents this phase: the dependence of the colonized on the colonizer is noted, and a theory is evolved to explain it. The 'colonizability' of the colonized is said to derive from the dependent relationships fostered by ancestor worship and its complementary family system. The colonizer's true task, if he can be enlightened, is not to perpetuate and bask in dependence, but to assist in the birth of a full personality in the colonized, launching his ego upon the troubled ocean of the inferiority complex. He must learn to endure the trauma of abandonment and stabilize his personality through desperate achievements. He must learn, as Western man has learned, to live out the myth of Tom Thumb.

In the third stage the initiative passes to the colonized, whose stirrings — Garveyism, negritude — have ushered in the second stage. The dependence theory of Mannoni and other notions of 'colonizability' are angrily and summarily rejected. Colonization itself is revealed as the creator of its dependents, and a full psychological analysis of the colonial situation is undertaken. The reader for whom Fanon and Memmi write their descriptions is the colonized man, the man who now seeks to re-make himself by destroying the situation which created him as colonized, and, in an expression which they both use, to 're-enter history'. (1976: 121-122)

What Kirkwood does here — in a brilliant piece of rhetorical inversion — is rewrite the three phases identified by Fanon in the development of the national culture of indigenous peoples, namely, assimilation into the colonial culture, followed by reaction and immersion in the indigenous culture, followed by revolutionary commitment, from the point of view of the colonizer, who finds himself, as settler, having witnessed and lived through, if not in living memory then in folklore, all three phases, with the effect that he grows in self-awareness as he observes himself being posited as the object of the emergent discourse of the colonized. This self-objectification is of course also a self-critique, and Kirkwood goes on to discuss some of the worst features of the colonizer self: what he calls 'the Nero complex' ('Nero, the usurper of the birthright of Britannicus'); the relationships of intimacy which develop with the colonized, but which are abused or repressed in the colonizer; the reliance on a language of dependence, full of imperatives and hierarchical modes of address; the mediocrity of colonial culture as the consequence of its provincial relationship with the metropolis and of the process whereby the colonizer ego is constituted on the assumption of superiority (125-131). The critique must eventuate, says Kirkwood, in self-transcendence, but he adds that 'a life-technique, as well as an art-technique, will be required' (131-132).

In the year of the conference on 'Poetry '74', Ravan Press — publisher of the SPRO-CAS Reports, closely linked to the Christian Institute — brought out *Dusklands*. It, too, develops a colonial history critique; moreover, it does so by positioning the subject within the colonial narrative and pursuing it through degrees of painful self-consciousness. Coetzee is therefore, both in his mode of access to the culture as well as in his themes, an intimate and effective participant in the opening up of the new discursive possibilities.

6 Coetzee, Linguistics and Colonialism

And yet, Coetzee's point of contact with the other developments was oblique. It was oblique for reasons, firstly, of personal history, in that it came about via his exposure to America in the years of the bombing of North Vietnam; it was oblique also because it was filtered by philological studies. In the cultural estrangement of Texas, and linking different threads of his personal history and current situation, Coetzee brought aspects of his graduate linguistic studies to bear on the question of colonialism. In a biographical sketch of this period written fifteen years later for *The New York Times Book Review*, he tells of writing a paper for the linguist Archibald Hill on the morphology of Nama, Malay and Dutch, exploring their interconnections by sifting through documents of colonial discourse such as travellers' reports on the territory of South West Africa, accounts of punitive raids against the Nama and Herero, anthropological and linguistic descriptions, and missionary and other historical records. In another study, he examined the syntax of exotic languages and discovered for himself what was already well known, 'that every one of the 700 tongues of Borneo was as coherent and complex and intractable to analysis as English'. He then speaks of the curious effect of generative grammar on his emerging ambition to write:

> I read Noam Chomsky and Jerrold Katz and the new universal grammarians and reached the point of asking myself: If a latter-day ark were ever commissioned to take the best that mankind had to offer and make a fresh start on the farther planets, if it ever came down to that, might we not leave Shakespeare's plays and Beethoven's quartets behind to make room for the last aboriginal speaker of Dyirbal, even though that might be a fat old woman who scratched herself and smelled bad? It seemed an odd position for a student of English, the greatest imperial language of them all, to be falling into. It was a doubly odd position for someone with literary ambitions, albeit of the vaguest — ambitions to speak one day, somehow, in his own voice — to discover himself suspecting that languages spoke people or at the very least spoke through them. (1984: 9)

The Chomskyian hypothesis that there are rules governing discourses at the level of deep structure seems to have initiated the drift in Coetzee away from both realist and Romantic conceptions of authorial creativity. Instead of being the independent producer of literary language, the writer — perhaps a more suitable term now than author — sets discourses in motion, pursuing their inner logic, sometimes setting several discourses in parallel, as in *Dusklands* where part of the interest lies in the critical distance that is set up between different discourses, from different periods and historical contexts and from different genres. (Jameson's notion of *transcoding* finds a different relevance here.) And yet, another implication lies in the influence of generative grammar, namely, its underlying demotic aspect. It appears in Coetzee's ark; it is also there in a work like Chomsky's *American Power and the New Mandarins*, which in questioning the role of liberal 'objective' scholarship in the context of the war, is close to the concerns represented by Eugene Dawn.

Coetzee's precursors in bringing linguistic studies into the field of colonial relations, however, go back to the period of high imperialism, and the work of Orientalists like Silvestre de Sacy and Ernest Renan. In Said's account in *Orientalism*, the successes of the Orientalist philology of the nineteenth century included 'comparative grammar, the reclassification of languages into families, and the final rejection of the divine origins of language'; these achievements, in Renan especially, linked Orientalism definitively with the ideals of progress and scientific knowledge (1978: 135). While Renan's 'philological laboratory' was a significant contribution to the extension and consolidation of European discursive authority, Coetzee, in a limited way, projecting now into the end of colonialism, follows the tracks left by this tradition, in order both to diagnose the source of the process that so severely shaped the history he knows, and simultaneously, to find Europe's authority relativized in the dispersed languages of the colonial world.

In conclusion, I wish to draw attention to the congruence between Coetzee's linguistic interests and his scepticism about the forms of political affiliation that are sometimes demanded of him in South Africa today. Insofar as these interests were given definition by generative grammar, they would tend to work against a pragmatic conception of the forms of political association that writers might try to develop, since, as the Speech Act theorist John Searle points out, generative grammar's weakest area was semantics which involves, by implication, an unwillingness to address the communicative functions of language (1974: 23-31).[13] Similarly, to the extent that Coetzee was influenced by continental structuralism, the principle of the arbitrariness of the sign must extend to an apprehension about the assumption of immanence that underlies linguistic conventions. *Competence* over *performance, langue* over *parole*; this emphasis is consonant with a statement like the following: 'I am hesitant to accept that my books are addressed to readers. Or at least I would argue that the concept of the reader in literature is a vastly more problematic one than one might at first think.' (Morphet interview, 1987 (1983): 456) Coetzee's caution about political association translates into a caution about the notion of community. In the South Africa of the nineteen seventies and eighties, the only community that a writer like Coetzee could envisage would be a community-to-be-created. If some of his readers do not sense in Coetzee's fiction the possibility of his sharing, as an authorial presence, in the work of construction or reconstruction that is required by such a prospect, then it is still incumbent on them to follow Coetzee into the break with the filiative colonial structure, to understand the terms of that break and to grasp the historical cogency of the fiction it produced, and to examine the affiliative connections that follow from it in the light of the historical pressures to which they are both a response and a judgement.

Notes

1. Coetzee's interest in the mathematical dimensions of Beckett's prose accords with his own background in mathematics as an undergraduate and as a computer programmer. His early publications include essays in stylostatistics and experiments with computer-generated poetry.

2. Nomenclature involving the concept 'history' will inevitably shift from one context to another in this essay, but I shall offer here certain basic distinctions which I try to adhere to in the course of argument. The term 'history' generally refers to reality, the Real, the datum of the individual and collective experience of the past. Of course, it will be recognized that in this sense the term is always used in the as-if mode. This contrasts with Coetzee's use of 'history' in recent polemics, where it refers to what I call historical discourse. (I shall have to refer the reader to the contexts of discussion when terminology by other writers and theorists is used.) 'Literary history' is used in the most widely accepted sense. I use the term 'History' to denote the radical historicization that accompanies the politicization of culture in South Africa. In this sense, there is paradoxically a transhistorical element in that the urgency of the immediate past governs the meanings that are available in the present, forcing them into accountability. I also use the terms 'historical engagement' and 'historicity'; these provide a sense of subjective engagement in the field of historical discourse. Finally, I use the term 'historical narrative' to refer to the diachronic sequence colonialism-

decolonization on which Coetzee's whole oeuvre is constructed.
3. 'Much of my academic training was in linguistics. And in many ways
    I am more interested in the linguistic than in the literary side of my aca-
    demic profession. I think there is evidence of an interest in problems
    of language throughout my novels. I don't see any disruption between
    my professional interest in language and my activities as a writer' (In-
    terview with J.D. Sévry, 1985).
4. Coetzee's remark about making sense of life in a novel being different
    from making sense of real life is in the interview with Alan Thorold and
    Richard Wicksteed. On the constitutive implications in generative gram-
    mar, see Noam Chomsky, *Cartesian Linguistics*: 'In short, then, man has
    a species-specific capacity, a unique type of intellectual organization
    which cannot be attributed to peripheral organs or related to general
    intelligence and which manifests itself in what we may refer to as the
    ''creative aspect'' of ordinary language use — its property being both
    unbounded in scope and stimulus-free' (1966: 4-5).
5. I borrow Nadine Gordimer's terms here, in particular her use of Gram-
    sci's *Prison Notebooks* in her epigraph to *July's People*: 'The old is dying
    and the new cannot be born; in this interregnum there arises a great
    diversity of morbid symptoms.' At what point we might call an inter-
    regnum a suspension is perhaps an open question. There are two fur-
    ther, related questions that one might take up concerning the narrative
    of colonialism that Coetzee employs: the first is the extent to which this
    narrative occludes the process of industrialization and class-formation
    (making Coetzee a writer with a regional, Cape emphasis in his han-
    dling of historical processes); the second is how this narrative compares
    with CST, the theory of colonialism of a special type, which in the past
    has been of paramount importance in directing resistance (Bundy, 1988).
6. In the social sciences in South Africa a similar tension is reflected in
    a polarization between social historians and social theorists, between
    the adherents of an E.P. Thompsonian position which produces under-
    class and 'people's' histories — characteristic of the African Studies In-
    stitute and the History Workshop at the University of the Witwaters-
    rand — and political sociologists, the local heirs of Louis Althusser and
    Nicos Poulantzas who, through theory, privilege the structural relation-
    ships between capitalism and apartheid. See Mike Morris, 'Social His-
    tory and the Transition to Capitalism in South Africa'. My brief discus-
    sion of the emergence of revisionist historiography will have to exclude
    a more detailed account of the different factions and streams within rad-
    ical historicism in the social sciences in South Africa. I am indebted to
    discussions of some of these differences with Michael Green, Peter Koh-
    ler and Michael Vaughan.
7. I am grateful to Jaqueline Henkel for this point. I am not suggesting
    of course that a functional approach to the sign is discovered by Coet-
    zee in advance of the fiction.
8. I am indebted to a conversation about this debate with David Schalk-
    wyk. I do not intend to rehearse the arguments of Michael Ryan's
    Marxism and Deconstruction. While I accept that a philosophical articula-
    tion of Marxism and deconstruction is possible (though in a language
    theologians call dogmatics), my interest lies in the way contexts over-
    determine conceptual allegiances.

9. Lacan has appeared in discussion of Coetzee in South Africa before, in Menán du Plessis's exceptional (in both senses) review of *Waiting for the Barbarians* in *Contrast* 52. Du Plessis precedes Dovey in arguing, with reference to a passage from Anthony Wilden's commentary on Lacan's *The Language of the Self* — referred to extensively by Dovey — that the dialectics outlined in Hegel's *Phenomenology of Mind* are recreated in all of Coetzee's novels. Du Plessis might not have predicted where a similar argument might lead, for while her argument evolves towards a political defence of Coetzee on the grounds of his concern with 'a true materialism' (by which is meant a materialist account of subjectivity, located in discourse), in Dovey's hands similar materials lead to a break with Marxism (although on occasion the need for such a break is disclaimed) and to a position that is arguably anti-historical.

10. I am indebted here to a conversation with David Bunn.

11. I agree with Stephen Watson and Neil Lazarus who, independently of one another, have written about an affinity with mainstream forms of modernism in Coetzee. This affinity, at its simplest level, is evident in the attempt to use the resources of narrative, of aesthetic form, to project beyond the immediately apparent or the immediately 'real', the all too familiar landscape of apartheid, in this case. (I have located the source of this emphasis in Coetzee's linguistic interests, rather than in modernism, but the positions are nevertheless analogous.) In Lazarus this point is generalized to all contemporary white South African writing which is critical of apartheid, and dealt with in terms taken from Adorno. This seems to me to be more persuasive than Watson's argument, which while providing a very insightful commentary on some of the texts, explains the fiction as originating from Coetzee's biographical position as 'a colonizer who refuses'. This blanket category is too close to its source in Albert Memmi to be useful, and requires elaboration and finer contextualization. Stephen Watson, 'Colonialism and the Novels of J.M. Coetzee', and Neil Lazarus, 'Modernism and Modernity: T.W. Adorno and Contemporary White South African Literature'.

12. I am grateful to Tony Morphet and Andrew Nash for their valuable assistance at several points in this characterization of the period and the role of Turner within it. I am also grateful to Andrew Nash for a valuable discussion on Hegel's relationship with the Enlightenment.

13. In *Unspeakable Sentences: narration and representation in the language of fiction*, Ann Banfield develops a generative grammatical theory of narrative style, predicating its essential division between the subjective and the non-subjective, or represented speech and thought and narration *per se*, on the argument that the 'communicative intent' is not intrinsic to the language of narrative.

References

Banfield, Ann. 1982. *Unspeakable Sentences: narration and representation in the language of fiction*. Boston: Routledge and Kegan Paul.

Barthes, Roland. 1966. 'Introduction to the Structural Analysis of Narratives'. *Image-Music-Text*. London: Fontana. Reprinted 1977, 79-124.

Bundy, Colin. 'Around which corner? Revolutionary Theory and Contemporary South Africa'. 1988. Unpublished. African Studies Seminar, Centre for Research on Africa, University of the Western Cape.

Chomsky, Noam. 1965. *Aspects of the Theory of Syntax*. Cambridge: MIT P.

Chomsky, Noam. 1966. *Cartesian Linguistics: A Chapter in the History of Rationalist Thought*. New York: Harper and Row.

Chomsky, Noam. 1969. *American Power and the New Mandarins*. Harmondsworth: Penguin.

Clingman, Stephen. 1986. *The Novels of Nadine Gordimer: History from the Inside*. Johannesburg: Ravan.

Coetzee, J.M. 1969. 'The English Fiction of Samuel Beckett: An Essay in Stylistic Analysis'. University of Texas at Austin: unpublished Ph.D. dissertation.

Coetzee, J.M. 1973. 'Alex La Guma and the Responsibilities of the South African Writer'. *New African Literature and the Arts*. Vol. 3. Ed. Joseph Okpaku. New York: Third World, 116-124.

Coetzee, J.M. 1974a. *Dusklands*. Johannesburg: Ravan.

Coetzee, J.M. 1974b. 'Man's Fate in the Novels of Alex La Guma'. *Studies in Black Literature*, 4(4) [should be 5(1) (Spring 1974)], 16-23.

Coetzee, J.M. 1978a. *In the Heart of the Country*. Johannesburg: Ravan.

Coetzee, J.M. 1978b. 'Speaking: J.M. Coetzee'. Interview with Stephen Watson. *Speak*, 1(3), 23-24.

Coetzee, J.M. 1981. *Waiting for the Barbarians*. Johannesburg: Ravan. Reprinted Penguin 1982.

Coetzee, J.M. 1983. *Life & Times of Michael K*. Johannesburg: Ravan.

Coetzee, J.M. 1984. 'How I learned about America — And Africa — in Texas'. *The New York Times Book Review*, 15 April 1984, 9.

Coetzee, J.M. 1985. *Interview de J.M. Coetzee*. J. Sevry. Societe des anglicistes de l'enseignement superieur. Atelier commonwealth. Colloque de Brest, 9-11 May 1985.

Coetzee, J.M. 1986. *Foe*. Johannesburg: Ravan.

Coetzee, J.M. 1987. 'Two Interviews with J.M. Coetzee, 1983 and 1987'. Tony Morphet. *TriQuarterly*, 69, 454-464.

Coetzee, J.M. 1988a. 'The Novel Today'. *Upstream*, 6(1), 2-5.

Coetzee, J.M. 1988b. *White Writing: On the Culture of Letters in South Africa*. New Haven and London: Yale U P.

Coetzee, J.M. n.d. 'Grubbing for the ideological implications: a clash (more or less) with J.M. Coetzee'. Interview by A. Thorold and R. Wicksteed. *Sjambok*. University of Cape Town: a *Varsity* publication.

Derrida, Jacques. 1985. 'Racism's Last Word'. *Critical Inquiry*, 12(1), 290-299.

Derrida, Jacques. 1986. 'But, beyond . . . (Open Letter to Anne McClintock and Rob Nixon)'. *Critical Inquiry*, 13(1), 155-170.

De Saussure, Ferdinand. 1959. *Course in General Linguistics*. Ed. Charles Bally and Albert Sechehaye, in collaboration with Albert Riedlinger. Trans. with Introduction and Notes by Wade Baskin. New York: McGraw-Hill. Reprinted 1966.

Dovey, Teresa. 1987. 'Coetzee and His Critics: the Case of *Dusklands*'. *English in Africa*, 14(2), 15-30.

Dovey, Teresa. 1988. *The Novels of J.M. Coetzee: Lacanian Allegories*. Johannesburg: Ad Donker.

Du Plessis, Menán. 1981. 'Towards a true materialism'. Review of *Waiting for the Barbarians*. *Contrast*, 52, 13(4), 77-87.

Galan, F.W. 1985. *Historic Structures: The Prague School Project, 1928-1948*. Austin: U of Texas P.

Gordimer, Nadine. 1979. *Burger's Daughter*. New York: Viking.

Hutcheon, Linda. 1980. *Narcissistic Narrative: the metafictional paradox*. New York: Methuen.

Jameson, Fredric. 1972. *The Prison-House of Language: A Critical Account of Structuralism and Russian Formalism*. Princeton: Princeton U P.

Jameson, Fredric. 1981. *The Political Unconscious: Narrative as a Socially Symbolic Act*. London: Methuen.

Kenner, Hugh. 1961. *Samuel Beckett: A Critical Study*. Berkeley, Los Angeles, London: U of California P. Reprinted 1968.

Kirkwood, Mike. 1976. 'The Colonizer: A Critique of the English South African Culture Theory'. In P. Wilhelm and J. Polley (eds). *Poetry South Africa: Selected Papers from Poetry '74*. Cape Town: Ad Donker, 102-133.

Kohler, Peter. 1987. 'Freeburghers, the Nama and the Politics of the Frontier Tradition: an analysis of social relations in the second narrative of J.M. Coetzee's *Dusklands*. Towards an historiography of South African literature'. Unpublished. History Workshop on 'The Making of Class', University of the Witwatersrand.

Kuhn, Thomas S. 1962. *The Structure of Scientific Revolutions*. Vol. 2 No. 2 of International Encyclopaedia of Unified Science. Chicago: U of Chicago P. Reprinted 1970.

Lazarus, Neil. 1987. 'Modernism and Modernity: T.W. Adorno and Contemporary White South African Literature'. *Cultural Critique*, 5, 131-155.

Marcuse, Herbert. 1964. *One Dimensional Man*. London: Abacus. Reprinted 1974.

Marks, Shula. 1986. 'The Historiography of South Africa: Recent Developments'. In B. Jewsiewicki and D. Newbury (eds). *African Historiographies: What History for Which Africa?* Beverly Hills: Sage, 165-176.

McClintock, Anne and Rob Nixon. 1986. 'No Names Apart: The Separation of Word and History in Derrida's "Le Dernier Mot du Racisme" '. *Critical Inquiry*, 13(1), 140-154.

Morris, Mike. 1987. 'Social History and the Transition to Capitalism in South Africa'. *Africa Perspective*, 1(5) and (6), 7-24.

Ndebele, Njabulo. 1984. 'Turkish Tales, and Some Thoughts on S.A. Fiction'. Review of Yashar Kemal, *Anatolian Tales*. *Staffrider*, 6(1), 24-25, 42-48.

Nkosi, Lewis. 1967. 'Fiction by Black South Africans: Richard Rive, Bloke Modisane, Ezekiel Mphahlele, Alex la Guma'. In Ulli Beier (ed.). *Introduction to African Literature: an anthology of critical writing*. London: Longman, 1979, 221-227.

Nkosi, Lewis. 1988. 'Resistance and the Crisis of Representation'. *South African Literature: From Popular Culture to the Written Artefact*. Second Conference on South African Literature, December 11-13, 1987. Evangelische Akademie, Bad Boll, West Germany.

Press, Karen. 1988. 'Towards a Revolutionary Artistic Practice in South Africa'. University of Cape Town: unpublished dissertation.

Rich, Paul. 1984. 'Apartheid and the Decline of the Civilization Idea: An Essay on Nadine Gordimer's *July's People* and J.M. Coetzee's *Waiting for the Barbarians*'. *Research in African Literatures*, 15(3), 365-393.

Ricoeur, Paul. 1975. *History and Truth*. Trans. Charles B. Kelbley. Evanston: Northwestern U P.

Ricoeur, Paul. 1981. 'The narrative function'. *Hermeneutics and the Human Sciences: Essays on Language, Action and Interpretation*. Trans. and Ed. John B. Thompson. Cambridge U P, 274-296.

Said, Edward W. 1978. *Orientalism*. New York: Vintage. Reprinted 1979.

Said, Edward W. 1983. *The World, the Text, and the Critic*. Cambridge: Harvard U P.

Schlebusch Commission. 1974. *Fourth Interim Report of the Commission of Inquiry into Certain Organizations*. Pretoria: Government Printer.

Searle, John. 1974. 'Chomsky's Revolution in Linguistics'. In G. Harman (ed.). *On Noam Chomsky*. New York: Anchor Books, Doubleday.

Sepamla, Sipho. 1981. *A Ride on the Whirlwind: A Novel of Soweto*. Johannesburg: Ad Donker.

Serote, Mongane. 1981. *To Every Birth its Blood*. Johannesburg: Ravan.

Siegle, Robert. 1986. *The Politics of Reflexivity: Narrative and the Constitutive Poetics of Culture*. Baltimore: Johns Hopkins U P.

Stadler, Alf. 1987. *The Political Economy of Modern South Africa*. Cape Town: David Philip.

Study Project on Christianity in Apartheid Society (SPRO-CAS). 1973. *South Africa's Political Alternatives*. Report of the Political Commission of SPRO-CAS. Johannesburg: Ravan.

Turner, Richard. 1970. 'Marcuse: The Power of Negative Thinking'. *Radical*, 1, 29-33.

Turner, Richard. 1972. *The Eye of the Needle*. Johannesburg: Ravan. Reprinted 1980.

Vaughan, Michael. 1982. 'Literature and Politics: Currents in South African Writing in the Seventies'. *Journal of Southern African Studies*, 9(1), 118-138.

Watson, Stephen. 1986. 'Colonialism and the Novels of J.M. Coetzee'. *Research in African Literatures*, 17(3), 370-392.

Waugh, Patricia. 1984. *Metafiction: The Theory and Practice of Self-conscious Fiction*. New Accents. London: Methuen.

White, Hayden. 1973. *Metahistory: The Historical Imagination in Nineteenth Century Europe*. Baltimore: Johns Hopkins U P.

The Human Sciences Research Council contributed towards the costs of this research. The opinions expressed are my own and are not to be attributed to the HSRC.

Raising Goose-Pimples: Wilbur Smith and the Politics of Rage

David Maughan-Brown

Referring to *Rage* in an interview in 1988 Wilbur Smith commented: 'It's not a political thriller and I'm no "message writer". The thought of being labelled one gives me goose-pimples.' (Bagnall, 1988: 10)

Rage takes the Courtney family saga through the 1950s and early 1960s. It tells the story of Shasa Courtney's crossing the floor from the United Party front bench to become a Nationalist Cabinet Minister; of his wife Tara's sexual involvement with Moses Gama, the novel's main rival with Nelson Mandela for the leadership of the ANC, and her complicity with Gama in a plot to blow up the Houses of Parliament while Macmillan is delivering his 'Winds of Change' speech; and of Gama's betrayal of his ANC colleagues, including Mandela. The novel provides detailed accounts of the Defiance Campaign, the murder of Sister Aidan in Duncan Village, the Sharpeville shootings and the formation of Umkonto we Sizwe and Poqo. Apart from making extensive use of non-fictional characters such as Malan, Verwoerd, Mandela and Sobukwe, the novel also features characters who are transparent fictionalizations of Joe Slovo (Joe Cicero in the novel) and Winnie Mandela (fictionalized as Vicky Gama). It ends with the assassination of Verwoerd by a Russian-brainwashed Demetrio Tsafendas whose 'Manchurian Candidate' conditioning is triggered outside the Houses of Parliament by Joe Cicero/Slovo. But the novel is not, according to Wilbur Smith, a 'political' thriller.

'Our Wilbur's' was the name on everyone's lips at the 1988 Frankfurt Book Fair, the *Sunday Times* tells us with chauvinistic pride. Given that Smith's twenty novels have sold over fifty million copies and that *Rage* sold 980 000 copies in paperback in Britain alone in 1988, it seems very probable that in the English-speaking world

outside Africa Wilbur Smith, via his fiction, is having a greater formative influence on the popular conception of Africa in general, and
of South African society, history and politics in particular, than any
other single individual.

Given popular fiction's potential for ideological reinforcement, the
immense popularity of Wilbur Smith's novels with the English-
speaking popular-fiction reading public in this country should be
of immediate concern to literary critics and social psychologists.

With popular fiction, as with any other fiction, the confirmation
of myths and stereotypes, the shoring-up of ideologically constructed
world-views, the vindication of prejudices, are all part of the ideological baggage which is carried in, often unnoticed, on the backs
of characterization and, in particular, plot. The faster-moving and
more seamless the story-line, the greater the likelihood that the informing ideology will pass unnoticed and the author's claims to an
apolitical neutrality remain uncontested. Wilbur Smith is now
regarded in some quarters as 'the best story teller in the world' (Bagnall, 1988: 10). That claim would be of no particular concern were
it not that being 'the best story teller' paradoxically carries with it
the attribution of being a reliable authority on whatever geographical locale or historical period the author happens to choose for his
or her setting. As Robert Ruark's two novels about 'Mau Mau' lent
him the status with the popular-fiction reading public of being the
single most reliable 'expert' on the Emergency in Kenya (Ruark, 1955
and 1962), so *Rage* is likely to lead to Smith's being accorded the
status of an authority on the history of South Africa in the 1950s
and 1960s.

Even the most conservative estimate of the proportion of the South
African reading public which chooses to read Wilbur Smith in preference to either the classics of English literature or the novels of writers
such as Coetzee and Gordimer, suggests that some kind of responsibility lies with South African literary critics to attempt to unpack
the ideological baggage, examine the ideological determinants and
potential ideological effects of the fiction, and analyse the fictional
techniques and devices employed by authors of popular fiction like
Wilbur Smith to serve their ideological ends.

This essay will concentrate its attention on just one of Smith's
twenty novels, rather than surveying a wider selection of either his
work or the novels produced by other writers of popular fiction in
South Africa since 1976. There are two main reasons for the close-
ness of focus. Firstly, though popular fiction will be cruder in its
effects and less demanding on its readers than more self-consciously
'serious' fiction, the ways in which it seeks ideological assent are

by no means always self-evident, and any attempt to do justice to
an analysis of the sometimes complex and sophisticated interpella-
tory devices Smith employs in even this one novel will strain the
limits of the space available for this essay. While it is not contended
that *Rage* is 'typical' of post-1976 South African popular fiction, it
is hoped that the kind of analysis embarked on here is broadly applicable to other novels in the genre.

Secondly, *Rage* is deserving of close attention at this particular
juncture because the ideological effect it seems likely to be having
on most readers has a very specific and immediate political currency: it will be strongly supportive of the Nationalist government's
rationale for many of the repressive measures implemented under
the current State of Emergency. The novel's plot is overtly political; its effect on many of its readers will be to confirm received interpretations of South African history and politics designed to justify
and reinforce the ideology of white supremacy. *Rage* is unquestionably a 'political' novel, and, regardless of the risk of giving Wilbur
Smith goose-pimples, it is important to disregard his denials and
examine the messages encoded in the fiction.

I will start by examining the strategies Smith adopts in attempting to establish for himself the posture of balance and neutrality on
which he presumably bases his claim not to be a 'political' writer
or a purveyor of 'messages'. To illustrate the kind of 'message' to
be found in the novel I will then discuss *Rage* in its capacity as cautionary tale and examine two significant examples of the manipulation of history in the novel. This will lead on to an identification
of the traces in *Rage* of some of the more significant of the myths
underpinning what can best be described as the 'colonial settler'
ideology which informs Wilbur Smith's fiction. It is hoped that this
will provide some insight into the general ways in which the novel
serves to reinforce the racism of the 'total-onslaught' rhetoric of the
South African government and its supporters. The essay will conclude with an examination of the specific ways in which the novel
gives assent to the political analysis underlying the imposition and
continuation of the current State of Emergency in South Africa,
declared in June 1986.

Strategies of Balance and Neutrality

An uncritical reader of *Rage* might be surprised at the assertion that
the ideological effect of the novel as a whole on many readers will
be to confirm them in views which coincide with those of the governing party in South Africa. Wilbur Smith allows his narrator and the

protagonists with whom the reader is invited to identify not only
to voice criticisms of the ruling political dispensation from time to
time, but also apparently to be taken seriously and treated sympathetically in so doing. Thus, for example, while the majority of
members of the Black Sash are written off as 'wealthy, privileged
and bored', and as joining political protests 'for the excitement of
defying established authority and outraging their peers', or simply
in an attempt to gain their husbands' attention, it is allowed that
some 'were moved only by revulsion at injustice' (1), which implies
an acceptance of the existence of injustice.

Criticism is levelled in varied tones at a number of different facets
of government control and 'social engineering' (455), ranging from
censorship — 'to the South African censors the female nipple was
every bit as dangerous as Karl Marx's Communist Manifesto' (83)
— to the description of a township as an 'Orwellian vision of bleak
and soulless order' (128). By the end of the novel the reader is intended to feel a very strong antipathy for Moses Gama, yet he is
allowed substantive criticism of the South African government —
as, for example, when he identifies Verwoerd as 'the man who had
elevated racial discrimination to a quasi-religious philosophy' (342).
The validity of his criticism is frequently, but not always, brought
into question by the exaggeration and bitterness of his rhetoric, and
the ambivalence with which his political analysis is presented to the
reader produces one of the more complex issues of interpretation
posed by the novel, but there can be no doubt that, in terms of structure, one of his main functions in *Rage* is to provide the appearance
of 'balance'.

Prophetic utterances attributed by the fiction to characters living
in the 1950s, but stamped with the authority of hindsight, crop up
fairly frequently in *Rage* and are normally taken to be definitive.
Moses Gama is credited with a number of such utterances. For
example:

We have all heard it said that the whole concept of *apartheid* is so
grotesque, so obviously lunatic, that it can never work. But . . . the
men who have conceived this crazy scheme are so fanatical, so ob-
durate, so convinced of their divine guidance that they will force it
to work. Already they have created a vast army of petty civil servants
to administer this madness, and they have behind them the full
resources of a land rich in gold and minerals . . . [T]hey will not hesitate to squander that wealth in building up this ideological Frankenstein of theirs. There is no price in material wealth and human suffering that is too high for them to contemplate. (43)

Perhaps more surprising from the author of novels like *The Sunbird*, which appears obsessed with 'hosts of darkness . . . spawned in darkness in the forests of eternal night to the north' (Smith, 1974: 316), is the sporadic sympathy elicited for Moses Gama. This sympathy persists even after his abortive attempt to blow up the Houses of Parliament, an attempt perceived by Shasa Courtney's mother Centaine (obviously correctly in terms of the broad ideological thrust of the novel) as '. . . murder and treason and attempting to assassinate a head of state. It is fostering bloody revolution and attempting by force to overthrow a government.' (401) Moses Gama's autobiographical statement from the dock describing 'his loss of innocence and how he had learned the bitter truths of his existence' (415-416) is treated sympathetically, even if it is undermined by the device Smith uses most frequently to discredit Gama's political stance — the attribution to him of the view that the end justifies the means: 'The struggle for liberation is all, in the name of liberty any deed is sanctified' (416).

At the end of the novel, immediately after being sprung from Robben Island and before being assassinated as a traitor by one of his Umkonto we Sizwe 'comrades' (who hopes to put the blame for the murder on the South African Police), Gama is allowed a television interview in which he speaks with 'a sincerity and depth that was devastating: "There are no prison walls thick enough to hold the longing of my people for freedom . . . . There is no grave deep enough to keep the truth from you."' The reader is told that '[h]e spoke for ten minutes and Kitty Godolphin who was old in experience and hardened in the ways of a naughty world was weeping unashamedly as he ended' (617).

In this way sympathy for the oppressed can be evoked in the abstract, allowing the novel to accrue 'balance'; but any significant risk to the novel's ideological project is avoided by denying the political position being espoused any but the most minimal content: 'Moses Gama's words were poignant and moving, spoken in that deep thrilling voice, as he described the agony of his land and his people, so that Tara, listening to him in the darkness, found tears running down her face' (200). Gama can talk for ten minutes and his 'deep thrilling voice' can make white women weep, but the novel remains crucially silent about what precisely it is that he says in those ten minutes.

Similarly, ANC supporters arriving by bus at Gama's trial — representatives of the earlier 'hosts of darkness' if ever there were any — are carried into the restricted enclosure of the reader's sympathy on the wings of song: 'The sound of singing grew louder as it approached, the lovely haunting chorus of African voices rising and sinking and weaving the intricate tapestry of sound that thrilled the ears and raised the gooseflesh on the skins of the listeners' (407). The sound of the singing distracts attention from Smith's silence with respect to the content of what could only be protest songs. When the bus stops the cameramen rush to capture Vicky Gama's 'dark beauty, and the sound of her voice as she sang the thrilling hymn to freedom. *Nkosi Sikelel' iAfrika* — God Save Africa.' (407) The 'thrilling hymn to freedom' is announced, but simultaneously voided of all content.

To balance the novel's apparent sympathy for the oppressed and rejection of the 'ideological Frankenstein', *Rage* contains a good deal of explicit support for the Nationalist government, which tends to follow the defensive propaganda strategies favoured by the SABC. To balance the unflattering description of a 'shanty town' on the Cape Flats (46) there is Shasa Courtney's uncontested assertion that '. . . the material existence of the black people in this country is five or six times better than any other on the African continent. More is spent on black education, black hospitals and black housing, per capita, than in any other African country.' (250) To balance the Orwellian vision of bleak and soulless order, the reader is informed of Nyanga, and there is no suggestion that Nyanga is atypical: '. . . although aesthetically ugly and uninspiring, the accommodation was adequate and offered reticulated water, mains sewerage and electricity' (45). Stress is laid on 'the complete independence of our press and the impartiality of our judicial system' (406) and Shasa manages, as a Cabinet Minister, to convince a vehement opponent of the government that he 'truly had the best interests of all the people at heart, [and] that he was especially concerned with improving the lot of the black and underprivileged sections . . .' (436).

As so often in colonialist popular fiction, it is left to a black person, whose pigmentation is presumed to be sufficient to establish his authority, to provide the clinching argument which appears to 'balance', but is intended to outweigh, the adverse criticism: Joseph Dinizulu 'reminds' his sister that 'without the white man we would still be living in grass huts. Look to the north and see the misery of those countries which have driven out the whites.' (540) Vicky, needless to say, is given no room to ask which countries those might be. It is notable that where supporters of the political dispensation in South Africa are concerned the novel focusses not on their 'thrilling voices' but on what they say.

The balancing act involves not only the political sympathies invoked by the narrative but also the attribution of 'evil' characters to the white race group as well as the black, and an ostensibly even-handed treatment of the violent actions of protagonists from both groups. Joe Cicero is repeatedly characterized in terms of a 'passionless evil' (578) or a 'passionless malevolence' (608) which is intended to be representative of that of men '. . . from a cold bleak land in the north [who] do not understand the African soul' (618) but plot the violent overthrow of the South African government nonetheless.

'Evil' is even attributed to one of the Courtney family, Shasa's eldest son Sean. He is expelled from Bishops for charging his classmates to watch him copulating with his art mistress on a secluded lawn on the family estate, and then has to flee the country when the police discover that he has been arranging for an accomplice to burgle the houses of wealthy Capetonians while he makes love to the housewives. It is said of him that '. . . he had a streak of genuine brutality and inherent evil in him' (318) and this is graphically illustrated in the following description of his behaviour after being involved in the killing of a 'gang' of Mau Mau:

> He had seen Sean do this before and although Ray Harris was a hard, callous man who for thirty years had made his living out of blood and gunfire, still he gagged as Sean squatted over the corpse and stropped the blade on the palm of his hand.
> 'You are getting soft, old man.' Sean grinned at him. 'You know they make beautiful tobacco pouches,' he said, and took the dead girl's breast in his hand, pulling the skin taut for the stroke of the knife blade.' (520)

The apparent 'balance' implicit in attributing evil to whites, and in particular to Sean, as well as to blacks is illusory. Joe Cicero's evil is representative of communism. The 'cruel and depraved' Mau Mau (518), who, in the best tradition of the colonial fiction about Mau Mau, are made (wholly without historical foundation) to disembowel the white overseer of a coffee plantation and 'stuff his severed genitals into his mouth' (514), are representative of those who resort to violence to further their political cause. The Gagool-like *sangoma* who eats the liver of Sister Nunziata in Smith's fictional version of the murder of Sister Aidan in Duncan Village is representative of black 'witchcraft' and superstition. But Sean's evil is not representative, it is a purely individual, idiosyncratic, and therefore atypical, depravity. Its *raison d'être* is to be deviant and aberrant. Whereas the novel invites the reader to generalize out from the representative instances of communistic or black evil and depravity, nothing is being said about white South Africans in general through Smith's treatment of Sean except, crucially, that they are not all like Sean.

Nor is neutrality achieved by the simple expedient of devoting space to the depiction of acts of violence perpetrated by whites as well as blacks. Leaving aside for the moment Smith's treatment of police responses to black mobs, one can take as an example of the 'balancing' of black violence by white violence the description of the violence of Umkonto we Sizwe 'intimidators' as against Sean's killing of the band of Mau Mau.

The violence employed by Raleigh Tabaka and his 'small task force' in enforcing a bus boycott is both bloody and personalized. A 'woman in middle age, large and matronly' defies the order to go home so Raleigh hits her with his fighting stick which

> split her shiny black cheek as cleanly as the cut of an axe, so for an instant Raleigh saw the bone gleam in the depths of the wound before the swift crimson flood obscured it. The big woman screamed and fell to her knees, and Raleigh felt a strange sensation of power and purpose, a euphoria of patriotic duty.

Raleigh hits her again and we are told that: 'The joint of her elbow shattered, and her forearm dropped and twisted at an impossible angle as it hung helplessly at her side' (467). We are then told:

> The woman screamed again, this time the sound was so filled with outrage and agony that it goaded the other young warriors and they fell upon the bus passengers with such fury that the terminus was strewn with the wailing and sobbing injured and the concrete floor was washed sticky red.

Blacks in Wilbur Smith are prone to going 'crazy with blood lust' (136), are repeatedly subject to a 'killing madness' (209) and are susceptible to being 'enraged' by the sight of blood (208) and 'goaded' by cries of agony.

The violence of the group of whites in the Mau Mau episode is treated very differently, even though Smith places a question mark against their attitude towards what they are doing by having them treat the whole exercise as a hunt: 'Only a fool walked directly up to dangerous game no matter how dead it appeared to be . . .' (519). The tone of the descriptions is one of detached interest in the effects on the targets of the different weapons used. While following the 'spoor' of the Mau Mau the 'hunters' engage in some discussion as to the most suitable guns to use and the reader is effectively invited to decide who made the best choice. So, for example, we are told:

> She was so close that he did not have to lift the Gibbs to his shoulder. He shot her in the stomach. The heavy rifle bounded in his grip and the bullet picked the girl up and while she was in the air it broke her in half, blowing a hole through her spine into which her own head would have fitted, and she folded up, loose and floppy as a suit of discarded clothing as she fell back onto the muddy forest floor. (518)

Sean's Gibbs makes a 'sound like the slamming of a great steel door' (518); 'Raymond's Stirling buzzed and cut him down' (519); the muzzle flashes of the Bren and Stirling 'were bright and pretty as fairy lights in the gloom, twinkling and sparkling, and the bullets went *frip! frip! frip!* amongst the leaves and sang shrilly as they ricocheted into the forest' (519). The focus is on the aesthetics of muzzle flashes, not the outrage and agony of the victims; the sounds described for us are the booms, buzzes and 'frips' of the guns, not the screams, wails and sobs of the people being shot. Unlike the woman who screams when her elbow is broken, one of the Mau Mau soldiers would appear to have remained totally silent when a bullet hit him in the shoulder joint and blew his right arm off so it hung by a tatter of torn flesh and flapped against his side as he spun around' (519). There is no 'swift crimson flood' when holes the size of people's heads are blown through their spines. In fact, in marked contrast to the 'sticky red' floor of the bus terminus there is no blood to be seen anywhere amid the carnage. The woman who folds up 'loose and floppy as a suit of discarded clothing', is as bloodless, and as unimportant to the narrator, as a rag doll.

Wilbur Smith can be seen here to be employing exactly the same fictional technique as Robert Ruark in the attempt to convey the impression of 'balance' to his reader without allowing the possibility that whites are prone to a 'killing madness' or 'blood lust', or, for that matter, even 'patriotic euphoria'. Whites may be guilty of violence but their killing is impersonal; attention is distracted from what is actually being done to people by a fetishization of the weaponry being used; death and mutilation may be involved but pain and bloodshed are absent.

It is not surprising to find Smith employing the same techniques as Ruark, as this whole scene bears much more than a passing resemblance to an episode in Ruark's *Something of Value* (438-439). In fact, the tradition in which this novel takes its place is signalled not only by this seemingly gratuitous, Ruarkian Mau Mau interlude, but also by the narrator's reverential announcement, when describing Sean's campsite, that 'Legend had it that both Hemingway and Ruark had camped at this very spot and breakfasted beneath this same wild fig' (543). The techniques are being employed to identical ends. Over thirty years on from *Something of Value*, under another State of Emergency, the aesthetic of 'balance' and the posture of neutrality are being used to gift-wrap an essentially colonialist ideology built on the triple pillars of white superiority, anti-communism and 'law and order'.

Rage *as Cautionary Tale*

The story of what happens to Tara Courtney in *Rage* constitutes a cautionary tale which is in itself enough to give the lie to Smith's denial that he is a purveyor of 'messages'.

The novel opens with a description of Tara protesting with the Black Sash at the opening of Parliament. The white dress she wears with her black sash carries connotations of political innocence and naivety. We are told that she '. . . had not worn white since her wedding day . . . the white dress she wore today made her feel like a bride again, tremulous and a little afraid . . .'. The relationship between political and sexual innocence is explicit, even if the need to establish the link results in semantic contortions: 'although she had carried four children, her waist was slim as a virgin's [sic]'. Her 'youth and beauty' are exemplified by her 'thick chestnut hair' which 'crackled with ruby lights in the bright Cape sun-shine' (1). Hair is a reliable index of moral health in Wilbur Smith: Joe Cicero's hair is described as 'black and lank and lifeless' (577) and as 'dead black hair' (607), and Jakobus Stander, who kills little girls with bombs, has hair which is 'long, flecked with dandruff' (579).

Tara is allowed her 'revulsion at injustice'; her cardinal error is that this revulsion leads to a loss of political innocence which is simultaneously a loss of sexual innocence and 'honour'. She allows Moses Gama to become her lover:

> He was so huge that he terrified her, and though she had borne four children, she felt as though she was being split asunder as his blackness filled her, and then the terror passed to be replaced by a strange sense of sanctity. She was the sacrificial lamb, with this act she was redeeming all the sins of her own race. (48)

Further acquaintance with Gama's 'blackness' leads to a rapid loss of the tremulousness and passivity of the sacrificial lamb:

> He lay naked upon his back on the stretcher, and he was like a pinnacle of black granite. Tara hurled herself upon him to impale herself. She was sobbing and uttering little cries and yelps . . . her body . . . thrashed and churned above him as he lay quiescent and

> unmoving, and she went beyond physical endurance, beyond the
> limits of flesh, insatiable and desperate for him, until exhaustion over-
> came her and she rolled off him and . . . there was a thin pink colour-
> ing of blood on the front of her thighs, so wild had been her passion.
> (194)

It is inconceivable that a white woman endowed with 'youth and
beauty' could behave in this way entirely of her own volition, so
the possibility is allowed that it is the black man who is responsible
for her fall, represented essentially as a loss of control. We are told:
'His voice was low and compelling, it thrilled like a drug through
her veins and the cruel images faded, she looked beyond them to
the paradise, the earthly paradise they would build together' (75).
Nevertheless this is clearly no way for a white woman to behave,
and the immediate wages of sin is an illegitimate child called Ben
Afrika. Just how far down the road to damnation Tara has travelled
as a result of impaling herself politically and sexually on the 'black
granite' spear of the nation (Moses Gama is, for the purposes of
this novel, the inspiration behind Umkonto) can be seen from the
reaction of Molly Broadhurst (Blackburn?), one of the founder members of the Black Sash, to the news that Tara is carrying Moses Gama's child: 'Molly was a militant liberal, as colour-blind as Tara was
herself, and yet Molly was stunned by the idea of a white woman
bearing a black man's infant' (142).

In keeping with the imperative for 'balance' discussed earlier, sexual endurance and 'huge' penises are not attributed solely to blacks
in *Rage*; the Courtney males are also endowed with these totems
of the masculinity appropriate to the heroes of popular fiction. Sean
is described as sexually inexhaustible (317), and Shasa comments
admiringly to his second son: 'Well at least Garry . . . you've got
a wanger on you that would make old General Courtney himself
turn in his grave with envy' (325). But the apparent 'balance' should
not distract attention from the significance of the repeated fascinat-
ed return to descriptions of Moses Gama's penis, as for example
in: 'He was so thick that she could barely encompass him within
the circle of her thumb and forefinger, and he was hot and hard
as a shaft of black ironstone that had lain in the full glare of the sun
at midday' (347).

The psycho-sexual myths which underlie Wilbur Smith's anxious
portrayal of the white bride hurling herself to her bloody, 'insatiable and desperate' doom on a gigantic black phallus are succinctly
identified by Fanon and Hoch. Fanon argues that: 'For the majority
of white men the Negro represents the sexual instinct (in its raw
state). The Negro is the incarnation of genital potency beyond all

moralities and prohibitions.' (Fanon, 1970: 125) Hoch suggests why the cautionary tale should feature a 'monster' (see Smith, 1987: 412) who can lie unmoved while the fallen and impaled bride 'thrashe[s] and churn[s]' herself to exhaustion on top of him:

> Thus, in white civilization which considers many forms of sexuality to be immoral — and consigns them to the dark dungeons of the un-conscious — the 'devil', dark villain or black beast becomes the receptacle of all the tabooed desires, thereby embodying all the forbidden possibilities for ultimate sexual fulfilment and becoming the very apotheosis of masculine potency. (Hoch, 1979: 44)

Tara may lose her political innocence, she does not lose her naivety. It is a constitutive impossibility of the ideology within which the novel was produced for a black man, let alone a black political activist, to love a white woman: '''Love?'' [Moses Gama] said. ''That is not an African word. There is no word for love in my vocabulary.''' (220) Gama is interested only in 'cynically and . . . calculatingly' using Tara, whom he regards simply as an 'instrument'. 'His vast sexual appeal', we are told, 'was to Moses Gama merely another weapon in his arsenal, another means of manipulating people. He could use it on men or women, young or old, no matter how attractive or unappealing.' (50) Marcus Archer's *raison d'être* in the novel is to hint obliquely that Gama does, indeed, use his sexual appeal on men. In terms of the colonialist ideology within which the novel was produced, this can be interpreted in the light of Hoch's: 'What seems to be at stake in all this is the attribution of certain dark and unclean . . . sexual practices to rebellious, outsider or subordinate groups, thus justifying (according to the prevailing sexual ethic) their repression' (1979: 53).

In keeping with a dominant ideology obsessed with racial difference, miscegenation is shown to be unnatural. Tara's 'soft pale flesh' quickly begins to revolt Gama and we are told that 'each time it took more of an effort to feign passion' (301). Not that any noticeable effort was being made to feign passion in the central 'granite pinnacle' passage quoted earlier. The contrast between white and black is heavily underlined in the account of Gama's return to Vicky after being with Tara:

> For a moment he thought of the woman he had left in London, and his senses cringed as he compared her humid white flesh, soft as put-ty, to this girl's glossy hide [sic], firm and cool as polished onyx. His nostrils flared to her spicy African musk, so different from the other woman's thin sour odour which she tried to disguise with flowery perfumes. (306)

While Tara's love for Gama 'multiplie[s] a hundredfold' (299), he regards her simply as a 'besotted woman' whose brutal interrogation by the security police would not matter; indeed Gama's indifference to Tara's fate is total: 'It did not matter if they tried and hanged her' (385).

Tara's fate in terms of the desiderata of popular fiction is worse than hanging, as it would have to be given the extent to which her insatiable sexual desire for a black man transgresses the novel's (still essentially colonial) ideal of white womanhood. She becomes a 'blowsy middle-aged drab' (627) whose hair, far from being chestnut with crackling ruby lights, is 'grey . . . streaked brassy ginger and violent mulberry red' (572). Just what fate awaits well-meaning but misguided Black Sashers, who go astray, impale themselves on black men, and end up running boarding houses for the ANC in London is made all too clear when Tara is visited by her daughter:

> They embraced. Isabella recalled how her mother had smelled, it was one of her pleasant childhood memories, but this woman smelled of some cheap and flowery perfume, of cigarette smoke and boiled cabbage, and — Isabella could barely credit her own senses — of underclothing that had been worn too long without changing. (572)

This novel may not have what Wilbur Smith would call a message, but it is quite clearly a cautionary tale which makes it clear that people who consort with communists and the ANC, and white women who sleep with blacks, must not expect the process to allow them to retain enough decent values to remain concerned about washing their underwear.

The Manipulation of History in Rage

The paperback blurb declares that *Rage* is 'an unforgettable blend of passion, power, history and intrigue'. Where history is 'blended' with passion, power and intrigue as just one among a number of ingredients of popular fiction, it is obviously necessary to examine what integrity it retains as history once the mixture has been processed. Where the writer stands to be regarded as an authority on the history of the country and period in question simply by virtue of being a writer, never mind being the best-selling author of an historical novel, there is an added urgency to the need for an analysis of the accuracy of his or her 'history' and the ideological use to which it is being put.

Wilbur Smith clearly researches the 'background' to his novels fairly thoroughly, and uses a variety of sometimes quite surprising sources in the process. It seems clear, for example, that Smith consulted Tom Lodge's *Black Politics in South Africa since 1945* and used that as the skeleton for his account of the Sharpeville massacre, though one would not want to hold Lodge in any way responsible for the outcome. It is safe, then, to assume that where there are significant departures from history they are purposeful and will be found on analysis to be serving very specific ideological ends. There are two major distortions of historical chronology in *Rage* on which I want to focus attention briefly here: firstly, and most crucially, there is the bringing forward of the date of the formation of Umkonto we Sizwe; secondly, there is the postponing of the date of the effective end of the armed revolt in Kenya known as the 'Mau Mau'.

For the purposes of 'history' in *Rage* the formation of Umkonto we Sizwe is proposed by Moses Gama at a meeting of the executive of the ANC, held at a farmhouse in Rivonia 'for the final planning and co-ordination' of the Defiance Campaign (61). This would have been in April/May 1952. The proposal is for 'a fighting force of trained men, ready to die for the struggle. Let us call this army *Umkhonto we Sizwe*, the Spear of the Nation. Let us forge the spear secretly. Let us hone its edge to razor sharpness, keeping it hidden but always ready to strike.' (65) An account of Bram Fischer's resistance to Umkonto at a later meeting, still before the start of the Defiance Campaign, seems to imply that '*Umkhonto we Sizwe*, the military branch of the ANC' is already in existence (191). By mid-1959 when Moses Gama returns to South Africa after undergoing Russian-sponsored training overseas, Umkonto is well established and one finds its 'high command', who have 'already accepted the principle of armed revolt', discussing a campaign of economic sabotage (310-311). In fact, Umkonto we Sizwe was only formed after an initial proposal put to a meeting of the ANC national executive in June 1961 and the campaign of economic sabotage was not planned until the second half of the same year (Lodge, 1983: 233-235).

Wilbur Smith is not simply 'taking liberties' with history in the interests of dovetailing this history of South Africa with that of the Courtney family, he is deliberately manipulating and distorting history. The ideological ends to which this is being done are immediately apparent. If the military wing of the ANC can be seen to have been mooted and established prior to the Defiance Campaign, then the passive resistance rationale of that campaign can be called into question. If the campaign of economic sabotage and bombings mounted by Umkonto in late 1961 can be brought forward to a date prior to Sharpeville and the banning of the ANC, that effectively discredits the argument that the ANC only took to violence as a last resort after all efforts at negotiation and passive resistance had failed. If the ANC, through the agency of a military wing, can be shown to have been engaged in violent intimidation, the enforcement of boycotts and the planning of bombings, then the banning of the organization and the detention of its leaders can be shown to have been justified. The potency of popular fiction as an instrument of propaganda lies in its capacity to accomplish that 'showing' far more effectively than non-fictional polemic via the vivid realism of its portrayal of fictional scenes from the 'history' of, for example, 'ANC intimidation'.

Wilbur Smith is thoroughgoing in his project of discrediting the argument that the ANC was non-violent prior to its banning. Not only does he try to provide cover for himself against the accusation of being anachronistic in his dating of the formation of Umkonto by Gama's stress on secrecy and keeping Umkonto 'hidden' in the speech quoted above, he also allows the assertion of the ANC's essential non-violence to be given voice in dialogue so that it can be refuted by the appropriate 'authority', in this case the Minister of Police, Manfred de la Rey:

'The ANC,' Shasa interjected. 'But surely they aren't behind this? They have been around for forty years or so, and they are dedicated to peaceful negotiations. The leaders are decent men.'
   'They were,' Manfred corrected him. 'But the old leaders have been superseded by younger more dangerous men. Men like Mandela and Tambo and others even more evil.' (119)

The fictional Moses Gama may be 'even more evil', but the reader will come away with a strengthened perception that the wholly non-fictional Tambo and Mandela are possessed of an undefined metaphysical 'evil'. This perception will obviously be useful to a government intent on depicting the ANC as so 'evil' that any utterance which might serve to enhance its image in the eyes of the public can justifiably be deemed illegal in terms of emergency regulations.

The historical distortion involved in the fictional prolongation of the Mau Mau revolt in Kenya serves very similar ideological ends. The at first sight entirely gratuitous hunt for 'members of the notorious gang run by the self-styled General Kimathi' (514) takes place, in the chronology of *Rage*, in the second half of 1961. Kimathi — whose rank, as it happens, was not 'self-styled' but assigned to him by a meeting of the Kenya Defence Council in August 1953 (Barnett and Njama, 1966: 225) — was arrested in October 1956, which is the latest possible date at which the novel's fictional attack on the Nyeri coffee plantation could have taken place. In practice, to have any historical plausibility Smith's Mau Mau raid would have to have taken place before mid-1954.

In the overall design of *Rage*, Sean's Mau Mau hunt is not gratuitous and the seven-year chronological distortion involved is not inadvertent. Mau Mau exists in the novel as a bogey which is used to discredit the ANC by association. Apart from playing on male white South African castration anxieties — 'Nobody is going to get a chance to stuff my knackers down my throat, matey!' (516) — Mau Mau is used to evoke fears about what black revolutionaries are liable to do to white children. In arguing for the ANC to direct its violence against human life and not simply against symbolic targets, Gama draws his inspiration from Mau Mau:

> We have no patience with symbolic acts. In Kenya the warriors of Mau Mau took the little children of the white settlers and held them up by their feet and chopped between their legs with razor-sharp pangas and threw the pieces into the pit toilets, and that is bringing the white men to the conference table. That is the type of symbol the white men understand. (311)

The fact that the speaker is a black man will probably be presumed to give the statement historical authenticity, or at least credibility, in spite of the fact that there is no vestige of historical foundation for this particular claim about Mau Mau 'atrocities'. Nor is there any basis whatever for Gama's earlier assertion that Mau Mau obtained support, implying material support, from Russia (193). Wilbur Smith is deliberately cultivating thirty-year-old colonial myths about Mau Mau, most of which have been long since discredited, in the interests of condemning the ANC by association. What is more, this time perhaps inadvertently, he allows Sean to make it clear precisely what the function of Mau Mau is in the ideological diagram of this novel: 'Let's talk about fun things. Let me tell Mickey about the Mau Mau in Kenya, and what they did to the white kids. Then he can tell me about his commie ANC friends here, and what he wants them to do to our kids.' (554) Mau Mau exists unhistorically in the novel for the sole purpose of nurturing the race fears of white readers — the nightmare visions of black beasts breaking through the defences of civilization to attack 'our' women and children (see Hoch, 1979: 58).

History and fiction make a potent ideological combination. The full potential of the effect that can be obtained by the fictional 'fleshing-out' of history is best seen in Wilbur Smith's heavily fictionalized account of the murder of Sister Aidan, renamed Sister Nunziata to make sure nobody overlooks the fact that she is a nun, in Duncan Village in November 1952. After the 'enraged' crowd has 'dragged the nun in the road . . . worrying her like a pack of hounds with the fox' (an unusual image for a nun), a *sangoma*, whose sacrilege is compounded by the fact that Sister Nunziata is not only a nun but also a 'handsome blond woman' (198), cuts through the nun's grey habit and 'split[s] her belly open from groin to rib cage'. She then pulls out 'something wet and glistening and purple . . . cut[s] a lump from the still living organ . . . thrust[s] the purple lump into her toothless mouth and chew[s] upon it' before throwing it to the crowd which fights 'for the bloody scraps like dogs' (208). The graphic and detailed fictional description of the murder; the stereotypical but nevertheless disturbing portrayal of the 'screaming', 'howling', 'bestial', 'insensate' mob with its 'mindless animal roar' and its individual 'faces contorted in a cruel rictus of excitement'; the cannibalism and the primitivism; all combine to evoke in the reader who is receptive to Wilbur Smith's message precisely the response articulated by Manfred de la Rey: '''A nun,'' he said aloud. ''And they ate her! . . . Let the bleeding hearts of the world read that and know what kind of savages we are dealing with.''' (213) As Kitty Godolphin was heard to say earlier: 'Nuns always make good footage' (198).

It is Moses Gama's subsequent comment on the nun's death that most definitively damns him, and simultaneously glosses the novel's title:

> It was beauty — stark beauty, shorn of all but the truth. What you witnessed was the rage of the people, and it was a holy thing . . . It was a consecration of our victory. They ate the flesh and drank the blood as you Christians do to seal a pact with history. When you have seen that sacred rage you have to believe in our eventual triumph. (232)

In *Rage* Wilbur Smith is dealing with the history of the relatively recent past, and his use of that history has very clear implications for the attitudes his readers will take towards contemporary South African society and politics. In an author's note at the beginning of *Rage* Smith acknowledges that he has 'taken some small liberties with the timetables of history, in particular the dates on which the *Umkhonto we Sizwe* and *Poqo* movements began . . .' and articulates the hope that the reader will forgive him 'for the sake of the narrative'. What we are dealing with here is not 'small liberties' but seri-

ous distortions with very clear and predictable political consequences; nor is it possible to discern any abstract and overriding
'narrative' imperative which could have determined this rewriting
of history. What Wilbur Smith does to history in this novel, particularly the history of Umkonto we Sizwe, suggests that his denial
of the existence of 'messages' in his novels is more than a little
disingenuous.

Rage *and Colonial Mythology*

As one would expect from a novel which places itself so deliberately in the Robert Ruark tradition, *Rage* reveals that Wilbur Smith subscribes to many of the myths that underpinned the colonial settler
ideology of the majority of whites in pre-Independence Kenya and
Rhodesia, myths that are drawn on extensively by contemporary
Nationalist and Conservative Party ideologues in South Africa. These
myths, and the fictional techniques through which they are conveyed, all serve to stress the essential 'otherness' of blacks, and
thereby provide an implicit rationale for political strategies which
seek to enforce separateness and deny blacks the right to political
and social equality.

Political enlightenment, where *Rage* is concerned, is represented
by Shasa Courtney's advocacy of the creation of a black middle class
(somewhat anachronistic for a Nationalist Cabinet Minister in the
early 1950s): 'Blacks don't need votes, they need a slice of the pie.
We must encourage the emergence of a black middle class.' (119)
Hendrick Tabaka and his chain of shops exist in the novel as vindication of Shasa's argument: '. . . now the frosts of wisdom were
upon Hendrick's head . . . [and] he was a man contented. True he
was not free — but then he was not sure what free really meant.'
(308) Give blacks a slice of the pie and they will discover not only
that they don't need a vote, but that they don't want it. The meta-
discourse overarching the 'liberal' desire for a stable black middle
class is one of racial superiority and separateness.

Many of the instances of colonial myths in *Rage* can be identified
and passed over fairly rapidly, as their individual contribution to
the overall ideological project of the novel is a relatively incidental,
if cumulative, one. However, rather more space will need to be
devoted to the obsessive focus on 'tribal' difference, as this forms
the basis for the novel's political analysis of the resistance movement.

Blacks in *Rage* are seen as essentially animalistic. Not only are they,
as a crowd, prone to being 'enraged' by the sight of blood, to 'bay-
ing like a pack of hunting dogs' (209), and to fighting like dogs over

scraps of nun's liver, they are also individually compared to animals. Moses Gama is likened to a leopard (6) and a black panther (41, 199); we are told that Hendrick 'bred' all his wives regularly every year; Vicky and Matatu have 'glossy hides' rather than skins (306, 513). Matatu — whose characterization bears an uncanny resemblance to that of !Nxui, the hero's dog-like 'Bushman' tracker in Al Venter's *Soldier of Fortune* (1980) — is the faithful retainer to be found in most colonial adventure fiction and is, here, the supreme example of the tendency to animalize blacks. He not only has a 'glossy black hide', he has 'the same instinct and superhuman sense of sight, smell and hearing, as one of the wild animals of the forest' (513), and he regards Sean 'with the patent adoration of a hunting dog who ac- knowledges the most important being in its universe' (515). This last is an appropriate response on the part of Matatu, who is prone to 'trembling with eagerness . . . like a bird dog' (517), as Sean treats him precisely 'as though he were a tired gun dog' (516).

Where blacks are depicted in human rather than animal terms, they are frequently seen as children, in keeping with the ideology of trusteeship which provided the colonizers with the justification for denying blacks the right to self-determination. The doctor ac- companying Sister Nunziata is trapped in the cab of his burning pick-up while the crowd chants and dances round him 'like chil- dren round the bonfire on Guy Fawkes night' (209). Shasa draws an analogy, again apparently acceptable to the highly critical and aggressive television interviewer, between Smuts's relationship to 'the native people' and a 'strict headmaster['s]' relationship with his 'children'. Moses Gama is highly critical in his speech from the dock of those who refer to blacks as children (415), but this obvi- ously doesn't carry much weight either with Wilbur Smith or with Gama's own wife: 'You cannot die, my husband, for without you we are children without a father' (309).

Cannibalism, whose attribution to blacks is frequently employed in colonial fiction as the ultimate device for consigning the 'other' to the outer darkness of 'barbarism' and savagery, is invoked on more than one occasion in the novel. Sister Nunziata's murder is the most obvious instance, but that was a one-off moment of 'mad- ness' on the part of an enraged crowd. It cannot convey adequately the casual acceptance by blacks of cannibalism in their everyday lives. That is achieved, as in George Harding Raubenheimer's nov- el about the Rhodesian war, *Crossfire* (1980), by reference to the Balu- ba who 'have always been cannibals' (374) and, where South Afri- can blacks are concerned, via the narrator's description of what they are wont to drink: 'These home brews were powerful concoctions known generally as *skokiaan*, and according to the recipe of the individual distiller, could contain anything from methylated spirits to the corpses of poisonous snakes and aborted infants' (457).

Rage subscribes to the quintessential colonial myth, that of the empty lands. This myth, which is central to Nationalist historiography, is introduced in an assertion accepted as 'historical fact' made by Shasa Courtney in a television interview with Kitty Godolphin: 'When the white settlers moved northwards, they came upon a land denuded of all human life. The land they staked was open, they stole it from nobody.' (87) This myth is so central that Wilbur Smith has it restated, this time by the omniscient narrator, later in the novel (492).

The most pervasive of the core myths of colonial settler ideology to be found in *Rage* is the myth of an all-subsuming tribalism to which all blacks inevitably subscribe and which, paradoxically coupled with an irredeemable individualism and private ambition, will forever vitiate effective national political action on their part. These two ineradicable traits are revealed to the reader in Smith's first description of the ANC executive:

> There was not a single black man present who did not cherish, somewhere in his soul, the dream of one day leading all the others, of one day being hailed as the paramount chief of all southern Africa.
>
> Yet the fact that Mandela spoke in English pointed up the single most poignant fact that they had to face: they were all different. Mandela was a Tembu, Xuma was a Zulu, Moses Gama himself was an Ovambo, and there were half a dozen other tribes represented in the room. (62)

The 'difference' is depicted in the novel through an insistent stress on the 'traditional' enmity of Zulu and Xhosa: 'History did not record . . . how many thousands of times over the centuries armed impis of Xhosa and Zulu had faced each other thus' (134). Shasa asserts in his television interview, again apparently unanswerably: 'If all the blacks in this country were given white faces, they would still think of themselves as Zulus and Xhosas and Vendas . . .' (250). Tribalism inevitably extends to personal relations: 'Raleigh returned [Vicky's] greeting with polite reserve, for even though she was the wife of his uncle, she was a Zulu. His father had taught him to distrust all Zulus.' (403) So much is 'tribal' enmity a part of 'tradition' that when, at his wedding feast, Moses Gama proposes a 'unification of the tribes' in the interests of sloughing off white domination, this is deeply resented by the older men on the grounds that 'what he was suggesting was a destruction of the old ways, a denial of the customs and orders of society which had held together the fabric of their lives' (181).

Not only will 'tribal' feuding and rivalry always call the potential for unified black political action into question, it makes it imperative to ensure government by whites, who can maintain law and order in the face of tribal 'faction fighting'. The underlying ideological thrust is given succinct expression by Swart Hendrick:

> 'The police are the enemies of the people, they too will perish in the flames,' Moses said, and Hendrick remembered that when the faction fighting between the Zulus and the Xhosas had swept through Drake's Farm . . . it was the police who had separated them and prevented many more than forty dead. . . . Now Hendrick wondered just who would prevent them killing each other after the police had been burned, and just what day-to-day existence would be like in the townships when each man made his own laws. (308)

For a novel which is not 'political' *Rage* manages to make it abundantly clear that all that can be looked for from black politics in South Africa is personal ambition on the part of the leaders and an inveterate 'tribal' consciousness on the part of the led. Any attempts to dislodge the state's security apparatus can only result in a return to the dark ages of cannibalism, tribal warfare and anarchy.

Rage *and the State of Emergency*

Wilbur Smith's invocation of the 'eternal rhythm', 'the promise and mystery' and the 'grandeur and savagery' of Africa suggests that he is trying to cultivate the appeal of the exotic (159). Further hints that the putative audience in *Rage* is an international one can be gleaned from some of the more improbable imagery: we are told, for example, that Vicky's 'large perfectly round buttocks oscillated like the cheeks of a chipmunk chewing a nut' (229) and that Matatu 'was like a bird dog with the scent of the grouse in his nostrils' (517). But it seems clear from the pains Wilbur Smith has taken to use this novel to provide the rationale and justification not only for police shootings but also for many of the repressive measures enacted under the 1986 State of Emergency regulations that the audience he has in mind for *Rage* is chiefly a South African one.

The lengths Smith goes to in the process of attempting to discredit the ANC are obviously part of this project; they have already been looked at and nothing further needs to be added here. I will examine the novel's exoneration of police violence; its very full and critical coverage of journalism, clearly designed to justify restrictions on the press; its endorsement of the government's 'agitator' thesis in respect of black political action; and the logical extension of this which is the justification of detention without trial, which specifically includes the detention of children. I will conclude this essay with a brief survey of some of the events and issues of South Africa in the 1980s which Wilbur Smith manages to prefigure and pass implicit judgement on in a novel which is ostensibly about the 1950s and 1960s.

The riot which led to the murder of Sister Aidan is not provoked in *Rage*, as it is for Tom Lodge, by the 'extraordinarily aggressive behaviour of the police' (Lodge, 1983: 60). It is the result of the police 'struggling ineffectually' to stem a 'wild torrent of humanity' (in which the pathetically 'white faces of the constables bobbed like flotsam') which is intent on breaking the law (204-205). When the police are forced to fire it is in the face of a mob which has worked itself up to the 'killing madness' by chanting '*Jee!*' — a magically inflammatory 'battle cry' which actually exists in no vocabulary but Wilbur Smith's — and the constables are described as 'some on their knees, all of them dishevelled and terrified' (206). 'Down on their knees', the attitude of prayer, signifies that shooting is very much the last desperate resort.

Sharpeville is covered much more fully, as it would need to be given that Smith is trying to exonerate a police action infamous the world over. Smith's strategy here is three-pronged. First he stresses 'how very young' (492) and inexperienced the police are; how 'the tension and the fear' rise in the police 'with the heat and the thirst and the dust and the chanting' (495); and how, long before the actual shooting, the police 'were reaching the point of nervous exhaustion' (496). Second, he once again has the crowd utter 'that murderous war cry '*Jee!*' which 'made their blood smoke with the fighting madness' (497) so that what the police are again confronted with is a maddened mob. Third, he explains the episode very fully in terms of the psychic history of the Afrikaner: as the police captain faces the crowd we are told that what he was

> looking upon was the nightmare of the Afrikaner people that had recurred for almost two centuries . . . . He felt his nerves crawl like poisonous insects upon his skin as the tribal memories of his people assaulted him. Here they were once more, the tiny handful of white men at the barricades, and there before them was the black barbaric host. (492)

When he shoots on the 'breaking and turning' crowd it is 'without his conscious volition' and in the grip of the ancestral nightmare: 'He tried to stop himself, but it was all a nightmare over which he had no control, the weapon in his hands shuddered and buzzed like a chain saw' (498). His response when he wakes from the nightmare is to choke: 'Oh, God forgive me. What have we done?' (498) Sharpeville is referred to as a 'massacre' (502) but Smith's fictionalization of the events cultivates sympathy for the police, reveals the black host at the gate to be, indeed, barbaric, and seeks assent to the proposition that police action in such circumstances is never brutal or callous but simply the result of fear, difficult working conditions and troubling ancestral memories.

The riot during the course of which Sister Nunziata is murdered would, according to *Rage*, never have taken place but for the interference of the foreign media. Without the police there would have been no riot, and the police are only there because they have been warned to be there by the novel's representative journalist, Kitty Godolphin, who justifies herself on the grounds that: 'These people want to get themselves arrested. That's the whole point. And I want film of them getting arrested.' (202) Kitty is only there herself because she has been told: 'The confrontation could turn to violence and even bloodshed' (197).

Where *Rage* is concerned, newspapers are prone to 'strident and partisan pronouncements' (246) and to 'pettiness and subjectivity' (327); we are told that 'in South Africa the English press was hysterically anti-government, while the Afrikaans press [by way of 'balance'] was fawningly and abjectly the slave of the National Party' (378). Shasa, who is proved consistently right in his assessment of Kitty by the action of the novel, tells her: 'You know it isn't like you make it sound, and you don't care. As long as you get a good story, you don't give a damn whether it's true or not or who it hurts, do you?' (89) Hank, Kitty's cameraman, is shown 'kneeling beside a wounded man, shooting into his tortured face, panning down on to the pool of blood in which he lay' (206). Here sympathy is directed towards the victim being subjected to the 'shooting' of the camera, but no account is given of him being shot, unmetaphorically, by the police in the first place. Kitty's later response to Shasa's comment, 'Your job is to report reality, not to attempt to restructure it. You are a reporter, not the God of judgement' is definitive: 'If you believe that, you are naive . . . We make and destroy kings.' (251)

The extensive coverage given in *Rage* to the media's misrepresentation and, indeed, 'creation' of unrest fits in perfectly with such statements as that of Major Nel, the branch commander of the security police in King William's Town in 1987: 'such publications contribute to the further public unrest and disorder' (*Weekly Mail*, 30 October 1987: 5). The ideological effect of *Rage* in this regard, and it is an effect which Smith is calculatedly striving for, will be to reinforce an attitude of hostility to the local press and overseas television and thereby contribute to a climate of (white) public opinion which will, in general, welcome restrictions on media access to designated areas, the censorship of news and the banning or suspension of newspapers like *New Nation* and the *Weekly Mail*.

The third facet of the determining ideology of *Rage* which bears directly on the political situation in South Africa under the State of Emergency is its endorsement of the thesis that where the media cannot be held responsible for unrest there are bound to be 'agitators' around who can. Prior to the Defiance Campaign, *Rage*'s Minister of Police, De la Rey, identifies a 'new breed of black agitators' (118) who are described as 'the bringers of darkness. . . . As the Marxist monsters destroyed the social fabric of Russia, so they seek to destroy all that the white man has built up in Africa.' (117) The 'they' of the last sentence is happily ambiguous in its context, as it is unclear whether it refers to the 'agitators' or the 'Marxists' and the effect is to elide the one into the other. De la Rey is proved right. Were it not for Moses Gama the benevolent paternalism of the police captain would have defused the crisis which leads to the murder of the nun (204). The agitator thesis is given the final, rather improbable, stamp of authenticity via Raleigh Tabaka's girlfriend's words to him just before she is killed in the police massacre at Sharpeville: 'I am so proud of you, Raleigh. Without you these poor people would never realize their misery, would never have the will to do anything to change their lot, but look at them now.' (485)

If agitators are responsible for unrest, the obvious way to put an end to the unrest is to detain the agitators. People have been detained under 'security' legislation for decades, but it is only in the 1980s that the detention of children has become an issue. Wilbur Smith uses *Rage*'s 'history' of the 1950s to endorse the government's frequently articulated view — see, for example, a speech given by Minister of 'Law and Order' Adriaan Vlok in October 1987 — that the ANC uses 'children to carry out revolutionary crimes and murder' and that in detaining children the state has 'no other choice than to protect law-abiding citizens and take action against the transgressors' (Adriaan Vlok, quoted in *Weekly Mail*, 30 October 1987). Smith fosters the white public's acceptance even of the detention of children by attributing to Moses Gama a calculating cynicism with regard to the political exploitation of children:

> The children are the future . . . . They are like fresh clean sheets of
> paper. You can write on them what you will . . . . Children lack any
> sense of morality, they are without fear, and death is beyond their
> conception. . . . They make perfect soldiers for they question noth-
> ing . . . . If an enemy strikes them down they become the perfect mar-
> tyrs. The bleeding corpse of a child strikes horror and remorse into
> even the hardest heart. Yes, the children are our key to the future.
> Your Christ knew it when he said 'Suffer the little children to come
> unto me' . . . . If a child cannot grow up a free man, then he may
> as well die as a child. (189)

Vicky responds to Gama by saying that his 'words are cruel and
blasphemous', but the cynicism, if not the blasphemy, of course is
Wilbur Smith's. Writing after 1976 he is drawing on such deaths
as that of Hector Peterson, and the image of that death carried by
the media around the world, in an attempt to discredit the ANC.
In the process he devalues the anguish of those deaths and exoner-
ates those responsible for the shooting. He uses the hundreds of
children shot down by agents of the South African state in the last
decade for his own 'messageless' political ends with as much cynicism as he imputes to his fictional ANC representative.

Smith uses *Rage* to confirm the essentially political prejudices of
the white South African popular-fiction reading public in a number
of other areas, all of which have some contemporary political significance. Readers will be confirmed, for example, in their views of
English-language universities as hotbeds of radicalism: the novel's
equivalent of John Harris — a member of the African Resistance
Movement hanged for the murder of a little girl after planting a bomb
on the Johannesburg railway-station — is a Senior Lecturer in Sociology at Wits University (579); and the arrangements for Gama's
escape after blowing up parliament involve a 'lecturer in political
philosophy' at Wits who is 'a secret member of the South African
Communist Party' (373).

In its denigration of the Anti-Apartheid Movement as communist-
inspired, *Rage* also clearly prefigures the United Democratic Front
and reinforces contemporary government propaganda claims that
it is a front for communism and the ANC: 'Lenin himself taught
us that we cannot move immediately to the communist revolution.
. . . We have to create a broad front of liberals and churchmen and
students and workers under the leadership of the vanguard party.
Oliver Tambo has gone to create that vanguard party — the anti-
apartheid movement in exile. . . .' (542)

Rage can also be seen to prefigure the political rhetoric of the 1980s:
Moses Gama is made to say 'We must goad the land, we must make

it wild and ungovernable' (308), which coincides perfectly, for example, with the assertion of the Chief of Security Police in February 1988 that the 'revolutionary onslaught' has as its aim 'making South Africa ungovernable' (*Weekly Mail*, 26 February 1988: 3). The term 'comrades' is anachronistically given its contemporary township usage and applied to 'the young comrades of *Umkhonto we Sizwe*' engaged in boycott enforcement and intimidation (467). We even find, right at the end of the novel, 'necklacing' being prefigured and justified in a speech attributed, inevitably, to Vicky Gama: 'Fierce and strikingly beautiful, she told them, ''We must devise a death for collaborators and sell-outs, that is so grotesquely horrible that not one of our people will ever dare to turn traitor upon us''' (623). This speech incites the crowd to strip naked and beat unconscious a woman identified as a police informer, whereupon 'they doused her with petrol and set her alight and kicked her while she burned. Afterwards the children urinated on her charred corpse.' (623) Smith manages to restrain himself from including an anachronistic tyre.

So strong is the relationship between Wilbur Smith's 'history' of the 1950s and the political developments in South Africa in the mid-1980s that there are good grounds for speculating that had the November 1988 verdict on the UDF leaders in the Delmas treason trial been forthcoming before the completion of *Rage*, Smith would have had Judge Villiers, the judge in Moses Gama's trial on charges of High Treason, deliver a verdict different from the one he does deliver: 'I have therefore reached the conclusion that no duty or loyalty exists towards a state in which the individual is denied the basic democratic right of representation. Accordingly, on the charge of high treason I find the accused not guilty.' (417) The verdict in Gama's case is obviously designed to vindicate Shasa's claim about the 'complete . . . impartiality of our judicial system' (406). Evidence from the rest of the novel suggests that such general arguments in support of the government tend to take second place to the imperative of providing the ideological justification for specific political developments such as the detention of children and the banning of newspapers, or, in the Delmas case, the finding that the organizing of black resistance to apartheid is, in itself, treasonable.

There is a great deal more that could be, and perhaps needs to be said about *Rage*. I have, for example, said virtually nothing about the very extensive, and highly imaginative, use Wilbur Smith makes of black superstition, 'witchcraft' and ritual, in particular the circumcision ritual, as a device to win the reader's assent to the irredeemable primitivism of blacks. But I hope that I have said enough

to locate Wilbur Smith firmly in the tradition of colonialist popular
fiction and to show the extent to which this novel endorses the race
ideology and the political repression which prevail in South Africa
today. Wilbur Smith's bottom line in *Rage* is clearly articulated by
Hendrick Tabaka in the fatherly advice he gives Raleigh:

> If the gods and the lightnings intervened and by chance you destroyed
> the white man, think what would follow him. There would come a
> darkness and a time without law and protection that would be a
> hundred times worse than the white man's oppressions. We would
> be consumed by the rage of our own people. (465)

When one reads such passages of popular fiction, and most of the
others quoted in this essay could stand as examples, and then encounters statements to the effect that 'It's not a political thriller and
I'm no "message" writer' one could wish that authors like Wilbur
Smith would confine their fictions to what they write in their novels and not what they say about them.

References

Bagnall, Gorry. 1988. 'Wilbur Smith: Best Seller'. *Edgar's Club*, November,
   1988.
Barnett, D.L. and K. Njama. 1966. *Mau Mau from Within*. New York: Modern
   Reader.
Fanon, F. 1970. *Black Skin White Masks*. London: Paladin.
Hoch, P. 1979. *White Hero Black Beast*. London: Pluto.
Lodge, Tom. 1983. *Black Politics in South Africa since 1945*. Johannesburg:
   Ravan.
Raubenheimer, G.H. 1980. *Crossfire*. London: Arrow.
Ruark, Robert. 1955. *Something of Value*. London: Hamish Hamilton.
Ruark, Robert. 1962. *Uhuru*. London: Hamish Hamilton.
Smith, Wilbur. 1974. *The Sunbird*. London: Pan.
Smith, Wilbur. 1985. *The Burning Shore*. London: Pan.
Smith, Wilbur. 1987. *Rage*. London: Pan.
Venter, Al. 1980. *Soldier of Fortune*. London: W.H. Allen.

Part of the Struggle: Black Writing and the South African Liberation Movement[1]

Martin Trump

1

Much black South African writing forms an important component of a developed counterhegemonic culture.[2] This counterhegemonic culture pits itself against a discourse of colonial capitalism[3] which it continually seeks to subvert and deconstruct. I shall be examining black fiction within this context and using the short story to illustrate black South African literary trends. I suspect that the conclusions reached here would be little changed if the genre I had chosen had been different. This in turn suggests the relative unimportance I attach to formal differences between literary texts. What's of relevance to me is the content of the form.[4]

2

How has black writing contributed distinctively to the South African liberation struggle? Before answering this question with reference to texts themselves, I would like to consider how one of the characteristic features of literary discourse lends itself very well to certain of the key processes, transformations and objectives of the South African democratic movement.

A major way in which literary discourse distinguishes itself from other social discourses (say, the discourses of history and the social sciences) is that literature tends to give precedence to the experiences of individuals. On a scale that stretches from institutionalized to personalized discourse, literature usually takes its place towards the side of personalized expression. Forms of self-reflexive and subjective consciousness are the usual distinguishing qualities of literary works. Stephen Clingman notes that 'fiction deals with an area of activity usually inaccessible to the sciences of greater externality: the area in which historical process is registered as the subjective experience of individuals in society' (1986: 1).

The importance of literature being able to deal in this way with the subjective experience of history is stressed not only by Clingman in his exemplary study of Nadine Gordimer's novels (1986) but also in recent writings of Njabulo Ndebele (1984, 1986). As part of an extremely sophisticated polemical analysis, Ndebele describes what he sees as two divergent currents within recent black South African writing: a tendency, on the one hand, to use fiction as a vehicle for overt politicization by means of character and situational stereotypes, with a heavy reliance on political slogans; and, on the other hand, a more traditional approach to storytelling in which the political content of the fiction arises from the carefully described workaday lives of the characters. The distinction he draws is not quite as clear, in practice, as he would like us to believe. Nevertheless an exceptionally valuable feature of his analysis is the emphasis it gives to the distinctiveness of the contribution fiction can make to the resistance movement precisely by the record it offers of the everyday experiences and feelings of people in various parts of the country. For, as Kelwyn Sole has observed: 'There is a realisation in South Africa that working-class people's everyday activities are as important politically as any amount of slogans and rhetoric, and are a force to be reckoned with' (1987: 267).

In an essay written in 1949, Herbert Dhlomo commented about the black writer's role in the liberation movement: 'It is he [the writer] who can touch the mind, heart and spirit of the people. He can speak to a greater audience than many a politician. . . .' (1977: 71-72) The inspirational force of the writer to which Dhlomo refers, stems largely from the 'history from the inside'[5] that he/she describes; a history which usually goes unrecounted in most social records. It is one which is of critical importance with regard to the mobilization of people on the scale that is essential for the resistance movement.

3

In essence, fiction writing is a mythologizing activity. The writer abstracts and, to a certain extent, invents views and experiences of history. De-mythologizing fiction frequently involves measuring fictional representations of history against conventional or hegemonic views of history. In the case of black South African fiction, which participates in a counterhegemonic discourse, the 'distance' between its representations of history and those offered by the colonial capitalist discourse is particularly marked. What the counterhegemonic discourse in fact does is to engage in a form of dialogue with the hegemonic discourse and offer a view of society and history which is its opposite in many ways. Black fiction is intensely involved with mythologizing, particularly in its presentation of a social vision that is markedly different from that promoted by colonial capitalism. Any assessment of the fiction, in my view, has to take this consideration very seriously.[6] For the mythologizing process itself is critically bound up with the political transformations implicit in the counterhegemonic discourse.

In looking closely at the nature of the counterhegemonic discourse given representation through the fiction, we need to bear in mind that, as the hegemonic discourse can be deconstructed and problematized, so too the counterhegemonic discourse itself is not immune from this kind of analysis. During the course of my examination of the counterhegemonic discourse I shall be attentive to problems, simplifications and dissonances within it: in short, to the ways in which black fiction can be de-mythologized.

4

How has black South African writing subverted colonial capitalist discourse? In the first place, the writing offers a view of history significantly different from that disseminated by the ruling class. Within black fiction one sees colonial capitalism challenged by a history of the working class that draws significantly upon a history of collective struggle against oppression.

The South African social formation is a complex structure within which various modes of production coexist and interact.[7] There remain, for example, a small number of pre-capitalist black communities in the country. And in the black community as a whole there is a recognition of there being a continuity between pre-capitalist and capitalist black societies. For the white ruling class this kind of continuity and consciousness has virtually been erased, through historical and geographical distance. In their case, a pre-capitalist mode of existence occurred in most instances centuries ago and in a different continent — Europe.

The presence of pre-capitalist modes of production in South Africa is a critical element in the construction of a coherent, oppositional account of history. The experiences and memories of pre-capitalist, collectivist society loom large in black South African consciousness and frequently form part of the basis for a transformed vision of the future. A communalist past and the residual traces of communalism in the present feed into the possibility of creating a communalist future. This vision of history is set against a narrative of colonial exploitation leading to the present dislocations of late capitalism.

This counterhegemonic history is most evident in explicitly historical works of fiction such as Sol Plaatje's *Mhudi* (1930) and Peter Abrahams's *Wild Conquest* (1950). Similarly, many of Mtutuzeli Matshoba's stories (1979) offer accounts of history from an explicitly black viewpoint. 'Three Days in the Land of a Dying Illusion', for instance, recounts the experiences of Mantatisi, Matiwane and the Xhosa girl, Nongqause, from a perspective of black resistance history. In the case of the latter, for example, Matshoba transforms ruling class accounts of the Xhosa cattle-killing episode of the mid-nineteenth century. Conventionally seen as a crushing defeat of the black people of the Eastern Cape, Matshoba turns the story into a symbolic record of the people's courage and inventiveness in circumstances of enormous hardship. History here is being mythologized.

A counterhegemonic history is also present in less obvious but crucial ways in virtually all black fiction. Much of the rest of this essay deals with the ways in which oppositional accounts of history are embedded in the works of fiction. In this regard, it is important to note that there has been a terrible uniformity to the oppression forced on black South Africans. This has had major effects on their writing. In the first place, this uniformity has contributed in a fairly obvious way to the force of the argument that there has been an unbroken history of social oppression in South Africa. Further, the unfolding of colonial capitalist exploitation, while attempting to divide the oppressed, has at the same time tended to minimize differences within the black community. This has meant that in the field of black writing, writers from a variety of regions and backgrounds, with a range of different experiences and ideas about what constitutes significant literature, have harnessed their individual creative powers in an attempt to chronicle the common experience of black people living together under oppression. The situation is comparable with that of the negritude writers and of early black nationalist writers for whom shared experiences meant more than ethnic, tribal or even political differences. Nadine Gordimer has commented: 'It is comparatively easy to create a ''people's art'' — that is to say aesthetic expression of fundamentally-shared experiences of all, intellectuals, workers and peasants alike, in oppression: in South Africa, the pass laws are a grim cultural unifier' (1981: iv).

The nature of the oppression and its tendency to minimize the perception of differences in an essentially broad and diverse community has had at least one further effect on black writing. There has been an almost overwhelming, and often not unproblematic, identification of petit-bourgeois writers with the black working class.[8] Almost willy-nilly the writers (virtually all of whom are petit-bourgeois) have been dragged into a necessary commitment to the aspirations of the working class. As I have suggested, this is far from unproblematic and there are frequent traces of internal tensions within the works of black writers about the historical necessities facing them, the most pressing of which is this radical commitment. Nevertheless, many black writers, forced to make a virtue of necessity, have unequivocally, and often not without a certain amount of irony, contributed to the most important work being produced in the country.

5

A particular sense of a history in opposition, a frequently troubled awareness of a shared destiny under oppression and of efforts to end that oppression and transform the society, are the qualities that most commonly characterize black writing. In addition, the writing is informed by an attachment to communal storytelling traditions. This attachment, which is intimately bound up with the community's memories and experiences of pre-capitalist society, adds to the strength of the writing as an oppositional discourse.

Mbulelo Mzamane (1984) has pointed out that there is a clear line of continuity between the oral traditions of pre-capitalist black societies and the written works of later generations of black writers using English as their medium of communication. And one of the points of connection here is the use of devices from and references to traditional storytelling by contemporary writers.[9] The role of the traditional storyteller or poet as the community's spokesperson and critical voice against social excesses and abuses of power has passed to modern black writers who find themselves in an analogous position to that of their non-literate forebears. Again, the notion of a counterhegemonic South African history which will ultimately transform existing structures towards the collectivism that characterized traditional African societies is strongly reinforced by this conscious link with a tradition associated with pre-capitalist society. Fiction works here as part of a transformative mythology.

I will now look at these patterns as they occur in the essays and fictional works of the writers.

6

Es'kia Mphahlele has written:

> There is a definite line of continuity in African cultures which acts on individuals and groups like the string by which a kite is held to the ground; it tacks and weaves and noses up, a toy of the wind while it remains up there; and yet it responds to the continual tug the boy gives it toward the ground. Again, the stresses and tension and segregated existence of South African urban life have the effect of evoking the traditional African sense of community so that the individual draws strength from the group. . . . (1972: 156)

The spirit of communalism suggested in this passage is frequently celebrated in Mphahlele's fiction. In his story 'Grieg on a Stolen Piano', for example, Mphahlele's central character embodies the link between traditional African societies and the new urban culture: 'There was in Uncle a synthesis of the traditional and westernized African' (1967: 46). Uncle, a popular figure in his community, regularly dispenses a form of folk wisdom that clearly represents certain of Mphahlele's ideas about society. 'A black man never starves if he lives among his people unless there is famine . . .' (1967: 50), Uncle tells us at one point. Similarly, in another story we are told: 'You are a person because of other people . . .' (1967: 109), and further that '. . . a hand cannot wash itself, it needs another to do it' (1967: 175).

A bitter sense of loss forms an undertow in much of Can Themba's short fiction, which is most clearly revealed when measured against the kind of certainty assured the individual in a communally-governed society:

> . . . those of us who have been detribalized and caught in the characterless world of belonging nowhere, have a bitter sense of loss. The culture that we have shed may not be particularly valuable in a content sense, but it was something that the psyche could attach itself to, and its absence is painfully felt. . . . (Themba, 1972: 8)

Many of Themba's characters, most of whom are projections of his own personality, find themselves cast adrift in the cities, bewildered and unable to protect themselves in the face of vicious urban practices and temptations. Interestingly, storytelling is the one activity that brings comfort and certainty to the characters. Here is a notable illustration:

At the bus-stop he was a little sorry to see that jovial old Maphikela
was in a queue for a bus ahead of him. He would miss Maphikela's
raucous laughter and uninhibited, bawdy conversations in fortissi-
mo. Maphikela hailed him nevertheless . . . Philemon considered this
morning trip to town with garrulous old Maphikela as his daily bulletin. All the township news was generously reported by loud-mouthed
heralds, and spiritedly discussed by the bus at large. Of course, 'news'
included views on bosses (scurrilous), the government (rude), Ghana
and Russia (idolatrous), America and the West (sympathetically
ridiculing), and boxing (blood thirsty). But it was always stimulating
and surprisingly comprehensive for so short a trip. And there was
no law of libel. (Themba, 1972: 38)

The shared destiny of South Africa's black people and their struggle against oppression are key concerns in Mtutuzeli Matshoba's
stories (1979). They inform the very way Matshoba tells his stories.
His first-person narrators find common cause with fellow black people in whatever situation they find themselves. These narrators,
often closely identifiable with Matshoba, take readers on journeys
which frequently illustrate experiences that are shared widely by
black South Africans. In this way each story exemplifies a particular aspect of South African oppression.[10] For instance, 'A Glimpse
of Slavery' describes the system by which pass offenders and criminals are forced into becoming farm labourers ('slaves' is Matshoba's term) for the duration of their sentences and the horrors this
involves. 'Three Days in the Land of a Dying Illusion' describes conditions in a bantustan; 'To Kill a Man's Pride' deals with the plight
of men in the massive single-sex Soweto hostels; and 'A Pilgrimage
to the Isle of Makana' treats the response of the community to political detentions and the way in which detainees react to their
confinement.
   Like much black fiction, Matshoba's stories draw liberally on oral
storytelling traditions. In many of them there is a direct conversational approach in which readers are familiarly addressed either as
'friends' or 'brothers and sisters'. Discussions, often of great length,
between the characters typify the stories. One notable instance occurs in 'Three Days in the Land of a Dying Illusion', where the narrator reports a long debate which takes place on a bus between a
group of men and a woman about the role of women in a society
where men are forced to seek work in the cities. In similar fashion,
Matshoba breaks the narrative flow of a story to discuss one or more
features of the country's history, politics or customs. In 'A Glimpse
of Slavery' alone, there are discussions about white South Africans,
black servitude, the role of the educated in society, the pleasures

of cigarette-sharing, and the wisdom of oppressed people. A notable feature of these discussions is the way Matshoba's narrators debate the issues from the point of view of the black community, using commonly voiced opinions to impart their particular sense of history.

Throughout his stories Matshoba celebrates the support black people offer one another, particularly in adverse circumstances. 'To Kill a Man's Pride' describes how men of the township hostels come together to sing traditional songs and to dance:

> As I continued going there, I discovered that song was the only solace of those lonely people. At least two days a week they sang traditional choral music. . . . After an evening of invigorating talk and untainted African traditional song I went away feeling as if I had found treasure in a graveyard. (Mutloatse, 1980: 123)

Similarly, on a train journey to the Transkei in 'Three Days in the Land of a Dying Illusion', the narrator records how groups of passengers join one another to share poetry and song:

> When the train pulled out we settled back in our compartment. I read *Africa My Beginning* aloud to my friend and I felt that I was going to 'sleep courage' that night. There was courage in other passengers too, for as we lay on our chosen bunks we heard singing in the corridor. Two or three sisters led a traditional lyric of joy, which became movingly voluminous as brothers picked up the tune. (1979: 147)

The mutual involvement of the black characters with one another is fittingly described as 'courage' by Matshoba. Finally, there is the following moment in 'A Pilgrimage to the Isle of Makana' in which the narrator tells a group of black women with whom he is travelling to Cape Town that he is hoping to visit his detained brother, a political prisoner on Robben Island. One of the women bursts out, spontaneously, illustrating the way in which black society has a deep sense of its history and mission:

> So he's there with *bo*Mandela *le bo*Sisulu *le bo*Mbeki? Tell him to say *bayethe* for us to all the great men there who have sacrificed themselves for us. *Molimo!* I remember the days of the Congress. I was this small then. (1979: 108)

Njabulo Ndebele's collection of stories *Fools* (1983) is a celebration of life in the black townships. The stories are set entirely within the world of the townships and white people remain a distant, almost irrelevant presence for the black characters. Within the collection there is a great diversity of characters drawn from virtually every class and sector of the black township population. This is part of Ndebele's vision of a diverse, yet united black community. For all the violence in the township (the student activist Zani in the story 'Fools' is stabbed, for example, and a young boy is viciously kicked by Church elders in 'Uncle'), Ndebele offers a view of this world which revels in its communalism and vibrancy.

The collection's best story 'Uncle', for example, ends with a scene of triumph in which people from all corners of the township gather together in an informal way to enjoy the music of a variety of performers. The work ends with the young narrator's delighted cry: 'Oh, Uncle, everybody is here' (1983: 123). Here one has an affirmation central to Ndebele's thinking about society (and one might add, to that of many black writers): namely the need to include and incorporate everybody within one's sense of community. And, obviously following from this, the necessity for socialist transformations within society that take into account the broad spectrum of needs of that society.

Interestingly, as in many works of black fiction since the students' uprising of 1976, the central characters or narrators in the majority of Ndebele's stories are young children or teenagers.[11] Ndebele is clearly addressing himself in the first place to a new generation of young black South Africans, the people for whom his vision of a unified community is of greatest relevance.

One senses throughout *Fools* that the small triumphs of the characters over a range of hardships in their everyday lives stand for the confidence of black people in their greater struggle against oppression. Again, it is in the story 'Uncle' that Ndebele establishes most explicitly a connection between the actions and sayings of his characters and the broader context of black people's lives. Uncle's statements, in particular, have a resonance for the entire community.[12] This is especially so in his words of advice to the young people about the effort needed to master a musical instrument. Here is one such instance:

> 'You see, when you are improvising you are free. Completely free. But I'm telling you, you've got to learn to be free. You've got to struggle hard for that freedom. You see, if I can give you this trumpet and say to you: play something, you'll soon tire of playing anything, because your playing will have no direction. Unlearned freedom frustrates; nothing elevating ever comes of it . . . .' (Ndebele, 1983: 76-77)

This quiet, unobtrusive, often humorous form of guidance and illumination, indicating the future role for the black community in South

African history, and its celebration of communalism, are the most distinctive features of Ndebele's volume of stories.

7

The very language of black South African writing challenges and subverts the hegemonic discourse. The widespread use of English by black writers can be seen as a gesture of rejection of the state's enforced policy of tribalism (the ruling class's 'divide and rule' programme) and as an affirmation that English is an element in the move towards the creation of a unified national culture, both as a unifying vehicle in the process of mobilization and as a likely contender for becoming the national language of the new political state.[13]

There are, however, other important dimensions to the writers' use of English. For certain writers, English has been seen as a means that can link them with writers in other parts of Africa.[14] At the same time, English is closely identified with the petit-bourgeoisie in South Africa. Moreover, English is a language of capitalist exchange, inextricably associated with forms of capitalist domination. On a level of mechanical causality there is a close relationship between the writers' use of English, the forms of their writing, and market forces in South Africa that have promoted the use of the language and certain literary forms and styles among an emerging petit-bourgeoisie.[15] This is especially evident in the case of popular tabloids which have been tremendously influential in the field of black writing. Magazines like *Drum* and *Staffrider* are an important part of the history of recent black fiction, and particularly short fiction.

Not all of the paradoxes mentioned above are resolved (or able to be resolved) in black fiction. There are, as I have suggested earlier, tensions and areas of contradiction in the writing. But there is little doubt that the linguistic component is important and integral to the wider ideological process of challenge, subversion and assertion. In this light, I think one can accept the claim that black South African writers have adapted English for their own particular purposes, as part of their articulation of a counterhegemonic discourse, and, in many ways, have made of English an African language. Barnett suggests that in their hands English becomes 'a new language with symbols and terms of its own' (1983: 36).

Certainly English is frequently used in unorthodox ways by black writers, possibly to greatest effect in poetry.[16] We have noted in prose, for instance, Matshoba's unconventional use of the word 'courage' in one of his stories. Similarly, English usage is defamiliarized in the fiction of Can Themba. A graduate in English and a teacher of the language, Themba expressly uses English in deviant and ultimately subversive ways. There are frequent instances where standard usage is wilfully distorted. Laughing at linguistic and literary convention is clearly a strategy for laughing at the society's laws. In 'Crepuscule' Themba refers to the 'horrificiency' of the law (a nice portmanteau term) (1972: 2). In 'The Will to Die' he plays with literary convention, turning the style of imperial boys' adventure stories against itself. By interrogating notions of heroism that typify them, he ultimately subverts the ideology which they inscribe.[17]

The subversive potential of language is finely illustrated in the following passage from Mphahlele's novella 'Mrs Plum' (1967). The black narrator reports a conversation she had with a white woman. Mphahlele uses the language barrier that exists between the women as a means of differentiating between their ideologies and of satirizing that of the white character:

> She [the white character] says to me she says, My mother goes to meetings many times. I ask her I say, What for? She says to me she says, For your people. I ask her I say, My people are in Phokeng far away. They have got mouths, I say. Why does she want to say something for them? Does she know what my mother and my father want to say? They can speak when they want to. Kate raises her shoulders and drops them and says, How can I tell you Karabo? I don't say your people — your family only. I mean all the black people in this country. I say Oh! What do the black people want to say? Again she raises her shoulders and drops them, taking a deep breath. (1967: 168-169)

The use of imagery drawn from the violence and social deprivation of the society is a widespread feature of black writing. Matshoba, for instance, describes the sparse landscape of the Karoo in terms of a suffering child: 'I woke up to ragged and uninhabited country. It seemed that God had forgotten that part of the earth, for he had apparently sent no rain to it for centuries. The shrubs were widely spaced like the hair on the head of a black child suffering from malnutrition.' (1979: 108)

Black speech patterns and dialects are often more than simply a vehicle for social realism in the writing, but also bear witness to the kinds of identification many of the writers wish to establish with the working class. There are few works of black fiction in which the influence, if not the direct use, of working class speech is not present.

8

One of the ways the counterhegemonic discourse engages in dia-

logue with the hegemonic discourse is to emphasize differences between the black and white South African communities. In the first
instance, black writers indicate the differences between the lifestyles
of the two communities and the value systems that underlie each.
Earlier in this essay I described the way a collection of stories by
Ndebele celebrates the qualities of township life. It sees tremendous
virtues in the close community lifestyle of many black South Africans. In doing this, Ndebele's collection makes a statement not only
about the black community, but also, by negative implication, about
the white one. The silent voice in Ndebele's stories is that of the
white community. There are, however, works of black fiction that
engage more directly with the ruling class community.

A regular trope in black fiction is a satirical examination of the dis-
ordered lifestyle of the ruling class. Mphahlele's 'Mrs Plum' (1967)
offers a devastating attack on the jumbled values of this class and
the political ideologies that inform them. The main white character
'love[s] dogs and Africans and [says] that everyone must follow the
law even if it hurt[s]' (Mphahlele, 1967: 164). In the white community Mphahlele depicts, animals are treated with more favour than
people, family members quarrel bitterly with one another and people commit suicide. Nothing could be further removed from this than
the lifestyle of the black characters portrayed in the novella. In the
black community, there is a vast informal network of support and
camaraderie. Here is a collectivist society battling to maintain its
identity in the midst of a dominant capitalism which sets its values
at naught. An important point in Mphahlele's novella and in much
black writing is how the collectivist society offers the individual a
more satisfying style of living than the exclusively capitalist society.

Mango Tshabangu's story 'Thoughts in a Train' (Mutloatse, 1980)
offers a graphic account of this. Here two black boys work in the
white suburbs of the city and the experience teaches them much
about the differences between 'white' and 'black' South Africa:

> . . . Ever since they'd discovered Houghton golf course to be offer-
> ing better tips in the caddy business, Msongi and Gezani found them-
> selves walking through the rich suburbs of Johannesburg. Their ex-
> perience was a strange one. There was something eerie in the sur-
> roundings. They always had fear, the like of which they had never
> known. . . . There was a time when they impulsively stood right in
> the middle of a street. They had hoped to break this fear. . . . But
> the attempt only lasted a few seconds and that was too short to be
> of any help. They both scurried off . . . .

However, we read of the change which occurs when the boys enter
the busy city centre:

Why, as soon as they hit town proper, and mixed with people, the fear the like of which they'd never known disappeared. No, Msongi was convinced it was not they who had fear. Fear flowed from somewhere, besmirching every part of them, leaving their souls trembling; but it was not they who were afraid. (Mutloatse, 1980: 157-158)

The narrator continues to ponder the differences between the white and black communities and how these affect the way their inhabitants think and behave:

They did not have stone walls or electrified fences in Soweto. They were not scared of their gold rings being snatched for they had none. They were not worried about their sisters being peeped at for their sisters could look after themselves. Oh, those diamond toothpicks could disappear you know. . . . Those too, they did not have. They were not afraid of bleeding, for their streets ran red already. On this day Msongi stared at the shut windows. He looked at the pale sullen faces and he knew why. (1980: 158)

Similarly, Ahmed Essop's collection *The Hajji and Other Stories* celebrates the robust and colourful community life of Fordsburg. This area of Johannesburg was a rich centre of Indian life and culture until its black residents were expelled. In a story significantly entitled 'In Two Worlds' Essop distinguishes two South African lifestyles. The black narrator records his responses to an affluent white suburb in this way:

Henry's parents lived in Sandown. On several occasions I accompanied him to his home, but I found the atmosphere of the suburb with its avenues of trees and solitary mansions amid acres of gardens, chilling. It lacked the noise — the raucous voices of vendors, the eternal voices of children in streets and back-yards — the variety of people, the spicy odours of Oriental foods, the bonhomie of communal life in Fordsburg. And it was not long before Henry too was attracted by our way of life. . . . (Essop, 1978: 99)

The virtues and resilience of black community life form a sub-text in virtually all black writing. The perceived difference between the vibrancy of black communities and the lifelessness and moral bankruptcy of white ones, offers a partial explanation of why humour is such an important ingredient in black writing.[18] The prevalence of humour in black writing can be more clearly understood in the context of a community confidently en route to liberation.

Casey Motsisi's humorous sketches (written from the 1950s until his death in 1977) project a picaresque view of black urban life. The 'underworldism' forced upon black people serves both as a point

of departure and a metaphor for his vision of a community peren-
nially engaged in roguish conflict with the ruling class and their law-
enforcing agencies. Life, in Motsisi's sketches and in much black
fiction, is frequently a set of comic engagements with a rather stupid,
oppressive class. Many of Mbulelo Mzamane's stories are written
in this spirit. His 'Jola' stories, in particular, celebrate their central
character's resourcefulness in the face of adverse circumstances:

> [Jola's] been arrested and deported to the Transkei several times. Once
> the police managed to guard him as far as Bloemfontein. He came
> back to Johannesburg on a goods train. . . . He has remained in the
> township, where his wits have sharpened with exposure to the vicis-
> situdes of life. What's more, he's lived so long under the shadow of
> the vagrancy laws, the Influx control regulations and the rest that he
> has come to consider such hazards as a shield and an umbrella. (Mza-
> mane, 1980: 12-13)

The following comment in one of Mzamane's stories succinctly conveys this picaresque view of the black South African response to
oppression: 'There are people, I believe, who take misfortune in their
stride and can turn it to their advantage, people who'll make faces
at adversity and get away with it' (1980: 172).

The image of black people as spirited survivors resisting oppression has obvious political implications and is projected in a great
deal of the writing. Yet viewed in isolation from other elements (as
this essay has done until now), one might feel uncertain about the
transformative value of the work. In order for writing to be truly
revolutionary, a positive projection about society needs to be related closely to the real struggles of people within and against oppression; frequently these are violent and end in defeat. In many instances this problematizes elements of the positive projection of society. Yet in doing this, as I hope to show, it brings, paradoxically,
a tremendous strength to the writing.

9

The positive projections of history and society in black writing are
necessary idealizations. Yet they stand in need of qualification. The
most useful model for understanding the relationship between counterhegemonic and hegemonic discourses, seems to me to be that
of a dialogue — where the terms of exchange are frequently intensely
hostile. I would also like to use this paradigm to consider the relationship *within* the counterhegemonic discourse, between the positive projections of history and society in black writing, and those

factors which at every point threaten to deconstruct such a project. In order to understand this dialogue, let us consider the way it is treated in the fiction.

Bessie Head's *The Collector of Treasures* deals with various complicating factors in the relationship of individuals to the community. The kinds of conflicts Head describes in Botswanan villages have special relevance within the South African context, not simply because of the closely linked histories of the countries, but also because of shared features in their social formations.[19]

The volume opens with a description of a pre-capitalist society, totally untroubled by conflict:

> Long ago, when the land was only cattle tracks and footpaths, the people lived together like a deep river. In this deep river which was unruffled by conflict or a movement forward, the people lived without faces, except for their chief, whose face was the face of all the people; that is, if their chief's name was Monemapee, they were all the people of Monemapee. (Head, 1977: 1)

Head goes on to describe the way the calm of the community was disturbed by the eldest son of the chief who insisted on displaying his individuality in the face of traditional practice: his love of the deceased chief's youngest wife runs counter to a tribal taboo. Eventually, this man leaves the community with his wife and followers to form a new tribe. This kind of stress, between individual need and communal demands, forms the essential dynamic of the collection. In the rest of the book, Head looks at the contemporary social situation — the Botswanan village — in which pre-capitalist values and practices contend with those engendered by colonialist and neo-colonialist capitalism. The relationship is often harmonious. Here, for example, is a description of the relationship between new structures of authority and traditional ones:

> [The new administration] had taken over, from the chief, the duty of land allocation, water rights and things like that, but they hadn't yet taken over people's affairs — the kgotla [village court] was still the people's place. It was the last stronghold where people could make their anguish and disputes heard, where nothing new could be said about human nature — it had all been said since time immemorial and it was all of the same pattern, repeating itself from generation unto generation. There, at the kgotla, it wasn't so important to resolve human problems as to discuss around them, to pontificate, to generalize, to display wit, wisdom, wealth of experience or depth of thought. All this made the kgotla world a holy world that moved at its own pace and time. . . . (1977: 62)

For the most part, however, relations are not quite so happy. In 'Life', Head explores discontinuities between traditionalist and commercial value systems. Set in the period shortly before Botswana's independence in 1966, the story deals with tensions that arise in Tswana villages after the return of large numbers of a long-urbanized class from South Africa. This incoming class brings back to their country of birth a number of urban customs and affectations. 'Village people reacted in their own way [to this influx]; what they liked, and was beneficial to them — they absorbed, for instance, the faith-healing cult churches which instantly took hold like wildfire — what was harmful, they rejected' (1977: 37). The murder of one of the urban returnees, Life, we are told, 'had this complicated undertone of rejection' (1977: 37).

The story of how Life is murdered in the village serves as an illustration of how the rural people reject certain aspects of the urban culture which new settlers such as Life have brought with them. Yet Head is also concerned to indicate the way the rural community, with all its mutual aid, traditions and generosity, fails to accommodate this young woman from the city. Head suggests that the murder of Life illustrates a failure on both sides: the young woman fails to make the adjustment to village life, while the community fails to offer her any meaningful alternative to the city pleasures and values with which she has grown up. (Interestingly, Life's murder follows directly from her prostitution — a practice of capitalist society, unknown and ultimately unacceptable in this communalist society.) Here is part of Head's account of this mutual failure:

> On the surface, the everyday round of village life was deadly dull in its even, unbroken monotony; one day slipped easily into another, drawing water, stamping corn, cooking food. But within this there were enormous tugs and pulls between people. Custom demanded that people care about each other, and all day long there was this constant traffic of people in and out of each other's lives . . . . It was the basic strength of village life. It created people whose sympathetic and emotional responses were always fully awakened, and it rewarded them by richly filling in a void that was one big, gaping yawn. When the hysteria and cheap rowdiness were taken away, Life fell into the yawn; she had nothing inside herself to cope with this way of life that had finally caught up with her. (1977: 43)

Incongruities and incompatibilities between pre-capitalist and capitalist societies also play an important part in Can Themba's 'Kwashiorkor'. In this case, the dislocations facing the newly urbanized are the subject of concern. Themba traces the cycle of violence which envelops a black family in one of the Johannesburg townships. He describes the harsh process of adjustment the grand-father was forced to go through on arriving as a young man in the city:

> First, there were the ordinary problems of adjustment; the tribal boy had to fit himself into the vast frenetic life in the big city. So many habits, beliefs, customs had to be fractured overnight.
> So many reactions that were sincere and instinctive were laughed at in the city. A man was continually changing himself, leaping like a flea from contingency to contingency. . . . (Themba, 1972: 16)

Although Abner Mabiletsa makes the shift to city living with the valuable aid of companions transplanted from his home-district, and in the process fathers a daughter, his stay is not long. He is killed in a motor accident. Abner's daughter grows up fatherless and in great poverty. She leaves school at fourteen and maintains a promis-cuous life among underworld figures of the township. Soon a daugh-ter is born and although she shows the baby much affection for a few months, the lure of her former lifestyle draws her back and the child is left with the grandmother. The impoverished old woman cannot feed the young child properly and it becomes a victim of mal-nutrition. Later, the child starves in one of the rural slums.[20]

The conflict that arises in the coexistence of pre-capitalist and capitalist modes of production and ways of life is one area for scru-tiny in the fiction. Conflicts within *each* of these modes are also sub-jects for fictional investigation. Head's collection, for instance, fre-quently explores the ways in which traditionalist society oppresses women and thus generates conflict:

> The ancestors made so many errors and one of the most bitter-making things was that they relegated to men a superior position in the tribe, while women were regarded, in a congenital sense, as being an in-ferior form of human life. To this day, women still suffered from all the calamities that befall an inferior form of human life. (1977: 92)

'The Collector of Treasures' tells how a young woman murders her husband. Abused and powerless in the society, Dikeledi adopts this extreme measure as a way of ending and redressing her terrible op-pression.[21] Head starts the story by describing Dikeledi's incarcer-ation with other women who have acted in similar ways against their men. Dikeledi's act is therefore carefully shown not to be a freak action of passion, but part of a pattern of female resistance in the society.

Accounts of how colonial capitalism has oppressed people in

South Africa are legion. The existence of a massive oppressed class, little able to alter its status, has generated very high levels of violence within the society. In stories by Themba and Mzamane, for instance, the daily violence confronting black urban commuters is described in graphic detail.[22]

In this world, being a member of the black petit-bourgeoisie in no way guarantees protection from the violence and discomforts of the community. In James Matthews's 'A Case of Guilt' (1983), for instance, a wealthy black businessman is rudely awakened early one morning by the police and finds himself cast into prison with common criminals. The charge that he has not paid his tax is later revealed to be bogus and his detention is shown to be part of a police procedure setting out to humiliate successful black people.[23]

The South African prison, that microcosm of the wider society, is the site of terrible violence. Here is one account of this, in a story by Alex La Guma:

> There had been the 'case' of a prisoner who had given offence to a cell-boss and his gang. It had been said that he had complained of them to a guard, an unforgivable offence. The gangsters 'tried' him, found him guilty and sentenced him to . . . he wasn't told. That, as some sadistic refinement, they kept secret among themselves.
>
> The terrified man died a hundred times over before, finally, unable to hold back weariness, he was forced to lie down to sleep. As he lay shivering in some unknown nightmare, a blanket was pressed over his head and face, and a half-dozen knives driven through the one in which he slept.
>
> The next morning the guards found a dead man wrapped in a bloody blanket. No trace of blood on any of the rest of the packed humanity in the cell. There was no sign of a knife. Nobody had a knife, despite searches. The prison inquiry revealed nothing. (1967: 99-100)

The oppression of colonial capitalism and its effects on people within the black community is also the subject of Essop's 'The Hajji' and 'The Commandment' (1978). These stories offer antithetical views of black communal responses to oppression. 'The Hajji' tells of a black man's reaction to a request from his dying brother. Karim 'crossed the line' ten years before the events in the story take place, found a white lover and had no further contact with his black family: that is, until he found himself gravely ill. Karim's final request is that he be able to return to his people, to be buried in a Muslim cemetery according to Muslim rites. This request is directed to his elder brother Hassen. After a certain amount of vacillation, Hassen decides to spurn his brother. Significantly, Hassen's attitude finally hardens after an incident in which he is racially abused by a group of white boys. He links the present attack on his dignity with Karim's journey across the colour-bar: 'The enormity of the insult bridged the gap of ten years when Karim had spurned him, and diminished his being. Now he was diminished again.' (Essop, 1978: 5)

Hassen's resolve to have nothing to do with Karim is unacceptable to the black community. Members of the community see to Karim's removal to the local mosque where he is tended day and night. Hassen's wife Salima is among those who maintain a vigil at the dying man's bedside. Throughout this time, black community leaders implore Hassen to relent. Karim's lover is assured: 'Don't worry . . . I'll speak to Hassen. I'll never allow a Muslim brother to be abandoned.' (1978: 7) One of the community leaders upbraids Hassen: 'Hajji, can't you forgive him? You were recently in Mecca.' (1978: 8) The request falls on deaf ears and the story concludes with a portrait of Hassen excluded from his brother's funeral procession:

> The green hearse, with the crescent moon and stars emblem, passed by; then several cars with mourners followed, bearded men, men with white skull caps on their heads, looking rigidly ahead, like a procession of puppets, indifferent to his fate. No one saw him. (1978: 13)

'The Commandment' describes the events that follow when the authorities serve a black man with an order to leave Johannesburg and move to a bantustan. Moses has worked as a servant for the Rehman family for many years. He is virtually one of the family, and speaks to them in fluent Gujarati. As the date of his banishment approaches, so Moses's anguish increases. On the actual day set for his departure he is found hanging from a roof beam in an outside lavatory.

As a kind of counterpoint to Moses's misery, Essop traces the responses of the families and people around him in the black community. Most significant is the shift in their attitudes towards him as his fate becomes inescapable and his solitary anguish more evident. Towards the end of the story, with Moses's anguish at its deepest, Essop observes of the people:

> And then a queer thing happened to us. We began to hate him. Vague fears were aroused in us, as though he were exposing us to somebody or something, involving us in a conspiracy — he spoke our language — threatening our existence. Indefinable feelings began to trouble us. Of guilt? Of cowardice? We wanted to be rid of him as of some unclean thing. Suddenly everyone avoided him and the children were sternly told not to go near him. . . . (1978: 71)

Within the context of colonial capitalism, both stories illustrate the complex nature of the relationship between the black individual and his community. This is often a troubled one.[24]

In stories such as these, one sees a dialogue taking place between positive projections of and sensibilities about history and society, and recognitions of failures within the present society. There is no complacent vision of a unitary black society here. (Having said this, one needs to comment about the fact that differences and conflicts between groups within the liberation movement, such as between supporters of AZAPO and the UDF, go virtually unremarked in black fiction. This is clearly problematic and is an area of silence which requires careful investigation. I would be wary of speculating — without more careful research — about the reasons for this silence, yet one could infer that it is related to that powerful urge to idealize a popular, unitary front of resistance in South Africa.)[25] Victories and defeats take place within contexts of oppression and division. It is in this way that black fiction distinguishes itself. Its commitment to a positive projection of society, to a society in virtually every respect the antithesis of colonial capitalism, is located within the texture of the lives of people battling against and within oppression. In black writing, the gesture towards the creation of socialism in South Africa is being made with reference to people living within and struggling against forms of capitalist domination, and not simply in terms of utopian conjurings. And that, when all is said and done, is the most valuable gesture and commitment that can be made.

Notes

1. This article is closely based on a chapter in my book *Literature & Liberation: The Politics of South African Writing* (forthcoming).
2. The notion of hegemony is discussed in the works of Antonio Gramsci. The phrase 'counterhegemonic culture' is used by Hein Willemse with reference to the South African situation (1988: 101-102).
3. The term colonial capitalism will be used frequently in this essay to typify the South African situation and requires some elucidation. Conditions in South Africa are closely analogous to those in countries subject to colonial or imperial domination in which national liberation struggles are being (or have been) fought. The major differences between the South African instance and most other cases are that the colonizer and the colonized here live in the same country, and that most of the colonizers have no direct recourse to a 'mother country'. The colonial condi-

tion and status of the majority of the people in South Africa has persisted despite juridical, constitutional and economic changes which have followed the Act of Union in 1910. Power remains in the hands of a small class of people. This ruling class — until very recently almost exclusively white — has all the features of a colonial or imperialist class living in a context of advanced capitalism. At the same time, the majority of South Africans — who are denied the vote — live under conditions of severe oppression and poverty. Typical also of colonialist or imperialist rule is the fact that the state relies heavily upon brute force and repressive legislation to maintain its position.

4. The implications of a critical practice chiefly concerned with interrogating 'the content of the form' are discussed in Jameson (1981) and the phrase offers the title of a collection of essays by Hayden White (1987).
5. The phrase 'history from the inside' is the subtitle of Stephen Clingman's study of the novels of Nadine Gordimer (1986).
6. In his demythologizing of recent black South African fiction, Kelwyn Sole (1988) tends, in my opinion, to underemphasize the importance of the mythologizing aspects of the works he is considering. As we shall see there is a crucial political role to the forms of mythologizing in black fiction.
7. The term 'social formation' as used here is drawn from the writing of Nicos Poulantzas (1973).
8. See Sole (1979) for an interesting exploration of this phenomenon.
9. These concerns form the corner-stones of Njabulo Ndebele's critical theory and fictional practice. See Ndebele (1983, 1984, 1986).
10. See Michael Vaughan's comments on this point:

   '[Matshoba's] concern [is] to produce a fiction closely in touch with popular experience. . . . Each story has an exemplary quality: it treats the situation that is its subject matter as a model situation, from which a lesson can be derived. . . . If we consider the significance of this collection of stories, taken as a whole rather than separately, we can see that Matshoba has given a model-like prominence to a *range* of situations. The stories move between town and country, metropolis and homeland, romantic love and political repression. Matshoba is using his stories to evoke a *map* of experience.' (Vaughan, 1982: 131-132)

   Also see Robertson (1980: 19-20).
11. Cf., for example, Mzamane's 'Jola' stories from *Mzala*, his novel *The Children of Soweto*, Miriam Tlali's *Amandla*, and Mothobi Mutloatse's *Mama Ndiyalila*. Also see Sole (1988).
12. In calling his central character Uncle it might not be improbable to suggest that Ndebele is recalling Mphahlele's popular hero, of the same name, in the story 'Grieg on a Stolen Piano'. See earlier discussion of Mphahlele's story.
13. For discussion of the reasons lying behind black writers' choice of English as their literary medium and the historical evolution of the language debate, see Barnett (1983), in particular the opening chapter, 'A History of Black Writing in English in South Africa'. Also see Sole (1979), particularly where he writes that the use of English 'as a possible cul-

tural unifying force among urban blacks, with political and ideological implications is one which goes back to Plaatje and John Dube' (160). See Mphahlele (1962) in the chapter, 'The Black Man's Literary Image of Himself': 'Now because the Government is using institutions of the fragmented and almost unrecognizable Bantu culture as an instrument of oppression, we dare not look back. We have got to wrench the tools of power from the white man's hand: one of these is literacy — the sophistication that goes with it. We have got to speak the language that all can understand — English. . . .' (193) For a discussion of English as South Africa's national language of the future, see Ndebele (1987).

14. See Ngugi's dismissal of this position (1986).
15. The term 'mechanical causality' is used here in an Althusserian sense. See Althusser *et al.* (1970: 186-189).
16. For an analysis of the subversive use of language in recent black South African poetry see Cronin (1985, 1988).
17. For a close reading of this story see Trump (1985: 402-404).
18. By contrast with its use in black writing, humour is merely a fugitive strain within the white English writing tradition. Sobriety is the characteristic quality of the latter. For Afrikaner writers, humour is mainly a means of satirizing the follies of their community. It forms part of that literary tradition's 'negative gesture' against repression.
19. One might also add that Head was born in South Africa and her 'ways of seeing' doubtless stem from her South African experiences.
20. Themba's description of the dying child is among the most powerful indictments of the failures of South African capitalism. Painful as it is, it is worth quoting in full:

> There sat a little monkey on the bed. It was a two or three years' old child. The child did not cry or fidget, but bore an unutterably miserable expression on its face, in its whole bearing. It was as if she was the grandmother writ small; pathetically, wretchedly she looked out upon the world. . . . The belly was distended and sagged toward the bed. The legs looked bent convexly and there were light-brown patches on them, and on the chest and back. The complexion of the skin was unnaturally light here and there so that the creature looked piebald. The normally curly hair had a rusty tint and had lost much of its whorl. Much of it had fallen out, leaving islets of skull surfacing.
>
> The child looked aside towards me, and the silent reproach, the quiet, listless, abject despair flowed from the large eyes wave upon wave. Not a peep, not a murmur. The child made no sound of complaint except the struggling breathing. (1972: 20-21)

21. An exemplary, detailed analysis of the story appears in Harlow (1987: 134-136). Also see my account of the story in Trump (1985: 464-475).
22. See Themba's 'The Dube Train' (1972) and Mzamane's 'The Dube Train Revisited' (1980), the latter being Mzamane's account of the same violent phenomena taking place some twenty years after those recorded by Themba.
23. The ironic position of the black petit-bourgeoisie as part of a wider oppressed group is the subject of satirical treatment in a number of sto-

ries by Mzamane (1980) and Richard Rive (1983). For critical discussion of these, see Trump (1988: 51-53).

24. For further detailed critical discussion of stories by black writers dealing with the violence generated by the South African state see Trump (1985: 433-464).

25. A more critical perspective on liberation struggles is in evidence in the works of certain Zimbabwean and Angolan writers: one thinks particularly of the writings of Pepetela (Angola) and Nyamfukudza and Hove (Zimbabwe).

References

Althusser, Louis *et al.* 1970. *Reading Capital.* Translated by Ben Brewster. London: NLB.

Barnett, Ursula A. 1983. *A Vision of Order — A Study of Black South African Literature in English (1914-1980).* London: Sinclair Browne; Amherst: University of Massachusetts Press.

Clingman, Stephen. 1986. *The Novels of Nadine Gordimer: History from the Inside.* Johannesburg: Ravan Press.

Couzens, Tim and Nick Visser (eds). 1985. *The Collected Works of H.I.E. Dhlomo.* Johannesburg: Ravan Press.

Craig, David (ed.). 1975. *Marxists on Literature: An Anthology.* Harmondsworth: Pelican.

Cronin, Jeremy. 1985. ' "The law that says/Constricts the breath-line (. . .)'': South African English Language Poetry Written by Africans in the 1970s'. *The English Academy Review*, 3, 25-49.

Cronin, Jeremy. 1988. ' "Even under the rine of terror": Insurgent South African Poetry'. *Research in African Literatures*, 19(1), 12-23.

Dhlomo, Herbert. 1977. 'The African Artist in Society'. *English in Africa*, 4(2), 71-72.

Essop, Ahmed. 1978. *The Hajji and Other Stories.* Johannesburg: Ravan Press.

Gordimer, Nadine. 1973. *The Black Interpreters.* Johannesburg: Spro-Cas/Ravan Press.

Gordimer, Nadine. 1981. 'Apprentices of Freedom'. *New Society*, 58(997/8), 24/31 December, ii-v.

Gramsci, Antonio. 1971. *Selections from the Prison Notebooks.* Edited by Hoare, Q. and G. Nowell Smith. London: Lawrence & Wishart.

Harlow, Barbara. 1987. *Resistance Literature.* London: Methuen.

Head, Bessie. 1977. *The Collector of Treasures and Other Botswana Village Tales.* London: Heinemann Educational (AWS).

Jameson, Fredric. 1981. *The Political Unconscious: Narrative as a Socially Symbolic Act.* Ithaca: Cornell University Press.

La Guma, Alex. 1967. *A Walk in the Night and Other Stories.* London: Heinemann Educational (AWS).

Lodge, Tom. 1983. *Black Politics in South Africa since 1945.* Johannesburg: Ravan Press.

Matshoba, Mtutuzeli. 1979. *Call Me Not a Man.* Johannesburg: Ravan Press.

Matthews, James. 1983. *The Park and Other Stories*. Johannesburg: Ravan Press.

Motsisi, Casey. 1978. *Casey & Co*. Edited by Mothobi Mutloatse. Johannesburg: Ravan Press.

Mphahlele, Es'kia. 1962. *The African Image*. London: Faber.

Mphahlele, Es'kia. 1967. *In Corner B*. Nairobi: East African Publishing House.

Mphahlele, Es'kia. 1972. *Voices in the Whirlwind and Other Essays*. New York: Hill and Wang.

Mutloatse, Mothobi (ed.). 1980. *Forced Landing. Africa South: Contemporary Writings*. Johannesburg: Ravan Press.

Mzamane, Mbulelo. 1980. *Mzala: The Stories of Mbulelo Mzamane*. Johannesburg: Ravan Press.

Mzamane, Mbulelo. 1984. 'The uses of traditional oral forms in black South African Literature'. In Couzens, Tim and Landeg White (eds). *Literature and Society in South Africa*. Cape Town: Maskew Miller Longman, 147-160.

Ndebele, Njabulo. 1983. *Fools and Other Stories*. Johannesburg: Ravan Press.

Ndebele, Njabulo. 1984. 'Turkish Tales and Some Thoughts on South African Fiction'. *Staffrider*, 6(1), 24-25; 42-48.

Ndebele, Njabulo. 1986. 'The Rediscovery of the Ordinary: some new writings in South Africa'. *Journal of Southern African Studies*, 12(2), 143-157.

Ndebele, Njabulo. 1987. 'The English Language and Social Change in South Africa'. *The English Academy Review*, 4, 1-16.

Ngugi wa Thiong'o. 1986. *Decolonising the Mind: The Politics of Language in African Literature*. London: James Currey.

Poulantzas, Nicos. 1973. *Political Power and Social Classes*. Translated by Timothy O'Hagan. London: NLB.

Robertson, Katharine. 1980. Review of M. Matshoba's *Call Me Not a Man*. *New Statesman*, 100(2580), 19-20.

Sizwe, No. 1979. *One Azania, One Nation. The national question in South Africa*. London: Zed Press.

Sole, Kelwyn. 1979. 'Class, Continuity and Change in Black South African Literature: 1948-1960'. In Bozzoli, Belinda (ed.). *Labour, Townships and Protest. Studies in the Social History of the Witwatersrand*. Johannesburg: Ravan Press.

Sole, Kelwyn. 1986. 'Authorship, Authenticity and the Black Community: The Novels of Soweto 1976'. African Studies Institute paper No. 197. Johannesburg: University of the Witwatersrand.

Sole, Kelwyn. 1987. 'Oral Performance and Social Struggle in Contemporary Black South African Literature'. *TriQuarterly*, 69. *From South Africa*, 254-271.

Sole, Kelwyn. 1988. 'The Days of Power: Depictions of Politics and Community in Four Recent South African Novels'. *Research in African Literatures*, 19(1), 65-88.

Themba, Can. 1972. *The Will to Die*. London: Heinemann Educational (AWS).

Trump, Martin. 1985. 'South African Short Fiction in English and Afrikaans since 1948'. University of London (SOAS): dissertation.

Trump, Martin. 1988. 'Black South African Short Fiction in English since 1976'. *Research in African Literatures*, 19(1), 34-64.

Vaughan, Michael. 1982. 'Literature and Politics: Currents in South African Writing in the 1970s'. *Journal of Southern African Studies*, 9(1), 118-138.

White, Hayden. 1987. *The Content of the Form: Narrative Discourse and Historical Representation*. Baltimore: Johns Hopkins University Press.

Willemse, Hein. 1988. Review of *The World of Can Themba*. *Research in African Literatures*, 19(1), 101-103.

Storytelling and Politics in Fiction

Michael Vaughan

This essay is part of a larger study of the theme of 'storytelling' fiction. My original intention was to include in the essay discussion of works by John Coetzee and Njabulo Ndebele of South Africa, and Fazil Iskander of the Soviet Union. The section on Ndebele grew too long, however, to allow for this. In this section, which forms the first part of this essay, I look critically at some of Ndebele's claims for 'storytelling' fiction, in the light of his own fictional practice. In the second section of the essay, however, I consider the implications of 'storytelling' fiction both more broadly and more positively.

1

I am concerned here with two publications by Njabulo Ndebele, a critical article, '*Turkish Tales*, and Some Thoughts on South African Fiction' (1984) and a collection of stories, *Fools* (1983). In the article, Ndebele develops a thesis about storytelling, and the relationship between storytelling and fiction-writing. He takes his admiration for the stories of the Turkish writer, Yashar Kemal, as the basis for a diagnosis of what is wrong with fiction by African writers in South Africa. Kemal's strength lies in his understanding of the conventions of storytelling, and in his ability to draw on the oral storytelling traditions of Turkey in the composition of his own written stories. Kemal's stories are critical stories, exploring the predicament of an impoverished rural population dominated by a ruthless, if paternalistic, land-owning class of Aghas. Because Kemal understands the conventions of storytelling narrative so well, and because

Originally published in G.V. Davis (ed.), *Crisis and Conflict: Essays on Southern African Literature*, African Literatures in English 2, Essen, 1989.

of his familiarity with local storytelling traditions, he can draw his reader into an 'imaginative' yet critical reflection upon the social processes of rural Turkey.

What of local African writers? They are not like Kemal, says Ndebele. They also want to write critical stories. The apartheid laws by which a minority white population holds a majority black population down in impoverished subjection offer as pressing an occasion for critical reflection as the predicament of rural Turkey. Unlike Kemal, though, local writers show little regard for the conventions of storytelling, and little interest in the oral storytelling art that is so popular amongst the wider African population. Instead, in order to provide their stories with the desired critical character, they resort to sloganizing, and to a journalistic rather than a storytelling mode of narrative, presenting the reader with 'evidence' of the cruelty of apartheid rather than composing a thought-provoking story.

Some of the blame for this Ndebele attaches to the conception of political commitment that is prevalent amongst African writers. The inadequacy of this conception he in turn explains in terms of the predicament of the radical African intelligentsia. On the one hand, this intelligentsia is denied access to the centres of intellectual research and analysis in South Africa. This means that the ideas of this intelligentsia are overly dependent upon the work of white intellectuals who, though critical of the apartheid society, are necessarily Eurocentric in their conceptual orientation, and who research African experience of apartheid from a vantage point outside that experience. The limitation of this kind of work by white intellectuals, valuable as it may be, is that it cannot resonate very far into the wider African society, and neither can it be very sensitive to the 'inner' initiatives and processes of this society. It cannot help this society become more truly conscious of itself. A radical African intelligentsia which is heavily dependent on work suffering from these limitations is thus severely cramped in its capacity to offer intellectual support or guidance to popular initiatives against the apartheid order. On the other hand, this intelligentsia, denied significant access to the centres of intellectual research and analysis, which are consequently dominated by Eurocentric categories of analysis, has also allowed itself to become cut off from its own wider African constituency. Ndebele comments, for example, on the absence of a literature which, like Kemal's, deals seriously with the predicament of the African rural population.

In this context, an inadequate conception of political commitment is prevalent amongst writers. Political commitment comes to mean, broadly, condemning apartheid and its agents, especially African 'sell-outs', and sympathizing with the plight of the majority of the African population, who are the victims of this policy. It does not involve a serious analysis of the *culture* of this 'victimized' population, of the themes that resonate in the daily lives of the people. It fails largely to connect with these resonances, to engage with them imaginatively or analytically.

Political commitment has overlooked culture; it has confined itself to a comparatively narrow range of attitudes and slogans, shared or debated amongst the intelligentsia. This is where Ndebele's conception of 'storytelling' comes in as an antidote. Storytelling requires precisely the cultural insight or capacity for imaginative analysis — analysis which engages seriously with the resonances of popular experience — that has been wanting in the literature of African writers.

Storytelling is the antidote suggested by Ndebele for the ailing condition, as he sees it, of African fiction-writing. This antidote arises out of a profoundly critical reflection on prevailing conceptions of how to express political commitment in literature. How well does Ndebele's own book of stories, *Fools*, accord with his recipe for politically committed fiction?

What characterizes each of Ndebele's stories is its prominent and sensitive treatment of the 'inner life' — the intellectual and emotional processes — of the protagonist. This concern with the inner life, focussed upon a strategic theme or incident, provides the principle of coherence of each story. It also differentiates Ndebele's stories from those which he criticizes for their sloganistic and journalistic ambience. Little of the fiction published by African writers in South Africa shows the same degree of concern with the exploration of the inner life that Ndebele exhibits. Clearly, it takes a lot of skill and insight into the craft of fictional narrative to compose the fascinating accounts of personal experience that distinguish the stories in *Fools*. Furthermore, the skill involved in composing these accounts is inseparable from the practice of cultural analysis.

This is so because the issues that preoccupy the mind of the protagonist are issues of culture. In each story, without exception, the protagonist is male, 'middle class', and a member of the intelligentsia (this membership may be either nascent or achieved). By middle class, I mean that the protagonist's parents are teachers, doctors or nurses, and the protagonist is himself destined for or occupies such an occupation. The issue in each story revolves on the problem of identity of the protagonist. This problem of identity turns out to be the problem of negotiating the total culture of the African township, and of establishing a meaningful position, in an 'inner' sense — a sense of self-ratification — within this total culture. The child or youth protagonist is thrown into crisis, for example, by his inability to endorse the way in which his parents affirm their middle-class position. This is because he is so keenly aware of the other cultural modalities in the township, such as those of the tsotsis (the 'juvenile delinquents'), modalities which are hegemonic over large areas of township life. In sum, the nascent middle-class intellectual is confronted, in his struggle to achieve a meaningful sense of identity, by the powerful presence of working-class and, especially, 'lumpen-proletarian' cultures.

There is an implicit agenda for the intellectual in these stories. This is the agenda of leadership. The destiny of the intellectual as Ndebele imagines it, is to provide an intellectual guidance and leadership for the wider, largely non-intellectual society of the township. To fulfil this destiny, however, the intellectual has to undertake a serious analysis of the cultural life of the township in its every aspect, as the basis for guiding this cultural life onto a higher plane of self-consciousness and mutual co-operation.

This 'serious analysis' is not to be conducted in the study — or only there. On the contrary, the intellectual can only conduct his analysis of the cultural life of the township on the requisite level if he engages with the 'inner' quality of this life. He must engage with the terms on which this life proposes itself to its participants, the terms in which they think, feel, and act. He must engage with its idioms, and enlarge his own idiom accordingly. (It is perhaps just this concern with the 'inner' quality of patterns of living that defines a 'cultural' level of analysis.)

What this means in storytelling terms can be illustrated by an example from the story 'Uncle'. The protagonist of this story is a schoolboy whose uncle, a musician, comes to visit. Uncle assumes the role of intellectual counsellor and guide to his nephew. In the course of his stay, he comes into conflict with the local tsotsi leader, Nzule. He wins Nzule's girlfriend away from him. Things get to the point where Nzule decides to exact a violent revenge on Uncle. He advances upon him, bearing a knob-kerrie and a shield. The protagonist is astounded when he sees that Uncle has left himself defenceless, or at least has only thought to protect himself with a small pile of stones. As Nzule comes on, so Uncle retreats, until he is in full flight, with Nzule pounding after him. What a humiliation for his watching nephew! But then the situation changes. Nzule begins to tire, as Uncle draws him back to the place where he has his pile of stones. He begins to pelt Nzule with them, and now it is

Nzule, thoroughly winded and outmanoeuvred, who is finally in retreat!

This little episode is an interesting example of how Ndebele translates his concern with intellectual leadership within the African population into 'storytelling' terms. It also illustrates his concern in his stories with culture, with the 'inner' dimensions to the patterns of township life. It seems, then, that he is at least in some respects successful in following up in his stories the advice he gives to African writers in his critical article, '*Turkish Tales*, and Some Thoughts on South African Fiction'. The stories show that Ndebele takes care over the composition of his narrative, so that it has a fascinating fictional texture, and also that he makes his stories a medium of cultural analysis. However, in some other respects, the stories diverge from the criticism — or perhaps more exactly, they exemplify some ambiguities or 'silences' in the criticism.

Although the stories are well crafted, so that they establish their subject matter in effective fictional terms, the skill with which they are composed seems to owe little to the 'timeless tradition of storytelling' to which Ndebele refers in his article. What he has particularly in mind when he uses this phrase, I suppose, is the oral traditions of storytelling which he believes to be very much alive in both Turkey and South Africa — or if not these oral traditions alone, then also a practice of fiction-writing that maintains a close relationship with oral traditions. Oral tradition, however, seems to contribute little to the composition of Ndebele's stories. It is true indeed that the oral culture of the African township contributes to the *subject matter* of the stories. The story 'The Prophetess' provides an example. This story opens with the visit of a young boy to the home of the prophetess, to have her bless a bottle of water with which to cure his ailing mother. The prophetess is an imposing and mysterious woman, about whom many township stories, acquiring an almost legendary character, have grown up. The narrative evokes the superstitious awe and fear of the boy in the company of the prophetess, as well as his insight into her perhaps more human and vulnerable aspects. The prophetess is an important figure in the oral culture of the township — the boy remembers overhearing a dispute amongst the passengers on a bus concerning the reality of her powers, the great majority being persuaded of this reality — and Ndebele acknowledges, through his characterization of such figures and through the roles they play in his stories, their significant 'resonance' in this culture (Nzule is another such example).

Oral culture enters into the subject matter of the stories, then, rather than into the principles of their narrative composition. Indeed, Ndebele seems to me to be a skilful composer of stories in a *Western, realist tradition* of fiction-writing. I cannot see any significant element in the composition of the stories that is extraneous to this tradition; only the subject matter is distinctively South African. Characteristic of this Western, realist tradition is its close-up focus on the inner life of the protagonist, a focus which provides the narrative with a significant principle of organization. What particularly is focussed upon in this inner life is its problematic relationship with the world around it. The protagonist, in other words, finds the meaning of life problematic rather than given. That meaning has to be negotiated through experience of relationships in the world, as the protagonist pursues the realization of a self-ratified identity. This is the characteristic agenda in the Western, realist tradition of fiction-writing. I doubt whether the stories that arise out of oral storytelling traditions, or that are closely modelled on these traditions, share this agenda.

That Ndebele should compose his stories according to the agenda of a Western, realist tradition is not surprising. It seems to follow 'naturally' from an English-language education, and from the decision to write stories in English. Ndebele's education enabled him to make a close study of literature in the English language, and it would be difficult, if not impossible, for him to be unaffected by the fruits of such a study in the composition of his own work.

Ndebele has, however, omitted any consideration of the part played by the Western, realist narrative tradition, in the fiction-writing of African writers in English, from his discussion of the practices available to the 'politically committed' writer. He juxtaposes two possibilities only for such a writer, one to be rejected, the other to be supported. What is rejected is what, according to Ndebele, most writers have been doing up to now; this involves a practice of fiction-writing which is overly dependent on the 'information' supplied by white intellectuals about the apartheid society. What is advocated, in place of this, is a 'storytelling' practice of writing, which maintains a close, even an 'organic', relationship with oral culture and oral narrative traditions.

At this point, a perhaps symptomatic ambiguity in Ndebele's deployment of the concept of 'storytelling' needs to be clarified. This concept seems to have *two* functions in his argument. One function is to refer to the skill required of the fiction-writer in the composition of stories. The writer, as storyteller, must be a skilful composer of stories. It is possible to arrive, on a level of the utmost generality, at certain 'universal' conditions of such skilful composition. These, then, become the basic conditions, the tools, of the writer's craft. Another function of the 'storytelling' concept, however, is to refer to oral traditions of narrative, and to the writing of stories which maintain a close affinity with these oral traditions. These two functions of the 'storytelling' concept are quite distinct, yet, in Ndebele's argument, they overlap and become confused. The net result of this blurring of the concept is that one function is enabled to stand in the place of the other. One function refers to what it is quite possible for the African fiction-writer to achieve: the skilful composition of stories. The other function refers to what is quite impossible, or at least far more doubtful: an organic relationship with oral culture and oral narrative. Through the blurring of functions in the concept, however, it appears as though *both* functions are equally possible. The practicability of the one lends credibility to the impracticability of the other.

Why is an organic relationship with oral culture an impractical aim for the fiction-writer to pursue? Large issues are involved in this question, issues of culture and of class. These issues concern the cultural relationship between literacy and orality, with the added complication that literacy involves, at some stage, transition to education in a non-vernacular language; and also the contribution of the distinction between literacy and orality to the class differentiation of the African population. Some clarification of these large issues might be achieved, however, if we adopt a particular focus – a focus upon the adherence of Ndebele's stories to a Western, realist tradition of narrative.

This adherence indicates another possibility for the African writer, besides the two juxtaposed by Ndebele. Ndebele's stories are *not* overly dependent on white 'information'; they are skilful narratives with their own fictional centres, and they contain an 'inward' cultural analysis of South African township life. *Neither* are they organically connected to oral narrative traditions; they relate more closely to a Western, realist tradition. They are an example of a practice of writing in the English language in which a Western, realist narrative tradition is adapted to a South African subject matter.

This practice gives expression to one, but not to the other, function of 'storytelling'. This practice has no organic connection with oral culture; what it depends upon, what it is 'organically' connected to, is rather a specific, English-language literary education. When I refer to this practice as adapting a Western narrative tradition, I do not mean that the Western portion of the world's population has a privileged relationship to this tradition, in the form of an exclusive claim to it. Neither do I mean to imply that Ndebele is betraying his African identity, his roots in the African population, by writ-

ing in this tradition. What I mean, rather, is that this narrative tradition *originated* in the West. It has since been adopted, and adapted, all over the world, where European-language education systems
have been established.

This has both cultural and social implications. Let's take the cultural implications in the first place, and focus upon some aspects
of Ndebele's narrative. What strikes me is the sophisticated scepticism of the narrative voice. This sophisticated scepticism, this *realism*, of the narrative voice is transmitted, in some degree, to the 'inner life' of the protagonist, upon which the narrative concentrates.
The scepticism of this inner life is never as sophisticated as that of
the narrative voice. It serves, however, to liberate the protagonist,
at least provisionally, from the authority of custom, convention,
traditional belief. It is, indeed, the premise of the problematic identity, the painful yet also exhilarating freedom, of the protagonist.

The scepticism of the narrative voice is 'sophisticated', in the sense
that it involves the ability to entertain mutually conflicting positions
in the mind, without demanding the immediate resolution of this
ambiguity. The narrative delays judgement, and invites enjoyment
of the play of opposites. This scepticism does not, for example, lead
to outright rejection of custom, convention and traditional belief,
but rather to a more complicated position whereby the 'resonance'
of the practices is acknowledged, without being positively endorsed.

What is the significance of this subtle scepticism? What is the relationship between the sophisticated scepticism of the narrative voice,
and the organic connection with oral culture which Ndebele advises
the writer to aim at? Is there not a discrepancy here? The discussion can be given more point by a return to the story, 'The
Prophetess'. Here, the visit of the young boy to the prophetess involves an encounter with 'superstition', in the sense that the old
woman is attributed magical powers. The narrative entertains a teas-
ing ambiguity about this attribution. There is certainly no question
of treating the magical aura of the old woman with contempt, of
being brutally dismissive of the 'resonance' of this aura in the local
population. On the contrary, the narrative treats her with a certain
reverence. However, in the end there is also no question of the narrative's scepticism, its secular 'realism'. This becomes manifest in
the climax of the story. As the boy returns home with the 'holy'
water to cure his mother, he is knocked over by a cyclist, and the
water is spilled. Recovering from this calamity, the boy refills his
bottle with 'ordinary' water, which his mother believes to be 'holy'.
After drinking the water, she seems to be on the mend. In a sense,
it no longer matters whether the old woman has magical powers

or not. What is finally more important is the 'inner life' of the boy, his concern for his mother's well-being, his will to help her, an 'inner' force which appears to be transmitted to her, as she falls into a deep, peaceful sleep.

The concentration upon the inner life, the problematic identity of the inner life, the scepticism of the narrative voice — all these features of Ndebele's stories are entirely characteristic of the Western realist narrative tradition; indeed, I suspect, they are specific to it. They have no *organic* connection with oral culture and oral narrative. Rather, what they depend upon is the intervention of an English-language education. It is this which enables these stories to be written in the way they are, and which also creates a readership capable of understanding and appreciating the way these stories are composed. The education enables and encourages certain practices of reading and writing.

These stories are not composed for just anybody to enjoy. There is an agenda to them; the agenda of intellectual leadership. It is the members of this nascent intellectual leadership, as they conceive it, who can best enjoy the emphasis in the narrative on the problematic freedom of the inner self, which is a freedom from custom, convention and traditional belief, also articulated in the sophisticated scepticism of the narrative voice. Does this nascent intellectual leadership relate 'organically' to the wider African population? Whatever the relationship is — and it doubtless may be a very complex one, when all its factors are taken into account — it is not an organic one. This is so, because of the way in which non-vernacular, English-language education intervenes in the development of this leadership cadre. It is this education which introduces the particular agenda of a sophisticated scepticism towards the customs, conventions and beliefs which resonate in the largely oral culture of the wider population. That culture does not 'organically' give rise to an intelligentsia with a sceptical attitude towards its point of origin. It does not 'organically' give rise to a preoccupation with the problematic freedom, in the leader-protagonist, of the inner self. These are the effects of the intervention of a particular non-vernacular education system. It would seem, then, that Ndebele's stories are in various ways the product of an education that has no organic relationship with the wider African population.

What, then, of the claims Ndebele makes for the organicity of the writer's relationship to the wider society, and its largely oral culture? What of his advice to the writer to listen humbly to the oral teller's 'masterpieces of entertainment and instruction'? What of the acute diagnosis of the 'disembodied' conceptions of the wider population entertained by the radical intelligentsia, in for example the story, 'Fools'? Or the satire of the uneasy disdain displayed by the middle classes for the oral culture of the township? Or the respectful treatment of the 'resonance' of characters famous or notorious in that oral culture?

What these points indicate is that Ndebele believes that the 'politically committed' writer, the writer who wishes to commit the practice of writing to the cause of the emancipation of the African 'nation' from cultural and economic bondage, must forge a relationship of understanding and respect with the largely oral culture of this population, this 'nation'. In this, he deploys the agenda of intellectual leadership in a different manner from some African writers, particularly of earlier generations, who have adopted disparaging and dismissive attitudes towards the culture of the 'uneducated' people. It is certainly no part of Ndebele's intention to endorse such attitudes in any way. Furthermore, he is keenly aware of some of the difficulties the politically committed intellectual experiences in trying to forge this relationship, and of the mistakes made while in pursuit of this goal. It is therefore on the limitations of the intelligentsia, rather than on those of the general population, that Ndebele frequently focusses in his fiction and his criticism. To return to a point made earlier in this essay, a crucial example of this is where he criticizes writers for adopting too narrow a conception of political commitment, one which fails to engage with issues of culture in the general population.

All this does not mean, however, that Ndebele's idea of the 'organic' relationship between the writer and the African population, as expressed in the theme of the writer as 'storyteller', is not more an example of mythmaking than of clear-sighted analysis. Such an analysis, I have argued, must give greater attention, amongst other factors, to the role of English-language education in the development and definition of the literary intelligentsia. I would argue, further, that the 'storytelling' agenda might have the effect of endowing the practice of English-language fiction-writing with a more inclusive social legitimacy than it warrants. I say this because this agenda suggests that the practice contributes 'organically' to the self-liberatory momentum of the wider African population. Perhaps, though, all that can more reasonably be claimed for it is that it contributes to processes of cultural self-definition amongst a section of the population, an 'intellectual' section — and further, that it explains and advertises these processes, in an imaginatively 'inward' way, amongst an English-language readership inside and outside South Africa. What bearing this has on the wider African population may not at this stage be clearly evident.

In further pursuit of this point, I come to the last stage of this critical discussion of Ndebele's 'storyteller' theme. I suggested earlier that Ndebele sees the need for the politically committed writer to establish a relationship of understanding and respect with the largely oral culture of the African population. In summarizing his argument in this way, however, I left an area of ambiguity in the implication of this argument unexamined. Is Ndebele's concern really with the writer's forging of a *relationship* with the wider African culture, or of an *attitude* towards it? This distinction is pertinent, in that the essence of a relationship is reciprocity, whereas an attitude only comes from one side.

Of course, as a human being and as a political agent, the writer may, and must, enter into relationships of various kinds with people from various sectors of the population. However, *through the practice of writing*, the writer enters into a more specific and exclusive relationship: that is, with a readership. This readership engages in a reciprocal relationship with the writer's practice, in the sense that this practice requires the response — interpretation, internalization — of the readership in order to achieve its realization. The 'meaning' of a written story derives not only from the writer's composition of it, but also from the way this composition is interpreted by its readership. The wider, non-reading population cannot engage in a relationship of this kind with the writer's practice. This population may have a 'significant' role assigned to it in this practice, by means of the attitudes towards it or the images of it that are expressed there. However, the response of this wider, non-reading population is not required for these attitudes, or images, or the composition as a whole, to achieve their/its realization.

It follows that we can never derive the nature of the non-reading population's 'response', its 'relationship' to the writer's practice, from the terms in which this population is conceptualized in the practice. Thus, if the writer's stories conceptualize the non-reading population in terms that are 'positive' or 'sensitive', rather than 'disparaging' or 'patronizing' — terms which the narrative invites the reader to endorse — this is no basis for assuming that this population accepts, or takes pleasure from, being conceptualized in this way, or is positively influenced in its own self-conceptualization. It is no basis, in itself, for assuming *anything* about the response of this population.

My conclusion, then, in general, is that the writer cannot, through the actual practice of writing, enter into a relationship with the non-reading population. What the writer can do is more one-sided than this: it involves the composition of a conceptualization of the non-reading population. This conceptualization is 'realized' amongst a readership, and may influence the way this readership understands its social role, and acts upon this understanding. However, the significance of this for the non-reading population cannot be read off from the terms of this interaction, this relationship, between writer and readers. In saying this, I wish merely to insist on the difference in cultural modality between the fully literate and the barely- or non-literate sections of the population, and to suggest, on the basis of this insistence, that the responses of the latter cannot be subsumed under those of the former. In brief, the writer cannot, in a really organic sense, write *for* the non-reading population, but only *about* it.

This is all the more the case where, as in Ndebele's stories, the principles of composition derive from a Western, realist tradition of narrative rather than from local, oral traditions. Let us return once again to the concern in these stories with the inner life of the protagonist. Ndebele, the critic, links this concern with the inner life to the analysis of cultural processes. In order to understand cultural processes, we have to learn to respect the terms in which people think and feel, we have to form a conception of their identity as *subjects*. How are these ideas borne out in the stories Ndebele composes?

It is certainly true that these stories engage with cultural process, as focussed in the inner lives of various protagonists. However, these protagonists are, in each case, middle-class intellectuals or nascent intellectuals. Thus, the concern in the stories with cultural process seems, at the level of characterization, the inner life, or subject-identity, to have a particular social weighting. The overwhelming weight of the narrative is devoted to the growth of the inner life in one section only of the population. It is true that this weighting is presented with a certain complexity. The inner growth of the protagonist generally involves a dramatic and challenging encounter with personalities in the oral, or at least 'non-intellectual', culture of the township: an encounter which may lead to self-criticism, and an altered self-perception. Such personalities may be more or less vividly dramatized in the stories, so that a sense of their cultural 'resonance' is communicated to the reader. In some cases, these personalities may be attributed more valuable human resources, for example, more moral power or human wisdom, than the protagonist possesses.

This does not mean, however, that the narrative of cultural process, with its focus on the growth of the inner life, passes over to these personalities, who then displace the middle-class intellectuals. On the contrary, these personalities remain in a marginal narrative position, stimulants to the growth of the protagonist's inner life in a certain direction, rather than potential alternatives to it. As readers, we do not experience them with the same narrative 'inwardness'. In consequence, we are forced to 'realize' the theme of cultural process as a middle-class intellectual phenomenon, rather than as one embracing the whole population.

Earlier, I discussed some of the ways in which an English-language education provides the basis for an agenda in Ndebele's stories. It seems appropriate, at this point in the argument, to consider some of the more specific effects of the English-language *medium* of the stories.

The narrative of a work of fiction in the realist tradition is probably composed of a number of different voices, each with its own distinctive elements of vocabulary, idiom and intonation. This is so, even if we regard the prevailing voice of the narrator as being a single one, consistent and homogeneous throughout the narrative. There are various ways in which other, subordinate voices can be introduced into the narrative, such as by means of the direct or indirect speech of characters in the story. The most dramatic means available within the realist tradition, and much used therefore, is the direct speech of characters. Important effects are derived in this way. One effect is to give the impression that no constraint is put upon the expression of the characters by the prevailing narrative voice. The characters are enabled to speak in their own voices, no matter how different from that of the narrator. The use of dialect is a forceful example of this: different principles of expression, derived from region and class, are allowed free play within the narrative. This effect of freedom within the narrative, the freedom of characters to speak in their own voices, makes possible another effect. This is the setting up of tensions between the prevailing narrative voice and the subordinate, but 'free' voices. This state of narrative tension, this disturbing of a set narrative pattern, can play a central role in the reader's enjoyment and understanding of a story.

What we now have to ask, with respect to Ndebele's stories, is: what is the significance of these two effects of the interplay of narrative voices in realist fiction, the effect of freedom, and the effect of tension? The most important linguistic characteristic of Ndebele's stories is that they are in English, and the significance of the effects of freedom and of tension has to be considered in the context of the English-language medium of the stories. The point I wish to make about this reinforces points made earlier in this essay. In linguistic terms, Ndebele's narrative invites the reader to enjoy and reflect upon tensions and issues that are relevant to an English-language readership, rather than to the African population as a whole. To this degree, any direct analogy between the oral storyteller and the 'storytelling' writer is misleading.

The prevailing narrative voice of the stories is one which employs English with absolute ease and sophistication. This establishes a norm for the reader: the reader's narrative attention is 'centred' on the easy, fluent, sophisticated deployment of English. The agenda here would seem to be that this deployment of English enables access to the 'real' life of the African township, despite the predominantly vernacular character of this life. There can be no question of the ability of English to 'translate' at least some aspects of vernacular culture, otherwise Ndebele would not have chosen English as the medium of expression for his stories of township life. Ndebele counsels the politically committed African writer to pay serious attention to the modes of thinking and feeling, the cultural modes, of the African population. If he practises his own counsel, and if he nevertheless allows his characters to express themselves in English, it follows that he believes a thoroughly English-language story has the capacity to translate at least some aspects of vernacular culture without significant distortion.

In the context of this issue of translation, or the role of English vis-à-vis the African vernacular, the effects of freedom and of tension established through the diversity of narrative voices in the stories seem to me to have somewhat contradictory implications. The effect of freedom, the freedom of characters to speak in their own voices, no matter how different from the prevailing narrative voice, seems to imply that the English-language medium of the stories places no constraints upon the subject matter. Township characters can still express themselves authentically. If they speak English, this means that, within the scope of the story, some quality of their vernacular subject-identity can be adequately rendered. Thus the capacity of the English-language medium to encompass the 'reality' of township life is actually reinforced by the freedom allowed to characters to speak in their 'own' voices.

On the other hand, the effect of tension seems to me to have a rather contrary implication. This narrative tension is established both within the prevailing narrative and between it and the direct speech of characters. What it involves is both the 'stretching' and the 'limiting' of the fluent, faultless, sophisticated English of the prevailing narrative through its encounter with the speech patterns of vernacular township culture. The stretching of this narrative to acknowledge the idioms and inflections of the vernacular, albeit in a translated form, indicates the necessity for the English-language medium to 'renew' itself, to become Africanized. Its capacity to translate depends upon its Africanization. The limiting of the narrative arises from the use of direct speech in the stories. The speech of the tsotsis and the speech of the members of the educated middle class who define themselves in opposition to vernacular culture, rather than in solidarity with it, limit the prevailing narrative from opposite sides. The speech of the tsotsis claims a more direct, organic relation to vernacular culture than the prevailing narrative has, and thus calls into question the ability of this narrative voice to 'translate' the totality of the township culture effectively. The speech of the members of the educated middle class who distance themselves from the culture of the classes below them, aggressively asserting their own superiority, associates the acquisition of education with alienation from popular vernacular culture, and thus calls into question the ability of the prevailing narrative voice to assert on convincing terms its solidarity with the vernacular culture. So tensions are set up in the narrative, as the role of an English-language education in African intellectual life is simultaneously affirmed and negated, or, at least, limited.

The point would seem to be that, at this linguistic level of the narrative, the cross-currents within it have a particular relevance for an English-language-educated section of the population. The narrative explores issues and problems which are specific to this section. For such readers, the significance of the characteristic tensions in the narrative, tensions between the language of vernacular culture and the language of the educated, will be plain. There is, however, a limit to the exploration of these tensions in the stories, a limit that is set by their medium of expression, the English language. The cultural difference between English expression and vernacular expression has to be represented *in English*. It can only be represented so far as English can be 'stretched'. It has to be explored by limited analogy, rather than in its actual dimensions, in the actual differences between the way English and the vernacular are spoken, thought and felt. It follows that the formation of vernacular subject-identity, in language and speech, can also only be addressed in the terms of a limited analogy, rather than 'organically'. Earlier arguments are thus reinforced. English-language fiction does not stand in a direct, organic relation to the culture of the general African population. It intervenes in the culture of a section of this population, and may come to have an organic significance in the cultural identity of this section. This section of the African population itself, furthermore, relates to the general population in ways that are both organic and non-organic. The mode of entry of English-language fiction into African culture has a complexity which requires a great deal more careful analysis. One criticism I have of Ndebele's 'storytelling' advice to the African writer in English is that it serves at least partially to obscure this complexity.

2

The previous section was concerned with a critical analysis of Ndebele's near-identification of the art of fiction-writing, as practised by African writers in the medium of the English language, with the art of oral storytelling. Both practices he refers to as 'storytelling', which has some misleading implications. My interest in Ndebele's emphasis upon 'storytelling' is not exhausted by my sense of the need to disentangle these implications, however. Rather, my own insight into what the agenda of literary criticism might be has been greatly amplified by this emphasis. Other writers besides Ndebele, though in very different contexts, intellectual and political, place an analogous emphasis upon storytelling. This emphasis is juxtaposed by them to other ways of developing political conceptions in writing, ways which are predominant amongst Western radical intellectuals. It is associated with a critique of the predominance of these ways, a critique which exposes their limitations and dangers. In this context of critique, the 'story' becomes an alternative means of conceptualizing a specific population, its political situation, and the relationship between the conceptualizing intellectual and this conceptualized population. The writer, as 'storyteller', conceptualizes the population which is the subject of the story in such a way as to challenge, or limit, predominant political conceptions, at least amongst the radical intellectuals, about this population. By this means, political thought is problematized. It is no part of the intention of these writers to compose 'apolitical' fiction.

The story establishes itself as an alternative means of conceptualization for two main reasons, I believe. The first reason has to do with *culture*. The story places the dimension of culture on the political agenda. Some definition of culture seems necessary here. Culture, then, refers on the one hand to human beings as subjects, and, on the other hand, to the customary practices which connect human beings to each other in collective, or collaborative, entities. Cultural analysis tries to co-ordinate these two terms of reference, the human being as subject, and customary social practices. It is concerned with the constitutive nature of the human 'presence' in social practices, and more specifically, therefore, with particular categories of social practice in which the human presence is given more or less elaborate formal expression (in what we might call narratives of the human subject, such as those of religion, or art). This is in contradistinction to economic analysis. Economic analysis is concerned with a specific set of customary social practices, that set which involves the organization of human labour and the distribution of the fruits of this labour. In economic analysis, however, the nature of the human presence in these practices is disregarded, or, more accurately, is reduced to a skeletal notion of such a presence. In economic analysis, the human subject is a rudimentary mechanism, powered by 'interest', or 'reason' ('rational calculation') or some such simple and elementary notion.

This comparison, lopsided as it is for the sake of the emphasis required by the argument, explains why the story should be proposed as an alternative means of conceptualization of the political situation of a specific population. Economic analysis has provided the basic discourse of radical political commitment. Because economic analysis has founded itself upon a rudimentary notion of the human subject, though, radical political commitment has tended, at least until recently, to push consideration of the constitution of the human subject to the periphery of its attention. Since, as recent theories have emphasized, the human subject has a complex constitution, this tendency has deprived radical political thought of the capacity to engage with political situations in all their significant complexity.

The argument for 'storytelling', which is an argument for the restoration of culture and the human subject to the political agenda, can therefore be seen as an initiative to enable this capacity. This argument starts from the position that stories are narratives of the human subject, of the human 'presence' in social practices. Stories are a specific type of practice that is concerned with the human subject, and thus they provide a means of conceptualizing this area of concern with a more adequate complexity. Oral storytelling traditions give expression to ways in which societies with a predominantly oral culture understand this question of the human subject. The argument for 'storytelling' urges the politically concerned writer to compose fiction which is in analogy to oral storytelling. Such a writer composes on the basis of earlier narratives, either oral or written, that take the human subject as their focus. This composition reshapes and reinterprets the understanding expressed in earlier narratives. This reinterpretation involves, within the work of fiction, a cross-fertilization between the concepts of the radical intellectual, and the concepts embodied in the narrative tradition, concepts which, at least if they come from oral narrative tradition, may be close to those entertained within the wider, non-intellectual population. The most interesting example I know of a work composed in this spirit, and one which has guided my argument in this section of the essay, is Fazil Iskander's *Sandro of Chegem*.

This takes me to the second main reason why the story should be proposed as an alternative means of conceptualization to those predominant amongst radical intellectuals. This has to do with the nature of the relationship between the intellectual and the non-intellectual population, and with the way this relationship is perceived amongst intellectuals. The 'storytelling' writer finds inspiration for the composition of stories from the interaction of a number of preoccupations. For example, the political thought of the radical intelligentsia, a traditional stock of story-material, and memories of the influence of a particular society on the formation of the writer's personal identity, may interact to form a basis for story-composition. In this case, a strong tension is set up in the narrative between the mode of conceptualization of the radical intelligentsia and that of the non-intellectual culture of the society the writer intimately knows/remembers from childhood.

An intimate cultural relationship — expressed in deep-seated memories of situations and relationships that contributed to the formation of moral and social preoccupations from the impressionable years of early childhood, and in shared narrative experiences — is an essential ingredient for 'storytelling'. We cannot imagine Iskander's stories, or Ndebele's stories, being written without the pressure of this cultural relationship. This marks a difference between the relationship the 'storytelling' writer has with the population conceptualized in the fiction, and the relationship the radical political theorist or analyst has with the population conceptualized in theory or analysis. I do not mean that the radical theorist is not inspired in any way by cultural relationships, but rather that these cultural relationships do not enter into the practice of conceptualization, and do not problematize this practice. Thus the practice of producing theoretical concepts is understood as being quite separate from the cultural practices of the non-intellectual population, and as in no way depending on these practices for conceptual inspiration or corroboration. This means, finally, that the non-intellectual population are seen as the objects, rather than the subjects, of knowledge. The production of knowledge seems to circle round its centre in institutions dominated, if not monopolized, by the educated middle class, institutions of a middle-class, bureaucratic intelligentsia.

The contribution of 'storytelling' fiction to radical political thought may therefore lie in its ability to foreground tensions between the conceptual practice of intellectuals and the cultural practices of the non-intellectual population. 'Storytelling' fiction posits both the relevance of culture to political thought, and the significant complexity of culture.

A line of Marxist literary criticism, which was influenced by the work of Louis Althusser, tended to identify literature as occupying a mid-station between 'ideology' (misperception) and 'science' (knowledge). Literature, in this view, serves to arouse doubts in the reader about the adequacy of customary perceptions (misperceptions) of society. It cannot, however, provide the reader with the conceptual basis for a true perception (knowledge) of society. My argument in this essay, vis-à-vis 'storytelling' fiction, accords literature a more active cognitive capacity than this. It broadens the agenda of knowledge by limiting the scope of the 'knowledge' produced by intellectuals at a distance from the culture of the wider, non-intellectual population.

In my detailed analysis of Ndebele's stories, the weight of evidence was tending in a somewhat different direction. There, my argument stressed the limiting of this fiction by its English-language medium, which made implausible the 'organic' relationship with oral storytelling and oral culture that Ndebele seemed to be claiming. There is a tension between the tendency of the argument in the first and second sections of this essay, which indicates the need for further clarification of the issues raised by the 'storytelling' theme.

References

Iskander, Fazil. 1985. *Sandro of Chegem*. Harmondsworth: Penguin.
Ndebele, Njabulo. 1983. *Fools*. Johannesburg: Ravan Press.
Ndebele, Njabulo. 1984. '*Turkish Tales*, and Some Thoughts on South African Fiction'. *Staffrider*, 6(1), 24-25, 42-48.

The Marabi Dance: *A Working Class Novel?*

Kelwyn Sole and Eddie Koch

Modikwe Dikobe's novel *The Marabi Dance* was published in 1973, at a time when interest in African literature was burgeoning in South Africa and elsewhere. Yet the arrival of Dikobe's novel was treated with scant regard by some literary critics. Nadine Gordimer does not mention the book in her 1976 'English-Language Literature and Politics in South Africa'; Lewis Nkosi remarked that its 'combination of bad taste, clumsy construction and wooden characterisation must seem . . . to exceed anything we have yet encountered in African writing' and, more recently, the poet Farouk Asvat has dismissed it as 'mere reminiscences of the Doornfontein removals of the 1930s' (Gordimer, 1976; Nkosi, 1981: 80; Asvat, 1981).

These remarks, we would suggest, demonstrate a fairly conventional approach to literary study; an approach which implies *inter alia* a conviction that literary forms of 'high' art are aesthetically more pleasing and analytically more significant than more popular and technically less polished works. However, the mid-1970s was also a period during which noteworthy shifts were occurring in political and intellectual life in South Africa, and these shifts tended to allow *The Marabi Dance* a space for continued regard by many readers beyond the dictates of the dominant literary critical ideology of its time of publication.

There was interest shown in Dikobe and his work by writers of a Black Consciousness persuasion — that combative populist ideology which had burgeoned in South African oppositional politics from the late 1960s onwards. Black Consciousness stressed the need for a revival of self-generated black cultural and intellectual activity; and included calls for black people to rediscover their own history and the history of their literature, both of which had fallen foul of white disregard and misconception. This urge to rediscover led, for example, to a visit paid to Dikobe in his rural home by several *Staffrider* writers during that magazine's early years. This interest in Dikobe has, however, remained ambiguous, as we will show below.

The 1970s was also a time when radical, often Marxist, often white, historians and sociologists were developing a keen interest in the class constituents of South African society. This newly-reaffirmed focus among scholars in the historical and social sciences quickly spread to a similar methodology of concern among younger literary critics within the country. This group of scholars paid Dikobe's novel attention principally because of the fascinating insights it displays into the conditions of working class black existence in Johannesburg during the 1930s. Indeed, this feature of the book has led to a belief that *The Marabi Dance* is the first 'working class novel' to come out of black South African literature (Couzens, 1979: 97). The rest of this essay attempts to explore and evaluate the assessment of the novel in such a light.

In order to do this we will look at several aspects of the making of the novel. Firstly, we will sketch out the social and cultural milieu which Dikobe writes about. Secondly, we will outline the author's life history and his connection to this milieu. Thirdly, we will look at the process wherebv the book was written and published. Finally, we will suggest criteria that may be useful in siting the book in class terms, and examine *The Marabi Dance* in relation to these criteria. In the course of this we will refer back to incidents in the novel itself from time to time: we will not, however, subject the themes of the novel to a close examination here, as this has already been dealt with adequately elsewhere (Hofmeyr, 1977).

The Slumyards

The Marabi Dance is situated within the social and cultural milieu of the Johannesburg slumyards in the 1930s. In an era when only a few black townships existed near to the city, these slums were home to a large number of urbanized black working class people. They were also the surroundings in which Modikwe Dikobe spent most of his early life. An analysis of the specific socio-economic conditions under which people lived in the slumyards, the class composition of these yards, and the various cultural expressions which the slumyard dwellers created to cope with and humanize their conditions will allow us a closer and more sympathetic reading of the novel. It will also give some understanding of the observations and insights given individual expression by Dikobe in his work.

(i) The Making of the Yards

By the beginning of the twentieth century a permanently proletarianized African population of some size existed in Johannesburg, along with semi-proletarianized migrant workers. The increase in the size of this workforce was fuelled by the expansion of available jobs in areas other than mining, especially in a growing industrial, manufacturing and service sector. Pressure on black rural dwellers increased dramatically early in this century as well. Tax demands forced more and more people to seek work in the cities, and sharecroppers and others were forced off the land. The effect of the 1913 Land Act in particular was to move whole families into the cities.

Class formation among black people took place under conditions which both differentiated them from whites and subjected them to excessive political and economic control. The small urban black middle class was subjected to legal and economic restrictions on its potential for capital accumulation, and the much larger working class to extreme repression and restriction on movement. However, from early on a sizeable number of people managed to eke out a living outside of the ambit of white control. Beer-brewing, hawking, trading, furniture-making, prostitution, crime and other activities proliferated (Proctor, 1979: 75-80). Black people did not form an undifferentiated group. Ethnic and class differences existed and were in some cases exploited by whites to prevent too close an identification of interests from emerging. The forces of proletarianization and urbanization were experienced by different people in different ways, and a variety of transformed cultural identities and expressions emerged. For example, one can point to the difference in self-identity between migrants housed in controlled compounds, the *abaphakati* (those in between) who moved between rural and city life, and the permanently urbanized people creating new ways of life in the towns.[1]

White capitalists and government spent very little on providing the goods and services needed by this black workforce, as the rural Reserves were officially supposed to bear some of the cost of maintaining the black worker. Generally black workers were paid a wage below subsistence level, and not supplied with adequate family housing in the city. Attempts to house permanently urbanized blacks in separate locations were made as early as 1904; and this impetus towards segregation in the cities became official in the 1923 Urban Areas Act, which proclaimed the implementation of urban segregation and said that the existence of blacks within towns should be solely to fulfill white needs. However, a 1926 court decision stated that no blacks could be removed from their present places of abode without alternative accommodation being provided. This hamstrung the Johannesburg Municipality's ability to implement the 1923 Act, as it could only house a small proportion of blacks in the existing segregated hostels and locations. Furthermore, a conflict of interests between the central State and the Municipality occurred as to who should bear the costs for providing alternative accommodation, and disagreements took place among different sectors of capital as to the advisability of housing workers in locations so far away from town. This increased the difficulty of implementing segregation.

The lack of alternative accommodation for blacks also resulted in a burgeoning rack-renting business. White landlords would rent or buy a piece of ground in the inner city, erect shanties on this land (usually around a central courtyard) and let these out at high rents. A belt of slumyard areas developed in this way, stretching across the western, central and eastern city in places such as Doornfontein, Marshalltown, Fordsburg, Vrededorp and Prospect Township (Koch, 1983b: 153-154). Despite high rent, these yards were popular because they were closer to the city than the locations and so cut down on transport costs, and because the alternatives — outside of the few freehold tenure areas like Sophiatown and Alexandra — i.e. the hostels and locations, were strictly controlled and policed.

The 1920s and 1930s were times of great rural impoverishment and the further breakdown of social and welfare structures within the Reserves: this created a surplus population of unemployed and marginalized people in the town, many of whom gravitated towards the slumyards. By the 1930s the yards had become a main form of housing for the black population of Johannesburg.[2] In the slumyards lived a mixture of classes: semi-urbanized workers, the self-employed, the unemployed and a small number of middle class people. They came from a variety of rural origins, although some slumyards did have a preponderance of inhabitants from the same area (Dikobe, 1984e). In *The Marabi Dance* Modikwe Dikobe describes Molefe Yard in Doornfontein during the 1930s: here lives Martha, fictional heroine of the novel; and here Dikobe himself spent several years as a young man.[3]

(ii) 'Marabi' Culture

'Marabi' was the name given to the cluster of activities and culture which emerged in these slumyards in the years before the yards were demolished. Through these activities, the inhabitants created a sense of meaning and more secure social conditions for themselves in a squalid and overcrowded environment. 'Marabi' also refers to the music which accompanied the parties in the yards where women illegally made and sold beer to visitors, mostly over the weekends. Beer-brewing was the focus of marabi culture. At the time there were few ways for black women to earn a living in town, other than by laundrying, domestic service or prostitution. Many families bridged the gap between the husband's low wages and the family's survival needs through the wife's beer trade, which also helped during times of unemployment. Doornfontein especially did a thriving beer trade because of the diversity of its population and its proximity to many potential customers — domestics from white suburbs (including members of *amalaita* gangs), municipal, cartage and commercial workers (the CNA Compound and Electricity Department were nearby), and so on.[4]

In addition, marriage patterns geared themselves to the new conditions of urban life — indeed, a debate on the relative merits of different kinds of marriage is one of the central themes of *The Marabi Dance*. A type of common-law marriage, called 'vat-en-sit', became popular among people in the yards, rather than traditional, Christian or civil marriages. 'Vat-en-sit' allowed many working class families to meet subsistence requirements, harnessing together the man's wages and the woman's beer profits. Children engaged in a variety of activities to make money too, like begging, caddying, pickpocketing and selling newspapers. Gangs of 'laaities' formed (such as the Black Cat Gang in the novel) and controlled areas of operation. Furthermore, reciprocal relations developed in the yards, which helped bring down costs. Child care was often shared; women avoided giving parties which clashed with each other; friends would brew beer and make collections for women who were ill or in jail; and people would help with selling food or take money at the door during their friends' marabi parties. Marabi culture, therefore, emerged in response to the same forces that went into the making of Johannesburg's early black proletariat — rural impoverishment, the demand for ultra-cheap labour, the inability of capital to pay subsistence wages, the lack of basic services and housing for people in the city. In the yards, the culture of marabi was the most noticeable way in which this early black proletariat responded to their impoverished conditions.

However, while the vast majority of agents who forged this culture were working class, marabi was the product of a rather wider range of influences. In the slumyards where it was born, workers rubbed shoulders with members of the middle class and lumpenproletariat; and a variety of traditional, European, and urban social influences went into its making. Social mobility across class lines was notable among many black people at this time. The middle class was in an exposed position and many of its members relied on the security of marabi culture during times of unemployment and stress. Black workers' lives were also bound up with the everyday struggles of unemployed wives, parents and relatives. So marabi catered for a very mixed population, and was in many ways geared to the needs of the industrial reserve army in the city.

Music was very important to marabi, enlivening the parties and giving employment to young musicians — some of whom, like the legendary Ntebejaana, Ernest Mochumi and Zulu Boy Cele (whom Dikobe says he based the character George on), became well known in their own right. Music was provided by a single pianist or various types of combo. The result was infectious:

> Gashe . . . was bent over his organ in one corner, thumping the rhythm from the pedals with his feet, which were also feeding the organ with air, choking the organ with persistent chords in the left hand, and improvising for an effective melody with his right hand . . . you get a delirious effect of perpetual motion . . . perpetual motion in a musty hole where a man makes friends without restraint. (Matshikiza, 1957)

Marabi music drew on a range of traditional and western influences. It has been suggested, for instance, that marabi was influenced to a large degree by the *amatimiti* found in shebeens and mine compounds at the time. These *amatimiti* were themselves a lower class appropriation, with alcohol added, of the more sedate tea parties encouraged by missions as suitable entertainment for their flock (Dikobe, 1984g; see also Sole, 1983). Various forms of syncretic dance tunes, church hymns, European marches and traditional music have also been cited as influencing marabi (Coplan, 1979: 184-185; Coplan, 1982: 368).

However, while it is possible to trace the cultural influence of many groups in the making of marabi, it is striking that black and white middle class commentators continuously vilified and denigrated marabi culture. For example, a black critic from the newspaper *Umteteli wa Bantu* remarked in 1933:

The problem of African music must eventually be solved by Africans. The 'Marabi' dances and concerts, and the terrible 'jazz' music banged and wailed out of the doors of foul-smelling so called halls are far from representing real African taste. They create wrong impressions. The Transvaal Bantu is to be complimented in the circumstances on the annual Eisteddfod, which, to a great extent, will help to abolish the 'Marabi' menace. (Musicus, 1933)

There was, by this time, an ideological struggle in progress for the minds and allegiance of black people. A number of institutions had been set up by white liberals as a response to the black political militancy that followed the First World War. Among these were the Institute of Race Relations, the Joint Councils and the Bantu Men's Social Centre (BMSC). Through these institutions, liberals hoped to co-opt the allegiances and tastes of the educated black middle class and create conditions for the improved productivity of black workers (the liberal press frequently blamed marabi for workers' malnourishment and drunkenness).[5] In *The Marabi Dance*, Martha stands between, and is attracted to, different cultural forms and the social milieux which surround them: the eisteddfods, dances and singing competitions at the BMSC; the variety shows, concerts and dances staged at the African Hall in Doornfontein; the choral singing *makwaya*, heavily influenced by Christianity; and marabi itself, which eventually loses its hold over her as she becomes more upwardly mobile by the end of the book.

Marabi dwindled and vanished at the end of the 1930s, as the conditions which supported its existence disappeared. In 1933 the whole of Johannesburg was proclaimed under the Urban Areas Act. This, and the Slums Act of 1934, cleared the way for the demolition of the slumyards and the removal of their inhabitants to newly built townships like Orlando. The Johannesburg municipality took measures to monopolize beer sales for blacks, and municipal regulations in the new townships required residents to produce a marriage certificate before they were allowed a house, thus effectively putting an end to 'vat-en-sit'. Beer brewers were further discouraged by the prohibitive distances between these new townships and their prospective customers in the suburbs and compounds. Marabi music was replaced by large jazz bands better adapted to playing at organized dances in township community halls. Fictionally, Dikobe poignantly alludes to the demise of marabi at the end of the novel, in the figure of the single marabi dancer asked to leave the church during Martha's wedding.

It was Dikobe's ability to capture the social constituency and flavour of marabi culture that makes his novel stand out. However, this does not mean his work is a mechanical reflection of social conditions, nor that it is free of the disparate and sometimes contradictory influences that went into the making of the culture he was observing. Before asserting that the novel is 'working class', it is important to consider Dikobe's life story and the process whereby he came to write the novel. This will allow us to proceed to a more precise assessment of the class nature of the novel.

Modikwe Dikobe: Biography[6]

Modikwe Dikobe was born in Seabe, Northern Transvaal in 1913, an illegitimate child. The first languages he spoke were Setswana and Sepedi. Dikobe came to live in Johannesburg with his mother and stepfather at about the age of ten, first in Sophiatown, then in a backyard in Newlands. In approximately 1926 the family went to live in Molefe Yard in Doornfontein.

Dikobe was eager for education from the first, attending St Cyprian's in Sophiatown and later the Albert Street School in Doornfontein, where he passed Standard Six. When his stepfather died in 1929, his mother became a live-in domestic worker and Dikobe lived separately in the CNA Compound. Later he moved to Jeppe Hostel, then to Newclare with his first wife, briefly again to Sophiatown and then, from 1937, he lived in Alexandra for ten years. Thereafter he lived in Orlando West.

Dikobe's first job was as a part-time newspaper vendor. Later on he worked for himself as a hawker, first of religious pictures and later of clothing. In 1942 he was involved in the Alexandra Bus Boycott, and from 1946 was Secretary of the Alexandra Squatters' Committee led by Schreiner Baduza. In 1948 he contested the Advisory Board Elections in Orlando, and in the same year was Secretary of *Asinamali*, an organization which opposed high rents.[7]

His involvement in politics caused his hawking business to suffer; so he lost his economic independence and became a clerk in a furniture factory. Here he was badly treated and was consequently attracted to the trade union movement. He joined the Shop and Office Workers' Union in the late fifties and became involved in organizing black shopworkers and writing for the union newsletter. After the State of Emergency in the early sixties he was banned for a while and lost his job. He later found employment as a domestic worker, a night-watchman, and a clerk in the City Treasurer's Time Office. In 1977 he retired back to Seabe (now in Bophuthatswana), where he still lives.[8] As his attempts at farming have been destroyed by drought he works as a boarding master at one of the local schools.

History of The Marabi Dance

Dikobe recollects a desire to write from the 1930s. However, he felt he lacked sufficient English vocabulary and so read a great deal (he remembers a marked preference for Charles Dickens). *The Marabi Dance* was written in the 1950s and early 1960s when, according to Dikobe, a second marriage made his life easier and gave him more time to write. *Fighting Talk* published an extract from *The Marabi Dance* in the 1950s, based around the figure of Rev. Ndlovu, and he began writing for newspapers such as *Inkululeko* and the *Shopworker*. His confidence grew as he appeared more often in print: Norman Levy, who worked for the same union, also played an important role in encouraging his efforts. The publication of Mphahlele's autobiography *Down Second Avenue* in 1959 seems to have spurred him on (Dikobe, 1984c).

The Marabi Dance was finished while Dikobe was working as a night-watchman in 1963, and thereafter the manuscript was read and commented on by several people, and some editing was done.[9] The manuscript was unsuccessfully submitted to at least one publishing house overseas and then vanished for a while in London, at which point Dikobe started on another novel based on much the same material (since discontinued). Finally, *The Marabi Dance* was serialized in the magazine *South African Outlook* in the early 1970s and published by Heinemann Books in 1973.

A Working Class Novel?

The debates that surround attempts to identify the 'proletarian' characteristics of people's consciousness, their literature and art, their political practices and their culture are complex and unresolved — there is no one satisfactory definition of all the ingredients that would make a piece of literature working class. A number of factors can nevertheless be isolated which, we feel, would be important to consider or have been previously thought significant in the debate on working class literature. These factors would include the author's class position and ideological proclivities; the ideological and social content of the work and the form/genre in which it is created; its audience and means of dissemination; and what is called the 'proletarian world-view' of the work. It should be noted right from the beginning, however, that the concept 'proletarian world-view' is problematic. The phrase means, in effect, 'socialist outlook', and seems to embody a belief that socialism is the essential ideology of the working class — therefore, if the cultural expressions of working class people do not conform to this standard, they are a kind of 'false consciousness'. Such a conception leads to the danger of overtypifying working class literature by assuming that it will generally deal with and expose social issues in a defined (usually didactic or mimetic) manner and with preconceived ideological goals in mind. Furthermore, it ignores the fact that there is usually an interplay of identities, ideologies and individual preoccupations at work within any piece of literary expression: and significant ideological silences and contradictions as well.[10]

Bearing these qualifications in mind, we will now look at *The Marabi Dance* in the light of some of the above criteria.

(i) Social Content

It is obvious that *The Marabi Dance* is a rich, mainly realistic, sketching of the day-to-day experiences of black people and the cultural and social determinants affecting them in the slumyards in the late 1930s. It shows a number of sides to life among the black lower classes in Johannesburg at the time and, principally through Martha, their striving for social betterment. While fictional, the novel has something of the nature of an autobiography about it. The depth of the work's insights into its milieu can almost certainly be attributed to Dikobe's personal experience and knowledge.[11] Characters in the novel are either easily recognizable general types or specific historical people: in some cases fictionalized, in others not. Makgato of the ANC and Zulu Boy Cele (aka George) rub shoulders with totally imaginative characters like Martha. Dikobe clearly does not see a big split between fact and fiction in the book:

> I have a feeling, I cannot define. My imagination of characters is 'real' . . . they're occupants of my mind. I still clearly see Martha and George from Prospect Township . . . I can't lay down a pen once this notion enters into my mind. (Dikobe, 1984b. See also Dikobe, 1984c and 1984d, and Couzens, 1979: 100-101.)

Many of the social and cultural determinants we have alluded to in the social and historical overview of the slumyards are present in the novel. *The Marabi Dance* is based around the young woman Martha in order to allow Dikobe to focus on the home and family life of lower class black people, where women predominate.[12] In the main, he deals with Martha's search for identity as she is attracted to marabi on the one hand and desires respectability on the other. The story shows graphically the discontinuities of working class life in the city and the struggle people had to survive; the reasons for proletarianization; the battle of the generations as traditional values are broken down; the status of black working class women in society; the vexed question of marriage in the context of the breakdown of traditional society; the Draconian legislation that controlled the working class; and the emergence of new cultural forms among blacks in the cities. The author is patently aware of the process of cultural and social differentiation taking place between middle and working class black people, and between the rural and semi-urbanized. One need only point here to the textual juxtaposition of the dance at the Bantu Men's Social Centre with a Zulu migrant dance taking place at the same time in a nearby field:

> On a certain Friday night, Charlie Chaplin in *City Lights* was shown. When it was over Mr Phillip, the organizer, switched on the lights and announced to the yelling youngsters that *Rin Tin Tin* would not play. There was going to be a concert. Then there was whistling and pushing to leave.
> Gangs stood in groups on the street. A large board advertised

> CONCERT AND DANCE
> HERE TONIGHT
> COME AND HEAR
> MISS V. THEMBA
> AND
> MISS M. MABONGO

> Another poster displayed a jazz band, with George shown playing a piano . . . The floor of the Social Centre was already crowded with dancers:
> My dog loves your dog,
> And your dog loves my dog
> And if our doggies love each other why can't we?
> Next to the Social Centre a Zulu war dance was in progress. Feet stamped the ground in time to the rhythmic singing and clapping of the men and the dust rose high in the air.
> The contrast between the western and the African dance was notable. The one, a shuffling of the feet, and the other, a vigorous stamping. The latter a dance of people witnessed by a large crowd and the other of dancers unwitnessed, men and women locked to each other. The free air swept away the perspiration of the Zulus. The closed air polluted the hall and when the music stopped there was coughing (Dikobe, 1973: 72-73)

The continuing connections, and differences, between rural and urban people which accompanied the process of proletarianization are also skilfully portrayed by the placing together of images associated with town and rural life throughout the novel:

> The dancers swayed from side to side like mealie stalks; the right and left feet moving forward and back like springbok crossing a river. They sang as loudly as they could, singing for joy to the spirits of their forefathers. George ran his short fingers over the black and white keyboard as if they were moved by an electric charge. He sang with his face pitched to the ceiling. Martha moved like a cocopan full of mine sand turning at an intersection. Her round female baritone voice filled the hall and made it vibrate with sound. The flies, which had become a nuisance to the dancers, buzzed in harmony, and the rats and mice between the wall and the false front of the hall, scrambled into the ceiling. (Dikobe, 1973: 6-7)

However, the author's finely drawn understanding of the social life from which the novel springs is not enough to render it a 'working class novel' in any strict sense of the term.

(ii) 'Proletarian Outlook'

If one views the working class collectively as the bearers of a number of identities which are not necessarily reducible to 'working class consciousness' (identities of sex, race, region and so on) the class delineation of literature becomes rather more complicated. The social conditions that the working class experiences will vary from place to place: the political and ideological directions of working class literature and culture will therefore depend on the socio-economic and political milieu in which they arise and to which they address themselves (Williams, 1984: 246). Dikobe writes about a slumyard culture in which workers, the self-employed and unemployed predominated as cultural agents. This culture emerged as distinct from, for instance, the middle class culture of the Bantu Men's Social Centre and Inchcape Hall; but the conditions of racial oppression and the diversity of classes present in the yards allowed a culture to emerge which drew on a variety of social and class influences. This culture was self-contained and largely self-sufficient because no alternative cultural means were available to lower class blacks at the time, and because commercial culture and the media had as yet made few inroads into black society. (A recording industry which appropriated black music only became significant in the late 1930s; the first Zulu broadcaster on SABC only appeared in 1941.) The novel describes, then, a culture that is mainly, but not completely, working class.

Neither can it be said that the novel displays a socialist political consciousness. Hofmeyr has pointed out that there 'is a significant

absence of a collective political consciousness which . . . manifests
itself through organised movements and bodies' in the work —
which seems to reflect a low political awareness in the yards, as well
as a low profile there by the relevant political organizations of the
time (Hofmeyr, 1977: 8; see also Koch, 1983b: 165 and Dikobe, 1984a:
3-4).

(iii) The Author

Dikobe was self-employed during the 1930s and much of the 1940s.
Later he worked as a clerk. His class position shifts slightly as his
material circumstances and possibilities alter. Neither as a hawker
nor as a clerk did he see himself as working class, but regarded himself as better educated and closer to the petit-bourgeoisie. He now
believes that his difficulties in making a living during the bus boycott and his experiences of wage labour under a white boss built
up his sympathy for and identification with black workers:

> I hadn't been working class since school days. I had imbibed 'col-
> lege' class of scholars: wearing a shirt-collar, speaking English. My
> outlook of life changed in Alexandra Township where I had to pro-
> tect myself against high rental. Read left-wing papers. I became fully
> fledged in the Alexandra (1942) Bus Boycott. In spite of self-
> employment, I suffered with the working man. . . . I was in a word:
> a petty bourgeois running with the working class. . . . During the
> bus boycott I sympathise with the working man. I could still run my
> business without having to take a bus. [But] my business depended
> on him, who boards a bus to earn a living. A human's mind changes
> with situations. I left the City Council being a worker. I farmed. . . . I
> am today a housemaster. A middle class institution. What am I if not
> a middle man? (Dikobe, 1984b; see also quote in Couzens, 1979: 93-94)

(iv) Intended Audience and Chosen Literary Form

Dikobe's education and love of books set him apart from many of
the people in his immediate surroundings. In 1940 he attended classes at the Mayibuye Night School, and later registered for correspondence courses and typing lessons.[13] He thus emerges as a self-
educated intellectual from circumstances which supplied few opportunities for betterment. Although Dikobe cannot be described
as a member of the educated elite of the time, the success of his
efforts at self-advancement and knowledge distinguishes him from
many other slumyard dwellers. He joined the BMSC, for instance,
because it made him 'feel like a gentleman' (Hofmeyr, 1977: 9). He
was obviously subject to some of the same social stresses and pulls

that affect Martha in the novel. It is striking that Dikobe sees himself as somewhat apart from the marabi culture he was describing. He says, 'I was a spectator: watching, admiring and seeing [the] declining of old custom.'[14]

What is more, his choice of an established literary form such as the novel sets him apart from much of the black working class, who were generally (and many still are) not fully literate and therefore could not read his work. Black workers then, as today, tended to gravitate towards more communal, oral forms of expression such as music, song and dance.

Moreover, Dikobe dedicated *The Marabi Dance* to his former schoolmates at Albert Street School, in order, he has since remarked, that they could feel pride that a black man had written a novel about their experience of life. His intended audience when he wrote the book was as follows:

> When I wrote the book, I hoped the white [man] will take note of [the] blackman's feeling, perseverance, his culture. I was erasing an idea that the blackman is not yet ripe to say his feelings distinctly. (Dikobe, 1984c, and in conversation with the authors 3 March 1984)

In the light of this it is simplistic to describe the novel as 'working class'.

The Importance of The Marabi Dance

Nevertheless, this novel is in many ways unique, and stands in a fairly unusual relationship to the existing corpus of black South African literature. While the novel cannot be defined as strictly working class, as we have shown, it does not fit into the preoccupations and discourse of many of the black writers in this country, even today. While in the 1930s and 1940s there was a small amount of middle class black literature in sympathy with or referring to working class issues, much of the contemporaneous literature denigrated working class life (see Hofmeyr, 1980: 34-39 and Couzens, 1978: 3-12).

The Marabi Dance also stands apart from a great deal of literature being performed and written at the time of its later publication, as this was a literature largely informed by Black Consciousness; and, despite its radical and anti-Eurocentric nature, this literature still emerged more often than not from a more privileged class of black writers (see Sole, 1987). The novel focusses little on questions of political persuasion, black unity or identification (as Black Consciousness does), but rather deals with the social and cultural life of less privileged blacks in an urban situation, showing processes of social change and class differentiation at work. It is unusual in that it views working class life from a close personal experience.

Conclusion

Debates about the exact class status of literature (whether specific works should 'be allowed into the rather empty Hall of Fame occupied only by such rare examples óf "proletarian writing" as can be found' (Croft, 1980: xiii)) can, if used as a lynchpin of all subsequent analysis, quickly become hair-splitting rather than helpful. In South Africa today, though, such scrutiny does seem to fulfil a purpose. A great deal of previous literary analysis which deals with the country's literature sees it only in terms of racial determinants or, in more radical cases, with reference to a vaguely defined oppositional populism of the 'oppressed' — and this serves, in effect, to obfuscate class differences in black cultural and social life.

There are practical considerations at work as well, which make further understanding of works such as The Marabi Dance imperative. Debates about the nature, limitations and possibilities of 'working class culture' have begun to appear in local journals and newspapers such as the Weekly Mail, South African Labour Bulletin and Cultural Worker since 1984 onwards; and many young cultural activists in the anti-apartheid movement inside the country now refer to and take inspiration from the creative resilience of the black working class in South African history, as well as recognizing the central importance of the working class in political and cultural issues in South Africa now and in the future. Dikobe's book is a significant historical forerunner to this movement away from 'high' art to more popular and class-specific concerns. Careful analysis of its contents and circumstances of production can possibly, therefore, throw some light on crucial questions which need to be asked about the present status of the creative forms and preoccupations of less privileged people in South Africa. It must be pointed out, though, that even now the amount of black *written* literature that can accurately be called working class is minimal: one would have to look at the recent short stories of Bheki Maseko, Joel Matlou and Mpumie Cilibe or the autobiographies of Mandlenkosi Makhoba and Petrus Tom for any likelihood of a black working class prose.

This makes The Marabi Dance, despite its ambiguities, an even more noteworthy phenomenon in the struggle to clear cultural space in which we may hear the voices of those writers discriminated against due to *both* class and racial factors. Analyses such as ours remain necessary, moreover, because of an ongoing compulsion over the last two decades on the part of many better-educated or more privileged black writers with a radical anti-apartheid stance to blur distinctions between themselves and the predominantly working class community they wish to speak to and on behalf of. While such blurring has tended, from Black Consciousness onwards, to take on the discourse of a radical populism or third worldism — a discourse of 'the people', or 'the oppressed' or 'resistance culture' in various permutations of the terms (Sole, 1987) — some writers have also begun to mobilize the presently favoured term 'cultural worker' to enable a more extreme claim that they are organic intellectuals of the working class.[15] In our view such obfuscation does not necessarily always have helpful analytical or political consequences.

The Marabi Dance has suffered more than its fair share from the vagaries of a formalist criticism which can be related back to the viewpoint of predominantly middle class critics, both black and white. Commentary on the novel swings wildly between extremes of disapprobation of its 'literary' shortcomings (which are rarely spelt out, except in relation to an arbitrarily conceived 'great literature') on the one hand, and a romanticization seeking to appropriate it into an undifferentiated discourse of 'black creativity' on the other. Among black critics, attitudes to marabi culture have varied from the denigration of earlier years to a more recent approval, as the black petit-bourgeoisie grows more radical and seeks an alignment of aims with lower class black people.[16]

One of the more persistent recent criticisms, generally from a Black Consciousness standpoint, has been the degree to which *The Marabi Dance* benefitted from the work of white editors. It must be noted, in reply, that patronage by literary or political sympathizers has often been the means by which lower class, unskilled writers gain access to the dominant culture's world of publishing and dissemination (Worpole, 1983: 82; Croft, 1980: xiv). One can add that, despite efforts to the contrary, a great deal of Black Consciousness theatre and publishing still remains indebted to expertise and money provided from outside the black community: as a recent example, two of the more radical young black playwrights in this country at present, Matsemela Manaka and Maishe Maponya, have built up their reputations considerably with overseas tours. Thus, although the editing *The Marabi Dance* received from white intellectuals makes its 'working class' pedigree questionable, the process of editing and perhaps influencing black writers' work is still widespread.

In addition, it has been our experience that black audiences seem to react to *The Marabi Dance* in different ways. Although this cannot be stated categorically, the readers who tend to react slightly unfavourably to the novel are black lecturers and literati; but in circumstances where the book has been used in trade union education groups or with immediate post-matriculants, the response has been far more positive. This potentially suggests an amount of difference in cultural response and ideology among black South Africans aligned, indirectly at least, with their social position and experience.

Whether its proponents are black or white, a purely textual criticism will not be able to deal with this novel. If there is no concern taken with its historical and social underpinnings and its conditions of production, sweeping generalizations may be forthcoming which show little grasp of the factors which went into the making of *The Marabi Dance*. This highlights an ignored but relevant principle: that in all literature there is an interplay of imaginative and sociohistorical components, and an emergence of the work from a cultural background, which can be understood only with reference to the text *and* its social and cultural bases. A careful reading of the novel and the history which informs it will be useful to the historian and literary critic respectively (Couzens, 1979: 90; Izevbaye, 1979: 10).

There remains the question of the literary value of *The Marabi Dance*. As some critics have suggested (Wolff, 1979: 19), it is perhaps not enough to remove literature from the realms of merely textual criticism and simply substitute a sociological or semiotic relativism in its place. In our opinion *The Marabi Dance* is a satisfactory work of art, and, as we have suggested, the manner in which some commentators have dismissed it says as much about their hidebound views as about the novel itself. An examination of how *The Marabi Dance* conforms, and does not conform, to middle class expectations of literature remains to be attempted, for

> It seems to me that what remains to be explored is the reasons why *The Marabi Dance* remains a scantily read novel; there is little doubt of its 'literary merit'. Answers perhaps lie in the domain of publishing policy, readership conditions and attitudes of readers — all of which are dictated by prevailing social conditions and values. A purely textual analysis could never answer or even pose these type of questions, because it takes its starting point from texts established by social precedent. (Trump, 1979: 75)

Notes

1. For a fuller discussion of this, see Coplan, 1982.

2. Between 1916 and 1927 the slumyard population is estimated to have increased from 10 000 to 30 000 (Koch, 1983a: 73, 86).
3. Dikobe describes the yard in Dikobe, 1973: 32. All further page references to the novel will be to this edition. For a full description of Rooi-yard, a short distance away from Molefe Yard, see Hellman, 1948: 8-9.
4. Dikobe, 1984f. Mabongo, Martha's father, had been a member of an *amalaita* group. For further information on these gangs, see Van Onselen, 1982: 54-60.
5. For further details, see Couzens, 1976 and 1982.
6. The following information was gleaned from Dikobe himself and Couzens, 1979: 91-94.
7. For further information on the Alexandra squatters' movement and *Asinamali*, see Stadler, 1979: 34-41.
8. For Dikobe's observations on life in Seabe, see Dikobe, 1980b.
9. It seems that the people who played a part in actually editing the manuscript were Lionel Abrahams and Valerie Phillip. According to Abrahams, the only aspects that were edited were those of style and presentation — the incidents, setting, characterization and dialogue were Dikobe's. Dikobe adds that the only assistance he got in content was from Monica Wilson (bride-seeking practices), his second wife Betty (Bridgman Nursing Home) and Norman Levy. (Dikobe, 1984c and Abrahams, 1988/9)
10. In the novel this point would be borne out by, for instance, the ambiguous tone in which the removals from the yards to Orlando are described, an ambiguity which seems to reflect Dikobe's own feelings on the matter.
11. In addition to *The Marabi Dance*, Dikobe has produced insightful prose works on other areas in which he lived in Johannesburg. For examples, see Dikobe, 1979a, 1979b and 1980a; as well as 'Sophiatown Kayalam' (unpublished manuscript).
12. Dikobe, 1984c and 1984d. He points out that the 'Rosie' sequence in his poetry collection focusses on a woman for the same reason (Dikobe, 1983: 20-27).
13. For information on these night schools, see Bird, 1984: 198-203.
14. Dikobe, 1984c. The sense of his 'standing apart' from marabi culture is not necessarily simply the outcome of class differences, but may say something about the position of an individual writer in relation to the culture he or she is exploring and giving expression to. A critic notes that one of the paradoxes of working class writers in Britain is that 'the act of trying to represent the culture and geographical community in which the writer has grown up and lived is the first step by which the writer is separated from that life almost irrevocably' (Worpole, 1983: 94).
15. A rather (in our opinion) idiosyncratic reading of Gramsci and Cabral is usually central to such claims. For an example, see Siers/Parenzee, 1988: 8-10.
16. Compare Mphahlele's depiction of the 'savagery' of marabi in 1959 with Manganyi's identification of marabi as a statement of 'continuity and change in African culture' some twenty years later (Mphahlele, 1959: 96; Manganyi, 1980: 17).

References

Abrahams, Lionel. 1988/89. 'The Saga of *The Marabi Dance*'. *Sesame*, 11.

Asvat, Farouk. 1981. 'A Critical Look at Black S.A. Writing'. *The Sowetan*, 26 June.

Bird, Adrienne. 1984. 'Black Adult Night School Movements on the Witwatersrand, 1920-1980'. In Kallaway, Peter (ed.). *Apartheid and Education*. Johannesburg: Ravan.

Coplan, David. 1979. 'The African Performer and the Johannesburg Entertainment Industry: The Struggle for African Culture on the Witwatersrand'. In Bozzoli, Belinda (ed.). *Labour, Townships and Protest*. Johannesburg: Ravan.

Coplan, David. 1982. 'The Emergence of an African Working-Class Culture'. In Marks, Shula and Richard Rathbone (eds). *Industrialization and Social Change in South Africa*. London: Longman.

Couzens, Tim. 1976. 'The Social Ethos of Black Writing in South Africa 1920-50'. In Heywood, Christopher (ed.). *Aspects of South African Literature*. London: Heinemann.

Couzens, Tim. 1978. 'Politics and Black Poetry in South Africa 1930-1950'. *Africa Perspective*, 7.

Couzens, Tim. 1979. 'Nobody's Baby: Modikwe Dikobe and Alexandra, 1942-1946'. In Bozzoli, Belinda (ed.). *Labour, Townships and Protest*. Johannesburg: Ravan.

Couzens, Tim. 1982. '"Moralizing Leisure Time": the Transatlantic Connection and Black Johannesburg, 1918-1936'. In Marks, Shula and Richard Rathbone (eds). *Industrialization and Social Change in South Africa*. London: Longman.

Croft, Andy. 1980. 'Introduction' to *Means-Test Man* by Walter Brierley. Glasgow: Spokesman.

Dikobe, Modikwe. 1973. *The Marabi Dance*. London: Heinemann.

Dikobe, Modikwe. 1979a. 'We Shall Walk'. In Bozzoli, Belinda (ed.). *Labour, Townships and Protest*. Johannesburg: Ravan.

Dikobe, Modikwe. 1979b. 'The People Overflow: A Tribute to Schreiner'. In Bozzoli, Belinda (ed.). *Labour, Townships and Protest*. Johannesburg: Ravan.

Dikobe, Modikwe. 1980a. 'Star Café'. *Staffrider*, 3(1).

Dikobe, Modikwe. 1980b. 'A return to the land — where minds grow stale'. *Frontline*, October.

Dikobe, Modikwe. 1983. *Dispossessed*. Johannesburg: Ravan.

Dikobe, Modikwe. 1984a. 'Class, Community and Conflict'. Paper presented to the History Workshop, University of the Witwatersrand, Johannesburg, February.

Dikobe, Modikwe. 1984b. Letter to Kelwyn Sole, 5 March 1984.

Dikobe, Modikwe. 1984c. Letter to Kelwyn Sole, 10 March 1984.

Dikobe, Modikwe. 1984d. Letter to Kelwyn Sole, 11 March 1984.

Dikobe, Modikwe. 1984e. Letter to Kelwyn Sole, 19 March 1984.

Dikobe, Modikwe. 1984f. Letter to Kelwyn Sole, 4 April 1984.

Dikobe, Modikwe. 1984g. Letter to Kelwyn Sole, 4 May 1984.

Gordimer, Nadine. 1976. 'English-Language Literature and Politics in South Africa'. In Heywood, Christopher (ed.). *Aspects of South African Literature*. London: Heinemann.

224 *Kelwyn Sole and Eddie Koch*

Hellman, Ellen. 1948. *Rooiyard*. Cape Town: Oxford University Press.
Hofmeyr, Isabel. 1977. 'The Marabi Dance'. *Africa Perspective*, 7.
Hofmeyr, Isabel. 1980. 'Perspectives on Working-Class Life Among Black and Afrikaans Writers, 1890-1930'. *Africa Perspective*, 16.
Izevbaye, Dan. 1979. 'Issues in the Reassessment of the African Novel'. In Jones, Eldred (ed.). *African Literature Today No. 10*. London: Heinemann.
Koch, Eddie. 1983a. 'Doornfontein and its African Working Class 1914-1935'. University of the Witwatersrand: unpublished M.A. thesis.
Koch, Eddie. 1983b. '"Without Visible Means of Subsistence": Slumyard Culture in Johannesburg 1918-1940'. In Bozzoli, Belinda (ed.). *Town and Countryside in the Transvaal*. Johannesburg: Ravan.
Manganyi, Chabani. 1980. 'Continuity and Change in African Culture — the Writer's Response'. In Mphahlele, Es'kia and Tim Couzens (eds). *The Voice of the Black Writer in Africa*. Johannesburg: U of Witwatersrand P.
Matshikiza, Todd. 1957. 'Jazz Comes to Jo'burg'. *Drum*, August.
Mphahlele, Es'kia. 1959. *Down Second Avenue*. London: Faber.
Musicus. 1933. *Umteteli wa Bantu*, 11 November.
Nkosi, Lewis. 1981. *Tasks and Masks*. London: Longman.
Proctor, André. 1979. 'Class Struggle, Segregation and the City: A History of Sophiatown, 1905-1940'. In Bozzoli, Belinda (ed.). *Labour, Townships and Protest*. Johannesburg: Ravan.
Siers, Rushdie and Donald Parenzee. 1988. 'A Dialogue on the Emergence of the Cultural Worker'. *Akal*, 1(1).
Sole, Kelwyn. 1983. 'The Study of South African Working Class Culture'. *Perspectives in Education*, 7(2).
Sole, Kelwyn. 1987. 'Identities and Priorities in Recent Black Literature and Performance'. *South African Theatre Journal*, 1(1).
Stadler, Alf. 1979. 'Birds in the Cornfields: Squatter Movements in Johannesburg, 1944-47'. In Bozzoli, Belinda (ed.). *Labour, Townships and Protest*. Johannesburg: Ravan.
Trump, Martin. 1979. 'Ghetto, Slumyard and Township: A Comparative Study of Urban Black Life in Chicago and Johannesburg, based upon the novels *Native Son* by Richard Wright and *The Marabi Dance* by Modikwe Dikobe'. University of the Witwatersrand: unpublished B.A. Hons thesis.
Van Onselen, Charles. 1982. 'The Witches of Suburbia: Domestic Service on the Witwatersrand, 1890-1914'. *New Nineveh*. Johannesburg: Ravan.
Williams, Raymond. 1984. *Writing in Society*. London: Verso.
Wolff, Janet. 1977. 'The Interpretation of Literature in Society: the Hermeneutic Approach'. In Routh, Jane and Janet Wolff (eds). *Sociology of Literature: Theoretical Approaches*. Keele University: Sociological Review Monograph No. 25.
Worpole, Ken. 1983. *Dockers & Detectives*. London: Verso.

M'a-Ngoana O Tšoare Thipa ka Bohaleng – The Child's Mother Grabs the Sharp End of the Knife: Women as Mothers, Women as Writers

Dorothy Driver

On 13 August 1976, a woman called Maria Tholo, a teacher of pre-school children in Guguletu near Cape Town, began to speak about her responses to the world so rapidly changing around her. Virtually the first words of Tholo's diary are 'We have Soweto with us' (1980: 10). The diary, which is largely to do with her day-to-day activities and thoughts as a parent, teacher and householder, deals specifically with her attitudes to 'the children of Soweto' and what they represent. Often with great difficulty but often also with excitement, Tholo negotiates the set of expectations placed on the adult world by these children, as well as the expectations placed on her by the world from which she received her education, a world represented – more or less – by Tholo's interviewer, an anthropologist called Carol Hermer. During the course of four and a half months, Tholo met with Hermer, sometimes weekly, often less regularly. Hermer transcribed and edited the taped interviews: *The Diary of Maria Tholo* was published in 1980.

   Not surprisingly, given the fact that Tholo was addressing a white interviewer, one can identify in Tholo's textual psyche a split similar to that, say, presented by Bloke Modisane in his autobiography *Blame Me On History*, published over twenty years earlier. Modisane characterizes himself as the 'eternal alien between two worlds', and speaks of a desire to be 'accepted into white society' (1963; rpt. 1986: 220). Tholo sometimes speaks like a person quite remote from her community, and sometimes speaks *against* that outsider's position. 'You know how Africans can scream', she says on the one hand (1980: 25), and on the other, scoffs at the way white authorities apply, to an African family, the alien concept 'close relative' (1980: 23). Tholo's editor speaks of the 'class' versus 'caste' conflicts evident in Tholo's language as she deals with the way the schoolchildren tried to clean up the townships (1980: 69): Black Power threatened the immediate material interests of the black middle class even while it engaged their psychological needs. What is at issue in this essay, however, is the considerably more complex question regarding the tensions between Tholo's position as mother/teacher/ authority and her growing deference to the children.

Tholo knows herself as mother, teacher and wife, as well as informant to a white anthropologist unable to see for herself what is going on in the townships: it is primarily from the positions these roles offer her that – according to the way she presents herself – she is accustomed to speaking. With Soweto 1976, the positions of authority implied by these roles begin to shift.

On 29 August 1976, at a parent/teachers' meeting in Guguletu, one of the teachers told the following story:

> The other day I went into class to start Social Studies and as I picked up the chalk one of the children asked me to please write down the word 'American' and when I'd done that to define the word. I said something like 'a person who belongs in America, who was born in America . . .'
> 'Define the word "African",' he said. I used a similar definition. Then they all shouted, '. . . are Americans only white or are Negroes also Americans?'
> 'Everybody is American,' I answered.
> 'Good. Now define the word "African" again.'
> . . . 'Well, here an African is usually taken to mean a black person.'
> 'Right. Now you are clever,' they chorused.

And then the children ask the teacher:

> 'Why, if we are all Africans, when some immigrant from Portugal, who has been thrown out of Angola, comes in, why is it that he gets all the rights that you can't have being born here, because of the colour of your skin? Why is it that he gets first preference in getting a job, he gets citizenship and we can't even be citizens in our own country? Teacher, if you can't answer those questions you are not fit to be a teacher, so leave the blackboard.' (1980: 34)

Allusions to the changed relations between parents and children are common in, and perhaps even fundamental to, the literature of the post-Soweto era. In Miriam Tlali's *Amandla*, Mmane Marta, who has just become a grandmother, says, 'We're in the hands of the children now. They are as good as our parents.' (1980: 35) And Noni Jabavu, who brought out a second edition of *The Ochre People* in 1982 (it first appeared in 1963), quite specifically turns in her preface to the '1976 generation' to seek their approval and to pledge her allegiance: 'I hope that in reading this book which one of your "grandmothers" wrote long ago and far away, you will see how vastly you have progressed and brought us forward from the views we beheld when we were your age in those times long-gone. We were scarcely peering, even dimly; whereas you see things clearly now.' (1982: n.p.) Tholo presents a considerably more detailed and complex picture: a world where the children have positioned themselves as the authorities – the teachers, the policemen, the judges, even the priests. Increasingly outraged at the behaviour and tactics of the police and the *witdoeke*, Tholo wishes to respond to what she often sees as the courage, clear-headedness and unanimity displayed by the children, these new authorities: yet she often has difficulty in constructing for herself a position not at odds with the demands they make and the dangerous world she feels they create for her and her family. She speaks frequently of the adults' fear of the children, and of their silence before them: 'One is quite scared to open one's mouth to a youth in the townships' (1980: 43). After a funeral she attends on 22 August she says: 'When we went back to the house for refreshments it was the children who were given first preference. I never thought I'd see that.' (1980: 26)

Tholo's sense of her place in the world is under continual interrogation. Near the start of her diary she sits guard outside the pre-school building, which has remained open as a place of safety for the young children, who would otherwise be with their 'brothers and sisters', and in danger. Yet she must also see herself as keeping a shelter available to the older children: 'Mr. M. says we mustn't lock our gates to keep out the students [running from police squads] because that will make it dangerous for us should they turn against us' (1980: 22). Later in the narrative her school has become established as a shelter: 'We ask, "Anything we can do?" and they shake their heads and say, "No, I'm just waiting." We just smile at them. You can't throw them out.' (1980: 54)

Again, near the start of the diary, she justifies her illegal presence at a funeral, a justification perhaps in part made with Hermer in mind. Because attendance was restricted, she first says that she was there since she felt she ought to help with the catering, for 'the mother was struggling on her own' with the sandwiches and tea.

Then she says, 'seeing that I was going to help with the catering I thought we should at least try and force our way to the ceremony' (1980: 24). As the diary progresses, her desire to see and be involved in as much as she can needs less and less excuse: 'I thought it was time we went to the graveyard. Gus [her husband] wouldn't budge. ''I'm not going anywhere. I'm not sticking my neck out another minute.'' So we did our own sort of Sabbath service in the house and just lay around. But I was feeling miserable.' (1980: 168) In a short time, she goes to the graveyard, and throws handfuls of earth on the graves of unknown people shot at random by police in the townships. But then she finally rebels: 'It was quite an effort, all that bending and throwing . . . . We were getting so tired that we tried to dodge the last row.' (1980: 169)

At the beginning of the schoolchildren's uprising, she very quickly begins to give the Black Power salute to the children, and urges her reluctant husband to do the same – '''Black Power'' is like a pass-word now' (1980: 13). Yet, at other points in her narrative, she speaks her doubts about the methods sometimes used and their motivation, and even admits that she says one thing to the police-man's wife and another to the children: 'because really you don't know where you stand' (1980: 108). She is sometimes clearly thrilled by the children's punitive actions; when she discovers that her neighbour's house is marked for looting, she says: 'In a way I felt sorry for the owner of the house because she is a neighbour. But inside I was happy, because without those shebeens we will sleep at weekends.' (1980: 87) Yet a little later, talking about house-burning, she says, 'Jealousies and personal fights are being decid-ed by petrol bombs,' and asks, 'Can there be as many informers as houses that have burned down? . . . You don't know what peo-ple think of you.' (1980: 156) Anxious herself about who she is seen talking to (1980: 129), for she knows, 'It's all so dangerous. Even a six-year-old can be walking around, but he has ears and he'll pass on the message' (1980: 138), she says, 'Nothing is safe anymore. Neither to be informing on this thing nor to be in it.' (1980: 130) Indeed, her diary returns again and again to the figure of the in-former (1980: 21, 115, 130), as if in anxious reflection about the thin line this revolutionary world is now drawing between informer and informant, informant and spy. To Hermer she says, 'As someone said, ''If Madam asks you what is going to happen you will say, 'The children are going to march', because you must tell Madam everything. Therefore we won't tell you.'' People respect someone who can keep a secret like that.' (1980: 56)

In *The Diary*, then, Maria Tholo does not establish a sense of a

stable and continuous identity, for her various roles continually contradict one another in their response to a changing community and
changing patterns of authority. Her role as teacher becomes inter-
rupted by her role as mother, for she has to run *out* of the pre-school
building to find her young daughter and take her to the safety of
their home (1980: 10). Then her role as mother conflicts with her
role as obedient wife, for she has to drive to Nyanga to look for her
son in defiance of the command given by her husband (1980: 173).
Then her role as dutiful and generous wife and mother conflicts with
her desire to obey the dictates of the schoolchildren, for she decides
to observe the ruling about a 'black Christmas' – a Christmas
without food and festivities – but then is called on by her family
to provide supper for them that night (1980: 170). And her role as
black sympathizer conflicts with her role as friend to a white woman: when the eruptions start, she drives to a Community Centre
to get a white friend out of Guguletu before she is killed (1980: 11).
One does not get a sense of splitting in this diary so much as an
endlessly deferred self, presented so aptly in the text by Tholo's criss-
cross of agitated movements, a body never at rest.

   Ellen Kuzwayo's *Call Me Woman*, published five years after Tholo's diary appeared in print, and nearly ten years after Hermer began interviewing Tholo, has ostensibly far less difficulty than does
Tholo in presenting the self as stable and coherent subject in terms
of Black Consciousness. In contrast to Tholo, a main project of her
text is to construct the image of a strong and active woman, placed
in a position of authority over the younger generation, whom she
admires but does not fear, and whose political activities she can
match. A particularly significant moment in her text is the elision
of a chronological gap, and therefore an elision of difference, between the detention of one of her sons and her own detention. Chapter 13, titled 'I See My Sons Grow Up', deals with events in 1971,
when her son Bokone Justice Moloto is detained. Chapter 14, 'How
the State Sees Me', makes a five-year leap so that her son's status
as a political activist is followed immediately by evidence of her own
similar status, for she was detained on 19 October 1977. Particularly revealing of Kuzwayo's intent here is the paragraph that acts as
a bridge between these two periods of time: 'As I write this chapter
in 1983,' she says, at the start of Chapter 14, 'I am sitting in full
view of the Atlantic Ocean, at a point where I can raise my eyes
and catch a glimpse of Robben Island where many of the political
prisoners from the black community are still serving jail sentences,
ranging from twelve years to life imprisonment. The irony of it all!'
(1985: 198)

But Kuzwayo's ostensible project is to celebrate women. She does so in various ways, drawing on the lives of contemporary women to show different kinds of political and domestic strengths. Many of her women are activists. She is unlike Miriam Tlali in this regard, who says that her women characters play a merely 'supportive' role to men in the struggle since, in reality, 'they are not allowed to come to the forefront' (1989: 75).

Kuzwayo also records moments from the lives of her grandmother and mother, whom she focusses on in order, again, to represent resilience and enlightenment rather than passivity or backwardness. Her project in *Call Me Woman* becomes particularly clear in comparison with Noni Jabavu's *The Ochre People*, for *Call Me Woman* also casts back in various ways to the world of pastoral harmony, a world permitted to relatively few black South Africans in the 1920s and 30s. Like Jabavu, who also came from a prosperous rural Christian community, Kuzwayo is clearly concerned with the breakdown of family life and with the absence of moral guidance for young girls entering puberty. Yet she does not present the 'new' urban woman in the terms set by Jabavu, whose world is threatened by women who remain outside the family structure. These urban women bear children but live without husbands: 'No marriage, cattle, nothing' (1982: 136). Jabavu calls them 'anti-social' (1982: 137). Nor does Kuzwayo present the 'new' woman in the terms set by Bessie Head in *The Collector of Treasures* – a woman made conceited by her education, as in 'Snapshots of a Wedding', or 'hysterical' in her gay individualism, as in 'Life' – although, like Head, she is concerned to keep women within a community. In fact, Kuzwayo's text focusses far less on the individual self than is usually the case with autobiography, for although it includes a considerable amount of personal narrative, with some introspection, it tries, largely through its portraits of other women, to proclaim an anti-individualist position that coheres with the philosophy of communalism proposed by Black Consciousness.

The title of her autobiography, *Call Me Woman*, reads as a response to Mtutuzeli Matshoba's *Call Me Not a Man*, published in 1979, whose main story opens with the words – *'For neither am I a man in the eyes of the law, / Nor am I a man in the eyes of my fellow man'* (1979: 18; emphasis in original). Matshoba's story presents the debasement of a man by police reservists. Kuzwayo's *Call Me Woman*, in contrast, provides an energetic reminder that *women* have not been debased, whether they are part of a group of YWCA women who frighten off the police and their guns (1985: 49-50), or part of a group of rural women left at home alone, taking 'the whole responsibility' (1985: 12). Kuzwayo goes so far as to say: 'Women somehow seem to cope with the pressures more successfully than men' (1985: 51).

Kuzwayo's text advocates the kind of female empowerment and female separatism which one associates with Western feminism at a certain stage of its history. In an interview published in 1984, she also speaks strongly about what she sees as a male 'vendetta' to 'blot . . . out' 'the tremendous contribution' made by women in their communities and to 'stifle' further contribution: 'the men, somewhere, are not playing a fair game. They don't give the black women an opportunity to honestly realise their potential and to recognise that potential when it does come forth. They're doing everything to thwart it.' (Lipman, 1984: 19) The word 'feminist' does not, however, come from her pen. In this regard she honours the current refusal by black South African women to assume a position whose ideology was formulated, largely, in white middle-class Europe and America: feminism has, historically, often been blind to the specific oppressions and exploitations suffered by black and working-class women.

I will, nevertheless, retain the term 'feminist' in relation to Kuzwayo, since different versions of feminism exist and since it has opened its eyes in recent years to its own Eurocentric and middle-class bias. There is, in any case, more point in expanding the concept where necessary than in abandoning it for another. I allude here to Alice Walker's term 'womanist' (1984: xi), sometimes posited as an alternative to 'feminist'. Retaining the use of the term 'feminist' draws attention to a set of important tensions and contradictions within the text which Walker's term 'womanist' might obscure.[1] If, indeed, new approaches need to be defined for black women's writing in South Africa, as the current mood seems to suggest, then these tensions and contradictions need to emerge, rather than to be silenced.

Kuzwayo's text is strongly motivated by Black Consciousness, for which she has been one of the primary advocates. In 1976 she was elected to the Committee of Ten in Soweto, was detained without charge or trial for five months in 1977-78, acted as expert witness at a 'terrorism' trial in 1978, and was a founding member of the Zamani Soweto Sisters Council and the Maggi Magaba Trust. At one point Kuzwayo apologises for seeing a white rather than a black doctor (1985: 207), just as she, as feminist separatist, apologises for employing a male accountant (1985: 231). We find embedded within this text, then, an analogy between feminist separatism (the desire not to use the services of a male accountant in a female-only organization) and the separatism of Black Consciousness (the desire not to use the services of a white doctor).

Separatism in feminism and in Black Consciousness is generally justified by the need for women on the one hand and black South Africans on the other to have a chance to develop their sense of self within a community (which may simply be an imagined or projected community) made up *only* of one another. Why has this been considered necessary? 'Self' is constructed in dialectic with others or another: one cannot see oneself in the absence of projections from the world around one. What the self is awaits its determination by or from those outside the self, those who say 'me' to me, and who constitute the self for which I strive (Derrida, 1985: 51). The search for an identity constructed through the black community has received particularly poignant expression in a recent poem written by Zim Mnotoza, one of the Chumani Writers Group in Grahamstown. Here the poet's sense of self depends on the self-image of the community:

> That is why today my existence
> is more like a research . . .
> That's why wherever I go
> I'm looking for children with the same identities
> So that I can finish my biography . . . (Berold, 1987: 13)

This search for a self-constituting community is important because of the damage done to black South Africans in an apartheid culture. But it is a process of extraordinary complexity. If 'self' is constructed in the terms provided by the symbolic system into which one is born, then South Africans are called upon to define themselves in terms of the oppositions offered by the symbolic repertoire of apartheid, a repertoire which includes the marks of imperialism and colonialism, of class exploitation, racial oppression, and gender stereotyped expectations. The search for, or definition of, self must negotiate, then, a set of particularly laden and particularly inflexible categories, for instance, *black* and *white*, *male* and *female*, terms rigorously ordered to their own 'group areas', their 'proper place', and held there by the concept of 'own affairs'.

Feminism and Black Consciousness have each felt the need, then, for a community which will not continually make them 'other', with all the negativities that term implies, and which will let them speak in the absence of the constraining and degrading hand of patriarchy, in the one situation, or of white domination, in the other. Thus we find Gcina Mhlope, short story writer, poet and dramatist, speaking of the need for women to speak to women and thereby create a world where they can write 'what they feel' and not what they have to pretend to feel 'when there's a man around' (Sigwili, 1980: 44).

In her preface to Kuzwayo's book, Nadine Gordimer acclaims the author for managing to 'define herself anew', not as a Westernized African woman but as an African woman who has 'Africanized the Western concept of woman and in herself achieved a synthesis'. Kuzwayo has thus attained 'wholeness' (Kuzwayo, 1985: xi). Kuzwayo does indeed make a significant adjustment and contribution to the Western concept of woman, which is why so many women, myself included, have responded with such pleasure to her text. However, the accolades of 'synthesis' and 'wholeness' not only give to her voice a stability and coherence that it does not, and cannot, have, but they also close, rather than open to scrutiny, the topic of women in contemporary South Africa and hence, of course, the topic of patriarchal domination. Much of the value of Kuzwayo's text, it seems to me, lies in the questions it poses about women: the nature of women, the status of women, the power of women, and the voices of women. It is these issues I wish to focus on, then, in the context of Black Consciousness.

Women and Black Consciousness

Any parallel drawn here between feminist separatism and Black Consciousness does not, of course, bring these two ideological positions politically closer: even within the contexts of separatism and solidarity, the terms 'black' and 'feminist' are kept apart rather than joined in a process of identification. In Kuzwayo's text, then, insofar as it is interested in both feminism and Black Consciousness, certain difficulties inevitably arise in the narrator's presentation of her female self.

Black Consciousness, which began to be articulated in South Africa from the late sixties, emerged as a coherent ideological, political and cultural perspective by the seventies. Black Consciousness is marked, above all, by the goal of reconstructing the self in terms offered by the black rather than the white community: the search for a social world as a matrix for self-definition takes the subject to a self-constituting black world, and a set of corresponding shifts get made as the concept 'black' itself is refined in order to slough off any negative attributes it may have carried. Thus Black Consciousness writers begin to make a point of characterizing the white world as individualistic, whereas the black world is characterized by means of the philosophy of *ubuntu*. Mongane Serote's novel, *To Every Birth its Blood* (1981), clearly marks the shift from 'individualistic' I to 'communal' I, as the prevailing philosophical position makes its return to the world of African communalism, signified by the well-known and widely-quoted African proverb: 'a person is a person because of and through other people.'[2]

While some writers have asserted this philosophical position to have realistic roots in African social life, others have recognized it only as a cultural ideal. Ellen Kuzwayo takes the second line:

> I have no intention of creating an impression that black people are in any way special; in terms of their attitudes of interaction with other groups; of their regard for sharing with others, be it knowledge, land or wealth; of their concern with their neighbours in times of common need and serious crisis. However, I am convinced that the impact of the philosophy of 'ubuntu' has played a major role in helping individuals, groups and communities of the black people of South Africa to still emerge with dignity, integrity, self-respect and determination in their relationship with others. (Kuzwayo, 1988: 133)

However, a closer look at Black Consciousness reminds one that any hospitality offered to women by its philosophy of *ubuntu* depends altogether on a particular definition of womanhood.

The personal pronoun which has predominated in the public statements of Black Consciousness is masculine. Only where the plural becomes logically necessary, that is, where the group or community needs to be named as such, is the third-person masculine amended. In the SASO Policy Manifesto (July 1971), Black Consciousness is defined as follows:

> (i) Black Consciousness is an attitude of mind, a way of life.
> (ii) The basic tenet of Black Consciousness is that the Black *man* must reject all value systems that seek to make *him* a foreigner in the country of *his* birth and reduce *his* basic human dignity.
> (iii) The black *man* must build up *his* own value systems, see *himself* as self-defined and not defined by others.
> (iv) The concept of Black Consciousness implies the awareness by the black *people* of the power *they* wield *as a group*, both economically and politically, and hence group cohesion and solidarity are important facets of Black Consciousness. (Khoapa, 1973: 42; emphasis added)

In the introduction to *Black Review 1972* the writer forecasts that two major trends will dominate the 1970s. The first has to do with 'the black man' engaging the problems of his community instead of 'trying for white' and depending on whites to help, and the second

– which is the one of interest here – concerns the way that black history will be written:

> 2. More important *he* will continue to address *his* black brother and sister because the events and the rich heritage that are their history have not been made fully available to them in the usual way in which a society informs its membership about the significant aspects of its development. (Khoapa, 1973: 1; emphasis added)

Quite clearly, the voice that speaks is envisaged as male, even if women – 'and sister' – are included in the community as those whose solidarity must be courted. At a rhetorical level, then, the emphasis on black experience and black perspective continually eclipses the female. And if women as a group are specifically referred to, it is in a way which reproduces them as voiceless.

By 1974, with the enormous growth in Black Community Programmes, a Women's Division had been established, dedicated entirely to 'women's work', which included 'spheres such as nutrition, child care, basic skills such as knitting, sewing, crocheting, cookery and gardening' (Mbanjwa, 1975: 121). Women were being defined, and/or were dutifully defining themselves, as domestic. The manifesto of the Black Women's Federation, formed in 1975, speaks of the desire to encourage and co-ordinate the efforts of black women and 'to present a united front' (presumably only among black women), and firmly recognizes 'that Black women are basically responsible for the survival and maintenance of their families and largely the socialization of the youth for the transmission of the Black Cultural Heritage' (Rambally, 1977: 109).

Any departure from the primary role of mother is tentatively expressed, so as not to disturb the concept of motherhood. In the Federation's statement comes the expression of a need 'to redirect the status of motherhood towards the fulfilment of the Black people's social, cultural, economic and political aspirations' (Rambally, 1977: 109). If women's duties are to fulfil the aspirations of 'the people', how should they do it? Besides passing on a particular cultural tradition, which they are positioned to do as mothers and child-rearers, they are allotted other duties too. Chabani Manganyi, whose *Being-Black-In-The-World* (1973) is one of the major texts of Black Consciousness, has spoken of the dehumanization suffered by black male South Africans in the following terms:

> In the life experience of the African, there is hardly any situation in his life in which his sense of self-esteem is nourished. His wife and children may have been forced by conditions beyond his control to

lose the modicum of respect which they had had for him as an effective, self-steering agent in his psychosocial environment. If we were
to formulate his psychic status in a phenomenological way, we could
say that his subjective experience is one of feeling emasculated. There
are other more positive sides to this picture such as the Africans' will
to survive. (1973: 10-11)

From this context of dehumanization, discouragement and demas-
culinization comes a plea to women on behalf of men. Recalling the
treatment he received as a South African classified 'coloured', Vernon February has said: 'Outside the family one could be de-
humanized and degraded even by the smallest white child. In this
situation the woman played an important part by re-encouraging
the man.' (79) If black males – universalized by Manganyi into 'the
African' – have been symbolically castrated by white patriarchal
government, women – excluded from the category 'African' – must
(instead of humiliating men further) restore to them their masculinity. This is a widespread view. Miriam Tlali's *Muriel at Metropolitan* distinguishes between the behaviour of the white clerks and
Muriel, who cannot bring herself to accept the messenger's offer
to get her something from the shops: 'How could I? He was a man
and I was a woman. According to our custom a woman does not
send a man. We reserve a place, an elevated place, for our men.'
(1975: 21)

Turning to feminism, then, we must ask whether it does not continue the act of castration perpetrated by the white world. Given
the virtual absence among black women of what Olive Schreiner
called 'parasitism' (see her *Woman and Labour* (1911)) – black wom-
en do not generally live the relatively dependent and pampered lives
of many white women in this country – the terms 'female' and
'feminine' have to adjust their meanings when they are applied to
black women as a group. Es'kia Mphahlele has said, 'When I think
of strong people, I don't think of men, I always think of women'
(Manganyi, 1981: 11). Of course, the idea of the strong mother occurs in British and American literature as well, but it has greater
currency here, and – more important – is nowhere contradicted.
Referring to the difference between North American and African
feminists at a gathering she attended, Miriam Tlali suggests that African women know their own power whereas North American wom-
en focus on their powerlessness. It is precisely because of their fearful
recognition of maternal power, she says, that African men try to
assert their own power over women:

> Everybody has had a mother and every man does not think his mother
> is something which can be overlooked. What makes them later try

to get out of that hold that their mother has over them, the power, the overwhelming power that the mother has over her offspring? (1989: 74)

The figure of the mother, then, signifies both the woman from whom the male separates in order to define himself as masculine, and the woman whom the male possesses in order to define himself as masculine. In Miriam Tlali's *Amandla*, Pholoso says to his girlfriend, Felleng:

> I *am* part of you already, Felleng. If you drank me and kept me inside you, then I would stop *coming* to you, and that alone would destroy me. I have to keep coming to you . . . You are like a prize. I must *fight* to get you. You are like a whole package of . . . of . . . what shall I say? A package . . . of sweetness . . . of bliss. And to think that you are all mine . . . You are Mother Africa – and how I love you! (1980: 71)

Separation and return: these are the movements through which the male subject defines himself. The return, here, is the return of possession: the body of the mother will give birth to all that is his: 'And to think that you are all mine . . . You are Mother Africa – and how I love you!' The idealization of motherhood is a crucial part, then, of the male's masculinity, and the strength of women is the strength of motherhood.

Even alongside her recognition that women must look to the community of women for self-definition, Gcina Mhlope says: 'Men can be physically strong, but our strength as women is our motherhood; men are always women's children. And their manhood doesn't show if women aren't there.' (Sigwili, 1980: 44) It is precisely to this assertion – the strength of motherhood – that women writers are currently addressing themselves, and it is only by passing through this assertion, it seems, that the possibilities for an African feminism begin to emerge. It is, at any rate, from this position that Ellen Kuzwayo speaks.

Call Me Woman

Given her occasionally scornful comments about men, Kuzwayo's focus on motherhood seems to be motivated less by the cultural imperative – voiced by such figures as Chabani Manganyi and Vernon February – to bolster the image of the father or husband, than by a feminist desire to insist upon the presence of the female self as a strong, courageous and resourceful mother on behalf of the children, whose image has been so radically reconstructed by Soweto, 1976. What Kuzwayo does *in* her text, then, is what Noni Jabavu could only do, and then hesitantly, in the 1982 Preface to her 1963 book: Kuzwayo constructs, for this new generation, the figure of the powerful and active mother, who now comes to be the Mother of Black Consciousness. (Kuzwayo is in fact widely known as 'the mother of Soweto' (Lipman, 1984: 18).) Whereas a writer like Miriam Tlali tends to bolster the image of masculinity, and to reiterate the need for women to stay at home minding the babies and tending the garden while men go out to fight for change, Kuzwayo more or less ignores the figure of masculinity, and gives to motherhood not just the spiritual power of immanent being, but an intelligent, active and angry political role. Whereas Maria Tholo made uneasy and contradictory adjustments to the authority of the children, Kuzwayo recognizes their stature, but then also insists on taking back her maternal authority, and even on occasions seeming to become the source of the children's power. The strategy is a fascinating one.

Barbara Johnson has suggested that those labelled 'black woman' threaten to disappear in a double self-division, being compelled to position themselves either as 'black', in which case they disappear as 'woman', or as 'woman', in which case they disappear as 'black'. Perhaps it is for this reason that Lauretta Ngcobo, in an introduction to an anthology of black women writers, finds it necessary to construct a new category called 'Blackwomen' (1987: 1 ff). Interestingly, Ngcobo's earlier statements about her own writing – *Cross of Gold* (1981) – foreground her inability to write about women in the way she had originally wanted to. In an interview after publishing the novel, Ngcobo said: 'I want to write about women. But I find it difficult to speak about the African woman . . . When I started the novel I wanted to write about my life, or in any case about the life of a woman . . . But whenever I began to write [she] would die on me. Then I let her die and continued my book.' (Vivan, 1984) Kuzwayo's autobiography, at its best, opens up a different space to women. What this space is, and how it does so, is the topic I now turn to.

In her autobiography Ellen Kuzwayo sometimes gives the impression that she feels it is in her interest to smooth over any contradictions between Black Consciousness and the consciousness of herself as woman. Kuzwayo's position in Black Consciousness and her anti-white statements proclaim her as black. Yet the title of her autobiography is a statement of feminist assertion; that the term 'woman' is used rather than 'mother' suggests that some space is being claimed for the voices of women beyond the careful definitions of the mother in the discourse of Black Consciousness. This feminist assertion is periodically adjusted in the text by references to the orthodox positions of mothers and wives within patriarchy. Yet, again, if one looks past these nervous adjustments to the way that Kuzwayo asserts 'motherhood' in the action of her text, where in the person of mother she disobeys a number of patriarchal strictures, one will see emerging, out of Johnson's self-collapsing self-divisions, the figure of a 'new' black woman: both mother and writer, and then (recalling Ngcobo's new category) the figure of 'Blackwoman', who speaks herself as both woman and black.

Conventionally, the figure of the mother spells silence. The mother, socially constituted as the place of nature within culture, as the matrix out of which the child's subjectivity is developed, and as the object of the other's desire, assumes a marginal position in culture, perpetually alienated from her own subjectivity. Rebecca Matlou speaks about the contradictions for black South African women between 'fighting, being mothers and writing' (1987: 79). Kuzwayo, on the other hand, begins to position herself as the mother who not only does not need to reject motherhood in order to voice her own subjectivity but who also insists on speaking from the position of motherhood, and whose motherhood has left its conventional bounds of the private and domestic. In order to win this position for herself, several different adjustments have to occur to her sense of self under the patriarchalism of Black Consciousness. They are adjustments made with considerable difficulty and contradiction.

In Kuzwayo's text marriage and motherhood are often referred to in terms that posit them as woman's natural and only destiny. Speaking of a schoolfriend whose future had seemed bright, Kuzwayo notes without any suggestion of disappointment that she 'got married and had two children' (1985: 94). At other times she lists marriages as, in themselves, achievements by women (see, for example, 94), all the more so when the women marry prestigious men. Even when she describes a woman who breaks the stereotypes of domestic femininity, such as Mrs Magdeline Sesedi, who was both in the forefront of political life and a director of a business company, she capitulates to these stereotypes by calling her 'a perfect model of womanhood, full of charm, beauty and dignity' (1985: 103), her epithets all too evocative of those used by Jabavu in *The Ochre People*. Kuzwayo calls up a cultural world where the terms 'woman' and 'mother' are used interchangeably, referring to 'the custom of my nation where every mother is every child's mother' (1985: 217), and eclipsing from view women who have not, for one reason or another, had children. 'I still wish to know what happened to such old mothers', she says of some women whose employers had not made provision for them in their old age (1985: 22); and, speaking about women potters, she says, 'The mothers took great pains to produce the best pots' (1985: 128).

If, then, it is part of Kuzwayo's project to give to black South African women a value all too easily denied them by contemporary society, this value often remains domestic. In a comparable way she regards it as crucial to appreciate aspects of black culture precisely because it has been undervalued and misunderstood: the extended family, for instance, is 'a pillar of strength to black people', however much 'other racial groups may deride [it] as being backward and outdated' (1985: 99). Such tendencies in her narrative perfectly accord with the tenets of Black Consciousness, and respond in important ways to the psychological needs of a nation which has been systematically victimized and belittled. 'Woman', for Kuzwayo, becomes one of the cultural terms which must, like the extended family, be re-evaluated as part of the national process.

Yet in certain ways Kuzwayo's attitudes to marriage and motherhood, and to the extended family, contradict the official line promoted by Black Consciousness and reproduced in her text. Indeed, her allegiance to this line sometimes takes on the status of a 'cover story', so familiar a strategy in women's fiction (Gilbert and Gubar, 1979: 146ff). Beneath the 'cover' of an orthodox appreciation of community work, Kuzwayo draws attention to the scope it gives to women like Sibusisiwe Makhanya to look after themselves 'away from their parents and free from dependency on a man' (1985: 90). Beneath the 'cover' of an orthodox presentation of the primacy of students' (the community's) needs, Kuzwayo acknowledges the 'great courage' of a woman who had to disobey the authority of her husband in order to fulfil community needs. Her example is Winnie Monyatsi, who married William Kgware, Rector of the University of the North, and sacrificed, says Kuzwayo, the 'security and peace of her own home' by engaging in student affairs apparently despite the wishes of her husband (1985: 99).

Such statements are not foregrounded or expanded. But the tensions exist. When Kuzwayo talks about her younger sister's marriage, for example, she negotiates with great difficulty her attitudes to women and marriage, women and patriarchy:

> I was upset to see Maria getting married at a young age. This was my beloved younger sister and the groom was Thari Pilane, son of Chief Ofentse Tlhabane Pilane of Saulspoort in the western Trans-

vaal. But the thought that Maria had not gone far with her education troubled me. I found it difficult to prevail on her to continue her studies since, as a married woman, she would have many additional responsibilities. In addition, they were to live in Saulspoort, miles away from the nearest town. I also realised that there were many restrictions and taboos she would be compelled to adhere to in her new role as wife of the chief's son who was next in line to take his father's office. However, her husband's education had liberated him from some of the most restrictive taboos and practices. For that I was very grateful. I finally resigned myself to the inevitable, but made a secret pact with myself: that I would keep in contact with my sister as much as possible and to the best of my ability. (1985: 116-117)

Kuzwayo's distress at her younger sister's marriage is negated by the prestigiousness of the match. Her pride is in turn negated by the realization that Maria had not gone far enough in her studies. Moreover, Maria's position in this rural community as wife of a chief would involve obedience to a set of restrictive practices, a point which further qualifies the prestige referred to earlier. Kuzwayo's anxiety is itself modified by the recognition that Maria's husband's education had liberated him from at least some of the 'most restrictive taboos and practices'. The skein of assertion and doubt created by Kuzwayo's words, which turn back and forth at 'But' and 'However', seems finally to settle into resignation 'to the inevitable', a resignation itself denied by the 'secret pact' she made with herself: to 'keep in contact with my sister as much as possible and to the best of my ability'.

Kuzwayo's own initial experience of marriage was not a happy one, and, for herself, fulfilment has not been measured in terms of marriage and motherhood. In another, even more interesting instance, the personal and individual experience of a woman is seen to interact with patriarchy's official story, contradicting and unsettling it.

Kuzwayo's personal story – and the story that provides much of the momentum of *Call Me Woman* – is one of homelessness: 'the trauma of a sudden severance from my roots and those I had known as parents and relatives' and 'the uncertainty about any place I could call home without hesitation for fear of being rejected' (1985: 122). Throughout the text she longs for the security of home and family repeatedly stripped from her, both in the days of her childhood and into her young adulthood. Whatever her text says about the value and stability of the extended family, her own experience stands in such denial as to give to her statements about the extended family the status of desire rather than of historical truth. It is this, above all, that interrogates the reality of communal life evoked by Black Consciousness.

When she speaks of rural communities (reminders of her childhood home) she draws attention to 'the unwritten common code of ethics, which is respected as the basis on which that community operates in its day-to-day activities' and 'the stability, tranquillity and security which permeated these villages before the introduction and enforcement of the relocation legislation' (1985: 89). Against this kind of eulogy, and the more specific presentation of the extended family to which she belonged as a child (1985: 65), she notes the periodic discrimination against her within that family. Her father's clan name differed from that of her siblings and cousins (her father and mother had divorced when she was a baby): 'sometimes I was clearly the odd one out. One of my cousins would count her sisters and brother . . . "One, two, three Setlogelos" . . . and would go on to count the Makgothi adults. When it came to me, however, I was alone. I was "one Merafe". They would laugh, leaving me alone staring into empty space, with no defence or explanation.' (1985: 65)

Now, in terms of Kuzwayo's text, there are two, closely related solutions to the anguish of homelessness suffered by the individual. The extended family on its own clearly has not offered a solution; indeed, in its very extension – with the entry of step-mothers, cousins and so on – it poses its own particular problems of disharmony. However, when Kuzwayo harks back to the extended family of her childhood, she claims that it was the generalized figure of the mother – the idea of the mother – that held the extended family together. 'It is amazing that despite differences of kinship within the family, none of those grandchildren born of Jeremiah's [her grandfather's] daughters addressed their own mothers' sisters as Aunt – we all called both our mothers and aunts "Mma" meaning "Mother", and this is how all Blanche's sisters' children address her to this day when they speak to her directly, myself included' (1985: 65). Significantly, the Merafe-Setlogelo/Makgothi split referred to earlier is healed by the invoked presence of the mother: 'But in a split-second the initiator of the unpleasant division would turn to me and shower me with love and kindness, saying, "Ngoanyana oa go Mme Mmutsi, eo montlenyane, tlo re tshameke" (Lovely little girl of Mama Mmutsi, come let us play). Somehow the feelings of unpleasantness and shock would vanish in me as fast as they had come.' (1985: 65)

Of course, as the reference to Blanche in the paragraph above reminds us, the ideal of harmony and embrace embodied within the term *mother* buckles under the pressure of social reality as Kuzwayo proceeds further with the narrative of her own extended family, for it is Blanche who has thrown her out of Thaba'Nchu. Her aunt Blanche, her mother's younger sister, married her step-father some time after the death of his wife. To Kuzwayo as child, the step-father had always seemed to be part of their family, so his formal entry into it through the marriage to her mother had caused no disruption of familial harmony. In relation to his second marriage, that is, his marriage to her aunt, Kuzwayo says: 'The change was smooth because, as young children, all grandfather's grandchildren had been taught to address all three sisters as "Mother"' (1985: 104). Yet, in due course, this relation becomes one of antagonism, for her new mother turns against her – 'I don't want to see the sight of you any more here' (1985: 105) – and she is turned out of her family and home.

Kuzwayo speaks of the way she was driven from home by her step-mother in the strongest possible terms:

> While I remained in Thaba'Nchu, I lost all sense of personal direction and identity. I felt so rejected by the people and surroundings I had once cherished as part of my very being. I was in a state of shock but had no one to share my hurt and shock with. Relatives and family friends who called at the homestead no longer seemed the same loving adults I knew. I began to see them in a new light. I gradually became suspicious of everyone around me and feared to share my feelings with them in any way. In short, I became paranoid. (1985: 107)

The concept of an all-embracing mother, otherwise elevated in Kuzwayo's text, is at this point interrogated, for the term becomes applied to Aunt Blanche ironically. 'I am sorry about this,' her step-father says. 'Your "Mother" wants it this way' (1985: 105). The author's quotation marks signal a decisive break in the relation between ideal and real. Even Mama Nnyelele, an old family friend also graced by the title of 'mother', 'was party to the whole plot', although Kuzwayo had looked to her for 'support or protection' (1985: 105).

Banished from Thaba'Nchu, she goes to the home of her father, on a journey which takes a day and a night, and is without external incident, yet whose telling is relatively prolonged: loss of family and home, with their attendant anguish and yearning, are an important part of the text's narrative focus. Then, in Pimville, she discovers that 'natural' father and 'natural' daughter lack, 'to a very large extent', the love that should 'naturally' occur; moreover, her relations with her other step-mother are strained. Again, Kuzwayo leaves.

She is not turned out, yet notes that she prepared her own provisions for her journey, as if this signals absence of care, and notes too that her send-off was, merely, 'reasonably warm and pleasant' (1985: 115).

As in the family drama which Jabavu depicts, through the eyes of the daughter returning to a patriarchal home, the behaviour of the father's second wife disrupts the family unit. The causes seem to be very different, but the personal and social costs are comparable, for the particular familial loss lets in a greater loss: loss of one's wider community, isolation of self from one's self-constructing 'other', rejection 'by the people and surroundings I had once cherished as part of my very being' (Kuzwayo, 1985: 107). Surely it is not by accident that the word 'split', though in some disguise, enters Kuzwayo's narrative at both those moments where she is talking about rupture from her childhood home. As regards the first episode she says: 'But in a split-second the initiator of the unpleasant division would turn to me and shower me with love and kindness' (1985: 65). As regards the second episode, the expulsion by Aunt Blanche, she says: 'Truth can be stranger than fiction in life sometimes. For a split second, I thought I was dreaming.' (1985: 105)

Dream and reality are turned upside-down. Kuzwayo puts them back the way she needs to, which means, to flip the terms back and forth across the 'split' that runs through their two contexts, the 'fiction' of all-embracing 'love and kindness' covers over the 'truth' of 'unpleasant division'. Kuzwayo needs to create family and home, and *Call Me Woman* is the story of that creation.

That there *is* the element of the fictive in Kuzwayo's project is clear enough to her when she speaks elsewhere – as quoted earlier – about the philosophy of *ubuntu*. Kuzwayo's autobiography also plays its part in the formation of *ubuntu*, largely by invoking the presence of the mother. And therefore, I suggest, when she calls upon traditional values which have been lost through the social disintegration consequent upon colonization and apartheid ideology, it is the mother, above all, who is in danger of being lost.

Kuzwayo argues that some of the sexist attitudes and behaviour handed down through the black cultural tradition would have changed with time had the white government not enforced them. In an interview published in 1984 she cites an incident where her elder son, approached by government authorities for permission for her to go overseas, said to her: 'If only people would realise that this home is where it is, we are where we are, because of you', as if demonstrating the adaptation her son and his generation have or might have made, if they had not been continually drawn back to the stasis of the past by the ethnocentric thinking involved in 'separate development' (Lipman, 1984: 19).

Again, the dynamic is one of exhortation or desire rather than mimesis, as in Kuzwayo's construction of *ubuntu*. And again, the text reveals moments of visible tension. When Kuzwayo speaks about the *timiti* sessions in the townships and the *famo* dances where women dance wildly into the night, she at first focusses on the particular way women are treated by men on such occasions: punished and insulted for transgressing the norms set out by patriarchy. Kuzwayo implies that this patriarchal response denies women's desperate efforts to fulfil their ascribed roles as dutiful mothers, for they are simply making money where they can in order to feed their children. Here, as elsewhere, the text is marked by a compassionate understanding of the lives of women in a profoundly difficult social context. However, despite the story told by male insult and the use of the sjambok, Kuzwayo finds it necessary not to dwell on the topic of black patriarchal oppression of women. The social context in which she places the *famo* dances is characterized, above all, by 'white legislation and control' (31), which force the women out of their rural homes into the cities, from one poverty into another. In this way the world of white oppression shifts into focus, and the complexity of a world in which women, as *famo* dancers, are both desired and punished by lovers/husbands/owners remains unexplored.

On another occasion, too, Kuzwayo elides male oppression of women into the oppression of women by the white patriarchal state, as if, again, only the second were an issue. She says: 'These women, these daughters, and their daughters' daughters have defied the cultural myth that black women are inferior to men and women of other racial groups' (1985: 241–242). The phrase 'and women of other racial groups' casts back to qualify men, who thus become white men and not black men at all. The reluctance to confront black men in feminist terms becomes all the more marked in the presence of statements made in the interview cited above. After saying that black men have done everything they can to 'stifle', 'blot . . . out', and 'thwart' the actual and potential contributions of women, she says, 'and the government has gone further: it has capitalised, in the legislation of this country, on the traditions and customs which all communities have had' (Lipman, 1984: 19), thus drawing attention both to the *prior* patriarchalism of black South African life and to the government's insistence that these traditions and customs be preserved. Black South Africans would otherwise have been ready to make the necessary adjustments to these traditions and customs:

'People have gone on, adapting their way of life to the life that is suitable now, for today . . . but the things retarding the progress of the black woman have been highlighted' (Lipman, 1984: 19).

In Bessie Head's fiction, and notably in *The Collector of Treasures*, there is a comparable contradiction between the yearning for an old (patriarchal) order and the recognition that patriarchy, which Head sees as having given a circumscribed space to women, breeds sexist abuse. Head castigates men for their irresponsibility and their maltreatment of women, characteristics which have flourished under the disruption of traditional life, and her solution to anti-female patriarchal tendencies is to correct or 'feminize' patriarchy (to use the terms used by feminist criticism of the 1970s). The new African community becomes one marked by gentle, loving, responsible men, with the standard gendered role divisions otherwise unchanged. This is the direction posited by the story 'Hunting' and the title story of the collection called *The Collector of Treasures*, for instance. In Kuzwayo's *Call Me Woman*, on the other hand, any contradiction between desire for and fear of a stable patriarchal order takes a different direction, for Kuzwayo's disruption of social stereotypes would issue in what one would call a 'masculinized' woman (to speak in terms of the masculine/feminine categories referred to above). Two textual moments, one at the beginning and the other at the end of the text, provide the necessary illustration.

Kuzwayo's autobiography opens with a letter written by Debra Matshoba, in detention in 1978 under Section 10 of the so-called Terrorism Act. Having already spent a period in detention under Section 6, and obviously having no idea how long her detention would last, Matshoba jokes in her letter about asking the Minister of Justice for 'conception leave'. 'Conception leave' is the term used by migrant workers for the few weeks spent at home each year. The detained woman thus jokingly positions herself as migrant worker, whose role as father and husband is disrupted by the combination of migrant labour, pass laws and the Group Areas Act. Thus, at the outset of the text, one's attention is drawn to the fact that, whatever gendered role divisions perforce exist in South African life, there are a number of women who cross over into the realm of the conventionally 'masculine'.

At the end of the autobiography Kuzwayo describes an occasion where she appeared as expert witness for the defence during the trial of eleven students under the 'Terrorism' Act. She spent two hours in the witness box. Here she performed in such a way as to make one of the fathers of the accused come to her, in court, and say, 'You are not an ordinary woman, you pleaded like a man, only a man could speak the way you did' (1985: 227). High praise indeed! Kuzwayo is touched and gratified, as if she has broken out of the stereotype of the feminine imposed on her by an African patriarchy. Yet she seems, at least unconsciously, to find something immobilizing in the man's praise, for – though the words recognize the way one woman is as good as a man – they nevertheless continue to fix women in the terms ordained by a patriarchal or phallocratic symbolic (see, for example, Cixous, 1981: 90ff; Irigaray, 1985: 13-129), where the only options given are masculine and feminine, where one is either a feminine man or a masculine woman. Kuzwayo says: 'I sat huddled in my seat as if nailed to it' (1985: 227).

Gordimer notes in her preface that Kuzwayo's text offers us an assertion of *woman* in terms other than those handed down through Western systems of thought and reproduced in the various forms of writing and speaking that make up South African culture, black and white. What Gordimer is probably alluding to is Kuzwayo's celebration of politically mobilized women, one which certainly expands the conventional role of mother. At a more complex level, however, *Call Me Woman* goes beyond defining women as the new and politically active mothers. In certain ways, it starts to open up a new space – a space where contradictions flourish, and the terms 'masculinity' and 'femininity' are tumbled about in disorder – and says of this space: *this* is woman.

One particular moment in the text illustrates the opening up of this complex space. This is the occasion when Kuzwayo is staying in Pimville with her father and his family, where she is drawn to comment on the attitudes to women that emerge during the *famo* dances:

> It is said to be a most ungodly, wild type of dance, where women dress in such a way that, as they dance and spin, their dresses fly up, leaving them exposed from the waist downwards. The behaviour between males and females, from hearsay, leaves much to be desired during such sessions. My own experience involved spending sleepless nights from the noise of the *timiti* sessions . . .
>
> It was a common occurrence to hear a woman's shriek in the middle of the night, pleading for help, whilst the sound of either a stick or *sjambok* (a rhinocerous-hide whip [sic]) rhythmically landed on her body. Then a male voice would hurl insults at the punished woman . . . This was one of the most disturbing and frustrating features of township life in the 1940s and 1950s: the *timiti*, an event which was both an entertainment and a living for many women of the community, compelled to participate for their survival. There is no doubt that on their return to their rural homes, such women found themselves misfits and out of place where they were once cherished and

> loved; but it is equally true to say that they coped as best they could
> in a very challenging situation in an effort to care for themselves and
> their families. (1985: 30-31)

Instead of reproducing the tensions between 'black' and 'woman',
and 'masculine' and 'feminine', reproduced elsewhere in the text,
this passage speaks of a variety of self-divisions. Above all, it reminds us of the multiple positions inhabited by black South African women as they speak to and within 'other' worlds. To take one
example of the developing complexity here: in this extract the relatively well-known term *sjambok* is glossed for an outside audience,
but *famo* and *timiti* remain in the vernacular. Within an English-
language text, and within a text that, the author has said, was intended for British consumption, the use of the vernacular gives voice
to an otherness that the narrator comfortably inhabits and does not
open to the outside. (In *The Ochre People*, by contrast, Jabavu's medi-
ating translations proclaim her audience as British, pulling against
the desire constantly expressed through the experiencing self to rein-
habit a Xhosa world.)

In the light of this moment of otherness, Kuzwayo again reaches
over to speak from the position of 'other'. As an educated, Christian woman of a certain class, she stands outside the activity of the
famo dance. The dance proclaims her as its 'other': 'the rigid class
distinctions of those days would have stopped me even from peep-
ing' (1985: 30). And yet she has access, if she wants it, even to the
extent that at a conscious level she must deny it. 'I never saw it',
she says, but describes it for our eyes. She knows about the behaviour 'from hearsay', which seems to keep her detached, but she
then represents 'hearsay' in a moment of apparent subjectivity and
immediacy through reference to the 'noise' of music, dancing and
sexuality that gave her sleepless nights. The woman's shriek, the
rhythmic sjambok, the male insults, the woman weeping: these are
the sounds which draw her into the scene, however much it is pro-
hibited to women of her class, and which draw her in, too, to the
imagined male and female positions. Given that other passage in
Call Me Woman where the young Ellen breaks free of her mother's
constraining hand and goes to watch young girls during an initiation ceremony, one's attention is caught in this passage by the reference to desire. Yet here the concept takes on an added complexity.
So 'much' is 'desired' in these *timiti* sessions that the nights become
'sleepless' for the restless listener. This obliquely articulated and in-
choate desire acts, it seems, as the bridge between Kuzwayo's
proclaimed self as educated woman of a certain class and her for-

bidden other, an other who remains shadowy, beyond her grasp, dangerous in many ways, for it is an other who travels a route between desire and punishment, and between the sexual bondage of the sjambokked woman and the apparent sexual freedom of the 'ungodly' *famo* dance, which is itself a sexual bondage, since women, says Kuzwayo, are 'compelled to participate [in it] for their survival' (1985: 31).

Authenticity of voice has sometimes been explained in terms of a unified self. However, as Barbara Johnson has said, a recognition of self-division is the sign of any authentic voice (1984: 212). Wholeness of identity is an illusion, and however strongly narrative itself desires wholeness, self-division is 'healed over' only at the cost of loss of the other. Johnson explains her claim regarding authentic voice through the example of black male writers in America. Speaking as a black male under white political domination, one may speak both from the position of the 'other' – acknowledging what Manganyi calls the existential facts of blackness – and from the assertion of the 'self', the other's other, which subverts the negativities of blackness. Double-voicedness, for the black male under white political domination, becomes a sign, then, of recognition of self, the kind of recognition that permits one to speak, as far as one is ever able, in one's own voice, or, to use Johnson's phrase, 'to assume and articulate the incompatible forces involved in [one's] own division' (1984: 212).

In the case of a male, whether black or white, constructed in the general terms offered by a patriarchal symbolic (aggressivity, personal success, power, independence from the constraints of 'apron strings') a degree of what may be called, variously, individualism, ambition, or a desire to make one's mark on the world, seems to be permitted. For the black woman, on the other hand, the call of *ubuntu* has placed a constraining hand on the development of aspects of self that cannot be justified by their link with the idea of family. For the black woman, the dominating and oppositional 'other' is doubled: white people on the one hand, and black and white men on the other. Moreover, if the black female subject can emerge from the double silence imposed upon her as cultural subject (as black, as female), the position from which she speaks (as black, as female) has still to be defined. To repeat, Johnson argues that this definition depends on a recognition and articulation of the incompatible forces involved in one's self-division. Kuzwayo's negotiation of these self-defining forces is, I suggest, often incomplete, for much of the time the black female self, as it has been defined in terms of Black Consciousness, still needs – in obedience to the demands of Black

Consciousness ideology – to dominate and repress the black female self that sees itself in opposition to patriarchal strictures. At other times Kuzwayo gives to these self-defining forces a considerably fuller voice, and it is in such moments that she starts to break down the categories imposed by a culture whose survival depends on the maintenance of rigid and artificial opposites, and to speak of the 'multiple displacements' which constitute the 'insouciant shiftings' available in the act of writing (Jacobus, 1986: 24).

As I noted earlier, the autobiography includes in its title the term 'woman' rather than 'mother', and thus opens up a space, although it is only occasionally exploited by Kuzwayo, between 'mother' and 'woman'. This is the space which Gcina Mhlope takes up.

Gcina Mhlope

By recognizing and starting to speak across the various self-divisions through which the self is constituted, Kuzwayo has begun to chart a world where the female self may begin to take up a position from which to speak and write without suppressing a substantial part of her experience of the world. In two autobiographical stories written by Gcina Mhlope, a writer far closer in age to the 1976 generation than is Kuzwayo, and thus in a different relation to Black Consciousness, the writer still has to struggle out of a world which divides 'mother' from writer. Before publishing these two stories, Mhlope had already published a story called 'Nokulunga's Wedding' (1983), where she exposes the voice of patriarchy that presides over the oral tradition, and thus exposes the voice of communal orality as a voice which curbs and controls female desire. In later stories Mhlope turns to address the act of writing. In the story called 'The Toilet' (1987), the text defines the autobiographical 'I' as a young urban woman who has no place to live and must stay in the room of her sister, who works as a domestic worker in Johannesburg. Here the narrator must remain invisible and silent for fear of discovery by the white employers. But there is another meaning to her mutedness and invisibility. Her sister feeds her with women's magazines, but then berates her for *reading* them too much: 'What kind of wife will you make if you can't even make baby clothes? . . . I suppose you will marry an educated man like yourself, who won't mind going to bed with a book and an empty stomach.' (1987: 1) The narrator finds a job, in a factory that makes women's clothing, and – to avoid the white employers – has to leave her sister's room at five-thirty each morning before she catches the seven-thirty bus to work. In this space between women's magazines and women's clothing, she finds a place to wait: a public toilet in the park, never locked, never used by anybody else. The toilet is her own: 'the walls were wonderfully close to me – it felt like it was made to fit me alone' (1987: 3). And it becomes a space not just for waiting, but first for daydreaming – about being the actress that the protagonist longed to be (and that Mhlope herself became) – and then for writing. 'Many . . . mornings saw me sitting there writing. Sometimes it did not need to be a poem; I wrote anything that came into my head – in the same way I would have done if I'd had a friend to talk to.' (1987: 7) In a sense the writing itself becomes her friend, the figure before whom she constructs herself, and most significantly becomes something that she 'was hiding' from her sister (1987: 7), even when her writing place shifts from private toilet to public park.

Mhlope's narrative, like the others I have discussed, is about finding a position from which to write, which is to say, about constructing an identity from which to speak, a place from which she may both view herself (as writer) and her sister (she who forbids writing) and from which she may dream of a world which offers, through acting, the assumption of many more roles than a wife who makes baby clothes and does not read too much. Although she presents some kind of 'resolution' at the end of this story (the writer who has found a place), in another story, called 'It's Quiet Now' (1987), she presents the self standing alone at a window, in the middle of the night. She remembers standing at the window earlier that day, watching the street-fighting on the other side of the glass – it is as if she has been there all the time, and as if she exists simply as a mind thinking about the children fighting. There is no apology at the stance of sceptical distance, no anxiety that focus on the individual self will be equated with individualism, no desire to romanticize the idea of community. Nor is there a focus on gender. There is just waiting: a self not marginalized so much as in a position of interrogation, a self not absent so much as marked by the transition at which night slips into day.

Deconstructive feminist criticism sets out to dismantle a system of thought that bases itself on a set of binary oppositions which are then posited as natural rather than socially constructed. In the phallocentric model of sexual difference, which is a model that comes out of and maintains systems of patriarchy, 'masculine' and 'feminine' are posited as polar opposites, with the feminine seen as the inverse or negative of the masculine. In a comparable way the apartheid model posits black and white as distinct categories, with black as the negative of white, a position that becomes reversed in Black

Consciousness. In both models the categories of feminine and black exist as the 'other' of the masculine/white self, functioning primarily to define for that self his/her sense of authority and identity.

But these categories are constructed as opposites, and thereby deny to each 'other' any attributes that slip out of the bounds thus defined. For the writer, as for the critic, these polar opposites tend to involve one in incessant linearity, where one's literary and critical reading of the world, and book, all too easily maintains itself as a reflection of the world of binary opposition. One is buffeted between white and black, masculine and feminine, in the back-and-forth movement of linearity. Black Consciousness denies to women a subjectivity that does not fit in with their assigned roles, and thus excises from them all that is different from what is called their 'femininity'. This difference is not masculinity; indeed, it is a difference that cannot be named in a language which continually offers us sets of opposites in place of a considerably more complex human and metaphysical spectrum. To label all difference in terms of oppositional categories continually preserves, in the desperate conservatism of patriarchal structures, the illusions of identity on which the male subject is based. But difference in fact disrupts these categories, in a radical movement being taken up within feminist criticism as well as in theories of colonial discourse. Two quotations, for example, which posit the system of opposites in slightly different terms:

> This century has shown that in every situation of organized oppression the true antonyms are always the exclusive part versus the inclusive whole − not masculinity versus femininity but either of them versus androgyny, not the past versus the present but either of them versus the timelessness in which the past is the present and the present is the past, not the oppressor versus the oppressed but both of them versus the rationality which turns them into co-victims. (Nandy, 1983: 97)

And:

> [The] crucial theoretical question, which undermines the foundations of traditional thought and whose importance the feminist writings have helped to bring out, pinpoints at the same time the difficulty of the woman's position in today's critical discourse . . . . Her problem is how to break out of this (cultural) imposition . . . *without* taking up the critical and therapeutic positions of reason . . . . The challenge facing the woman today is nothing less than to 're-invent' language, to *re-learn how to speak*: to speak not only against, but outside of the phallogocentric structure, to establish a discourse the status of which

would no longer be defined by the phallacy of masculine meaning. An old saying would thereby be given new life: today more than ever, changing our minds – changing *the* mind – is a woman's prerogative. (Felman, 1975: 10)

The voice of difference is a voice incessantly and constantly at odds with all that would fix it into stasis. The fluctuating positions of the female selves presented by Maria Tholo, Ellen Kuzwayo and Gcina Mhlope are moments which begin to offer us the difference that slips out of the repressiveness of orthodox alignments and takes us into a world beyond the rigid categories passed down to us in different versions of patriarchy. These are voices not usually available to us through the forms of mimetic or polemical literature, which adopts a severe and autocratic eye over reality. Instead, they emerge in what has been called 'literariness', where the writer speaks out of an unconscious at odds with the dictates of officialdom, and where the text, so to speak, 'knows more than it knows' (Jacobus, 1986: 233). Perhaps these are the voices which might start to change the South African mind.

Notes

Parts of this essay, in a very early form, were presented as seminars in the English Department, University of Cape Town, and the Institute of Commonwealth Studies, University of London; I am indebted to friends and colleagues there, and also to David Bunn and Jane Taylor at the University of the Western Cape, for useful discussion. I am also indebted to the University of Cape Town Research Administration for making funds available to the department which allowed me time off from teaching in order to work on this essay.

1. Walker defines 'womanist' at some length. Her definition includes these elements: 'A Black feminist or feminist of colour'; 'A woman who loves other women, sexually and/or nonsexually'; 'Appreciates and prefers women's culture, women's emotional flexibility . . . and women's strengths'. Cecily Lockett's South Africanization of the term erases such obviously feminist tendencies and simply quotes: 'Committed to survival and wholeness of entire people, male *and* female. Not a separatist, except periodically, for health.' (Lockett, 1989: 286)
2. The saying appears in Setswana, *Motho ke motho ka motho yoy mogwe*, Southern Sotho, *Motho ke motho ka motho e mong*, Xhosa, *Umtu nguntu nga banye*, and Zulu, *Umuntu ngu muntu ngo munye*, and has been translated in slightly different ways: 'A person is who he is because of another person', for instance (Kuzwayo, 1988: 133). I use Jabavu's translation here (1963: rpt. 1982: 69).

References

Berold, Robert. 1987. 'My heart camera'. *Upstream*, 5(4), 8-13.

Cixous, Hélène. 1981. 'Sorties'. In Marks, Elaine and Isabelle de Courtivron (eds). *New French Feminisms*. New York: Schocken Books, 90-98.

Derrida, Jacques. 1985. *The Ear of the Other: Otobiography, Transference, Translation: texts and discussions with Jacques Derrida*. Translated by Peggy Kamuf. New York: Schocken Books.

Felman, Shoshana. 1975. 'Women and Madness: the Critical Phallacy'. *Diacritics*, 5(4), 2-10.

Gilbert, Sandra and Susan Gubar. 1979. *The Madwoman in the Attic: the Woman Writer and the Nineteenth-century Literary Imagination*. New Haven and London: Yale University Press.

Head, Bessie. 1977. *The Collector of Treasures*. London: Heinemann.

Irigaray, Luce. 1985. 'The Blind Spot of an Old Dream of Symmetry'. In *Speculum of the Other Woman*. Translated by Gillian C. Gill. Ithaca, N.Y.: Cornell University Press, 11-129.

Jabavu, Noni. 1963. *The Ochre People*, repr. 1982. Johannesburg: Ravan.

Jacobus, Mary, 1986. *Reading Woman: Essays in Feminist Criticism*. London: Methuen.

Johnson, Barbara. 1984. 'Metaphor, Metonymy and Voice in *Their Eyes Were Watching God*'. In Gates, Henry Louis, Jr (ed.). *Black Literature and Literary Theory*. New York and London: Methuen, 205-219.

Khoapa, B.A. (ed.). 1973. *Black Review 1972*. Durban: Black Community Programmes.

Kuzwayo, Ellen. 1985. *Call Me Woman*. Johannesburg: Ravan.

Kuzwayo, Ellen. 1988. 'My Life Is My Neighbours'. *Monitor: The Journal of the Human Rights Trust*. Special issue on human rights in South Africa. 131-133.

Lipman, Beata. 1984. *We Make Freedom: Women in South Africa*. London: Pandora.

Lockett, Cecily. 1989. 'The Fabric of Experience: A Critical Perspective on the Writing of Miriam Tlali'. In Clayton, Cherry (ed.). *Women and Writing in South Africa: A Critical Anthology*. Marshalltown: Heinemann, 275-286.

Manganyi, N. Chabani. 1973. *Being-Black-In-The-World*. Johannesburg: Spro-cas/Ravan.

Manganyi, N. Chabani. 1981. *Looking through the Keyhole: Dissenting Essays on the Black Experience*. Johannesburg: Ravan.

Matlou, Rebecca. 1987. 'The South African Woman Writer: in so far as a separate entity'. In *South African Literature: Liberation and the Art of Writing*. Proceedings of the first conference on South African English literature, 7-9 November 1986, Bad Boll, FDR. Special issue of *Dokumente, texte und tendenzen*, 7, 65-79.

Matshoba, Mtutuzeli. 1979. *Call Me Not a Man*. Johannesburg: Ravan.

Mbanjwa, Thoko (ed.). 1975. *Black Review 1974/75*. Durban: Black Community Programmes.

Mhlope, Gcina. 1983. 'Nokulunga's Wedding'. In Brown, Sue *et al.* (eds). *LIP: from Southern African Women*. Johannesburg: Ravan, 82-86.

Mhlope, Gcina. 1987. 'It's Quiet Now' and 'The Toilet'. In Oosthuizen, Ann (ed.). *Sometimes When It Rains*. London: Pandora, 1-7; 8-9.

Modisane, Bloke. 1963. *Blame Me on History,* repr. 1986. Johannesburg: Ad. Donker.

Nandy, Ashis. 1983. *The Intimate Enemy: Loss and Recovery of Self under Colonialism.* Delhi: Oxford University Press.

Ngcobo, Lauretta. 1981. *Cross of Gold.* London: Longman.

Ngcobo, Lauretta. 1987. 'Introduction'. In *Let It Be Told; Essays by Black Women in Britain.* London: Pluto, 1-34.

Rambally, Asha (ed.). 1977. *Black Review 1975-1976.* Durban: Black Community Programmes.

Sigwili, Nokugcina [i.e. Gcina Mhlope]. 1980. 'Women Writers'. *Staffrider,* 3(1), 44.

Tholo, Maria. 1980. *The Diary of Maria Tholo.* Carol Hermer (ed.). Johannesburg: Ravan.

Tlali, Miriam. 1975. *Muriel at Metropolitan.* Johannesburg: Ravan.

Tlali, Miriam. 1980. *Amandla.* Johannesburg: Ravan.

Tlali, Miriam. 1989. 'Miriam Tlali: interviewed by Cecily Lockett, Johannesburg, 4 September 1988'. In MacKenzie, Craig and Cherry Clayton (eds). *Between the Lines: Interviews with Bessie Head, Sheila Roberts, Ellen Kuzwayo, Miriam Tlali.* NELM Interviews Series No. 4. Grahamstown: National English Literary Museum, 69-85.

Vivan, Itala. 1984. 'Lauretta Ngcobo: esilio e romanzo'. Interview. In *Tessere per un mosaico Africano.* Verona: Morelli, 191-204. Unpublished translation by T. Zambonini and W. Assam.

Walker, Alice. 1984. *In Search of Our Mothers' Gardens: Womanist Prose.* London: The Women's Press.

Ideology and the Study of White South African English Poetry

Dirk Klopper

I believe it is the case that our discipline, which not so very long ago seemed so vibrant, so liberatory, so, if I may invoke the dreaded word, relevant, now appears to increasing numbers of our universities' most creative students to be remote, defensive and incapable of providing them with the means to understand and deal with the almost over-whelming pressures their society thrusts upon them.

— *Nick Visser, 'English Studies in Transition'*

The development of literary criticism is making it increasingly difficult to ignore ideology. As a result, the theoretical dimension of criticism is becoming increasingly important, for it is at this level that the con-cealed ideological underpinnings of any given critical approach must be made manifest in order to understand both the approach and its subject better.

— *Michael Green, 'The Manifesto and the Fifth Column'*

1

If we are looking for a critical event to mark the first decisive challenge to the dominance of traditionalist literary criticism in the study of South African English poetry, there is the publication *Poetry South Africa: Selected Papers from Poetry '74.* Peter Wilhelm writes in the Introduction that the UCT conference from which these papers derive 'was a sequel to the 1973 conference of the Afrikaans Ses-tiger writers, and brought into the spotlight divisions of approach and outlook as irreconcilable, and as often bitter, among the Eng-lish poets as among their Afrikaans compatriots' (1976: 9). The selec-tion of papers bears this out: Ridley Beeton and Guy Butler are placed uneasily alongside Tim Couzens and Mike Kirkwood. Yet despite these 'divisions of approach and outlook' many of the papers

are marked by a common concern, in one way or another, with questions of ideology — even if only, as in the case of Douglas Livingstone, to defend poetry against what he terms 'Polit-Lit' (12). Given
the revolutionary political climate in Southern Africa in the 1970s
this preoccupation is hardly surprising. In addition developments
in Marxism, semiology and psychoanalysis were, at the time, providing new methods of enquiry into the relationships between literature, language and society.

For purposes of this study Kirkwood's paper 'The Colonizer: A
Critique of the English South African Culture Theory' is of particular interest. It represents one of the first attempts at introducing into
the study of South African poetry, in a fairly systematic fashion,
insights gained from studies on colonial ideology. In his paper Kirkwood adopts an existentialist-Marxist position and contrasts the false
consciousness and alienation of Eurocentrism (what he terms 'Butlerism') to the radical self-awareness of the 'awakened colonizer'
(127). He concludes his argument by collapsing the division between
'life' and 'art', thereby renouncing the claim to autonomy of the
literary work:

> 'Art for liberation' should indeed be the theme of the colonizer writer,
> in our view: the liberation of the colonized is the liberation of the
> colonizer also. The attempt to realize such a programme in the arts
> will demand, we contend, a self-transcendence in the colonizer writer,
> just as it will in the colonized writer. We stop short of advocating
> the techniques of that transcendence, but we point out that a life-
> technique, as well as an art technique, will be required. (131-132)

Despite the confidence with which Kirkwood announces the advent
of a radical literary critical programme, this was slow to gain momentum. Five years after the UCT conference Isabel Hofmeyr (1979) was
polemizing against the still 'lacklustre' results of critical enquiry into
South African literature:

> Instead of a dynamic critical approach, as one would expect from a
> 'new' discipline, we face a critical malaise. Article after article con-
> spicuously fails to elucidate any meaningful aspect of South African
> literature, past and present. Writers continuously resort to tired and
> hackneyed formulations that should by all rational standards have
> been obsolete years ago. Despite having come under heavy and con-
> certed attack, the phantoms of our peculiar brand of prac. crit. still
> go strong — universality, felt life — a naive empiricism and the use
> of generally shoddy analytical concepts that are incapable of articulat-
> ing their own premises. (39)

As exceptions to the theoretical naivety that characterizes traditionalist studies, Hofmeyr mentions the work of Tim Couzens, Kelwyn Sole, Mike Kirkwood and Stephen Gray (although she acknowledges that Gray works from a different paradigm to the others). The poverty of South African literary criticism is attributed to the fact that the 'dominant vision of this criticism belongs to the class-based practices of a privileged and insulated fraction that lives, perceives and understands the world through an ideology of liberalism' (42). She argues that we need a theory of literature that will 'explain the complexities of a dynamic society and its culture' (44), and that we must understand literature 'as an activity and process' where the writer is 'part of a "social context and the bearer of the weight of its beliefs, conformities and rebellions"' (44). Hofmeyr concludes by summarizing the conditions under which a vigorous critical practice is likely to emerge:

> South African literary criticism needs to be a rigorous and exacting discipline, placed on a respectable theoretical footing and grounded in a truly interdisciplinary approach. If we continue to use literature as easy philosophy for making moralistic judgements on 'universal human nature', or as an elitist pursuit for preening one's sensibilities, we might as well forsake any pretence of being interested in South African literary history and the society from which it comes, and go instead to join therapy groups. (48)

Three years later Nick Visser (1982) confidently proclaimed that alternative perspectives were fast gaining ascendancy over practical criticism. He singles out Marxist literary criticism as the most significant challenge to literary traditionalism:

> Whatever the merit of the various perspectives (and I believe open-minded and thorough examination shows each of them to have a great deal), the one that seems to be moving most strongly towards reorientating literary studies in this country, and the one that appears in quantity and quality of published research to be the most productive, comprises sociology of literature generally and Marxist literary criticism in particular. That this should be the case will be disquieting to many. We are unlikely, however, to make this state of affairs disappear simply by anathematizing sociology of literature and Marxist literary studies and all their adherents. (331)

Thus by the early 1980s a radical critical practice, distinguished by a concern with the socio-historical determinants of literature, had succeeded in establishing itself as a significant force in South African literary studies. In addition to the critics singled out by Hofmeyr in 1979, others had come to prominence, including Michael Vaughan, Mbulelo Mzamane and David Maughan-Brown. Yet, in many instances, this critical practice was characterized by ambiguity. Despite the materialist approach of these critics, many tended, paradoxically, to formulate the relation of social context to literary text in idealist terms. Beginning with Kirkwood, who retains the notion of the integral self in his existentialist-humanist formulations of alienation and guilt, through to such critics as Mzamane, for whom the socio-historical context is a transcendental determinant, radical critical practice in South Africa failed, on the whole, to challenge the idealist underpinnings of traditionalist criticism. This failure stems from the absence of a semiological conception of materialist processes. In terms of this conception the socio-historical is not simply opposed to the literary as the material exteriority of a mystifying interiority. Instead the socio-historical itself is seen as discursively produced and therefore as intrinsic to the signifying processes of the literary text. The socio-historical and the literary are not, in the semiological conception, simply antithetical terms in an ultimately idealist binary system.

Radical critical practice in South Africa in the late 1970s and early 1980s seems largely to have overlooked the impact of semiology and psychoanalysis on Marxism in the 1960s. Hofmeyr's observations on literature as an activity (a productivity) and a process (an endless signification) point to a semiological conception but she fails to explore these notions fully. It is not until the mid-1980s that materialism is explicitly deployed as a semiological conception. Jeremy Cronin's work in this field is of particular relevance to this study as he deals directly with South African poetry. Cronin's understanding of the relation between social context and literary text draws substantially on semiology. In 'Turning around: Roy Campbell's "Rounding the Cape"' (1984), for example, he applies techniques of semiological analysis to Campbell's poem in an attempt to demonstrate how political ideology articulates with discursive processes. Cronin's understanding of ideology, which is crucial to his critical practice, is explained at length in 'Ideology and Literary Studies in South Africa' (1985). To begin with he draws a functional distinction between 'aesthetic ideologies' and 'socio-political ideologies':

> Both varieties of ideology are liable to be at play within the same text. While they certainly interact in complex ways, it is important not to conflate them too readily. Not least because there are frequently disjunctures between these two varieties of ideology within the same text . . . . The reception of the text may also involve both aesthetic, as well as more directly socio-political ideologies. Such ideologies, at the reception end, may be considerably in agreement, or even completely at variance with those in the text. (2-3)

Cronin explores the implications of this distinction between the aesthetic and the socio-political through three sets of related antinomies: form and content, the universal and the immediate, and the private and the social. He sees South African literary criticism (particularly when confronted with black poetry) as falling into one of these opposed positions:

> On the one hand there have been polemical interventions which have attacked the 'formlessness', the 'excessive particularization', and the 'excessive public' character of this poetry. All of these attacks have been couched in the terms and categories of an aesthetic ideology. On the other hand, there have been defensive attempts at rehabilitating this literature. Such attempts have been dominated by socio-political criteria.
>
> In our view these two opposed positions have tended to fall into merely antinomic, mutually reinforcing ideological standpoints, the one taking its stand in the aesthetic domain, the other in the socio-political. (8)

Cronin contends that theoretical opposition to traditionalist literary criticism has tended to be 'merely reactive' (23). As evidence he cites the work of Couzens, Mzamane and Vaughan. Through careful elucidation of the theoretical assumptions underlying both aesthetic and socio-political criteria, Cronin endeavours 'to break through the antinomies' (8).

Cronin oversimplifies perhaps when he characterizes South African literary studies as falling neatly into two categories. Such a view does not account for the position of a critic such as Stephen Gray. Although Gray also favours a socio-historical approach, his criteria are not political. Moreover he incorporates the aesthetic into his perspective. As early as 1978 he had outlined the basic shape research into South African poetry ought to assume by urging a multicultural and multilingual reconstruction of its history in its full particularity. The project he proposes is daunting in its scope and detail, yet it offers a tantalizing prospect of what collective research into South African poetry could amount to in future:

> I have stressed that research should be undertaken from scratch . . . . I have suggested that it should be conducted on a comparative basis, so that all facets of the polylingual culture of this African subcontinent be explored in their dozens of permutations . . . . I have also suggested by implication that, although a thorough knowledge of the great tradition of mainstream English poetry is an absolute essential, it should by no means be used as the only referent in the search for patterning here . . . . Then, apart from money and time and energy, I feel one is going to need a team of linguistic polymaths, of histori-

ans and archivists and bibliographers, too, plus a very strong reliance on the librarians and documentalists who have the material for us to discover. (11-12)

To date Gray's socio-historical perspective has found its fullest articulation in *Southern African Literature: An Introduction* (1979), a study that breaks with practical criticism but not with its idealist underpinnings. Gray's interpretive method is mytho-poetical. It seeks to illustrate that 'there is in Southern Africa something of a central literary consciousness which can be seen to be sustained by myth' (34). The study fails, however, to examine (at least consistently) the ideological significances of the myths. Their enclosure in a transcendental literary consciousness ultimately severs them from the historical context that Gray otherwise amply invokes through his contextual approach.

Since 1981 Michael Chapman has exerted strong influence on the shape of South African poetical studies through numerous publications, papers and edited works. He is easily the most prolific writer in this field. Notwithstanding his having characterized his work as 'seeking to blend literary-critical and social-historical insights' (1983: 1), Chapman has vigorously defended formal literary criteria and has vilified what he calls the 'sociological idea':

Whereas an earlier textual criticism tended to neglect the poem as the construction of specific critical and ideological practices, the tendency among sociologically-orientated commentators in current South African literary debate is to go to the other extreme and collapse all textual signification into surrounding discourse. In focusing here on Campbell I want to defend the resilience of the poem as text and, by implication, literary-critical activity against the intrusions of the 'sociological idea'. In doing so it will be necessary to acknowledge several valuable insights and procedures of literary sociology, particularly those which reveal criticism as active social practice and which open the efficacy of any poet's self-declaring intentions to ideological investigation . . . . At the same time, however, I want to remain critically alert to the hidden agenda of literary sociology as a struggle in South Africa for new forms of dominance: particularly in those cases where it is held that one may not give assent to any writer whose 'message' does not accord with that of the socialist millennium. (1986a: 80-81)

These remarks are directed against Cronin, whose analysis of Campbell's poem 'Rounding the Cape' prompts Chapman's attack on literary sociology. In defence of the poem as literary artefact, Chapman assesses Campbell's achievements in terms of such categories as poetry's appeal to 'mythic consciousness' (79), imagination as 'the

highest form of the intellect' (80), the ability of poetry 'to invest indigenous forms of life with the full palpability of their being' (85),
and 'poetry's capacity to strip away the conditioned response and
to tap the primitive unities of words and things' (87). Yet it is precisely the semiological paradigm from which Cronin operates that
renders problematic the notions of transcendental consciousness,
autonomous being and the unity of words and things subscribed
to by Chapman. Chapman fails, however, to address Cronin's theoretical premises, seeing him instead as 'fairly representative of the
current sociological line' (82), and grouping him together with such
critics as Couzens and Vaughan (92), whose work, as we have seen,
Cronin himself views as 'reactive'.

In using Cronin's analysis as the basis of a sweeping polemic
against the 'sociological idea', Chapman reveals no sensitivity to the
complexity of materialist practice and Cronin's position within it,
and this despite Chapman's own reference to the gains provided
by 'the radical enquiry into semiotics of structuralism and Marxism
over the last twenty years':

> Cronin's critique usefully reminds us that, after the radical enquiry
> into semiotics of structuralism and Marxism over the last twenty years,
> no defence of poetry can simply offer tautologous pronouncements
> on 'beauty', 'truth' and 'life'. At the same time, however, his critique
> reminds us, by its very omissions, that poetry, indeed any imagina-
> tive literature, is a humanistic pursuit; a grappling at particular times
> with the complexities of experience, within various kinds of personal,
> historical and formal constraints . . . . Campbell the poet is a reminder
> to literary sociology in general that, while culture, ideology and con-
> vention govern individual roles in systems, every person's sociolin-
> guistic abilities are diverse. Language embodies ways, not one way,
> of looking at the world. Similarly literary criticism — especially in so-
> cieties of narrowly-defined political tolerances — should also perhaps
> set out to affirm, in valuable new ways, its own semi-autonomous
> relationships to iron sociological times. (91)

Chapman does not, however, specify what he means by the important concept of the 'semi-autonomous' status of literary criticism.
The term is central also to Althusserian Marxism, and thus demands
elucidation if it is not to undermine Chapman's argument. Moreover
Chapman's portrayal of Cronin's project itself constitutes the 'heresy
of paraphrase' (79) of which Cronin is accused. It distorts this project
by presenting it as a dogmatic application of a sociological master
code. Chapman sums up his case against Cronin by asserting that
'To reduce the paradoxes of Campbell's personality and practice to
a limiting ''colonialism'' is to fail fundamentally to restore his poetry

to the full imaginative and emotional pressure of its moment of creation and reception' (79).

The notion of a recoverable 'moment of creation and reception' raises epistemological problems which are simply ignored. Of greater importance, however, is the fact that Cronin's reading avoids precisely a reductivist interpretation by foregrounding what he calls a complex 'vertiginous play of subversions' (1984: 78) within the poem. He provides insight into how different meanings coexist while simultaneously undermining each other. Cronin is particularly alert to the ambivalences and disjunctures between structural oppositions in the poem (white and black, colonizer and colonized) which he examines in order to show that the poem is characterized by 'Denial . . . . of colonial oppression shadowed by a half-admission' (68). For Cronin it is 'in the resonance of this cognitive subversion that many of the poem's fascinations and shortcomings lie' (68). Far from denying the poem its 'imaginative and emotional' impact, these are retained and articulated in relation to another structure of meaning: colonial ideology as it is inscribed in the text. The 'shortcomings' that Cronin refers to are moments of ideological closure in the poem which are integral to, and not external to, its meaning. Rather than 'collapse all textual signification into surrounding discourse', as Chapman would have it, Cronin examines the discursive processes of the poem itself. He discovers in the poem not one voice but contradictory voices which speak, in a conflictual fashion, of 'ways . . . of looking at the world'.

Chapman ultimately rejects Cronin's reading on grounds that at a strategic moment he arrives at an interpretation 'according to the syntax of grammar rather than verse' (1986a: 83). Yet there is no reason why the syntax of grammar should be ignored. Along with other components it forms the basis of meaning in the poem, even if only to introduce ambivalence. In fact it can be argued, as Cronin does (1984: 68), that the syntax of grammar provides the literal meaning against which other meanings arise. Chapman's absolute distinction between the syntax of grammar and verse is unconvincing.

Chapman has made clear, in another context, that despite his gestures towards the socio-historical he seeks to uphold what he calls the 'dominant paradigm' (1985: 18), by which he means a formalist/new critical approach, arguing that 'literary studies may best serve students, whatever their race or ideology, by means of searching modifications and changes within the existing model; also, with the ever-challenging reminder of deconstructive practices: the implications of the text depending on our specification and, indeed, on theoreticization of its historical environment' (18). Deconstruction is co-opted into this practice but Marxism is excluded on grounds of being 'unassimilable' (18). What makes Marxism (and, we might add, deconstruction) unassimilable does not reside in the fact that Marxism fails to give attention to the intentionality of the work, as Chapman urges, but in the fact that it is grounded in materialist assumptions and is therefore incompatible with the idealist enterprise advocated by Chapman.

Chapman's defence of literary idealism, his defence of the unity of text and of subject on the basis of a harmonizing tension between opposing elements, as well as the idealism implicit in much socio-historical literary study, calls for re-examination of the theoretical underpinnings of materialist critical practice. Such re-examination is implicit in the work of Cronin. However, to discourage a mechanistic understanding of material determinacy, such as Chapman is left with, materialist practice needs to be grounded more explicitly in a semiological conception of material processes. This conception sees text and subject as irreducibly traversed by difference, displacement, contradiction and struggle.

2

The impact of semiology on contemporary materialist practice is highlighted in Rosalind Coward and John Ellis's *Language and Materialism: Developments in Semiology and the Theory of the Subject* (1977). They argue that semiology has led to the important perception that 'social practices can be understood as meanings, as signification and as circuits of exchange between subjects, and therefore can lean on linguistics as a model of their systematic reality' (1). Given this understanding of social practice as signification, ideology as double articulation of linguistic system and social formation takes on particular conceptual importance:

> Ideology can be seen as the form of representation that society gives to itself, on condition that this representation is seen as an active process of production within material instances, as a material force comprising 'the perceived, accepted, suffered cultural objects: objects of [men's] world' . . . . This representation has the character of tending towards a structural closure: it defines the limits for, and works to fix the individual with, a certain mental horizon. (74)

The above understanding of ideology can be termed discursive to distinguish it from the traditionalist view. The traditionalist view regards ideology as an autonomous body of ideas communicated between one expressive consciousness and another by means of a unified sign system. A discursive understanding of ideology abandons the notion of ideology as the content of words exchanged between individuals in favour of the notion of material processes which are inscribed in language and which serve to position the subject within the social formation.

Coward and Ellis's views, which are elaborated from a reading of Roland Barthes, Louis Althusser, Jacques Lacan and Julia Kristeva, have been developed in several directions. In *Critical Practice* (1980) Catherine Belsey leans heavily on their conceptual framework in her exposition of a radical literary critical practice. John Frow operates within a similar conceptual framework in 'Discourse and Power' (1985), although his immediate models are Umberto Eco and Michel Foucault. I invoke Belsey and Frow because each provides a useful synthesis of contemporary attempts to rethink the notion of ideology in literary critical terms.

Both Belsey and Frow premise their arguments on the theory of the differential nature of the sign, where meaning is perceived as dependent not on the correlation of a sign with a reality outside language but on the position of the sign in a differential system. Belsey explains:

> The most revolutionary element in Saussure's position was his insistence that language is not nomenclature, a way of naming things which already exist, but a system of differences with no positive terms. He argued that far from providing a set of labels for entities which exist independently in the world, language precedes the existence of independent entities, making the world intelligible by differentiating between concepts. (1980: 38)

If it is conceded that 'language precedes the existence of . . . . entities', it follows that ideology likewise does not exist in an autonomous realm of ideas but, as Belsey goes on to argue, 'is inscribed in signifying practices — in discourses, myths, presentations and re-presentations of the way "things" "are" — and to this extent it is inscribed in language' (42). According to this view ideology cannot be conceived of in essentialist terms because it is inscribed in language and language is a system of differences.

Louis Althusser is credited by Belsey with having broken with the conception of ideology as a set of ideas in people's heads. He is said to have acknowledged the role of discourse in the creation of 'reality' in his insistence that ideology establishes a relation of signification between the subject and the world (57). Althusser phrases this as follows: 'What is represented in ideology is . . . . not the system of real relations which govern the existence of individuals, but the imaginary relation of those individuals to the real relation in which they live' (1971: 165). In other words he uses the Lacanian notion of the imaginary order to argue that the relation between the subject and reality is articulated in discourse and determined by ideology.

Frow explains the effect of ideology by arguing that meaning arises from metonymic displacement, the substitution of one sign for another in 'an endless chain of semiosis' (1985: 208). Meaning is therefore perpetually deferred along a signifying chain. Ideology arrests this process by imposing closure (211). This closed meaning is projected in discourse as natural and self-evident, indicative of the way things really are. Frow claims that 'Ideological utterance is marked by . . . an automatization which appears as a kind of semantic crust proclaiming its authority and its status as second nature' (206). What ideology is seen to mask then is the social construction of meaning by positing instead a natural meaning.

Frow is particularly interested in the relation between power and discourse. He argues that because it is not possible to appeal to 'an extra-discursive real . . . as a final authority . . . [t]he decisive criterion of analysis could thus no longer be the relation between discourse and a reality which would be external to it, since discourse would be ''interpretable and intelligible only in terms of their own and other discourses' constructions and the categories of adequacy which they apply to them''. Instead, the relevant criterion would be that of the relations between discourse and power, the intrication of power in discourse.' (199-200) The 'categories of adequacy' and the power relations that sustain these categories operate therefore within a discursive formation of interwoven texts. The phrase 'categories of adequacy' should be understood to include the values, beliefs, concepts, linguistic devices and interpretive strategies by means of which truth is determined and judgements are made. Frow asserts that these categories of adequacy are ideologically motivated in that they are maintained through the exercise of hegemony in the discursive realm by a particular social formation. Following Michel Foucault, he emphasizes that hegemony, or power, should be conceived as asymmetrically dispersed within discourse and not as monolithic (204). Power is fragmentary. It is deployed from many positions within discourse and follows diverse routes.

Belsey, on the other hand, is interested in the way ideology interpellates the individual in discourse as a unified subject who is centred on an essence. This essence is defined as eternal human nature. Myths, images and scientific procedures all represent the individual to himself as an integrated complex of ineluctable instincts, desires, limitations and aspirations. Belsey contends that although the construction of the subject in language results in a split subject, ideology seeks precisely to suppress 'this contradiction . . . between the conscious self, which is conscious in so far as it is able to feature in discourse, and the self which is only partially represented there' (1980: 85). She argues that the subject is therefore constituted as 'not only a grammatical subject . . . but also a subjected being who submits to the authority of the social formation represented in ideology as the "Absolute Subject"' (62).

Belsey follows Pierre Macherey in speaking of the unconscious of the literary text, its silence or reverse side. What is concealed by the text is the process of production that makes it a text, including 'the strategies by which it smoothes over the incoherences and contradictions of the ideology inscribed in it' (129). She invokes Jacques Lacan in drawing a parallel between the construction of the unconscious in relation to the subject and the creation of the unconscious in relation to the text:

> The unconscious is . . . a construct, created in the moment of entry into the symbolic order, produced in the gap between the subject of discourse, the I of the enonce, and the subject of the enunciation, the I who speaks. Constructed of elements whose entry into the symbolic order is barred, the unconscious is structured like a language. Its discourse . . . threaten[s] the apparent autonomy of the ego . . . . [Likewise the] unconscious of the work is constructed in the moment of its entry into literary form, in the gap between the project and the formulation. The process is precisely parallel to the process by which the child enters the symbolic order. The text is a bearer of ideological meaning, but only in so far as literary form permits the production of meaning. To adapt Lacan's formula, the text speaks, but it is because literary form has made it a text. (131, 135)

The function of critical practice, as Belsey sees it, is to articulate that which is unspoken in the text, to decentre and to deconstruct the text, and in so doing to produce the text anew. This involves using the text to reconstruct the ideology that determines its silences. In the final analysis what is present in the text, she avers, is history, 'not as background, not as cause, but as the condition of the work's existence as ideology and as fiction' (136). To the practice of a kind of consumerist criticism, which projects itself as nontheoretical, neutral and objective (i.e. as transparent), she opposes a productive critical practice: 'No longer the accomplice of ideology, no longer parasitic on an already given literary text, criticism constructs its object, produces the work' (138).

Frow gives the name of 'resistance' to this type of critical practice. He argues that 'both "ideology" and "resistance" are uses of discourse, and both are "within" power' (1985: 206). A critical practice of resistance inserts itself into the fissures and figures of ideology, fracturing the discursive formation and turning its tropes against it, opposing power with power in numerous textual engagements with the intention of ultimately reappropriating ideology for counterhegemonic purposes. This involves the exposure of the omissions, gaps, contradictions, partial truths and self-serving value systems of the ideology inscribed in the text. A critical practice of resistance thus employs strategies of infiltration of, and confrontation with, the ideology inscribed in the text in an attempt to deconstruct this ideology.

According to Frow it is possible therefore to escape and oppose specific ideologies. Belsey endorses this view when she maintains that 'while no society can exist without ideology . . . and while it is impossible to break with ideology in the general sense, nonetheless it is possible to constitute a discourse which breaks with the specific ideology (or ideologies) of the contemporary social formation' (1980: 62-63).

A critical practice that does not address the question of the text's ideological formation and simply accepts it as given, as natural, acts in complicity with this ideology. Whether it is made explicit or not, ideology is inscribed in the text. By not exposing and questioning it, the critic subjects himself to it, is interpellated by it as a subject. Such a critic implicitly upholds the social formation on whose behalf ideology applies coercive force. No critical practice is ideologically neutral.

Terry Eagleton (1976: 68-73) maintains that the raw material of literature is not reality but ideology. This is because literature deals directly with modes of perception, cultural codes and conventions, social values and metaphysical beliefs. Better than any other form of writing, literature illustrates the specifically discursive means by which a society constructs reality. This reason alone is sufficient to justify examination of South African literature along the lines suggested by Belsey and Frow. Such examination, concerned with the ideological transactions between reader and literary text, could contribute significantly to current processes of cultural critique and transformation in South Africa.

3

Stephen Gray points out that it is possible to trace the historical construction of South African poetry by examining past anthologies

(1978: 9-11). In their selection and exclusion a tradition is created and a canon of poets comes into existence. An examination of anthologies from Alexander Wilmot's *The Poetry of South Africa* (1887) to Guy Butler and Chris Mann's *A New Book of South African Verse in English* (1979) reveals that the following poets, at least, qualify for inclusion in the canon of white South African English poets: Pringle, Scully, Slater, Campbell, Plomer, Butler, Currey, Eglington, Miller, Clouts and Livingstone. Critical studies on white South African English poetry suggest that of these poets the most significant are Pringle, Slater, Campbell, Butler and Livingstone. I shall confine my enquiry to a poem by each of these writers.

Michael Chapman argues that anthologists 'have continued to promote a traditional sensibility and style as the approved inheritance' (1984: 19). He characterizes this literary traditionalism as the exercise of reason and restraint:

> Although the liberal-humanist line has, then, its own internal divisions, the overall impression remains of a poetry in which moral discourse takes precedence over the image, mellifluous syntax over the cryptic utterance and an order of concepts over the imagination. Despite its use of African subject-matter, it is a poetry which does not entirely succeed in (or more likely does not altogether see the necessity of) severing itself from, or even transforming, its standard-English literary codes. (39)

I should like to take up the suggestion, offered in parentheses, that the poetry fails to sever itself from or transform the tradition from which it derives not because its attempts are unsuccessful, but because it does not set out to do so. Since Miller and Sergeant's *A Critical Survey of South African Poetry* (1957), it has become commonplace to view the poetry as attempting to devise new modes of poetic response which are somehow more appropriate than traditional ones in portraying conditions on the African sub-continent. The purported success or otherwise of such attempts is then used as a standard against which to measure the commitment, perceptiveness and originality of the poets in question. Thus Pringle, for example, is both praised and condemned, depending on whether it is his use of South African themes and diction that is foregrounded or his adherence to Augustan-Romantic styles of composition. Rather than adopt such antithetical positions perhaps we should accept, instead, that the poetry does not pretend to be anything other than colonial, and explore the implications of this premise. For it seems to me that it is precisely the double vision of colonialism, which brings into focus simultaneously the colony and the metropolis, that characterizes the poetry.

Thomas Pringle (1789-1834) resided at the Cape for six years. Leader of a Scottish group that arrived with the 1820 settlers, he spent some time farming on the frontier, travelled fairly extensively in the eastern Cape, and lived in Cape Town for several years. He distinguished himself as defender of the free press and vocal abolitionist. Before his arrival at the Cape he had published a volume of poems in Edinburgh where he had worked as editor of Blackwood's *The Edinburgh Monthly Magazine* and Constable's *Scots Magazine* among others. On his return to Britain after the failure of his plans at the Cape, he was appointed secretary of the Anti-Slavery Society. His complete African writing was published a few months before his death under the title *African Sketches* (1834), which comprises two sections: 'Narrative of a Residence in South Africa' and 'Poems Illustrative of South Africa'.

Pringle is commonly referred to as the 'father' of English poetry in South Africa, though Gray has pointed out that this distinction applies more accurately perhaps to Frederic Brooks (1978: 9). Pringle is elevated to this position partly at least because he embodies the qualities admired by the liberal-humanist tradition-makers. He is credited with having an enlightened attitude towards the indigenous people and is seen as exemplary in his defence of freedom and justice.

In a study of Pringle's depiction of the 'Bushmen', A.E. Voss identifies, however, a contradiction between Pringle's Christian sentiments and the colonial ethos to which he subscribes. Voss uses as example the much anthologized 'Afar in the Desert' and maintains that Pringle emerges in this poem as 'the archetypal white colonial: mounted, rifle in one hand, Bible in the other' (1982: 20). Previous commentators have praised the exotic lyricism of the poem, savoured its hypnotic evocation of a desolate waste-land, and discovered in its sentiments a universal need for meditational solitude. Voss does not ignore these aspects but sees them as symptomatic of a pathological tendency:

> The power of Pringle's poem is not in its 'local colour', but in its presumably intuitive following of the frustrations of colonial experience to their potentially horrifying and alienated conclusions: solitary identification with God and Nature can mean the elimination of society. Hence the tissue of paradox and opposition on which the poem rests: poet rides, bushboy runs; poet raves, bushboy is silent; bushboy is 'alone' yet 'by my side'; the 'death-fraught firelock in my hand' is 'The only law in this Desert Land', yet in this desert land

the 'still small voice' says 'GOD IS NEAR!' God, it seems, is on the
side of the firelock. (20)

I wish to take up some of these suggestions and elaborate on them.
In the poem the speaker (whom Voss identifies with Pringle) gives
his reasons for seeking solace in the desert:

> Afar in the Desert I love to ride,
> With the silent Bush-boy alone by my side:
> When the wild turmoil of this wearisome life,
> With its scenes of oppression, corruption, and strife . . .
>
> Dispose me to musing and dark melancholy;
> When my bosom is full, and my thoughts are high,
> And my soul is sick with the bondman's sigh —
> Oh! then there is freedom, and joy, and pride,
> Afar in the desert alone to ride! (ll. 25-28, 32-36)

Because despondency and rapture are equally insistent, the tone is
ambivalent. This ambivalence is paralleled by a contradiction in the
speaker's motives. He identifies social ills and injustices, especially
the sufferings of the slave, as the cause of his melancholy. He feels
spiritually contaminated by colonial society. Riding into the desert
is seen as a cure. Yet he takes with him the attitudes of the colonial,
the ills of which are therefore simply perpetuated.

Perpetuation of colonial attitudes occurs in at least two ways. In
the first place the speaker is patronizing towards the bush-boy. He
acknowledges his presence while simultaneously denying him his
full humanity. The boy's silence announces his presence/absence.
He does not speak, is not called upon to speak, and consequently
is not involved by the speaker in any form of human relationship.
In the second place the speaker describes the initial stretch of wilderness as a scene of pastoral serenity (ll. 47-48) while claiming at the
same time that the 'death-fraught firelock' which he carries is the
'only law of the Desert Land' (ll. 39-40). The purported law of the
desert, a law of violence, does not inhere in the landscape but is
what he brings with him. He holds the law, which is his own law,
in his hand: the law of the pioneer-settler.

Thus the bush-boy's brooding, disruptive silence is also the text's
silence. That which is unspoken, which is repressed, subverts the
text's conscious articulation. The speaker talks of the curative powers of solitary communion with God. But we detect in his words
not the remedy for colonialist ills but their apotheosis. Gun in hand,
sullen bush-boy at his side and yet absented, the speaker exults in
silent and childlike reverence over the solitary waste-land around
him:

> And here, while the night-winds round me sigh,
> And the stars burn bright in the midnight sky,
> As I sit apart by the desert stone,
> Like Elijah at Horeb's cave alone,
> 'A still small voice' comes through the wild
> (Like a Father consoling his fretful Child),
> Which banishes bitterness, wrath, and fear, –
> Saying – MAN IS DISTANT, BUT GOD IS NEAR! (11. 89-96)

The fact that by the end of the poem the bush-boy has been forgotten draws attention to the denial of his humanity. He has served his purpose as poetic device of the romantic colonialist imagination. He has accompanied (guided) the speaker to the mystery of the desert. In himself he is unimportant. His humanity lacks substance. He is simply another exotic element in a poem that owes much to the tradition of the picturesque travelogue.

The poem illustrates, in fact, the limit of the picturesque within which the speaker's response to Africa is contained. The deeper he moves into the African desert the more he encounters simply a void where articulation is impossible except in terms of a series of negatives which recall the absent picturesque:

> A region of drought, where no river glides,
> Nor rippling brook with osiered sides;
> Where sedgy pool, nor bubbling fount,
> Nor tree, nor cloud, nor misty mount,
> Appears, to refresh the aching eye: (ll. 81-85)

What this indicates is that the speaker's ideology is inscribed in the very conventions and techniques he employs. It is these discursive means, rather than some free-floating body of ideas, that determine his perception of his subject. It is through the discursive means that the subject is articulated. These cannot simply be left behind when he flees into the desert away from colonial society. For even flight into the wilderness on the part of the troubled prophet/reformer is a convention carrying a culturally specific meaning rather than a universal one.

Gray has published a poem in which the silent bush-boy muses to himself as he jogs next to the master's horse. The poem is called 'In memoriam: Thomas Pringle (bush-boy speaks)':

> he's never grown out of his Native Land
> he does not look as if he belongs
>
> here we offer him a kingdom of all
> he surveys down the sight of a firelock

an Eden puckered with bare spoor
over the border and into the dark

but this man — he rides in excursions
looking back through me for home

he says it is wrong to enslave me
yet he grows taller in my company (1977: ll. 5-14)

The reversal of perspective is startling. A century-and-a-half of silence is broken by the bush-boy's observations on Pringle the colonial, the hunter and the philanthropist. The bush-boy's speech is situated in the gaps in Pringle's discourse and exposes the ideology that
shapes it.

Pringle is seen by the bush-boy to view Africa 'down the sight
of a firelock' and to reduce it to 'an Eden puckered with bare spoor'.
By implication the desert is therefore of Pringle's own making. As
colonialist he contributes to the devastation of Africa and not, as
he believes, to its salvation. In addition Pringle is said to 'grow taller'
in the company of the bush-boy. Pringle's self-regard, the 'pride'
he speaks of in 'Afar in the Desert', is in direct proportion to the
degradation of the bush-boy. The colonialist measures his superiority by the distance between himself and the colonized.

Gray's poem forces us to take a fresh look at 'Afar in the Desert'.
We notice that the relationship between the speaker and the bush-
boy is paralleled by the relationship between God and man (father
and son). Accordingly the speaker implicitly aligns himself with
God. He conceives of himself as lord over Africa and pursues his
alienation and isolation to the point of creating around him a desert.
In the desert he communes with his own lonely self.

It is instructive to note how the critical ethos of the era concurs
with the poetry. The literary assumptions of colonial readers of the
mid-nineteenth century prove to be similar to those of their British
compatriots. Thus an anonymous contributor to the *Cape Monthly
Magazine* (the writer is believed to be W.R. Thomson) decries the
absence of meritorious poetry in the colony and espouses a poetic
creed founded on moral sensibility, enthusiastic description of nature and introspective contemplation of divinity:

> The moral atmosphere of colonial life is not considered sufficiently
> nutritive or conducive to poetic thought. We have too much of hard
> money-grabbing . . . and, withal, of narrow views and overwhelm-
> ing conceits to cultivate the amenities and refinements of the poetic
> spirit . . . . It is not every country that can prove, to the fullest ex-
> tent, a 'Meet nurse for the poetic child.' There must be the rugged

grandeur of the mountain and the flood, or the soft beauty of the wooded landscapes and the sunlit glades. There must be the stirring traditions of the historic past, and the kindred associations of the exciting present . . . . But though this be true, there is a still higher truth that must be remembered. The essential spirit of poetry is independent of external associations. It consists in the vision and the faculty divine . . . . (1858: 342-343)

Poetry is said to possess an 'essential spirit'. In other words it has a defining characteristic that is everywhere the same, whether the poem is composed in the Congo, in China, or in the Lake District of England. This common denominator can be abstracted as an autonomous quality independent of history and of culture. By implication the writer of the article is in the privileged position of being able to detect this spirit, perhaps because his spiritual faculties are appropriately refined. Paradoxically, however, this essential spirit, which has fixed and absolute qualities, is described in terms of, and predicated on, organic nature. The vegetable world is used to image the metaphysical world in so far as the spirit is said to require a 'nutritive' environment which will 'cultivate' it. Moreover the poetic spirit is alleged to flourish only where there are mountains, lakes and forests. Urban life, and by extension social life, is consequently regarded as inimical to poetry.

Clearly the poetic utterances and the theoretical reflections of this period are mutually reinforcing. Inscribed in this discursive formation, and projected as self-evident through a circular path of closure, are numerous essentialist and supremacist assumptions and beliefs about men and women, reality, moral values and culture. Practices and concepts that are contingent on history are presented as eternal and unchanging. Poetical studies is elevated to theology. Only by articulating the silences of the texts is it possible to reconstruct their ideological unconscious. This requires a strategy by which the texts are penetrated and subverted from within their textual operations.

A century of colonial versifying lies between Thomas Pringle and Francis Carey Slater (1876-1958). Born of settler stock, of which he says he is 'prodigiously proud' (1954: 5), Slater grew up on a farm near Alice in the Border district. Here he learnt to speak Xhosa and took delight in African folktales and legends. When he was eight years old his father brought home several volumes of verse: Shakespeare, Milton, Wordsworth, Scott, Burns and Longfellow. These volumes, he says, 'were to influence my future life to an undreamed-of extent' (33). Interestingly his appreciation of Scott is as enthusiastic as Pringle's had been: 'As a genius of universal stature he seems to me to approach nearest to Shakespeare of all British writers' (63).

Slater started publishing his best work in the 1920s, when he was already forty-eight years old, and continued publishing for more than twenty years. His important works are *The Karroo and Other Poems* (1924), *Drought* (1929), *Dark Folk and Other Poems* (1935) and *The Trek* (1938). While Roy Campbell and William Plomer were in the process of introducing modernist techniques into South African poetry, Slater continued to adhere to the Romantic and Victorian styles of his early influence. Seen alongside his younger contemporaries, he is essentially a nineteenth-century figure, a poet of the untrampled South African veld. In his major poems Slater sets out to preserve in poetry a pre-industrial, arcadian South Africa. Like Wordsworth, he uses the idea of the rural as a symbol of pre-industrial consciousness. Writing about the poem *Drought*, Sydney Clouts says that the theme is 'space, distance, vastness, controlled by the voice of a poet for whom the preservation of scenes with historic significance and the evocation of a heritage of myth are of importance in a structure which has mnemonic ends as well: it preserves the past' (1971: 96).

Slater was also an important anthologizer. In his Preface to *The New Centenary Book of South African Verse* (1945) he comments on the alleged derivative nature of South African poetry:

> The main fault in our poetry, according to English critics, is that it is too derivative in form. Apparently they look to new countries for a new technique — a new way of writing. This seems hardly fair. New forms are the natural development of a ripe culture, and a new country is the last place in which to seek them . . . . If, then, the poets of the younger countries introduce new themes and fresh and arresting imagery while handling old forms in a characteristic manner, is this not all that may be reasonably expected of them? (x)

His view of how a tradition develops is clearly conservative. In the early stages the old techniques and forms are maintained, and by implication the modes of perception to which they give access. Using primarily the Romantics as models for his own poetry, Slater seems partly to have himself in mind as he writes this. Yet several critics have viewed him as the first English poet to have spoken in a truly South African voice. Commenting on his work Anthony Delius, for instance, says that 'Whatever tendency there might have been to "colonialism" in S.A. English verse before Dr. Slater, there has certainly existed no excuse of it since his work during the '30's' (1954: 67). As evidence of this break with colonialism, Delius cites the distinctive South African imagery employed by Slater (67).

Nevertheless Slater is not a particularly popular poet today. To my knowledge there have been no recent articles on him. He has not provoked the kind of interest we find, for instance, in Pringle and Campbell. In fact one of his works, *The Trek*, published in 1938 to coincide with the centenary celebrations of the event, may even be a bit of an embarrassment today. The poem raises, in a particularly stark manner, the question of the relationship between English and Afrikaner in South Africa.

In view of the poem's aggrandizement of Afrikaner history and key personalities (though several are portrayed as bigoted and stubborn), it is interesting to note what Slater's later thoughts were on the Afrikaners, after the experience of the Ossewa Brandwag and the rise to power of the Nationalist Party:

> A number of my writings in verse — especially my longest poem *The Trek* — afford unquestionable evidence of my sincere admiration of great South Africans of Dutch descent and their heroic deeds. But whilst I honour the Voortrekker leaders of long ago, who were giants in courage, mind and spirit, I find it most deplorable that their mantle of leadership should have fallen upon the shoulders of those who, in comparison with them, are spiritual dwarfs . . . .
>
> We, South Africans of British descent, are not sufficiently numerous to rescue South Africa from the Afrikaner extremists, who are proving so harmful to her both here and in other lands . . . . In the circumstances, it seems to me that the salvation of South Africa mainly depends upon the better class of Afrikaners, who are worthy descendants of Dutch and French ancestry . . . . Inter-marriages between this type of Afrikaner and English-speaking South Africans are frequent, so let us continue to hope that such happy unions of young hearts and hands may ultimately result in a truly united and peaceful South Africa. (1954: 229)

It is understandable therefore that Slater should have admired a man like Jan Smuts, with whom he maintained a warm correspondence and friendship from the time of the publication of *The Trek*. In a letter dated 3 June 1947, Smuts, in turn, expresses his appreciation of the service Slater has done to South Africa through his poetry:

> I had so hoped to find an opportunity to see you and thank you for sending me a copy of your Oxford Edition. Alas, such an opportunity has not come. And so I send you this line to thank you and congratulate you on the honour you have thus brought South Africa . . . .
>
> Something of the intimate spirit of South Africa will be found there and be enjoyed by those who do not know the South Africa which is ours. You have been the interpreter of much that is best in the spirit of our country and our people and for this too I thank you. (Slater, 1954: 240)

Slater maintains an ambiguous stance towards the Afrikaners. He promotes an English liberalism while simultaneously transcribing the central Afrikaner myths. In *The Trek* he looks back nostalgically to an earlier age and endeavours to create an epic in which to encapsulate its heroism. That he chooses to do so by identifying closely with Trekker history rather than with Settler history, as Alexander Wilmot for instance had done in his heroic poem on the British settlers (1870), is unusual in South African English poetry:

Not locomotive-engines, snorting dragons
Belching black smoke, I sing, but tented wagons:
Wagons that like the battered caravels
Of Christopher Columbus by their spells
Wrested the unknown from its secret cells;
Wagons that conquered plain and mountain-belt —
Cradles that rocked the Children of the Veld
Into a nation stubborn strong and hard,
Narrow, suspicious, slow to give regard
To the rights and views of those of other race,
But, won to friendship, friends of steadfast breed.
Nor sing I petrol's toys of dizzy pace
But the slow-trudging ox and ambling steed.

The smoke-flagged factory, industrial town,
Temples of this machine-enchanted age,
I leave to budding bards of fame full-blown,
Or over-blown, and make my pilgrimage,
At trek-ox pace, through plains austere and brown.
Not of mechanics, masons, engineers
I sing, but of bronzed farmer-pioneers:
Men who were horsemen as by right of birth,
Who from their saddles grew, like trees from earth,
With swinging guns for branches, quick to flame
With deadly flowers; men who found living tame
Save on the brink of danger; men who won
Strength from the barren veld and burning sun.
('Theme', ll. 1-26)

These are forceful lines, and one senses that Slater has learnt from Campbell how to employ vigorous metrical expression. They are strong in cadence, resonant in sentiment, stirring in expression and vivid in imagery. To say that the lines are forceful is to concede to their power of persuasion and to acknowledge the coercive power of the language. Whereas previously South African poets had responded to their context mostly through incidental lyrical outbursts, *The Trek* constitutes a systematic reconstruction of an historical event along mytho-poetic lines. To this end a rousing rhetorical style is deployed, one that is able to carry with it a weight of importance absent from most earlier South African poetry in English.

The dignified and solemn tone is slightly compromised though by the vituperative reference to 'budding bards of fame full-blown,/ Or over-blown'. The defensive tone of this statement can be read as signalling a moment of self-doubt and self-justification. The speaker is regressing in time, escaping from the present to 'sing' of an earlier age, and for a moment he seems conscious that he is romanticizing and falsifying the achievements of this period. Witness his portrayal of the 'bronzed farmer-pioneers' as larger than life and his investiture of their actions with the sweeping grandeur of romance. They are 'men who found living tame/ Save on the brink of danger'. Most revealing of all is the description of their weaponry. The trekkers are like trees that have 'swinging guns for branches, quick to flame/ With deadly flowers'. This is a bold metaphorization of killing, a daring infusion of the act of slaughter with an effulgence of beauty.

Part of the reason why an Englishman could write so convincingly on a subject that is intimate rather to Afrikanerdom can be ascribed to rhetorical technique. In the first place the speaker projects himself as a fellow pilgrim into the interior. He speaks of himself in the first person. He is the 'I' of the poem and participates in the 'pilgrimage,/ At trek-ox pace'. But of course the speaker is, strictly speaking, absent from the poem. It is the reader who speaks on his behalf and who is therefore in the position of the speaking 'I'. Thus the reader is interpellated as subject of the poem-as-pilgrimage and is subjected to its ideological co-ordinates. The journey as pilgrimage is in pursuit of, as the speaker subsequently spells out, 'the Land of the Trekker's dream,/ Where milk and honey in plenty stream' ('Onward the Wagons Went', ll. 25-26). In other words he pursues in this allegorical journey an inner vision of the promised land. For this reason too it is a desert journey, like that of the Israelites, 'through plains austere and brown'. History is reconstructed as biblical myth and as such is seen to be the expression of God's will. Because the myth is subscribed to by both Englishman and Afrikaner, who share a belief in the Christian Bible, it serves to bind together the two groups in a common understanding of history. For socio-political reasons this is an important task in a country still suffering from the wounds inflicted by the Anglo-Boer war. This alliance is clinched in the naming of a common enemy, the 'swarming legions of savage men' ('Onward the Wagons Went', l. 24) encountered en route to the promised land.

In the second place, the speaker creates a convincing story through

skilful manipulation of realism. The grand epical gesture is carefully supported by meticulous attention to detail. Mimesis offers a
simulacrum of truth:

> Onward labours each caravan,
> Each plodding bullock, each patient man;
> Trek-chains rattle; jukskeis squeak;
> Wheels wake thunder in each stone-throated creek . . . .
>
> Koppies cackle to the crack of whip;
> See-sawing, heavily, tents rise and dip.
> ('Onward the Wagons Went', ll. 11-14, 17-18)

The noise of the trek, its rumbling invasion of the interior, speaks
triumphantly of colonial victory. Yet the heroism of conquest masks
the bloodshed by which subjugation of the indigenous people is ensured. It is noteworthy that the historical appropriation of the land
is paralleled in the poem by cultural appropriation of an indigenous
literary idiom. Cultural appropriation also ultimately serves
hegemonic purposes. On the whole the indigenous people are silenced by the discourse of the colonizers. At one point, however,
between episodes in the epic or white narrative, the Zulu warriors
are given a voice. This voice invokes the spirit of black death:

> 'Arise, great black Vulture,
> Devourer of other birds,
> Flap thy prodigious wings
> In the scorching face of the sun,
> And darken his dazzling eyeball.'
> ('Zulu Warriors' Chant', ll. 1-5)

Significantly, Slater's most frequently praised and anthologized
poems are precisely those that find inspiration in African idiom and
indigenous literary forms (the *Dark Folk* poems). Through their inclusion in anthologies Slater is acknowledged to have successfully
colonized the indigenous aesthetic. The choice of these poems is
testimony to their force. Slater knows the rhythms and expressions
of the native tongue, and uses them skilfully and, it would appear,
authentically.

In relation to the *Dark Folk* poems the image of the vulture and
sun is perhaps uncommonly subtle and complex. It is self-
consciously literary, and for that reason belongs arguably within a
sophisticated European rather than an African symbology. The dark-
ening of the 'dazzling eyeball' of the sun by the 'great black Vulture' has deep resonance in European culture and mythology. Pre-

eminently the eye, which is also the narrative 'I', suggests a divine faculty of reason and perception. It is the white eye of the blazing sun, which is also the Son who dies and is reborn in victorious glory. The vulture that swoops up from below on 'prodigious wings' is an awesome personification of death and the devil. It is an infernal spirit invoked by a heathen people.

The chant thus aligns the Afrikaners with Christendom and the Zulu warriors with the legions of hell. Ironically therefore the Zulu warriors damn themselves. Their speech is turned against them, betrays them. They speak, but in so doing they condemn themselves to hell. The very skill with which Slater reproduces the idiom and imagery of the indigenous tradition is used as a weapon against the people to whom this tradition belongs.

In terms of its ideological formation it is entirely appropriate that the poem ends with Afrikaner victory and Zulu defeat at Blood River, as this signifies a victory of Christianity over heathenism. The Day of the Covenant testifies to that victory, as well as to the victory of myth over history.

The poetry of Roy Campbell (1901-1957) has been studied extensively. In fact South African poetry is seen by some as beginning with Campbell. At least two anthologies of South African poetry start at this point, completely ignoring everything that had come before. The search for a founding figure of a 'true' South African poetry has led therefore to several poets: Pringle, Slater and Campbell (and recently Brooks). This absence of agreement on the origin is indicative of the displacement of the origin within the discursive field. The founding figure is original in the sense of not being derivative. He occupies the point of origin, where South African poetry supposedly springs to life in the fullness of authentic being. It would seem, however, that the question of a South African poetic identity is highly problematic. How can we identify the offspring if we cannot name the father?

Michael Chapman regards Campbell as a key figure of the modernist imagination in South African poetry, saying that he had realized the possibilities 'of utilising in tandem a sophisticated European imagism and the vitality of indigenous settings' (1984: 60). He argues, however, that the tradition of African exotica (which can be traced back beyond Rider Haggard to Pringle) is also an important feature of his poems:

> And if Campbell is more assured in his use of language, more technically proficient and more cosmopolitan than earlier South African poets, his affinities are not simply with an avant-garde European sym-

bolism, but in no small measure with the codes of hunter romance common to the last century. In reacting against the idylls of 'veld and vlei' poets, for example, he transformed such rural retreats into an equally romantic hunter's paradise, thereby displaying a flamboyancy which had antecedents within a British-South African Imperial tradition of African exotica (found especially in novels of Rider Haggard and the diaries of the frontiersman, R.C. Cumming). (63)

While accepting that Campbell draws on the Imperial tradition of African exotica, I would argue that he portrays an Africa that has been wrenched from the pastoral idyll not simply by the Imperial hunter code but also by the disruptive and alienating violence of the industrial age.

In an article attributed to Campbell, limp Victorianism in South African poetry is denounced in favour of energetic expression. The creed announced here describes accurately Campbell's own poetic practice, and indicates by way of Nietzsche and Rimbaud two important influences on his poetry and thought:

> It is curious that our country, so rugged and massive, should have produced such a polite, meagre, peeping, creeping, stealing style of poetry. The bushveld and the Karroo are no place for garden-rollers . . . . Nietzsche and Rimbaud with their tremendous zest and vigour would do much to relieve the emasculation that Afrikaans and English-African poetry seem to have suffered from too close a contact with Victorian literature. (1926: 1(2), 65-66)

In respect of this glorification of energy in nature, Campbell is perhaps best approached by way of contrast with Slater. Writing within a predominantly Romantic idiom, Slater conceives of nature in terms of the unity of the spirit. Thus nature is often personified. It is alive, in the same way man is alive, by virtue of the spirit. In Slater's poetry man perceives his own being in the being of nature and discovers the volition of the spirit in both (as in the case of *Drought* for instance). Campbell, on the other hand, finds in nature not spirit but brute energy. Moreover he conceives of this energy in terms of technological society with its electrical power and self-generating engines. Thus the stallion in his poem 'The Zebras' is described as a self-contained and self-generated 'engine of beauty volted with delight' (l. 13). In other words nature's energy is portrayed in ambiguous terms. Like the Zulu girl and the serf, the zebras symbolize a type of primeval power. But in some or other way they are assimilated into or conquered by European technological society.

In 'To a Pet Cobra' even the snake, one of Africa's most lethal offspring, has been domesticated, has become a pet whom the speaker engages in a dangerous game of seduction:

With breath indrawn and every nerve alert,
As at the brink of some profound abyss,
I love on my bare arm, capricious flirt,
To feel the chilly and incisive kiss
Of your lithe tongue that forks its swift caress
Between the folded slumber of your fangs,
And half reveals the nacreous recess
Where death upon those dainty hinges hangs. (ll. 1-8)

This is an apt image of the colonialist's flirtation with Africa. Africa
has been conquered and tamed. Savage nature has been outrivalled
by the energy of advanced industrialization. The cobra is awesome
in so far as its elemental power is ultimately comparable, as in the
case of the zebra stallion, with electrical voltage:

Dainty one, deadly one, whose folds are panthered
With stars, my slender Kalahari flower,
Whose lips with fangs are delicately anthered,
Whose coils are volted with electric power (ll. 25-28)

The snake is frequently used to represent Africa's menacing aspect.
In Pringle's poetry, for instance, it is used as a metaphor of the out-
cast 'bushmen' with their poison arrows. Commonly it inhabits a
desolate landscape of bare rock and burning sun. In Campbell's
poem, the speaker uses these associations but attempts in addition
to bring about an identification with the snake on the basis of a
shared experience as lonely and reviled outsiders:

I wish my life, O suave and silent sphinx,
Might flow like yours in some such strenuous line,
My days the scales, my years the bony links,
The chain the length of its resilient spine:
And when at last the moment comes to strike,
Such venom give my hilted fangs the power,
Like drilling roots the dirty soil that spike,
To sting these rotted wastes into a flower. (ll. 41-48)

The 'rotted wastes' symbolize colonial society, what the speaker
refers to earlier on in the poem as 'men of my dull nation' (l. 29).
The poem overtly celebrates the revolt of the Romantic individual
who in his solitude has built 'a tower of pride' (l. 40) from which
to strike out at colonial society. By way of identification with the
cobra it also enacts, however, a narcissistic fascination with the
alienated self. The speaker engages in sexual play with an Africa
that has been colonized, tamed and reduced to the co-ordinates of
his own being.

A fascination with primordial Africa as the epitome of primitivism is characteristic of the modernist imagination. In a sense the modernist imagination operative in this poem is neo-colonialist in that Africa is exploited for poetic ends. Contrary to its overt intention of intimacy with Africa and with nature, the poem registers their reification. Accordingly the tone, the style, the point of view and the sentiment are detached, metropolitan.

The Preface of the first issue of *Voorslag* magazine, co-edited by Campbell, asserts that one of the primary aims of the newly-launched publication is 'to keep in contact with contemporary thought in Europe and America' (1926: 1(1), 5). Campbell was deeply offended by what he perceived as the bovine torpidity of South Africans. In an article published in the second issue of *Voorslag*, entitled 'Fetish Worship in South Africa', he argues that whereas Europe has reached consciousness as a result of its social complexity, South Africa is still unconscious: 'There is no circulation, no nerve-telepathy. One aching stomach and that is all. The cells cohere in some sort of slipshod fashion but they all function in the same way. Mentally we have just arrived at the protozoic stage.' (1926: 1(2), 11-12) The energy of Africa, which he had celebrated in the poem 'The Flaming Terrapin', written when he was abroad in soggy England, has proved on return to South Africa to be fanciful, a myth cherished by exiles and romantics. Once here Campbell ironically turns to Europe for intellectual voltage. What he finds in South Africa is merely a mindless and enervating prostration at the feet of a colour fetish.

Campbell's texts are thus characterized by a contradiction between the metropolis and the province, Europe and Africa. This contradiction finds focus in the image of nature galvanized by industrial energy. Further instability occurs in that each of these two topographies embodies, at different stages, shifting and conflicting values of freedom and restriction, energy and emasculation. The texts speak therefore of rupture, uncertainty and transition. South African writing is moving, as is the society, from one formation into another, from the rural/agricultural to the urban/industrial, and in the process is reorganizing its co-ordinates.

Increasingly South African English poetry by whites shows awareness of a basic contradiction. The poetry becomes increasingly conscious of its colonialist status, its European identity. It becomes self-conscious. Guy Butler (1918-) mythologizes the contradiction, the inner conflict between Africa and Europe, as a cosmic battle between Dionysus and Apollo. His poem 'Home Thoughts' declares its intention to integrate the two modes of being, but succeeds only in defining their difference and upholding their mutual exclusion:

> Apollo, come!
> Oh cross the tangled scrub, the uncouth ways,
> Visit our vital if untamed abysm
> Where your old rival in the lustrous gloom
> Fumbles his drums, feels for a thread of rhythm
> To dance us from our megalithic maze . . .
>
> Oh let the lightning of your quickening eye
> And his abounding darkness meet and mate,
>
> Cleave, crack the clouds! From his brimming drum
> Spill crystal waves of words, articulate!
> (ll. 125-130, 137-140)

Without Apollo's lightning intervention, Dionysus is clumsy: he 'Fumbles his drums'. Apollo is invoked because he represents articulation. He will give shape and life to Dionysus's formless rhythm. His is a 'quickening eye' which will penetrate Dionysus's 'abounding darkness' and give birth to language. Apollo, who is aligned with the sun, is the active agent. Dionysus is passive. He is female, Africa as mother. The drum is his womb. Apollo is called upon to penetrate it violently: 'Cleave, crack the clouds!' This is a kind of rape of Dionysian Africa by Apollonian Europe. Once the womb, which is likened to clouds, has been violently penetrated, it will produce 'crystal waves of words'. What will have been born is discourse.

What has been born is the poem. The merging of Europe and Africa has not materialized. Instead it has been substituted by the poem. The poem is simply a metaphor of the union: it does not constitute it. Apollo and Dionysus, Europe and Africa, remain distinct, for they have been defined by the poem in mutually exclusive, dualistic terms. Their fusion is a linguistic sleight-of-hand, a myth. What is announced by the poem is their difference, their otherness, from each other. It is a poem of separation and longing. Europe yearns for, and simultaneously violates, its estranged other.

The poem was first published in Butler's *Selected Poems* (1975). Several years before this publication Butler had delivered a paper entitled 'The Republic and the Arts' (1964) where he examines at length the relationship between European and African in terms of Apollo and Dionysus, concluding that 'they cannot do without each other . . . they are complementary' (1964: 9). In dealing with conflict between white and black Butler invokes the Jungian notion of archetypes and sees this conflict as generated primarily by the projection of the shadow archetype: 'The characteristic emotion of South Africa is Fear. We are terrified of each other, not because we are so different, but because we are so alike . . . . [W]e dread the Black man because he symbolizes an anti-self, a portion of our natures suppressed and starved; and the Black man dreads us because we symbolize other human traits, mainly rational and intellectual, which his tribal culture did not develop.' (4)

Butler's paper illustrates the danger of the archetype petrifying into the stereotype. We are less inclined today to ascribe superior rationality to whites on the basis of a seemingly formal archetypal opposition derived from the Apollo-Dionysus myth. We see in it yet another evaluative Eurocentric conception in which the superiority of an intellectual Apollo over a bestial Dionysus is asserted.

In the first book-length study of South African poetry, Miller and Sergeant's *A Critical Survey of South African Poetry in English* (1957), the writers contend that the early poetry is derivative in style, but that it slowly gives way to a poetry that is individual and authentically South African. An important element in the attainment of this authenticity is said to be the ability to identify with the plight of blacks and the incorporation into the poetry of indigenous forms of literary expression:

> It is important to call attention to the truly significant note that was struck whenever the more outstanding of these poets contemplated the situation of the black races in a society organized and controlled by people of European descent. There is a curious sense of sympathy — one might even describe it as an intuitive understanding — which . . . finally appears at a later date as the aesthetic identification of the poet with his subject . . . . (101-102)

Significantly the phrase 'a society organized and controlled by people of European descent' is not developed. Instead liberal sentiments of identification with, and incorporation of, African perspectives are dwelt on. Yet this phrase is very significant. However earnestly the white poet sympathizes with blacks, and however skilfully he incorporates elements of their culture into his own, he operates from within a social formation that is organized and controlled by whites. By virtue of this social formation, whites are placed in a position of superiority over blacks.

By speaking on behalf of the oppressed, and by co-opting their discourse, white poets merely demonstrate the complete power exercised by whites to the exclusion of blacks. It is only when blacks begin to speak for themselves (i.e. when they renounce white patronage) that Eurocentricism in South African poetry in English begins to be replaced by Afrocentricism. The transition from European to African frames of reference constitutes a displacement of the established signifying systems rather than their extension, and thus enacts a rupture with the colonial past.

Douglas Livingstone (1932-) started publishing during the 1960s, an era when white and black were systematically segregated through legislative means, and when political dissent was violently suppressed and driven underground. Such intimations of reconciliation between white and black as expressed in Butler's poem are notably absent from Livingstone's poetry. Significantly when a poem does describe contact between white and black it is characteristically in a work situation, as in 'Dust'. This is notable because the site of labour exemplifies the contradiction that is characteristic of racial segregation: it demarcates the twin mechanism of exclusion and inclusion by which racial segregation operates.

The title poem of Livingstone's first important volume, *Sjambok and Other Poems from Africa* (1964), echoes, perhaps unintentionally, the idea of a whiplash expressed in the title of the journal *Voorslag*. The link is possibly more than gratuitous because, as Michael Chapman points out (1984: 73-74), Livingstone does appear to draw on the work of Campbell. One way of describing Livingstone is to say that he is a contemporary South African modernist who combines the symbolic resonance of Campbell with the ironic sensibility of William Plomer. These points of reference describe, within the context of South African poetry, the range of poetic technique that Livingstone deploys.

The poem 'The Lost Mine' was published in *Sjambok and Other Poems* (1964) but was omitted from *Selected Poems* (1984). It has, however, been anthologized by Guy Butler and Chris Mann in *A New Book of South African Verse in English* (1979). The narrative form of the poem in fact calls to mind Butler, particularly in the ironic concurrence of mundane external event and visionary inner experience (e.g. Butler's 'Myths'). Thus Butler, possibly, is another convenient point of reference. In the poem external event and inner experience are linked by an informal, conversational voice, one that is at once prosaic (empirical, sceptical) and poetic (imaginative, visionary):

> I suppose you could almost call it romantic -
> the way the dead wheel hangs there in the sky
> against the rusty blood-washed banner
> of a bat-stitched evening and the evening star
> (ll. 1-4)

The ironic tension established between empirical object and imaginative perception is sustained in the subsequent stanza and extended to include action and inaction, present and past:

> Clumping about, denting a tin with a kick,
> the solitudes enhanced, I might say, by the cry
> of a distant fisheagle and that flaky hammer
> stuck, mute and forgotten, in a hollow spar (ll. 5-8)

The speaker, whose actions are conveyed as everyday, down-to-earth ('Clumping about, denting a tin with a kick'), registers a series of perceptual disjunctures (dead wheel and bat-stitched evening, cry of fisheagle and mute hammer). These perceptual disjunctures suggest, in turn, conceptual disjunctures (death and mystery, spirit and materiality). It becomes increasingly clear that the space occupied by the speaker, the site of an abandoned gold mine, is a site of struggle. After recalling the past when the mine was the locality of an articulated human community, the speaker breaks the silence of the present by throwing a stone down the mouth of the mine shaft, thus forcing a response, even if only an echo:

> . . . this maw whose food
> has long been dust, perhaps a rotten cable, rats,
>
> Whispers somewhere in its tainted throat daft
> silent work-songs, the stilled smash of pick and bill
> and echoed grapplings from the ancient seamy feud
> of men and pits. Around me tack the triumphant bats.
> (ll. 19-24)

The struggle ('grapplings') about which the mine shaft whispers is twofold: it is a struggle between man and matter, and between man and man. It embraces the 'smash' both of 'pick' (instrument of labour) and 'bill' (instrument of war).

Concerning the struggle between man and matter, it is significant that gold has made possible the far-reaching material transformation of life in South Africa from the pastoral-agricultural to the industrial. Starting with its mode of extraction from the earth, it brings about a chain of material transformations across numerous social institutions (economic, legal, educational, cultural, etc.). The reverse side of these transformations, their 'seamy' side, is what is echoed in the tunnels underground: the stilled smash of the worker's pick, the long and arduous shifts in cavernous darkness, the danger and the hopelessness.

The struggle of man against matter has its corollary in the struggle of man against man and the exploitation of man by man. The discrepancies in power, privilege, aspirations and freedom between the owner of the mine and the mine-worker are enormous. The worker is subjected to his position both through force of necessity and through state violence. His descent into the pit is forced on him by a system of relations (social, political, economic, educational) by means of which he has been subjected. If he should protest against prevailing conditions, he is met by repressive measures.

Consequently the mine tunnels are both 'seamy', a kind of undesirable and repressed knowledge, and are seams, interfaces, demarcating lines of conflict ('the ancient seamy feud of men and pits'). However, the seaminess is only hinted at in the phrase 'the stilled smash of pick and bill/ and echoed grapplings'. It has had to be reconstructed as the unconscious of the text, the forgotten history of which the poem as voice purports to whisper. In the poem the historical echo is evoked only to be silenced by the tacking action of the 'triumphant bats'.

What is absent from the final stanza is a sense of historical particularity. In the fourth stanza this was evoked through reference to 'Saturday nights with fiddle and beer' (l. 14) and 'daguerreotypes of chinny maids' (l. 15). However, the perspective in stanza four is commercial, as a visit to Pilgrim's Rest will confirm: sepia photographs and Saturday night dances. The mine's throaty whisper seeks to refute the conventional historical view. But the refutation is cut short: the voice of history (the whispering mine shaft) is silenced by flight into romantic obscurantism (the tacking bats). What the throat seeks to whisper has already been proclaimed, and more trenchantly, by the 'blood-washed banner' in stanza one. The red banner of sky, backdrop to the ghostly feud in the mine tunnels, has a clear political significance that transgresses the silencing endeavours of the bats.

Chapman speaks of the tension between scientist and romantic in most of Livingstone's poems (1984: 106). In the first two stanzas of 'The Lost Mine' this tension can be said to be exemplified in the disjuncture between empirical and metaphorical perception. Over and above Chapman's antinomy, however, another kind of tension is discernible in the poem: the tension between poet and historian. This tension is the outcome of repression rather than of synchronicity. The bats that sew up the seam of conflict, and hence resolve it on a symbolic level, actively repress history.

Notwithstanding the political eloquence of the red banner, the impression remains of a mystique of violence. It is an 'ancient seamy feud', prehistoric in origin and non-historical in expression. Commenting on violence in the *Sjambok* poems as a whole, Chapman says that 'both animal and human life [are] governed mostly by an unremitting pattern of victimisation, with beast preying on beast and man on man' (85). A crude view of biological survival appears to have been elevated to a transcendental absolute and applied equally to animal and human societies.

This is in direct contrast to black poetry of the 1970s, where violence is depicted within the specificity of a particular socio-political context and a given historical moment. But then Livingstone has chosen to disavow what he scathingly terms 'Polit-Lit' (1976: 142) and has adopted, instead, a form of individualistic response which is directed at the discovery of universal (rather than historically specific) truths. Accordingly he continues the Romantic tradition that I have been examining in this article. In terms of this tradition the artist is deemed a highly developed and attuned individual who is in a position of privileged insight and uncommon talent vis-à-vis his society.

What sets Livingstone's transcendentalism apart from other transcendentalisms that I have been discussing is his privileging of science (rather than God or spirit or self or myth) as the ultimate source of truth. In his article '"Africa within us" . . .?' (1976), Livingstone uses science to counter political conceptions of literature. His parodic style is clever, subversive even, in its deployment of scientific jargon to undercut political jargon. But science turns out, finally, to be simply a metaphor, and a politically loaded one at that:

> A living body is of course subject to certain immutable laws. A body divided against itself, as someone I'm sure said, dies — as in various types of cancer for instance, where some cells, not content with their orderly dissimilarities yet underlying unity of purpose with the blokes over the road, differ yet again from their associates, and in trying to impose their ways on the others, destroy the whole world they occupy. Dying too in the process, of course: the inexorable final goal of which they are no doubt mindlessly unaware while the heady process of Antigone-like insurrection ensues. (143)

Livingstone's allegory of insurrection reaches back to Elizabethan notions of the body politic. The immutable law is both biological and socio-political. The implication is that social insurrection, like bodily insurrection, is a cancer. Perhaps at this point we should remind ourselves that the article was published in 1976. If, as Livingstone suggests, the body politic follows the immutable laws of the 'living body', June 1976 ought to be seen as a cancerous growth on

an otherwise healthy social body. This is clearly absurd. Livingstone's allegory is inadequate and misleading.

What Livingstone offers as an immutable law, supported by the
authority of 'science', is simply one interpretation of the available
evidence. To say, as he does further on, that individuals are 'organized together . . . with the single inherent determination (if we
are sane) to preserve life' (143) is based on his view of the healthy,
undivided, ideal body. Now it appears to me that another interpretation, equally 'scientific', is defensible — that the body is a site of
struggle between life and death. In this view death is not an aberra-
tion of life but its condition. It is not life gone wrong, become unnatural, fallen into insanity, or attacked exclusively from without.
Division, struggle, life and death: these are inscribed in the body
from the time of its emergence as body.

Livingstone has as much faith in his chosen literary-critical model
as he has in his scientific model. Commenting, in another context,
on the work of several black poets, he asserts that 'Poetry in
English, in Africa, must be judged . . . by internationally established
yardsticks. If the poetry is powerful enough and causes those same
yardsticks to change — so much the better! But we have some distance still to go in this direction.' (1982: 157) When he speaks of
'internationally established yardsticks' he means, of course, European yardsticks. These yardsticks, it transpires, are of a formalist
nature: they pertain to form, structure or technique. According to
Livingstone, African poetry in English is deficient in form (160). He
proceeds to establish an opposition between the poet as craftsman
and the poet as political pamphleteer, the latter being, in his opinion, 'a short-lived and grubby calling, and a sorry one for a poet
to descend to' (161). Livingstone's formalism, his exclusive consideration of European poetic techniques and his notion of the autonomy of the poet as craftsman are commensurate with the idealism
evident in the scientific allegory of the previous piece.

4

Despite the advances made by radical critical practice in recent years,
idealism continues to dominate the discourse of South African poetical studies. I have argued that its hegemony is felt particularly in
the work of Chapman, whose influence, through many important
publications, is considerable. The extent to which his views have
assumed institutional authority can perhaps best be gauged by his
anthology *The Paperbook of South African English Poetry* (1986b). Given
its format (critical introduction, notes, bibliography) we can assume

that the anthology is aimed primarily at students. Unlike Chapman's earlier anthology *A Century of South African Poetry* (1981), *The Paperbook* is not unwieldy and, from a student's point of view, is not prohibitively expensive. And unlike *Voices from Within: Black Poetry from Southern Africa* (1982), edited by Chapman and Achmat Dangor, *The Paperbook* is representative of the overall poetic output of the country. In many respects, therefore, it is eminently suitable for a general course on South African poetry.

The Introduction to *The Paperbook* contains a useful periodization of the poetry with comments on aspects of the social and literary context, the sort of thing that students need to orientate themselves historically. But the Introduction also contains Chapman's attack on Cronin, and through Cronin his attack on materialist critical practice in general. Given the assumption that *The Paperbook* is preeminently a student text, it would appear that Chapman means to entrench idealist practice in the classroom. I suspect that in some cases students have little more than this Introduction to guide them through the course on South African poetry, though some students might refer also to Chapman's *South African English Poetry: A Modern Perspective* (1984) and to a selection of essays in *Soweto Poetry* (1982), edited by Chapman. Few students, I suspect, would bother to consult Cronin's original article. Fewer still would attempt to pursue the intricacies of the debate between idealist and materialist positions as articulated in papers delivered at AUETSA conferences and published subsequently in journals ranging from *Critical Arts* to *English in Africa* and *Theoria*. From the student's point of view Chapman would appear to have pulled together the diverse threads of the scattered arguments rather usefully while remaining a champion of heterogeneity, of the complex response, of the freedom of the critic to kick himself loose from history and to confront, with the nakedness of his own self, the living poem in the full palpability of its mystical creation, a confrontation where one sensual intellect, one imaginative consciousness, is seen to fuse with another.

Through its adherence to Romantic aestheticism, Chapman's practice ultimately upholds traditional critical practice (as he himself acknowledges). Now Robert Scholes maintains that traditional practice leads invariably to the 'reverential attitude' (1985: 16), which he describes as 'the attitude of the exegete before the sacred text' (16). He argues that what is needed, instead, is a 'judicious attitude: scrupulous to understand, alert to probe for blind spots and hidden agendas, and, finally, critical, questioning, skeptical' (16). Such a practice can only come about, says Scholes, if literary exclusivity is renounced:

> The essential change — the one that will enable all the others — must
> be a change in the way that we define our task. To put it as directly,
> and perhaps as brutally, as possible, we must stop 'teaching litera-
> ture' and start 'studying texts'. Our rebuilt apparatus must be devoted
> to textual studies, with the consumption and production of texts
> thoroughly intermingled. Our favourite works of literature need not
> be lost in this new enterprise, but the exclusivity of literature as a
> category must be discarded. All kinds of texts, visual as well as ver-
> bal, polemical as well as seductive, must be taken as the occasions
> for further textuality. And textual studies must be pushed beyond
> the discrete boundaries of the page and the book into the institution-
> al practices and social structures that can themselves be usefully
> studied as codes and texts. (16-17)

Chapman's strict adherence to a Romantic aesthetic excludes this
contextual or intertextual approach. Such an approach is not unlike
the contextual project proposed, however, by Stephen Gray, to
which I referred earlier. But Gray fails to go beyond the purely verbal, or even literary, context, though his context is considerably
broader than Chapman's. A rigorously materialist practice ought to
attempt to examine the structural features of the field of discourse
as a whole, literary and social, textual and institutional, along the
lines suggested by Scholes. To divorce, as Chapman does, the study
of South African English poetry from a broader study of South African culture is to enclose the poetry in an idealist cocoon and to
deprive it of its diverse material levels of significance.

In my own teaching practice at a black university I have found
that students respond enthusiastically to a probing, questioning,
materialist approach to South African English poetry. Because they
frequently do not share the same cultural assumptions and values
as the white writers whom they read, and because I do not see my
role as simply legitimizing and instilling those assumptions and
values, knowing very well to what extent they have served the interests of domination, we attempt instead to identify and describe
the political unconscious of the text through examination of the text's
language and conventions. Following Scholes this practice can be
extended, with poetic texts examined alongside, for instance, travel writings and political speeches. Such a practice has the additional pedagogical value of foregrounding the techniques specific to the
poetic text. It also opens the way to integrating literature teaching
with language teaching, a practice that, particularly in the context
of English second-language teaching, is currently eliciting
widespread interest.

References

Althusser, L. 1971. 'Ideology and Ideological State Apparatuses'. *Lenin and Philosophy and Other Essays*. Translated by Ben Brewster. London: Monthly Review Press.

Anonymous. 1858. 'South African Poetry'. *Cape Monthly Magazine*, 4 (July), 342-355.

Belsey, C. 1980. *Critical Practice*. London and New York: Methuen.

Butler, F.G. 1964. 'The Republic and the Arts'. *The Republic and the Changing World*. Johannesburg: Witwatersrand University Press.

Butler, F.G. 1975. 'Home Thoughts'. *Selected Poems*. Johannesburg: Ad. Donker.

Butler, G. and C. Mann (eds). 1979. *A New Book of South African Verse in English*. Cape Town: Oxford University Press.

Campbell, R. *et al.* (eds). 1926. *Voorslag: A Magazine of South African Life and Art*. Facsimile reprint of numbers 1, 2 and 3. With an Introduction and Notes by Colin Gardner and Michael Chapman. Pietermaritzburg: University of Natal Press, 1985.

Campbell, R. 1981. 'The Zebras'. *Selected Poems*. Johannesburg: Ad. Donker.

Campbell, R. 1981. 'To a Pet Cobra'. *Selected Poems*. Johannesburg: Ad. Donker.

Chapman, M. (ed.). 1981. *A Century of South African Poetry*. Johannesburg: Ad. Donker.

Chapman, M. (ed.). 1982. *Soweto Poetry*. Johannesburg: McGraw-Hill.

Chapman, M. 1983. 'Nineteenth Century South African Poetry: A Modern Perspective'. AUETSA papers.

Chapman, M. 1984. *South African English Poetry: A Modern Perspective*. Johannesburg: Ad. Donker.

Chapman, M. 1985. 'Literary Studies in South Africa: Contexts of Value and Belief'. Inaugural lecture delivered in the University of Natal, Pietermaritzburg.

Chapman, M. 1986a. 'Roy Campbell, Poet: A Defence in Sociological Times'. *Theoria*, 68, 79-93.

Chapman, M. 1986b. *The Paperbook of South African English Poetry*. Johannesburg: Ad. Donker.

Clouts, S. 1971. 'The Violent Arcadia: An Examination of the Response to Nature in the Poetry of Thomas Pringle, Francis Carey Slater and Roy Campbell'. Rhodes University: M.A. thesis.

Coward, R. and J. Ellis. 1977. *Language and Materialism: Developments in Semiology and the Theory of the Subject*. London: Routledge and Kegan Paul.

Cronin, J. 1984. 'Turning around: Roy Campbell's "Rounding the Cape"'. *English in Africa*, 11(1), 65-78.

Cronin, J. 1985. 'Ideology and Literary Studies in South Africa'. AUETSA papers.

Delius, A. 1954. 'Slater and Campbell'. *Standpunte*, 9(1), 64-70.

Eagleton, T. 1976. *Criticism and Ideology: A Study in Marxist Literary Theory*. London: Verso.

Frow, J. 1985. 'Discourse and Power'. *Economy and Society*, 14(2), 193-214.

Gray, S. 1977. 'In Memoriam: Thomas Pringle (bush-boy speaks)'. *Quarry '77: New South African Writing*. Johannesburg: Ad. Donker.

Gray, S. 1978. 'A Critical Approach to the Interpretation of South African Poetry in English'. AUETSA papers.

Gray, S. 1979. *South African Literature: An Introduction*. Cape Town: David Philip.

Hofmeyr, I. 1979. 'The State of South African Literary Criticism'. *English in Africa*, 6(2), 39-50.

Kirkwood, M. 1976. 'The Colonizer: A Critique of the English South African Culture Theory'. In Wilhelm, P. and J. Polley (eds). *Poetry South Africa: Selected Papers from Poetry '74*. Johannesburg: Ad. Donker.

Livingstone, D. 1964. 'The Lost Mine'. *Sjambok and Other Poems from Africa*. London: Oxford University Press.

Livingstone, D. 1976. '"Africa within us" ...?'. In Wilhelm, P. and J. Polley (eds). *Poetry South Africa: Selected Papers from Poetry '74*. Johannesburg: Ad. Donker.

Livingstone, D. 1982. 'The Poetry of Mtshali, Serote, Sepamla and Others in English: Notes towards a Critical Evaluation'. In Chapman, M. (ed.). *Soweto Poetry*. Johannesburg: McGraw-Hill.

Miller, G.M. and H. Sergeant. 1957. *A Critical Survey of South African Poetry in English*. Cape Town: A.A. Balkema.

Pringle, T. 1834, 1970. 'Afar in the Desert'. *Poems Illustrative of South Africa*. Cape Town: Struik.

Scholes, R. 1985. *Textual Power: Literary Theory and the Teaching of English*. New Haven and London: Yale University Press.

Slater, F.C. 1938. *The Trek: A Poem*. London: Macmillan.

Slater, F.C. 1945. *The New Centenary Book of South African Verse*. London: Longmans.

Slater, F.C. 1954. *Settler's Heritage*. The Lovedale Press.

Visser, N.W. 1982. 'The Situation of Criticism in South Africa'. AUETSA papers.

Voss, A.E. 1982. 'Thomas Pringle and the Image of the "Bushmen"'. *English in Africa*, 9(1), 15-28.

Wilhelm, P. and J. Polley (eds). 1976. *Poetry South Africa: Selected Papers from Poetry '74*. Johannesburg: Ad. Donker.

'Even under the Rine of Terror ...': Insurgent South African Poetry

Jeremy Cronin

In the recent treason trial of sixteen United Democratic Front and trade union leaders, the apartheid prosecutor produced a weighty indictment running to over three hundred pages. The bulk of the indictment consisted in long quotations from the proceedings of political rallies. The speeches were taped, one presumes, by police informers and then transcribed: there are extensive quotations from speeches made and quotations and translations of songs sung and slogans chanted. There is also evidence on the wording on banners, T-shirts, buttons, pamphlets, and flyers. Among this mass of forensic detail, as part of the allegedly treasonable material, there are a few poems, also taped and lovingly transcribed from the same events.

Besides the obvious question (Just who and what *is* treasonable in apartheid South Africa?), there is another irony in this indictment. The state prosecutor has understood more about current black poetry in South Africa than many an academic commentator. The prosecutor has, unwittingly, anthologized the poetry more accurately than is commonly the case in academic appraisal, for this is a poetry that can only be understood and analysed in its relationship to a range of traditional and contemporary oral and verbal practices: songs, chants, slogans, funeral orations, political speeches, sermons, and graffiti. It can be understood only in terms of the context of its major mode of presentation and reception. The book and the small magazine are perhaps not entirely insignificant modes of presentation and reception for this poetry, but they are mostly secondary and excep-

This article first appeared in *Research in African Literatures*, 19(1), 1988, published by the University of Texas Press.

tional. When the book or magazine arrives within the university library, or in the academic's study, it tends willy-nilly to be collocated within a continuum that runs, if South African poetry is in question, from Thomas Pringle through Roy Campbell and William Plomer. Without wishing to disparage the academic reproduction and consumption of poetry, I find it necessary to understand that the conventional modes are more or less entirely inappropriate to deal with much contemporary black poetry in South Africa.

To talk about this poetry, written over the last two or three years, we must contextualize it within the rolling wave of semi-insurrectionary uprisings, mass stayaways, political strikes, consumer boycotts, huge political funerals (involving anything up to seventy thousand mourners at a time), factory occupations, rent boycotts, school and university boycotts, mass rallies, and physical confrontation over barricades with security forces. This wave of mobilization and struggle has spread into the smallest rural village. It has interwoven with a substantial organizational renaissance: youth, civic, religious, women's, trade union, and student organizations have sprung up and spread countrywide.

An emergent (and insurgent) national political culture is an integral part of this rolling wave of mass struggle. Journalists, photographers, and television crews are the only ones so far to have described some of the features of this emergent culture from the outside. Very little academic analysis has yet been done. The *South African Labour Bulletin* has had a brief and lively debate on working-class culture. There have been a few articles on trade union theatre. Some of the earlier academic writing on 'Soweto poetry' is relevant, but somewhat left behind by the speed of unfolding events.[1]

In the hope of assisting tentative beginnings, I shall present, descriptively, and to the best of my ability with all the limitations of the written word, a sampling of poetry performances that have occurred in the last two years. Through adopting this somewhat empirical approach, I hope to give at least an idea of the crucially important context of the poetry. I have drawn selectively, but I hope representatively, from the more than one hundred occasions when I have been either an active (it is difficult not to be that) participant member of an audience, or an actual performer of poetry at political rallies, funerals, protest meetings, and vigils in black ghettos all over South Africa.

A Student Conference

Glynn Thomas Hostel, Soweto, July 1984 — AZASO, the black

university and college students' organization is holding its national conference. Five hundred delegates from all over South Africa, some from AZASO branches in the bantustans where they are compelled to operate clandestinely, are present. The atmosphere is vibrant; for three days the student delegates are locked in intense political discussions, papers, reports, workshops, and elections. The debates and discussions flow over into the hostel rooms and reach into the small hours of the morning. The national question, socialism, Afghanistan, the trade unions — the topics are diverse. For plenary sessions delegates pack into the hostel canteen. There is barely enough space and not enough chairs; one-third of the delegates are left standing, crammed up against walls and into corners. Sometimes emotions run away, and the chairperson or an older guest speaker is compelled to ask for discipline. 'Please, comrades, our task is not to make it easy for the enemy to arrest us. This place is certainly bugged. Comrades must please refrain from wild rhetoric; let us preserve a militant discipline.'

At the end of a paper, or discussion, to give minds awash with stimulation a moment of relaxation, the hall takes off on a series of liberation songs. The singing unfailingly brings the half-dozen stout mamas on the kitchen staff dancing and ululating out from behind the sinks and dishes. They do a little swaying, clapping lap of honour, down the aisles, up to the makeshift stage and round again. Cheers, *amandlas*, vivas, and then silence again as delegates return to the next discussion paper.

The interludes are not all song. Through the three days of conference, there are several poetry performances, notably by two young students from the University of the North, Turfloop. In fact, their performances are in popular demand. 'Poem! Poem!' is a request that gets called out fairly frequently between breaks in the days' sessions. The poetry of the two Turfloop students consists in a set of chanted refrains, one voice leading: 'Cuppa-ta-lismmmma! cuppa-ta-lismmma! cummmma to me-e-e-e!' with the other voice weighing in behind in response, 'I-I-I-I a-m-m-m-m-a cuppa-ta-lismmma.' They have obviously worked out a broad structure and a basic set of refrains, but the performance is considerably extemporaneous. Sometimes the two voices are at separate ends of the canteen, more by chance than design, I guess. They then call to each other across the heads of the five hundred delegates:

Cuppa-ta-lismmmma, cuppa-ta-lismma
A spectre is a hauntinnnga you
This accordinnnnga the gospel

Of Marx and Engels
Cuppa-ta-lissssmmma!

The interplay continues for some time with the second voice
('Capitalism') finally fading away with a long groan to enthusiastic
foot stomping from those present.

The voices perform the poetry with a slow lilt, and from the reaction of the audience, much enjoyment is derived from the phonetic
exaggeration. The principal features of this are an increased stress
and duration of the repeated nasal sounds, particularly *m* sounds.
Some of these are held for a full two or three seconds. There is also
a tendency to lengthen penultimate syllables or to shift lengthened
final syllables (particularly nasals) into penultimates with the addition of a little, lilting schwa as in 'I'mmmmmmma', or 'cuppa-ta-
lismmmmmma'. This gives the English a pronounced, indeed, an
exaggerated African texture.

The poetic thickening of language carries a playfulness as well as
implications of appropriation and nationalization. 'Capitalism', the
signifier, is taken over, smacked about on the lips, and transformed.
Stylistically the poem bears all the marks of its context and function
— a relaxing interlude that is, nevertheless, in key with the political
ambience.

The Political Rally

Poetry performances somewhat like the above occur fairly often in
a variety of contexts, such as mass funerals for political martyrs, rallies, and commemorative church hall meetings. Perhaps the finest
current practitioner of this line of poetry is Mzwakhe Mbuli. It was
he who brought the house down with his poem, 'I Am the Voice
of International Anger', before an audience of fourteen thousand
at the national launch of the United Democratic Front in August
1983. Mzwakhe[2] is tall and angular with bulging pop eyes. His
rhythms are somewhat influenced by the reggae, or dub talking
poetry of Linton Kwesi Johnson.[3] He performs at speed, with a
heavily syncopated intonation, the mostly three- and four-beat
rhythms poked out in the air with two long forefingers.

Ig-nor-rant
I am ignorant
I am ignorant
I have been fortunate
In the business of ignorancy

I am South African
Without residency
I can read,
I can write,
However ignorant I may be
I know Mandela is in Pollsmoor jail
Though I do not know why.
Oh people of Afrika
Help me before it is too late
Eamancipate me
From my ignorancy.

Mzwakhe breaks the rhythm, stops, leans into the microphone, and whispers:

For freedom is getting rusty
On the pavements of oppression.[4]

Sometimes Mzwakhe performs alone. At other times he performs with his group, Khuvangano. Some of the poems are then spoken by one voice, pitched over a freedom song that has dropped down to a hum in the remaining three or four voices of the group. The audience will also tend to take up the humming, particularly if it is a well-known freedom song. This style of declamation over a backdrop of humming might derive from African church rituals.

I say this because I have seen very similar oral performances (he does not call them 'poetry' but 'prayers of remembrance') by Aubrey Mokoena. Mokoena is a well-known political figure and was one of the sixteen charged in the treason trial mentioned above. He is also a part-time preacher. The two occasions on which I have seen him perform were at a mass rally of the Cape Youth Congress (CAYCO), and at the funeral of seven alleged ANC guerillas gunned down in Guguletu, Cape Town. On both occasions Mokoena led the hundreds-strong audience in singing the mourning song, 'Thina Sizwe'. After a minute or so of singing, Mokoena asked those present to drop down to a hum while, microphone in hand, he paced the dais, invoking a long litany of fallen martyrs, of leaders languishing in jail, and of those forced into exile. Mokoena's phrasing is more preacherly, more grand compared to the jerky syncopations of Mzwakhe. But there are also many common elements.

A Trade Union Imbongi[5]

It is the AGM of the local branch of a trade union. The setting is the dance hall of the Belmonte Hotel in Bellville South, an industrial suburb outside Cape Town. Broken bottles and glasses from the night before have been shuffled away behind the stage as several hundred workers cram in under union banners and posters. In between reports, given factory by factory, on percentages of signed-up members, recognition agreements, strike actions (won, lost, deferred), there are cultural interludes. Among them are several African freedom songs. *'Manyanani basebenzi'* ('Workers, let us unite') is rendered as 'Money, not Mercedes Benzes' by some of the 'coloured' workers. An imported 'We shall overcome', sung by the whole hall, is drawn out in a true Cape Flats croon, 'some day-ay-ay'.

Later, an African shop steward in her mid-thirties steps forward. As she moves toward the platform, she is encouraged in song by other women workers from her plant. Some of the male workers cat-call, still others ('Jeyy, thulani, man!') hush them. She wears animal skins, or at least a cut-out and pinned-up plastic bag imitation of skins. On stage she takes the microphone boldly in hand and begins to pace to and fro as she incants at a furious pace, like an old-style *imbongi* (praise poet). She delivers a praise poem to the union and to the collective strength of the workers. Many do not understand all the Xhosa words but, with whispered help, we get the drift. At the end there is enthusiastic applause and shouts for 'More! More! Hmmm!'

A Poetry of Testament

There is another poetry which is fairly widespread, but which is first written down, or even scratched out, before it is performed. This is a poetry of testament, inscribed on cell walls, smuggled out of jails on rolls of toilet paper, or left behind under pillows in the townships. These are poems that involve a slight heightening of language to carry a special meaning, to give significance to the unspeakable. On what evidence I have, I would guess that all over South Africa there are black mothers with little pieces of paper, four- or five-line poems left behind by a son or daughter who has gone in the night to join up with the clandestine liberation movement. The poem, found a day later, is sometimes the last a parent will hear of a child. In the samples I have seen, the language is often clumsy, or formulaic ('for the motherland', 'shed my blood'). But, however spurious this may seem to a literary criticism that measures the 'authentic' in terms of 'individuality' and 'originality', the sincerity and meaningfulness of those little scraps is real enough. The existential acts with which they are integrated speak as loud as the words themselves.

A similar poetry is being smuggled out of jails. The following poem was written by a young member of the Bridgton Youth Organization, Bridgton being the 'coloured' ghetto in Oudtshoorn. The writer is probably a high school student. The poem, entitled 'Mothers of Bhongolethu' (which is the local African township), is dated '9.45 am, 30/6/85'; it is very much a poem of time and place. It was written in detention immediately after one of the countless massacres and widescale arrests:

> Mothers of Bhongolethu,
> You gave birth to the most
> oppressed youth of our nation.
> . . .
> The enemy rejoiced in their death
> But we don't mourn.
> Mothers of Bhongolethu,
> let us mobilize,
> to continue their struggle.
> Let us avenge their death.
>
> Our sons and daughters were
> not armed on that day.
> But the soldiers of Africa
> are marching into our
> townships.
> The day will come when we
> will be ready,
> ready to avenge the death
> of our martyrs.
>
> Mothers of Bhongolethu
> do not despair.
> Do not mourn . . .
> But take courage in the
> blood of our children.
> In the blood that nurtures
> the tree of Freedom.

The most moving of all are the short poems that come from the political prisoners on death row. On the eve of his hanging, young Benjamin Moloise sent out this poem:

> I am proud to be what I am . . .
> The storm of oppression will be followed
> By the rain of my blood

I am proud to give my life

My one solitary life.

The last poem of Moloise, like that of Solomon Mahlangu, another young guerilla executed in Pretoria Maximum Security Prison, has since been repeated at many mass rallies, and so, like most of the other poems we have considered so far, it achieves its major form of reception in public gatherings. Indeed the words of both Mahlangu and Moloise have been incorporated within dozens of longer performed poems.

Some General Poetic Features

I have, in passing, already noted many of the poetic features of the poetry I have been describing. In the interests of moving in the direction of a little more analysis, it is useful to consider in more general terms some of the notable features.

The gestural. The poetry is, clearly, largely a poetry of performance. The bodily presence of the poet becomes an important feature of the poetics. Arm gestures, clapping, and head nodding are often used expressively and deictically. The poets also draw freely from the current political lexis of gesture: the clenched fist salute of people's power (*Amandla ngawethu*); the index finger pointing emphatically down to signal *Ngo!* ('Here and now!') after the chanted call *Inkululeko* ('Freedom'); or the slow, hitchhiker-like thumb sign to signal 'Let it come back' (*Afrika . . . Mayibuye*). These latter collective gestures are used freely within poems and, more often, as framing devices before and after the performance of a poem. The slogans and gestures will be taken up by the whole audience. They act phatically, as channel openers or closers and as a means of focussing attention on the performer.

The clothing of the performer should also be noted. As often as not it is unexceptional. However, quite a few poets, especially those who adopt a more bardic tone, don dashikis as an integral part of their performance. The several trade union praise poets also tend to wear special clothing, traditional skins and ornamentation, or a modern-day facsimile of the kind already noted.

Verbal stylistic features. The most notable verbal stylistic features are those commonly associated with principally oral literatures: the style tends to be additive, aggregative, formulaic, and 'copious'.

In Qwa Qwa
I found no one

In Lebowa
I was unfortunate
In Transkei
I talked about pass laws
Transkei citizenship card
Was the answer
In Bophuthatswana
I talked about democratic and social rights
Sun City was the answer
In KwaVenda
I talked about people's security
The building of Thohoyandou police station
Was the answer
In Ciskei
I talked about trade unionism
The banning of SAAWU
Was the answer
(etc., etc.)
Ma-Afrika,
  I have travelled![6]

The repetitive and formulaic features assist the performing poet mnemonically. But these features also assist the audience to hear and understand the poem. Walter J. Ong notes the limitations of oral, as opposed to written, communication:

> Thought requires some sort of continuity. Writing establishes in the text a 'line' of continuity outside the mind. If distraction confuses or obliterates from the mind the context out of which emerges the material I am now reading, the context can be retrieved by glancing back over the text selectively. Backlooping can be entirely occasional, purely *ad hoc*. . . . In oral discourse, the situation is different. There is nothing to backloop into outside the mind, for the oral utterance has vanished as soon as it is uttered. . . . Redundancy, repetition of the just-said, keeps both speaker and hearer surely on the track. (1982: 39-40)

Apart from these universal features and limitations of the oral, it should be remembered that the poetry we are considering is often performed in the worst imaginable acoustic situations. It is sometimes performed, for instance, in open township soccer fields or crowded halls with no public address systems. The poets are also pitching their poems to audiences that are generally very different from the quiet, reverential salon audience that will occasionally receive poetry of another kind. The poets have to take their chances in between militant mass singing, rousing political speeches, or routine organizational business. They perform to an audience that, generally, warmly acclaims their poetry. But it is an audience which, nevertheless, does not sit tightly in respectful silence. There are women with crying babies on their backs; there are youngsters crawling and toddling underfoot. People are getting up or sitting down. And all the while, hovering just outside the venue, radio transmitters bleeping, are the police with, as often as not, a helicopter rattling overhead.

Agonistically toned features. Another significant feature of much of this poetry is, again, noted by Ong as typical of all oral cultures.

> Many, if not all, oral or residually oral cultures strike literates as extraordinarily agonistic in their verbal performances and indeed in their lifestyle. Writing fosters abstractions that disengage knowledge from the arena where human beings struggle with one another. . . . By keeping knowledge embedded in the human lifeworld, orality situates knowledge within a context of struggle. . . . Bragging about one's own prowess and/or verbal tongue-lashings of an opponent figure regularly in encounters between characters in narrative: in the *Iliad*, in *Beowulf*, throughout medieval European romance, in *The Mwindo Epic* and countless other African stories . . . in the Bible, as between David and Goliath (1 Sam. 17:43-47). Standard in oral societies across the world, reciprocal name-calling has been fitted with a specific name in linguistics: flyting (or fliting). . . . The other side of agonistic name-calling or vituperation in oral or residually oral cultures is the fulsome expression of praise which is found everywhere in connection with orality. (43-45)

There are, in South Africa, strong indigenous traditions of praise poetry. We have already noted the existence, specifically within the trade union movement, of a proletarian reworking and updating of this tradition. But strong agonistic tones are a feature throughout:

> Even under the reign of terror [pronounced 'rine']
> The land is still mine
> My land is immovable
> I am the beats
> Admire me
> I am the beats
> From the drums of change
>   In Afrika.[7]

However, the most notable case of agonistically toned performance is the marching, defiant *toyi-toyi* chant. It is the national favourite with militant youth on the barricades, in their street battles with the army and police armoured cars. The *toyi-toyi* involves a lead voice incanting a long litany of names, some admired like u-Nelson Mandê-ê-ê-êla, Ol-eeee-va Tambo, or Joe Slovo, with appropriate epithets: *ubaba wethu* ('our father'), i-chief commander, and so forth.

Other names are vilified: Le Grange, P.W. Botha, Gatsha Buthelezi. While the lead voice, mostly hidden anonymously deep within
the folds of the crowd, incants, the rest of the squad, group, or
crowd, as the case may be, replies to each name with approbation:

Hayyyiii! . . .
Hayyyiii! Hayyyiii!

or with contempt:

Voetsek! . . .
Voetsek! Voetsek! ('Go to hell!')

All the while, the entire group will be marching or marking time,
knees high, at the double. The *toyi-toyi* litany is also freely sprin-
kled with onomatopoeic evocations of bazookas and 'ukka four
seven' ('AK 47') assault rifles being fired off, of land mines exploding, and of 'freedom potatoes' ('grenati') going off:

Goosh! . . .
Goosh! Goosh!

Whether the *toyi-toyi* is a song, a chant, a march, a war cry, or a
poem is a scholastic point. Functionally, like much of the emergent
culture and all of the poetry I have described, it serves to mobilize
and unite large groups of people. It transforms them into a collective that is capable of facing down a viciously oppressive and well-
equipped police and army. In acting together, under the shadow
of the apartheid guns, the mobilized people are forcing open space
to hold proscribed meetings, to elect and mandate their own leadership, to discuss basic matters, to resolve crime in their streets, to
bury their dead, to raise illegal banners, to unban their banned organizations, to discover their strength, and even to make their own
poetry. In short, through it all, liberated zones are being opened
up in industrial ghettos and rural locations, where the people are
beginning — tenuously it is true — to govern themselves in this land
of their birth.

Notes

1. See Sole and Naledi Writers Unit. In addition to the first Sole article,
   the *South African Labour Bulletin* 9(8) has articles on trade union praise
   poetry and theatre. For a useful anthology of critical writings on con-

temporary black poetry, see Chapman. See also Cronin ('The law . . .').
2. Mzwakhe Mbuli is known by, and performs under, his first name.
3. An informant, Steve Gordon, tells me that Mzwakhe has also been influenced by tapes of Jamaican performance poetry, closely related to dub
poetry.
4. This partial transcription of a Mzwakhe poem is, like others quoted in
this paper, taken from performances I have listened to and from tapes.
Change is Pain is the title of a tape by Mzwakhe, distributed by Shifty
Records, Johannesburg. It was first released in 1986 and subsequently
banned for possession on Christmas Eve of the same year. It is currently
banned for distribution.
5. A version of the following description has already appeared in my review
of Jeff Opland's *Xhosa Oral Poetry* (Ravan Press).
6. From a poem by Mzwakhe Mbuli.
7. Ibid.

References

Chapman, Michael (ed.). 1982. *Soweto Poetry*. Johannesburg: McGraw-Hill.

Cronin, Jeremy. 1985. Review of *Xhosa Oral Poetry*, by Jeff Opland. *Social Dynamics*, 11(2), 91-93.

Cronin, Jeremy. 1985. '"The law that says / Constricts the breath line": South African English Language Poetry Written by Africans in the 1970s'. *The English Academy Review*, 3, 25-30.

Naledi Writers Unit-Medu Art Ensemble. 1985. 'Working Class Culture and Popular Struggle'. *South African Labour Bulletin*, 10(5), 21-30.

Ong, Walter J. 1982. *Orality and Literacy: The Technologizing of the Word*. London: Methuen.

Sole, Kelwyn. 1984. 'Class and Populism'. *South African Labour Bulletin*, 9(8), 54-76.

Sole, Kelwyn. 1985. 'Working Class Culture'. *South African Labour Bulletin*, 10(7), 43-56.

Collective Creativity: Theatre for a Post-Apartheid Society[1]

Ian Steadman

One cannot but be aware of the political context of a discussion of theatre in South Africa, and any such discussion coming at the end of a decade of rapid and radical social upheaval necessitates at least some illumination of contextual matters.

It is clear enough that South African theatre has changed rapidly during the 1980s. Responding to important political and cultural developments, the theatre since 1976 has not only asserted a vigorous new identity, but has also been marketed abroad to an extent where South Africa boasts a high profile at many international festivals.

Despite this high profile, however, it is necessary to question the extent of the proclaimed 'change' in South African theatre, if only because the ways in which South Africans use words like 'change' and 'reform' are ideologically loaded. It may be persuasively argued, for example, that despite opening doors to previously excluded constituencies, the theatre in some quarters has not fundamentally changed as an institution.

In recent years established theatre managements have assumed that their responsibility is to make up for past omissions by providing black theatre practitioners with those skills and opportunities (previously denied) which will enable them to make their way in the (now slightly reformed) theatre industry. Their error lies in assuming that their energies should be directed at educating others. They should, of course, rather focus on re-educating themselves. Like so much in South African cultural life, it is not what must be learnt that is important, but what must be unlearnt.

If there is something to be learnt, it is the difference between reform and change. Certainly, there have been many new developments in South African theatre based on the notion of 'reform'. It is always instructive, however, to compare the fundamentally 'new' with the merely 'novel'. I do not, therefore, want to discuss in any detail those new developments in South African theatre which have occurred within old structures, significant though many of them are. What I want to concentrate on are a few examples of those developments that can teach the established theatre how to unlearn many of its practices, and to abandon many of its old structural constraints.

One of the most important things that the established theatre can learn — one of the most important factors in understanding the changing relationship between South African theatre and South African society — is the value of collective practices in community theatre. But before investigating such a theme, it is necessary to take a closer look at the more established face of South African theatre.

1 *Marketing South African Theatre Abroad*

South African theatre enjoys prominent exposure on the international stage. Ranging from exploitative works which reinforce myths and stereotypes by re-producing on stage false images of black 'tribalism' (Vandenbroucke, 1976) to works by artists committed to exposing such myths and stereotypes, every year since the beginning of the 1980s South African theatre has elicited acclaim in Europe and the United States of America.

Often, the mere presence of a South African theatre group overseas provokes surprise. Why, it is asked, does the South African government, with its reputation for repressive state and ideological apparatuses, allow plays and players — often incisively critical of the status quo — the freedom to tour overseas? The answer is not difficult to find. In a context where the government proclaimed a dubious programme of 'reform', it was pragmatic to be seen to allow a certain critical licence, especially if it remained within the boundaries of art. The commodified forms of cultural resistance, especially if they are purveyed to members of a social group who can afford the price of theatre tickets, are unlikely to have any real effect on the black majority. At the same time, those productions which are considered worthy enough for invitation to the international stage provide a valuable diversion for the South African government. Successful plays about South African politics create the impression that the state endorses freedom of expression. Thus is the facade of 'reform' upheld.

The underlying political significance is not, however, my focus here. What is necessary to note is that the plays which have represented South Africa abroad tend to display some common features which point to new developments along the lines insinuated by myself when I mentioned 'collective' practices in the theatre. That is to say, the traditional guise of the establishment theatre in South Africa has been one rooted in individualism, whereas the new theatre reflects concerns of community and collectivity which point the way to the future.

The phenomenal success of a play like *Asinamali* is but one facet of this argument. It may be argued that of the many plays presented abroad by South Africans in the last ten years — of the many plays which might, therefore, be considered 'successful' in some way — the vast majority have been created in 'workshop' through the process of collaborative work rather than — in the mould of Athol Fugard's favoured approach — being produced by the writer at his or her desk. (Of interest, of course, is the argument that even Fugard's real successes were his collaborative plays with John Kani and Winston Ntshona — although I would not be prepared to reduce Fugard's work to such a simplistic basis for assessment.) What seems to be manifesting itself is a clear sense that South African theatre is most successful when it is created as an analogue of group experience: the experience of the oppressed. Is this perhaps homologous with a sense of the demise of liberalism? Has the emergence of popular democratic politics signalled the emergence of collective creative work and the end of a situation where an individual progressive artist is allowed to speak on behalf of the oppressed? Has the cult of individualism, of personality — with all its implications regarding a 'star' system — begun to fray at the edges?

One way of answering these questions is to investigate the emergence, during the 1980s, of forms of theatrical endeavour which demonstrate a collective approach. It is of further interest to note those occasions when an alleged adherence to group creativity is undermined by an unconscious ideological commitment to the cult of individualism. For the cult of individualism — or personality — inscribes, of course, a political ideal.

2 *Studying South African Theatre*

Before we proceed, however, it is necessary to discuss some of the difficulties involved in studying the theatre in South Africa.

In South African cultural studies the theatre is important in two ways. Firstly, it signifies a repressive society. Secondly, the study of theatre signifies the ways in which forms of domination and resistance undermine scholars' attempts to understand their society. The received traditions of theatre and of theatre scholarship have for generations reproduced South Africa's confusing network of political and cultural relations.

Authoritative histories of this theatre have approached their subject under the influence of a dominant notion of what theatre is and what it does: the published record largely trivializes creative work which challenges the status quo in South African politics. In journal articles, encyclopaedia, and critical monographs on the subject the same premise is operative: theatre is conceptualized within a Eurocentric vision of stage entertainment.[2]

Because of the operation, historically, of European hegemony, we know comparatively little about the ways in which oppressed people in South Africa responded to historical change and development. We know even less about the ways in which their responses influenced and were influenced by their forms of cultural expression. At a time when South African theatre is prominent in the international arena, this essay attempts to describe salient features of another kind of South African theatre — one which is not prominent because it does not have access to the media and marketing strategies employed by the professional theatre managements. The theatre under discussion here is created by practitioners who share at least one basic assumption: that theatre can be used as a form of oppositional cultural practice, and that it can therefore be described as 'resistance theatre'.

In filling a gap in our knowledge of South African culture by describing the major features of this theatre, this essay also contributes in some small measure to revising current critical attitudes about the role and function of theatre in a country caught in political crisis. In the context of the current political struggle in South Africa, the theatre has featured prominently in cultural debate. The notion of 'cultural struggle' in South Africa incorporates many features of the conflict presently being played out in the political arena. Lodge (1983: ix) suggests that whereas his book is about black political resistance, there is a further story to be told about other kinds of resistance. The theatre in South Africa tells such a story, elucidating aspects of political resistance in ways which are not immediately apparent to observers looking for direct political statements. Work has already been undertaken in this field in relation to music (Coplan, 1985) and in relation to theatre in the 1970s (Kavanagh, 1985). This paper focusses on three types of theatre in the 1980s which illustrate the theme of collaborative group creativity.

3 Community Theatre

The idea that the performing arts provide tools for social action has prompted fairly widespread work in community theatre. Kidd and Colletta (1981) have edited a representative collection of essays in the field, demonstrating the role of drama and performance in literacy programmes, community health and numerous other areas of community endeavour in the Third World. In South Africa community theatre is a phenomenon which has become increasingly prominent during the 1980s. This theatre has been described as 'goal-oriented' (Blecher, 1980) because it is seen to provide solutions to problems.

Such work is exemplified by a project at the Winterveld squatter camp, in which theatre was used to educate a community: not only to extend awareness, but also to provide skills for acting upon that awareness. Firstly, the day-to-day problems and needs of squatters emerged in role-playing exercises. Medical needs, the problems of unemployment and education, the psychological effects of squatter life and many other issues were explored through the medium of theatre. At this stage theatre was still functioning merely as a consciousness-raising medium. The project then moved from merely showing what the problems were, to showing the community how to cope with them. A nutritionist, for example, dramatized a scene showing the community-audience how to cultivate food with meagre resources. Such scenes are of practical use to the community because they extend the function of theatre from conscientization to social action.

A similar project was undertaken in 1983 with the Crossroads squatter community in the Cape peninsula. Here a play entitled *How long, Crossroads?* was created with a group of squatters and documented by a student who was one of the co-ordinators of the project (Fox, 1984). The group, dramatizing aspects of their lives as squatters, became known as the Squatter Players, and toured throughout the region, educating communities about the underlying causes of their situation, and demystifying media reports about it. The play was also performed during political meetings, and became an active ingredient in politicization. Like the Winterveld project, the Crossroads play was conceived as a strategy for social action.

Both the Winterveld project and the Crossroads project represented attempts to conscientize oppressed communities through means which were alternative to the mass media. The specific tools employed have been described as 'folk media' (Kidd and Colletta, 1981: 281). In each case, however, the initiative came not from the communities themselves, but from cultural agents: educated social workers and theatre practitioners who entered the communities as outsiders and attempted to use the experiences of community members in order to educate them. In the Winterveld project, the community was taught how to match needs with resources. In the Crossroads project, the community dramatized a view of their oppression. In both cases outside agents co-ordinated the work.

These cultural agents who co-ordinate the experiments bring to the work their own ideological perspective. There is a difference between theatre which shows the community how to survive in a system, and theatre which shows the community how to mobilize resources in order to confront the system. The former reproduces the relations of domination and exploitation while providing means for the exploited to survive within the system. The latter demystifies the relations of domination and exploitation and shows that they can be altered.

The Crossroads play demonstrates one aspect of this problem. Members of the community participated in the creation of a play which showed them various aspects of the exploitative relations which caused squatter camps to develop. Thus both participants and audience were re-educated. Such processes facilitate the growth of group consciousness: participatory theatre becomes an analogue for social action because the participants, by making their own play about resistance, are rehearsing, as it were, strategies of political resistance — and the very process of making the play involves the development of group solidarity and all the relations which that expresses. Thus the residents of Crossroads, when attending a performance and responding to it, joined in the singing of freedom songs, threw stones at the character of the policeman on stage, and expressed solidarity with the defiant squatters represented in the action (Fox, 1984: 13). Nevertheless, the play inscribed in its structure and discourse something of the values and ideology of the cultural agents who co-ordinated the project. Despite an alleged adherence to Paulo Freire's educational principles (Fox, 1984: 4), the project could not rid itself of a certain conformity to the logic of its co-ordinators. Thus, for example, the answer to the problem of oppression at the end of the play comes in the form of an enlightened decision by the law courts. Although a challenge has been made, the play ends by upholding the logic of the system.

While the practitioners of community theatre might claim that their work constitutes positive social action, community theatre can sometimes produce passivity instead of active critical understanding and response. In South Africa, effective community theatre is not that which shows communities that they are poor and must find ways to cope. Effective community theatre is that which demonstrates the

structural and ideological relations of oppression and exploitation
and which posits strategies of resistance to that oppression and exploitation. One of the ways in which this has been demonstrated
in South Africa is through trade union theatre.

4 Trade Union Theatre

One of the most innovative developments in South African theatre
in the 1980s has been the phenomenon of trade union theatre. The
significance of this development lies in its implications for a notion
of effective community theatre.

Unlike literature and film, theatre can be relatively free of the constraints of technology and capital and is accessible to the majority
in South Africa. It is able to show experience in dynamic ways. In
recent 'worker plays' the theatre has achieved an important educa-
tive function, as well as providing a context for solidarity within a
worker collective. Thus theatre is used not merely for conscientization but for material social action. In 1987, *The Long March*, work-
shopped and performed by workers striking for legal recognition
as a union, not only represented a lesson in union solidarity, but
also offered a way of raising money for the strikers. Following this
initial impulse, the workers created co-operatives, staged concerts
and started subsidiary industries for their community (who were
suffering deprivation as a result of the strike). *The Long March*
demonstrated that theatre need not remain a form of cultural 'expression', but could provide the context for community action.

The play *Ilanga Lizophumela Abasebenzi* ('The Sun Shall Rise for the
Workers') had its germination (Tomaselli, 1981: 14-33) in a role-
playing exercise devised by a labour lawyer for black workers of the
Metal and Allied Workers' Union. A dispute had arisen between
the management of an iron foundry and the union's shop stewards.
A decision was taken to call a meeting of workers who would discuss the problem prior to a meeting with the management. Interpreting the work-stoppage as an illegal strike, management called
in the police. Fifty-five workers were arrested and taken to the Boks-
burg police station. In preparing a defence on the basis that the work-
stoppage had been a legitimate meeting and not an illegal strike,
the lawyer decided to gather evidence from the workers by creating a few role-playing exercises in order to determine the nuances
of each stage of the action which led to the stoppage. These role-
playing exercises became the nucleus of a play which was then extended through rehearsals and workshops.

Ilanga eventually materialized into a play which was performed in numerous venues for other black workers. Included in the cast of the play were some of the workers who had originally been involved in the dispute and the subsequent role-playing exercises. When the play was performed, the performers/workers were reenacting events that had actually occurred. For worker audiences, then, the experience was qualitatively different from that which constitutes the normal play-going activity. What the theatre manages to do in such instances is to show the workplace from within: the relations of exploitation are demystified in ways which are not merely explained but dynamically shown. When performed for audiences of other metal workers, this process was extended. The audiences in such cases were drawn into the action. No longer passive spectators, they became active participants. The worker-actors on stage would ask the audiences for their opinions and advice on important issues: Should they strike? What are the possibilities of a collapse in worker solidarity? What are the answers to the exploitation of workers? The play elicited from audiences their own opinions regarding worker solidarity in the union, strike action, and strategies to resist exploitation. *Ilanga* became a forum for educating workers about trade unionism and for demystifying the exploitative relations of employment.

Because there is no text of the play, an example must be based on a rough paraphrasing of dialogue which, in any case, changed from one performance to the next, depending on the audience's response and the actors' imaginative improvisations. Based on the actual events at the iron foundry, one scene showed a Department of Labour official trying to defuse the workers' demands for a meeting with the management. The official, speaking through an interpreter, tried to persuade the workers to reject talk of union representation and to accept instead management's proposal for an in-house liaison committee. The dialogue progressed roughly thus:

> OFFICIAL: Tell them that talk about unions will make them lose their heads . . . tell them that industry is like Bantu society: the manager is their father. Do they talk to their father in Bantu society? No . . . they talk to their mother who talks to their father . . . and who is the mother of all black workers? The Department of Labour.

At this point, during one performance, the lively response from one member of the worker-audience brought cheers and laughter from his fellow spectators:

> Does the manager sleep with the Department of Labour?

The audience, then, are part-actors. They are asked their opinion about going on strike. If they urge the worker-actors to do so, then the latter argue with them, explaining the problems associated with a strike decision and making the audience consider the implications of a lack of solidarity, the cost of strike action to members of the union, and other factors. If the audience suggests that the workers should not strike, then the opposite point of view is argued. Either way, debate is encouraged amongst the audience until they begin to understand the ways in which industrial relations are structured and the opportunities which exist to resist the formal structures when necessary.

The emergence of theatre by workers and about workers' experiences has important implications for our understanding of political significance in South African cultural studies. The emergence of trade union theatre has generated much debate about the relative importance of phenomena like 'popular culture', 'working-class culture' and theatre as the 'authentic' representation of the viewpoints of particular 'groups' in South African society.[3] There is the insinuation, for example, that plays like *Ilanga*, dealing as they do with the experiences of workers, are more or less 'authentic' depending on the degree of interference by cultural agents from a more privileged social background.

For example, *Ilanga*, like the Winterveld project and the Crossroads project, did not germinate in spontaneous working-class activity. The initiatives which led to theatrical production came again from 'agents' or 'co-ordinators'. After the initial experiments in role-playing by the labour lawyer, the play was developed under the guidance of co-ordinators from a professional theatre group, the Junction Avenue Theatre Company. Leadership was provided by intellectuals. The cultural interventions of intellectuals in the processes of working-class culture can boast positive results, as our examples demonstrate. It is a fact, however, that such intervention gives the lie to the very notion that these projects represent independent working-class activity. To find, after community theatre and trade union theatre, a third category of theatre which can claim to avoid the problem of cultural intervention by non-oppressed white agents, we have to turn elsewhere.

5 *Popular Theatre*

A popularly-supported syncretic form of entertainment commonly known as 'the township musical' only came to the attention of academic observers of South African theatre comparatively recently, and it is perhaps symptomatic of the distortions of our cultural history that the international community is virtually unaware of the volume of theatre produced in the townships. The repressive political climate of the late 1980s ensures that there is nothing like the amount of work which was apparent in, for example, the 1970s, but it is nevertheless a fact that most white South African theatre-goers are unaware of the real traditions of their theatre.[4]

Melodrama, musical comedy and committed agit-prop theatre have long been the staple diet of black theatre-goers in the townships. Conventional critical methods based on a sociology of these performance pieces and on descriptive exegesis can yield fairly obvious features of a 'real' experience of life in the townships (Kavanagh, 1981). Beyond such conventional descriptive methods, however, there has been insufficient in-depth study of this work. One reason has been the scarcity of textual records of the work. The very nature of these theatrical performances demands research methods drawn from an 'archaeology' of theatre: excavating the record of performance, analysing the creative processes at work in relation to their wider implications, and studying the performances not as commodities but as social action of a specific kind (Clark, 1979: 43). Even the present restricted and word-bound description of such work falls short of what is required for a full appreciation of the dimensions of the work in performance. Nevertheless, it is still possible to present an impression of the kind of theatre under discussion here.

Reverend Mzwandile Maqina lives in New Brighton, a township outside Port Elizabeth. In 1975 and 1976 his play *Give Us This Day*, based on the murder by parcel-bomb of exiled student leader Onkgopotse Abraham Tiro, was performed to extraordinary acclaim in the townships. It was banned in May 1976. Maqina immediately created another play, *The Trial*, based on a young girl's struggles against repressive and discriminatory laws. The play was banned and Maqina detained. As soon as he was released he began work on another play.[5] This time Maqina was banned and put under house arrest for five years. As soon as his banning order expired in March 1982 he began work on his next production. He was again banned in June 1982 for a further period of three years. His banning order was lifted in July 1983 and he immediately began work on his play *Dry Those Tears*.

Maqina was clearly, during this period, a committed theatre practitioner. Quite apart from his stubborn determination, the nature of his work earned him the respect of the many thousands who knew what his theatre stood for. He was not only a theatre practitioner, but a community leader as well. He did not boast a company of professional actors. His plays were performed by unemployed black proletarians who lived off whatever donations were received at the door in community halls and church halls where they performed. They were people who were quite simply using the stage as a platform to express their solidarity with Maqina as cultural workers. While performing in November 1983, the leading actress in *Dry Those Tears* was five months pregnant. She told this interviewer that theatre offered her the opportunity to 'sing our grievances against the system'.

Dry Those Tears is a play incorporating numerous scenes in the tradition of the Brechtian *lehrstücke*, interspersed with songs in both Xhosa and English. The central song, which expresses the thematic core of the play, is 'We have the right to sell our labour'. The action of the play traces the adventures of Gift, a young man who attempts to find employment and is trapped by the vast web of bureaucratic laws and controls which frustrate the black work-seeker. The various scenes of the play explore the social and psychological alienation which eventually drives Gift to suicide, prompting the full cast to close the play in singing a song, with the audience participating in a solemn rite of resistance. Based on a simple newspaper report, the play depicts the typical status of the young black work-seeker, contradicting the many mystifying state pronouncements at the time regarding 'reform' in the labour market.

Only the context of performance can fully explain the nature of Maqina's theatre. The above description indicates little of the active participation of his audiences during the presentation of the play in 1983. Exclamations from the audience, shouts of solidarity, salutes and raised fists, the singing of freedom songs — these signified that the play was more than mere entertainment. Like the responses of audiences to *Ilanga*, the response of audiences to Maqina's productions made his theatre an active forum for the celebration of black resistance.

Maqina's theatre may be conceptualized as 'popular' theatre, in which a member of the majority oppressed group presents to a cross-section of that group a theatrical demystification of events in relation to a broad vision of structural change (Kidd and Colletta, 1981: 281). As such, his theatre can be distinguished from both community theatre and trade union theatre — at least in the forms we have described above. Maqina's plays contributed to a sustained critique of the dominant group and a reinforcement of political consciousness amongst his audiences, and the work was not generated by outside cultural agents.[6]

Nevertheless, in all three types of theatre under discussion here, there exists a similar problem. How is conscientization transformed into action? Within South Africa, discussions of the role of theatre in social 'change' have prompted unrealistic notions about the efficacy of cultural expression in political resistance. Sentimentality characterizes most of these discussions.[7] What can be said with some assurance is that theatre of the kind under discussion here contributes to effective 'change' only when it is part of a broadly-based social or political movement. The foregoing discussion of three types of theatre is cast in a more significant mould when we consider the notion of 'black' theatre in South Africa.

6 Black Theatre

Theatre seldom mobilizes people to act. It can, however, play an important part in that mobilizing process. In the 1974-1975 'Treason Trial' in South Africa, two of the five organizations listed in the charge sheet were theatre groups, and a number of the accused were charged on the basis of their activities in theatre.[8] The state clearly conceived of theatre as playing a significant role in the black liberation movement. Much of the impact of black theatre during the 1970s was the result of its identification with Black Consciousness. It was during this period that theatre was considered — and not only by the state — an integral part of the movement towards liberation. Theatre played a genuine role in mobilization. Dramatic sketches, performed poetry and didactic 'teaching plays' were presented at political meetings, on university campuses and at festivals, where they were an important factor in the rising tide of militant black resistance. After 1976, however, this theatre was co-opted in different ways. Initial retaliatory action by the state, cultural appropriation by the newly-launched television industry and 'multiracial' theatre groups, and crises within the ranks of Black Consciousness all helped to fragment black theatre. It was not until 1980, with the developments outlined in this paper, that the theatre again began to play a prominent role in 'resistance'. What has changed, however, is a network of relationships between class, race and nationalism: and this has important implications for a notion of resistance theatre.

The developments we have described above — in community, trade union and popular township theatre — have all taken place in an era when the earlier conception of political liberation based on Black Consciousness has been overtaken by a conception of liberation based on an alliance of progressive forces. It is not my intention to rehearse here the obvious merits of this development. What I wish to raise is one aspect of loss: to what extent has the effectiveness of black theatre been dissipated by a shift in emphasis away from Black Consciousness? It can be argued that in the 1970s Black Consciousness sponsored a truly emergent[9] theatre. Radically debunking tendencies in cultural expression which were associated with white norms and standards, black artists[10] responded to the Black Consciousness programme of creating works which were innovative expressions of 'black experience'. A 'new* wave of energy'[11] emerged in black theatre with 'blackness' as its point of departure. Audiences at this theatre, despite differences in language, class and status, shared a commonality — a mythology of blackness, as it were. An affirmation of blackness by both performers and spectators in the theatre was held by Black Consciousness theatre practitioners to be the source and the focus of a revolutionary collective consciousness. The very condition of that consciousness was blackness. Black theatre was both a product of this relationship and helped to mould it.

In the years following 1976 popular township musicals continued to be presented, but the focus of work in black theatre shifted to non-racial collaborations, mostly sponsored by white capital and under the artistic control of whites.[12] Militantly exclusive black theatre was temporarily anaesthetized.[13] The very notion of 'black' literature and theatre began to be critically scrutinized as an idealistic conception.[14] During the formative years of Black Consciousness, committed theatre practitioners had been harassed, detained, and banned, but despite such repression their work was prolific (though relatively unknown outside the townships and hardly at all known internationally). In the present crisis, despite the most sustained and systematic repression yet enacted by the state against progressive forces, theatre practitioners are relatively untouched, yet the volume of work in the townships has decreased (in inverse proportion to the increase in the volume of South African theatre presented both internationally and in theatres sponsored by white capital).

Perhaps one example will suffice to demonstrate the point being made here. In 1984 Maishe Maponya, a playwright who has produced much in the Black Consciousness mould, was informed by the state censorship authorities that he could continue to present his play *Gangsters* in small experimental theatres such as that housed in Johannesburg's Market Theatre, but that on no account was he permitted to perform the play elsewhere without first obtaining the permission of the authorities. Clearly the state considers the Market Theatre a 'safe' venue.

This essay has attempted to draw attention, at a time when South African theatre enjoys prominent exposure on international stages, to other types of theatre which do not have access to the capital and marketing strategies of professional companies. It is a time of political crisis in South Africa. While some South Africans are celebrating the death of apartheid, the theatre continues to signify the exploitative relations of social life which will long continue to be the heritage of apartheid.

Notes

1. A draft of this essay was read at the Winter School of the Grahamstown Festival on 9 July 1987.
2. Every encyclopaedia of world theatre up to 1987 exemplified this problem. See also Graham-White (1974) and Woodrow (1970).
3. The debates over this issue are exemplified in the pages of the *South African Labour Bulletin* from 1984 to 1985.
4. Kavanagh (1981) and Kavanagh (1985) contain the most detailed study of the subject.
5. Maqina told this interviewer that the play, *The Crack*, dealt with 'the crumbling edifice of apartheid'. Production plans were cut short by his banning order.
6. Maqina has recently become notorious for adopting a moderate political stance, and his work in theatre seems to have ceased.
7. See, for example, a special issue of the Johannesburg-based magazine for the performing arts, *Scenaria*, 1986, entitled 'The Arts in South Africa — A Force for Social Change'.
8. Documentary Exhibits for the trial and a copy of the Charge Sheet are housed in the archives of the National English Literary Museum in Grahamstown.
9. The term refers to Raymond Williams's (1977) distinction between dominant, residual and emergent elements.
10. In referring to black artists here I am by no means forgetful of important non-racial work by groups outside the Black Consciousness movement, for example, the group Workshop '71. See Kavanagh (1985).
11. The phrase is an umbrella term used for the special issue of *Theatre Quarterly*, 7(28), 1977, devoted to South African Theatre.
12. The Market Theatre of Johannesburg is the most prominent of these groups, and is the home for most innovative work in professional theatre in South Africa.
13. Benjy Francis, promoting a strong Black Consciousness line, formed a group in 1982 and eventually opened a new black theatre called the Dhlomo Theatre, which was soon closed down by the Fire Department on the grounds that it did not properly observe safety regulations.
14. See, for example, Sole (1983).

References

Blecher, H. 1980. 'Goal-Oriented Theatre in the Winterveld'. *Critical Arts*, 1(3), 23-39.

Clark, VeVe A. 1979. 'The Archaeology of Black Theatre'. *The Black Scholar*, 10(10), 43-56.

Coplan, D. 1985. *In Township Tonight! South Africa's Black City Music and Theatre*. Johannesburg: Ravan Press.

Fox, J.M. 1984. 'Community Theatre in the Western Cape: A Case Study'. University of Cape Town: unpublished undergraduate thesis.

Graham-White, Anthony. 1974. *The Drama of Black Africa*. New York: Samuel French.

Kavanagh, R. 1981. *South African People's Plays*. London: Heinemann.

Kavanagh, R. 1985. *Theatre and Cultural Struggle in South Africa*. London: Zed.

Kidd, R. and N. Colletta. 1981. *Tradition for Development: Indigenous Structures and Folk Media in Non-Formal Education*. Bonn: International Council for Adult Education.

Lodge, T. 1983. *Black Politics in South Africa since 1945*. Johannesburg: Ravan Press.

Sole, K. 1983. 'Culture, Politics and the Black Writer: A Critical Look at Prevailing Assumptions'. *English in Africa*, 10(1), 37-84.

Tomaselli, K. 1981. 'The Semiotics of Alternative Theatre in South Africa'. *Critical Arts*, 2(1), 14-33.

Vandenbroucke, R. 1976. 'South African Blacksploitation'. *Yale Theatre*, 8(1), 68-71.

Williams, R. 1977. *Marxism and Literature*. Oxford: O.U.P.

Woodrow, M. 1970. 'South African Drama in English'. *English Studies in Africa*, 13(2), 391-410.

Literature and Crisis: One Hundred Years of Afrikaans Literature and Afrikaner Nationalism

Ampie Coetzee

The history of Afrikaans literature has been very well document-ed.[1] But those who have traced its contours were so engrossed with their delineations that they apparently forgot the lay of the land. Theories based on aesthetic excellence dominated the interpretations and periodizations of that literature. Literary texts were described in their chronological order of publication and regarding their 'contribution to Afrikaans literature'; 'Afrikaans literature' thus became the literary canon against which texts were measured.

Why would one want to 'rewrite' the history of this literature? As another academic exercise, or as an attempt at being alternative and relevant? No, the exercise is necessary because eventually in one unitary, non-racial, democratic South Africa, Afrikaans litera-ture cannot have a history apart; Afrikaans literature has to become part of a national culture, a national literature, which would never exclude any text from our history, but which may shift the empha-sis from the pure and untouchable aesthetic text (as it may have been canonized) to other texts which may have more to say within a na-tional consciousness. There may be many reasons for deciphering the cultural monuments of the past from the perspective of histori-cal materialism. Walter Benjamin provides one when he says 'there has never been a document of culture which was not at one and the same time a document of barbarism' (Benjamin, 1982: 258). Jame-son provides another: ' . . . it is increasingly clear in today's world . . . that a Left which cannot grasp the immense Utopian ap-peal of nationalism (any more than it can grasp that of religion or of fascism) can scarcely hope to "reappropriate" such collective energies and must effectively doom itself to political impotence' (Jameson, 1981: 298).

At the time of the invention of a tradition of Afrikaner nationalism, and the conscious creation of a literature in Afrikaans at the beginning of the century, the importance of a national consciousness was recognized in the production of literature (Hofmeyr, 1987: 95-123). But this literature's slight movement away from narrow nationalism in the thirties, and the partial demise of Afrikaner nationalism in the seventies for the sake of capitalism, as well as the definite anti-hegemonic position of most Afrikaans prose in the time of militarization in the late seventies and eighties have not been explained. Furthermore, Afrikaans literature has always been viewed from a white, ruling class perspective. Historical events, race and class confrontations, the totality of South African history have only been mentioned in the introductory paragraphs of literary histories, as if Afrikaans literature existed in a sphere of its own. There has therefore never been an attempt to integrate this literature into the master narrative of South African history; it has thus far only been listened to as one half of an imaginary dialogue: 'A hegemonic discourse, in fact, has just this character: historically speaking we "hear" only one voice because a hegemonic ideology suppresses or marginalizes all antagonistic class voices, and yet the hegemonic discourse remains locked into a dialogue with the discourse it has suppressed' (Dowling, 1984: 131).

This essay will attempt to look at the history of South Africa from a materialist point of view, to look for a dialectic between Afrikaans literature and an infrastructure of class and race conflict, and where there is no apparent dialectic to try and explain the silences. I am fully aware that I am venturing onto dangerous ground. The debate on the relative importance of class within the orthodox Marxist paradigm is never-ending. Looking at South African history from a class point of view there is the innovative work of Frederick Johnstone. Deborah Posel's criticism of Johnstone (or this class perspective) takes the history of the Afrikaner into account; and recently the debate on class surfaced again in a book by Ellen Meiksens Wood.[2]

Because of the scope of the task I am proposing – Kannemeyer's recent history of Afrikaans literature consists of two volumes of over 500 pages each — this essay can only be a pilot study. One also has to keep in mind that reading Afrikaans literary texts in isolation can become a one-sided affair. The short history of this literature (particularly as canonized literature), the situations of crisis in which it has been produced, its 'apartness' from other literatures and cultures in South Africa and its consequent 'inbreeding' — all these suggest that the literature requires a total reading, as one text.

Regarding the concept 'literary text' I shall accept as literary those texts that have to a greater or lesser extent been canonized by Afrikaans literary critics, although an extensive rewriting of Afrikaans literary history would obviously have to explain the choice of texts in terms of the ideologies of the current aesthetics. My basic approach to the interpretation of the text would be that of Fredric Jameson, 'that all literature must be read as a symbolic meditation on the destiny of community' (1981: 70), and that these symbolic acts are resolutions of contradictions in society. The individual text should be seen as an individual utterance ('parole') in the wider system ('langue') of class discourse: 'The individual text retains its formal structure as a symbolic act: yet the value and character of such symbolic action are now significantly modified and enlarged. On this rewriting, the individual utterance or text is grasped as a symbolic move in an èssentially polemic and strategic ideological confrontation between the classes . . .' (1981: 85)

The 'appropriation' of the developing Afrikaans language round about 1875 as an incitement to national consciousness and the creation of a literature to strengthen that consciousness have sited this literature within a political arena from its beginning, and it is within this arena that I would like to view it — but then not only as the Afrikaner has seen it, or in terms of white ruling class values.[3] One would have to look at the class struggle between capital and labour, and racial domination would have to be seen in its class instrumentality, as a discourse of domination: 'The whole basis of our particular system in South Africa rests on inequality. . . . It is the bedrock of our constitution . . . .' (Marks and Trapido, 1987: 32) But because one is working at the 'superstructural' level a reductionist historical materialism has to be guarded against, as Johnstone clearly states: 'But the more we move from political economy into such areas as political sociology and social psychology — to issues of culture and subjectivity, of ideology and psychology, of meaning and identity, the more the Marxist approach is faced with the paradigmatic weaknesses of an essentially materialist approach confronted by the role of non-economic factors in history and society' (Johnstone, 1982: 23).[4] Furthermore, the role of Afrikaner nationalism cannot merely be read in terms of class as it was not originally devised for domination, but rather to promote coherence among a threatened people and define their identity.

The periodization of Afrikaans literature I would now like to suggest is made from a historical materialist paradigm but also takes into account Afrikaner nationalism:

1 1875-1922
2 1922-1948
3 1948-1961
4 1961-1976
5 After 1976.

The dates 1922, 1948, 1961 and 1976 have been decided upon following a reading of Antonio Gramsci's concept of crisis:

> A crisis occurs, sometimes lasting for decades. This exceptional duration means that incurable structural contradictions have revealed themselves . . ., and that, despite this, the political forces which are struggling to conserve and defend the existing structure itself are making every effort to cure them, within certain limits, and to overcome them. These incessant and persistent efforts . . . form the terrain of the 'conjunctural', and it is upon this terrain that the forces of opposition organise. (Gramsci, 1978: 178)

On these dates the terrain of the conjunctural was clearly defined within the dialectics of power: 1922 — the Rand Rebellion; 1948 — the beginning of the Afrikaner Nationalist dream state; 1961 — the coming of the Republic, the first attacks of the ANC's Umkonto we Sizwe, and the banning of the ANC and the PAC; 1976 — the Soweto Rebellion.

1 *1875-1922*

The discovery of diamonds and gold in South Africa in the 1870s and 80s can be seen as the serious beginning of industrialization and of a capitalist mode of production. At almost the same time reaction against British colonization and anglicization led to the creation of the Genootskap vir Regte Afrikaners (GRA — Association of True Afrikaners) in the Cape in 1875. Rallying around the 'kitchen patois', Afrikaans — which developed from Dutch, Malayan and a mixture of languages at the Cape (mostly spoken by 'people of colour' and slaves) — the men of the Genootskap were responsible for guiding the beginnings of a cultural and national movement. With their newspaper *Die Afrikaanse Patriot* (first edition 15 January 1876) they began the invention of a literary tradition in a new language, with 'alternative' Afrikaner history (*Die geskiedenis van ons land in die taal van ons volk*, 1877, The history of our country in the language of our people), and a first book for children (*Eerste*

Afrikaanse prentjies boekie vir soet kinders, 1879, First Afrikaans picture book for good children).

Although at the beginning of South Africa's history as a colonized country nationalism and capitalism were the forces contending for domination, the first literary products were aimed at educating and entertaining readers about history, social evils and race. The work of the leading person of the GRA, S.J. du Toit (1847-1911) also aimed at creating an awareness of 'literature' and the fictional. The 'profound and violent transformations' (O'Meara, 1983: 67) that growing industrialization and proletarianization brought about at the beginning of the century were not addressed in a literature that was preoccupied with a new language and with nationalism — but nevertheless the facts of language and ethnicity '. . . can perhaps best be understood as a response to the social dislocations and problems posed by the uneven development of capitalism in South Africa . . .' (Marks and Trapido, 1987: 10).

It was not the political and economic causes and consequences of the Anglo-Boer War (1899-1902) which were the concerns of the poems of the first major Afrikaans poets (Jan F.E. Celliers, 1865-1940; J.D. du Toit (Totius), 1877-1953; and C. Louis Leipoldt, 1880-1947), but the human suffering the war entailed, expressed in a poetic fashion, necessary to transcend that moment in history, to universalize suffering. The bitterness after the war was reflected in the work of Leipoldt and Totius. But very little was written in Afrikaans literary texts about economic realities, such as the endeavours of Sir Alfred Milner to make South Africa a place fit for capitalism after the war, and his fruitful attempts at bringing the mines back into full production. It is as if the Milner reconstruction period — with its allocation of African 'reserves', the control of urban influx, the ideology of segregation — and the beginning of a fatal discourse of racial domination, of white appropriation of the means of production, of surplus and the control of labour (Johnstone, 1982: 10), went totally unnoticed by the Afrikaans writer.

Why? Because Afrikaans writers were also busy with reconstruction, with cultural reconstruction, creating, especially in poetry, a monologic tradition of the aesthetic and of excellence; and in prose, entertaining, teaching their people to read. They were striving towards the confirmation of Afrikaans as a language, founding at the initiative of people like Gustav S. Preller (1875-1943) the Afrikaanse Taalgenootskap (Afrikaans Language Association) in 1905. Preller wrote eloquently on the grass-roots importance of Afrikaans:

The language living in a country, taking root in all the people, has in that country and among that people the best chance of survival, and will not be destroyed except with the destruction of the people in which it lives. . . . Afrikaans finds its roots deep and lives healthily in the whole Afrikaner nation. (Kannemeyer, 1983: 85)

The texts of the time situate the Afrikaans writer unambiguously on the side of the colonizer: *Jakob Platjie*, 1906, by G.R. von Wielligh (1859-1932), and *Klaas Windvoöl*, 1910, by Melt J. Brink (1842-1925). The theme of the first is summarized clearly in the words of one of the characters:

'Yes, we want to go and stick a white person's head on the shoulders of a Hottentot, but we will never succeed.' (Gerwel, 1983: 94)

These books tell the story of white benefactors who attempt to 'civilize' and assimilate the 'Hottentot', but who at the same time confess to the inherent inequality of the races and the impossibility of their project. Basically these texts state the case for cultural control over black ('coloured') people, '. . . a process whereby people of colour are relieved of any autonomous cultural way of living and consequently have to fall back upon the superimposed dominant culture, but at the same time their full assimilation into that culture is everywhere blocked' (1983: 74).

'Union transformed the main population groups — the Africans, Afrikaners and English — into monoliths, each of which had its own history, culture, definition of the so-called race problem and solution to it. Each had fundamental strengths, basic weaknesses and peculiar concerns which determined political goals, shaped policies, fixed priorities and dictated strategies.' (Ngubane, 1987: 141) Around 1910 new ethnic identities began to emerge, but the English controlled the state and dominated the economy. Ethnic mobilization would be the only means whereby an Afrikaner monolith would take control of the state.

The conscious response of Afrikaner nationalist culture was to set up publishing houses (J.L. van Schaik in Pretoria, 1914, and Nasionale Pers in Cape Town, 1915), to create the Afrikaner Broederbond (1918) and the Suid-Afrikaanse Akademie (1909), and to strive for the eventual acceptance of Afrikaans as an official language (1914-1925). With the institution of a prestigious prize for literature, the Hertzog Prize, in 1915, Afrikaans Literature was on the road to canonization, and the attainment of the aesthetic became a goal, although an unconscious and not yet clearly formulated one.

With Leipoldt's volume of poetry *Uit drie Wêrelddele* (1923, From

three parts of the world) a cosmopolitanism had been reached —
and the end of the creation of a tradition. While prose writing was
beginning to manifest an awareness of the 'literary' (as in the highly lyricized prose of D.F. Malherbe, 1881-1969) the preoccupation
was still with history (cf. Preller's *Piet Retief*, 1906) and the creation
of a taste for reading among the people. Here the didactic, humorous
and harmless satirical writing of C.J. Langenhoven (1873-1932), who
also wrote the Afrikaner's national anthem 'Die Stem', is important, especially in its introduction of an intimate association between
the narrator and the reader, thereby bringing the fictional and the
literary closer to the reader's perceptions. This narrative mode will
become popular in later years.

While the Afrikaner was striving for national mobilization there
was rural discontent among black people: rebellion in the Kat River
settlement and war on the eastern frontier. The coloured people in
the Cape were already experiencing faint threats of losing the fran-
chise, and an emerging black petit-bourgeoisie was striving towards
making use of electoral machinery provided by the Cape colonial
government: in 1880 a Native Educational Association had been
formed and by 1882 an association like the Afrikaner Bond, the Ibum-
ba Yama Nyama, had as its aim 'to unite Africans in political matters so they could band together in fighting for national rights'
(Marks and Trapido, 1987: 6). But Africans were destined to be excluded from the 'unification' of South Africa in 1910; the result was
the founding of the ANC, then called the South African Native National Congress, in 1912.

The texts of history and the texts of literature converge at this time
in attempting to find solutions to the growing contradictions caused
by race, class, industrialization and the growth of capitalism. These
various texts can merely be summarized here. There was the 1913
Natives' Land Act, which galvanized the ANC into action. This also
caused the production of one of the first documentary political texts
written by a black person, *Native Life in South Africa* (1916) by Sol
T. Plaatje (1876-1932). Plaatje states clearly what the Act meant:
'. . . to prevent the natives from ever rising above the position of
servants to whites' (Plaatje, 1982: 71). Afrikaners after the war, in
the industrializing areas, were divided between the dispossessed
poor and the new proletariat. There was the epic poem by Totius
(*Trekkerswee*, 1915) written in simple readable rhymes, lamenting the
past, the loss of paradise and the growth of urban poverty (this was
also the first winner of the Hertzog Prize). There were sketches on
the evils of the city by J. Lub (1868-1926); but especially a concern
for the demise of feudalism and the poverty of white share-croppers,

in the work of Jochem van Bruggen (1881-1957). Later the first farm novel, by D.F. Malherbe (*Die Meulenaar*, The Miller), tells about the waning of the idyll and the eventual loss of the farm and of that kind of existence.

The common denominators were land and proletarianization, but the texts differed in their solutions: protest from blacks; nostalgia, but the promise of a new, bourgeois future from whites.

The beginning of the transition to different realities can be seen in the writings of Eugéne Marais (1871-1936), who was still bound to the patriotic tradition by his active involvement in the Boer War, but who also agitated against conservative patriotism in his clashes with President Paul Kruger and in poems such as 'Die stem van Suid-Afrika' (The voice of South Africa), in which South Africa says words like:

Sy sê: 'Ek vorder as 'n heil'ge reg
Die vrug van eindelose pyn;
Ek smyt hulle oor die berge weg,
Ek smoor hulle in die sandwoestyn.' (Marais, 1941: 47)

(She says: 'I demand as a holy right / the fruits of endless pain; / I hurl them across the mountains, / I stifle them in the deserts of sand.')

Marais's solitary withdrawal into nature, his addiction to morphine, his texts on 'transformations', on human suffering and the insensitivity of supreme power, and the beginnings of an existential 'Angst' make of him the first 'schizophrenic' in Afrikaans literature.

With Marais, Toon van den Heever (1894-1956) can be called an 'early individualist' (Kannemeyer, 1978: 240). He is critical of God and of the Afrikaner, and although his preoccupations are 'philosophical' and his poetry personal he nevertheless reveals a sensitivity towards industrialization and the dream of the lost idyll (cf. the poem 'In die Hoëveld', On the Highveld) and a particular awareness of labour and class. In an idyllic setting the games played by two children (black and white, servant and master) are almost unnoticeably — at any rate to Afrikaans literary critics of the time — about labour relations, class, and strikes ('Werkstaking by die kleigat', Strike at the swimming place).

The miners' strike of 1921-1922 can perhaps be seen as the first South African crisis in which labour, class, race and nationalist politics (especially in the form of Hertzog versus Smuts) converge to create a terrain of conjuncture from which protest against capitalist and state domination can be made.

2 *1922-1948*

This period, culminating in the triumph of Afrikaner nationalism in 1948, also sharpened the contradictions in South African society, for the gains made by a small section of the population caused growing distress and conflict among the majority.

As the process of industrialization accelerated among black and white, poverty also increased; there was a dissolution of the tribal system, the breaking up of families, radicalism among the working class, and rural disturbances. Revolutionary talk of 'Africa for the Africans' and threats of 'swart gevaar' were prevalent. In 1928 the Communist Party of South Africa was talking seriously of 'an independent South African Native Republic as a stage towards the Workers and Peasants Republic, guaranteeing protection and complete equality to all national minorities' (Marks and Trapido, 1987: 260). The white Nationalists made new laws, new texts of the time: the Riotous Assemblies Act of 1929; the Industrial Conciliation Act; the Immorality Act; the Hertzog Bills.

Apart from the fact that Afrikaans literature, especially prose and drama, was reflective in nature, and involved with the demise of the idyll, the loss of nature, urbanization, poverty and the growth of the bourgeois class — apart from this close and obvious relation with socio-political developments, there was also the beginning of a transformation. Literature and society had developed to such an extent that one can now identify the second of Fredric Jameson's 'semantic horizons' ' . . . which mark a widening out of the sense of the social ground of the text through motions, first, of political history, in the narrow sense of punctual event and a chronicle-like sequence of happenings in time; then of society, in the now already less diachronic and time-bound sense of a constitutive tension and struggle between social classes . . .' (1981: 71).

Afrikaner nationalism made use of labour and the work-place for support, it thrived on ethnicity and believed completely in the colonial concept of Western civilization. In the words of J.B.M. Hertzog:

> As against the European the native stands as an eight-year-old against a man of mature experience. . . . Differences exist in ethnic nature, ethnic custom, ethnic development and civilization and these differences shall long exist. . . . When he achieves his majority in development and civilization, and stands on an equal level with the white man, his adulthood will be acknowledged. . . . (Marks and Trapido, 1987: 9)

It is clear that white people were going to be the civilizers, but to be able to fulfil that role they had to develop and maintain a definite level of civilization. Afrikaans literature became part of the civilizing process; its relationship to 'Western civilization' was formulated distinctly, and it had to contribute to Afrikaans culture, and therefore strengthen the ethnic grouping, but at the same time also become 'universal' as a Literature.

While the most admired prose texts of D.F. Malherbe still glorified idyllic and idealized pre-industrial labour, the changing means of production became a major conflict in his *Hans die Skipper* (1929), when a son refuses to take over his father's respected form of labour. The initiation of the backward and feudal class into a developing bourgeoisie is the preoccupation of Jochem van Bruggen's later work (especially the *Ampie* trilogy, 1924, 1928, 1942). With the initiation-trilogy Van Bruggen began a narrative mode that would find interesting parallels later, in the sixties, particularly in the work of Etienne le Roux. Class, industrialization, Afrikaner poverty were direct stimuli for the plays of J.F.W. Grosskopf (1885-1948), as well as the struggle against conservatism in the plays of H.A. Fagan (1889-1963).

But these reflections on socio-economic events were issues of the more old-fashioned literary products. Cultural developments were taking place, such as the founding of the Federasie van Afrikaanse Kultuurverenigings (FAK, Federation of Afrikaans Cultural Societies, 1929), an Afrikaanse Skrywerskring (Afrikaans Writers' Circle, 1934), and two literary magazines, *Tydskrif vir Letterkunde* (Magazine for Literature, 1936) and *Standpunte* (Viewpoints, 1945). There was a new generation of writers (C.M. van den Heever, 1902-1957; I.D. du Plessis, 1900-1981; N.P. van Wyk Louw, 1906-1970; W.E.G. Louw, 1913-1980; Elisabeth Eybers, 1915-) and a 'movement', the Dertigers (writers of the thirties), came on the scene. These cultural developments during the thirties happened at a time when black political militancy was declining dramatically, because of the actions of the state — but there was also famine and depression (Marks and Trapido, 1987: 30).

It is generally accepted in Afrikaans literary criticism that the Dertigers brought about a renewal in Afrikaans poetry — the Dertigers themselves have now become idealized literary figures. The persistent concern with 'renewal' in literary writing, which today is still the most significant norm for the literary critic in his/her quest for 'quality' and the aesthetic, can perhaps be traced back to these competitive times. The 'renewal' of poetry was seen in the lesser weight given to the typical 'Afrikaans' motifs (nature, the past) or to the language and its relation to literature, and an emphasis instead on the personal and the confessional, where the individual became central. Poets saw the writing of poetry as a conscious task, where every word, metaphor and sound had to be pure and aesthetically satisfying. The artist became a person with a role, and with a prophetic purpose.

It is significant to note that this greater awareness of the literary was not limited to Afrikaans literature only, because Plaatje's *Mhudi* (1930) and John L. Dube's *Insila ka Shaka* (1928) also tended towards 'elite' literature where the writer has a special role: 'It is in the late thirties that the notion of the black intellectual regarding himself primarily as a "writer" seems first to have surfaced. . . . Movements for cultural unity and advancement began to emerge.' (Sole, 1979: 151) There may be a correlation between decreased (suppressed) political militancy and therefore less political awareness, and an increase in an elite type of literature.

A brief look at the work of the canonized Dertigers should indicate literary developments.

In the prose productions of C.M. van den Heever a typical narrative pattern emerges, in which the main elements are: nature, the farm, the city and urbanization. There is always a loss, a destruction of the idyll. Opposed to powerful father-figures, central characters lead introverted lives — as internalized as the poetry of the time (especially that of Van den Heever). Often a text would be structured so that there are parallel character relationships: for instance, a love triangle among the owners of the farm will be echoed or shadowed or parodied by love triangles among workers (cf. *Somer*, 1935, Summer), thereby creating an awareness of class differences, although these were never perceived as such at the time. (The concept of class has not yet become part of the modern Afrikaans literary critic's language.) Often economic questions and ideological concerns were conveyed through the novels. These ecological, economic, political and class realities were combined within the 'literary work', where the literariness was given emphasis in the style, the modes of description and often the clearly 'structured' narrative. The writer was at the same time an intellectual, consciously co-producing an Afrikaans literary culture within a developing state (the father) and family (the Afrikaner).

The growing awareness of nationalism and the conscious cultivation of an own culture may at this time have resulted in the development of subconscious dialectical counterparts, or opposites, where an 'other' becomes clearly recognized, and is to be observed for its 'otherness'. It is significant that in these times of relentless advancement towards institutionalizing the separation of races, there was such an interest in other cultural and racial groups, especially in the work of I.D. du Plessis, Mikro (C.H. Kahn, 1903-1968), P.J. Schoeman (1904-) and G.H. Franz (1896-1956). Du Plessis wrote a thesis on the contribution of the Malays to the Afrikaans folk-song (1935), where the Afrikaner's culture is the norm and others contribute towards it, and where the implication is that the Malayan is another culture to be studied, to write about, and eventually to 'uplift'. In Mikro's trilogy about the coloured farm-worker, *Toiings* (1934, 1935, 1944, Tatters) he 'places . . . the Coloured centrally for the first time' (Kannemeyer, 1978: 349), although Toiings is initiated into the distinction between good and evil by the white farm-owner, his patronizing custodian. The accent is on the ideological, even in his progression from the portrayal of the coloured to a more politicized consciousness of colour. The ideological categorization of Schoeman's work in literary histories as falling under 'the depiction of the animal and the native . . .' (1978: 357) is indicative of the prevalent colonial attitude of literary critics. Franz's interest in the 'Bantu' and folklore, and the 'folkloristic' information given by these writers indicate the linking of the 'scientific' and the literary. This may have found its origin in Social Darwinism and 'Imagery derived from the biological sciences and the family [which] gave rise to ubiquitous notions of the "dependant" or "child races". In the imperial context this was later transformed into conceptions of "separate development" and "trusteeship".' (Marks and Trapido, 1987: 72) Added to this is the milieu, which is usually the farm or veld — the idyllic — where 'they' (the other races) belong, and where their class is affirmed.

While prose texts were concerned with race, the role of ethnicity within class domination (this was seldom a conscious matter) and growing urbanization, drama texts of this period were concerned with poverty and the upliftment of the poor-white. Afrikaans poetry of the time was striving towards a culture of aristocracy. The fact that this was happening at more or less the same time that, for instance, white Afrikaner women were moving out of the garment factories into white-collar and clerical positions, the time of the Ekonomiese Volkskongres, the Reddingsdaadbond and Volkskapitalisme (economic people's congress, rescue league and people's capitalism), can only mean that both economically and culturally the Afrikaners were developing into a bourgeoisie. This development in turn would strengthen the forced formation of a black proletariat, rising working-class militancy, and the escalation of trade union organization, culminating 'in the extraordinary African mine workers' strike of 1946' (Saul and Gelb, 1981: 14).

The poetry of this period can be characterized in Kannemeyer's words: 'The new artists look upon poetry as a conscious task and want to create poems in which every word and image is pure and artistically satisfying' (1978: 278). The Dertigers have become synonymous with poetry — the poetry of N.P. van Wyk Louw, W.E.G. Louw, Uys Krige and Elisabeth Eybers.

N.P. van Wyk Louw — 'as poet and essayist one of the very greatest personalities that Afrikaans literature has yet known' (Kannemeyer, 1978: 278) — was professor of Afrikaans and Dutch literature (first in Amsterdam, 1950-1957, and later in South Africa), literary theoretician and academic under whose guidance a whole generation of literary critics of the fifties, sixties and seventies was educated in the Formalist tradition, with special attention to the aesthetic and to the 'pure word'. His essays of 1939 (*Lojale verset* and *Berigte te velde*, Loyal protest and Reports in the field) formulate the aspirations of the new Afrikaans poetry: to have a 'high and compelling task', and to strive towards the 'aristocratic'. The ultimate aim of the poet should be the intellectual, and that would imply being the intellectual of his/her people. Perhaps Van Wyk Louw wished to create a kind of organic intellectual (there is no evidence that he had read Gramsci), just as in his time the creation of an aesthetic tradition became a primary aim, as did eventually — when Afrikaner nationalism had been established, with its reliance on ethnicity and division — the creation of liberalism. The title of his later book of essays and 'letters' is self-explanatory: *Liberale Nasionalisme* (1958), with a subtitle 'Thoughts on Nationalism, Liberation and Tradition for South Africans . . .'.

The poetry and plays of Van Wyk Louw written between 1935 and 1948 are centred mainly around the spiritual and metaphysical, poetry/writing, the 'national' and power.

Throughout Van Wyk Louw's poetry there is a search for spiritual clarity, a metaphysical struggle with God. This is the real beginning of a 'rule of thoughts', a Hegelian approach to reality, totally without a concern for or realization of the materialistic. The poet is the prophet, but the one who is not understood by 'them', the masses, one who has to resolve his struggle with God; and the solution is to be found in the perfect poem, in intellectual beauty. This is therefore the beginning of the self-centredness of the artistic (the beginnings of modernism in Afrikaans?). Even where Van Wyk Louw uses apparently 'materialistic' solutions, like the attack by a half-human, half-animal apparition on an organized tribe somewhere in Africa (*Raka*, 1942), the work becomes an idealistic construct about the destruction of a culture and a civilization, an epic poem, but written within the canon of the classical Greek drama, with protagonist, antagonist, heroic deed and tragic flaw. The attempt to reconcile Africa and the West ends in uncertainty, perhaps even tragedy. Van Wyk Louw's work on a national theme, like the play about the Voortrekkers' justification of their actions (*Die dieper reg*, 1938, A deeper justice) is allegorical, idealistic and poetic, without historical motivation. The later play, *Germanicus*, which is about power and domination, contemplates and intellectualizes the conflict between the aristocrat and the potentate, between the political leader and the person of culture; and the result is the withdrawal of the individual from the 'masses', and a disdain of power as base and evil. (Apparently Van Wyk Louw started *Germanicus* in 1947/48 but did not finish it then — perhaps he had political second thoughts? — and it was only published in 1956.)

With the exception of *Die dieper reg* Van Wyk Louw's literary production during this period did not have a direct relationship to the burgeoning Afrikaner hegemony (as was also the case with the other Dertigers, W.E.G. Louw and Elisabeth Eybers). But a reinterpretation of his work within that historical context may have to conclude that his aristocratization and intellectualizing of the poetic process, his 'universalizing' of literature, was eventually dialectically related to the strengthening and justification of Afrikaner nationalism. Although his work may have attempted to broaden that nationalism out from a narrow ethnicity, it also shied away from clear concepts on the possible abuses of political power. For Van Wyk Louw was very aware of power and its abuses, as shown in his later poem about the inquisitor and his prisoner, 'Die hond van God' (The hound of God).

The position of Uys Krige was different. He spoke out against political injustice, criticized the Afrikaner, and was involved in the Second World War, while the nationalist Afrikaner refused conscription. His poetry had none of the cultural and aesthetic fervour of his contemporaries, he did not have their sense of calling or their obsession with the intellectual and his/her role. He was a romantic, wrote poetry for the people, and — a world traveller — he brought the flavour of southern Europe into Afrikaans poetry, especially through translations. While Van Wyk Louw intellectualized about liberalism, Krige was the first liberal, but sceptical of nationalism — because he had seen it in its extremes during the war; and he wrote a memorable poem about it: 'Lied van die Fascistiese bomwerpers' (Song of the Fascist bombers). Where Van Wyk Louw was the aesthetic, liberal nationalist committed to an aristocratic ideal, Uys Krige was the liberal humanist moving out into the world, critical of nationalism.

M.E. Rothmann (MER, 1875-1975) was deeply involved in the material conditions and cultural development of the Afrikaner. Her participation in the Carnegie commission on white poverty in the early thirties, in the ACVV (Afrikaner Christian Women's Federation), the Voortrekker movement and the Cape National Party brought her closer to the people she wrote for and about than the poets of the time. Her concerns were much the same as those of Van Bruggen (poverty, the farm etc.) but with a greater emphasis on the recording of culture; and her prose was more sophisticated, in a 'literary' manner, with narrators associating intimately with the reader, narrating and informing. In her texts a literary culture developed from socio-economic conditions, in the sense that writing and the advance towards a hegemony went hand in hand. Although literature may be superstructural it seems a fact that the greater proficiency in literary production at this time cannot be separated from Afrikaner çohesiveness that would culminate in the Nationalist triumph of 1948. Just as nationalism accelerated the growth of capitalism the prose would move away from the people and from social matters towards the individual, and from realism to forms of premodernism (cf. the texts of C.J.M. Nienaber, P. de V. Pienaar, Willem van der Berg).

3 *1948-1961*

In a Basic Policy Statement in 1948 the African National Congress Youth League said:

> The majority of Europeans share in the spoils of white domination in this country. They have a vested interest in the exploitative caste society in South Africa. (Karis and Carter, 1973: 227)

If this statement is read with the following observation the dialectic of struggle becomes clear:

> The inclusion within the ruling Afrikaner coalition of a growing number of urbanized 'poor whites' guaranteed them a privileged status in the labor market and channeled to them some small fraction of capital's rising profits. On this basis, the living standards of all white South Africans rose rapidly after 1948. . . . (Saul and Gelb, 1981: 17)

Afrikaans capital began evolving, and several new parastatal corporations fell under the management of Afrikaners. In short: 'capital found that apartheid worked' (1981: 16). Capital and apartheid went hand in hand: the whites became bourgeois, the blacks were being consolidated as the proletariat. It should also be noted — as a contrast to Afrikaans literature — that this developing position of class domination caused disillusionment among the black elite of the 1940s, which was reflected in black literature by the growing use of Afro-American models rejecting white supremacy.

To ensure maintenance of their domination the Afrikaner Nationalists bombarded South Africa with laws: the Group Areas Act, the Population Registration Act, the Immorality Act, the Suppression of Communism Act; and later the Bantu Authorities Act, the Public Safety Act, the Bantu Education Act, the Promotion of Bantu Self-government Act. The great repression had begun. 'It is the situation of the 1940s which aptly deserves the appellation of "organic crisis"' (Saul and Gelb, 1981: 13). Most of the Afrikaans prose of the period carries on in the existing tradition — reflecting realities, without succeeding in producing symbolic solutions to the growing contradictions in society.

In contrast to the idyllic feudalism of the master-servant relationship of his former work Mikro now attempts to address the intensified racial problems. He does not, however, succeed in looking at colour within a political context. Instead he turns to the small-town, white world of old folks and writes with narratorial intimacy about their little tragedies. It is a significant declaration of inability to cope with new times: having had a humanistic, patronizing attitude toward blacks, he now writes patronizingly about whites.

W.A. de Klerk (1917-) in a play called *Die jaar van die vuur-os* (1952, The year of the fire-ox) wants Afrikaners to realize that they cannot remain isolated within the confines of race, but should reach out to their brown and black compatriots to work for a new solution. The confused mixture of ideology, caricature, type and the use of a *deus ex machina* indicates the uncertainty of some Afrikaans writers of the time as to what kind of interventions were needed. A mixture of various topical matters — industrialization, the development of a more complex society, colonialism, Africa, the Afrikaner in it — characterized De Klerk's other work as well. Later, in *Die laer* (1964, translated as *The Thirstland*), an historical novel about the Dorstlandtrek, narrated from the perspective of a person of 'mixed' blood, the problems De Klerk has with the perspective can probably be related to ideological 'silences' which may subconsciously have influenced the production of the text.

At this time the first of the black Afrikaans writers (Arthur Fula and Eddie Domingo) produced their prose texts, and we also see the first attempt by a white petit-bourgeois writer to project himself into the situation of the black peasant attempting to become part of an urbanized proletariat. F.A. Venter's (1916-) *Swart Pelgrim* (1952, Black pilgrim!) is the story of a Xhosa going to the city to work and to look for his brother. But he returns home a physical wreck. The ideological message has yet to be noticed by contemporary Afrikaans literary critics: there could be no black pilgrims to white people's land in the time of Verwoerd. It is significant that both De Klerk and Venter have in recent times become more conservative in statements they have made regarding the Afrikaner and the writer; and that there has been dissatisfaction at black schools concerning the prescription of Venter's *Man van Cirene* (1957), a novel about a black man helping Christ to carry his cross. This kind of racism, 'historical' of course, may have been in order during the heyday of Nationalist hegemony; but not today.

Afrikaans poetry was consolidating itself into a bourgeois poetry in tandem with South Africa's economic upswing after World War Two and the Afrikaner's growing acceptance of capitalist ideology. This is the development of a poetry which had consciously grown out of a Western tradition and was striving to attain equality with 'the best in the Western world'. Capitalism — more specifically, 'Volkskapitalisme' — was consciously being adopted as the Afrikaner's salvation, against the fear of black oppression and English superiority. The withdrawal of the poetry of the time from a national struggle or a social conscience into individuality and competitiveness can be read parallel to the development of capitalism — the real face of which the aesthetes had not yet seen:

> And what was . . . the essential problem in South Africa was what had been the problem for a long time: not nasty prejudiced whites and irrational Afrikaners and mysterious cultural forces, but a super-exploitative capitalism. (Johnstone, 1982: 16)

Despite ANC campaigns in the urban areas, the mass mobilization of the 50s, the Defiance Campaign, the Congress of the People and its adoption of a text of human rights (the importance of which other text-producers of the time should have noticed); despite protest against the Bantu Education Act and pass laws for women, removals of people, the consolidation of the proletariat and its organization, and industrial turbulence in the late 50s; despite the fact that an existing black elite, because of the ending of African rights to own property, was being reduced to proletarianism, and yet producing exciting prose literature ('In the 1950s and the larger portion of the sixties we experienced a literary renaissance for blacks in this country. But the renaissance was a celebration in prose' (Mphahlele, 1982: 89)); despite tremendous contradictions developing between a white bourgeoisie and an enforced black proletariat in the urban areas, and a cultivated black bourgeoisie in the 'bantustans' being alienated from their ethnic compatriots in the cities — despite all these upheavals there are no indications that the Afrikaans poets who had already gained a certain stature (Van Wyk Louw, Eybers and Ernst van Heerden) were in any way aware of or concerned about these matters.

Van Wyk Louw was striving towards the 'new' in *Nuwe Verse* (1954), reaching a synthesis of the past and the world of his youth with its colourful folk-language and magic. He was seeking a new poetic discourse for the 'changing of the times' (Kannemeyer, 1978: 422), very much aware of the poet's trade and the prophet's calling. He found that discourse in *Tristia* (1962), the poetry written during his 'exile' from 1950-1957, which is still considered today as the 'greatest' volume in Afrikaans poetry. The feeling of exile is ironical: it did result in a criticism of the Afrikaner and an 'odi et amo' emotional response to South Africa, but it was more of an enriching exile, made in terms of European consciousness. In almost elegiac verses he lamented the fact that South Africa possessed so little of Europe:

> my land, my dor verlate land:
> iets wens olywe groei in jou:
> dat alles klein, Latyns, gaan word
> en kalk-wit kerkies bou (1962: 14)

> (my land, my parched, forsaken land: / something wishes that olives would grow in you: / and everything would become Latin and small, / and build small chalk-white churches).

This volume represents the peak of refinement in the Afrikaner's poetry. The aristocratic ideal had been attained at the time that the Afrikaner had found his political republic. Of course, one cannot simply connect the two achievements in a straightforward cause and effect relationship — but in terms of the dialectics of power they would be the results of purposeful endeavours.

The words 'tense realism' have been used to describe the direction in which Elisabeth Eybers's poetry developed. This movement away from an earlier romanticizing of the mother, the child, the woman may accord with maturity, but there is a definite heightening of the ironical, not only regarding poetic technique, but also in her attitude towards life. Irony will become a ubiquitous element in Afrikaans poetry after Van Wyk Louw's frequently quoted lines from *Tristia*: 'Ons het ten minste heelwat ironiese ruimte', and 'eintlik moet ons leer ironies lewe: / én: binne ironie nog liefde hou' (At least we have considerable ironic space, actually we have to learn to live with irony: / and: within the irony still retain the love) (1962: 83 and 132). Although one can probably explain Eybers's predilection for irony with reference to her personal life, the fact that irony had become so important may also be seen as a symbolic solution to the great contradictions developing in South African society. Adapting Pierre Macherey's theory of absence ('We always eventually find, at the edge of the text, the language of ideology, momentarily hidden, but eloquent by its very absence' (1978: 60)) one could say that whereas the poetry of this period had little thematic material directly connected to the South African situation, it may be that poetic modes and personal attitudes of withdrawal of the aesthetic from the political could imply a silent awareness.

Although Ernst van Heerden's (1916-) poetry of the later 70s and the 80s indicates a growing concern with the political, his work in this earlier period is personal, internalized and very conscious of the poetic.

Poets who in terms of their themes and poetic execution have been more committed to their time than those above, are S.J. Pretorius (1917-) and D.J. Opperman (1914-1985) — and later S.V. Petersen, G.A. Watermeyer and Barend Toerien. Industrialization, labour and the alienation of capitalism are related topics in their work. Opperman (also considered one of the 'great' poets of Afrikaans literature) is the master of metaphor and the successor in the line of 'excellence' regarding poetry. While Pretorius was closer to the people, Opperman was a poet's poet.

To Van Wyk Louw the poet was the intellectual, to Opperman the poet was the academic, the scholar, the researcher and anthologizer (or accumulator). He was involved with literature even as a youth, and from the 60s onwards organized a 'literary laboratory' at the University of Stellenbosch where he was head of the Afrikaans Department. Many young poets sat at his feet, and many write poetry as he did. Through his anthologies as well as his association with the publishers of the hegemony he could exercise a certain amount of 'control' over poetic production, and canonize poems.

Opperman exploited South African reality (the political and nature) in order to transform it, to set free the 'angel from the stone', the infinite from the finite. His attachment to Africa was for the sake of transforming, metaphorizing, even 'universalizing'; and this would imply de-Africanization in fact. The purpose of literature was to interpret reality *sub specie aeternitatis*; and where he depicted industrialization, labour, class, capitalism and nationalism (as in 'Ballade van die grysland', Ballad of the grey land, 1947, and *Joernaal van Jorik*, Journal of Jorik, 1949) the materialist sources were ultimately reworked to become idealist constructions with impressive metaphors. In the latter poem — an epic on the history of the Afrikaner, but also on the human condition — the inevitable growing attachment of 'man' to his material conditions is seen as a betrayal of the spiritual and the religious; and in this epic Opperman sharpened the Afrikaans writer's already refined preference for the idealistic above the materialistic. He writes about 'the history and dilemma of the Afrikaner and eventually also of humanity and the poet in the light of eternity as building material' (Kannemeyer, 1983: 119). This exploitation of the material for the sake of the eternal also informs the 'layered' structure of his poetry, where more than one superstructure can be read off the poetic infrastructure.

Opperman therefore de-historicizes the text of history for the sake of an 'eternal meaning', and for the sake of aesthetic *écriture*. To him the poet is the scribe of the people, and he records their history so that it can be transcended. He is the guardian of civilization; and civilization is ultimately equated with the gains made from capitalism. An intensive study of Opperman's work, including his dramas written in the classical Greek tradition, which work is seen as part of the Afrikaner's growth from nationalism into capitalism, may well find a correlation historically between politico-economic and cultural development.

Opperman's poetry dominated the period; but because they aestheticized and de-historicized the major tensions and contradictions of his time his texts were, indeed, symbolic 'solutions', or pointers. On the other hand the less symbolic and more direct poetry of other poets recorded the emotions of the time. G.A. Watermeyer's (1917-1972) male Afrikaner workers demanded money, land, housing and bread, and refused to remain satisfied with being mere workers and 'anderman se kneg' (another's servant). Of the writings of S.V. Petersen (1914-1987), the first 'coloured' poet, it is said 'the life of the brown person with his feelings of protest and acceptance after the earlier . . . realistically humorous renderings becomes a reality for the first time in Afrikaans literature' (1983: 167). But here, at the beginnings of black Afrikaans writing, the racism of the Nationalist regime had already given rise to a sense of shame: Petersen initially spoke of 'die vloekstraf van 'n donker huid' (the curse of a dark skin); and although he protests against discrimination in a later volume, the title is still significant: *Die kinders van Kain* (The children of Cain, 1960).

The white Afrikaans poet's awareness of oppression and class difference did gradually find expression, notably in the satirical verses of Barend Toerien (1921-), written 'out of anger'. His poem 'Orlando landskap' (Orlando landscape) speaks in the voice of the black worker about unhealthy living conditions, labour exploitation, humiliation, pass laws, class and racial discrimination, group areas — all the discriminatory practices of the period after 1948. This text is a suitable transition from this period to the growing repression of that which followed. It both speaks about its present and provides an indication of a different kind of literature to come: a literature aware of oppression (to the extent of identifying in writing with the oppressed) and critical — but yet no more than comment or attack; reactive but incapable of producing symbolic solutions to contradictions, because the white Afrikaans writer had become totally bourgeois, totally distanced through class and culture from the oppressed.

Orlando landskap

Wat van ons wat woon in krotte
en dag na lange dag geruk
word deur die ritme van 'n pik,
of donker onderaards soos rotte
kap en dra en dril, met gasse
en ou lug ons pal metgesel,
met uitskei ondersoek word, afgetel,
op straat gestop word, visenteer vir passe?

Wat van ons, julle wat wette maak,
wat met 'n potlood, met 'n hand-
beweging op 'n kaart ons koers
neerlê, gevoelens en die land
haarfyn beplan, en bitter maak;
wat, wat van ons, jul donker broers? (1983: 17)

(What of us who live in hovels / and are shaken day by day / with the rhythm of a pick, / or deep, subterranean, like rats / chop and carry and drill, with gas / and bad air our constant companion, / when leaving work searched, counted, / stopped in the street, searched for passes? / What of us, you who make the laws, / who with a pencil, with a hand / movement on a map determine / our course, plan feelings and the land / meticulously, and cause bitterness; / what of us, your dark brothers?)

4 1961-1976

This period begins with a crisis: the attack by the state on people in Sharpeville on 19 March 1960; and ends with a crisis: the attack by the state on children in Soweto on 16 June 1976. Between these crises the pattern of repression and uprising clearly becomes the path of political history.

In the wake of Sharpeville gold reserves fell as capital flowed out of the country, and big business called for reform. The state responded by banning African nationalist organizations in 1961 and crushing opposition from the working class. Bantustans, the re-invention of ethnicity and its importance, social engineering, increased control over the labour force — all became part of a 'newly constructed state ideology' (Marks and Trapido, 1987: 390).

The consolidation of a sound Afrikaner Nationalist hegemony was taking place; but the contradictions building up around it were pointing towards the beginnings of another hegemony: in these times both the ANC and the PAC were abandoning their policies of non-violence. Nelson Mandela noted: 'It would be unrealistic and wrong for African leaders to continue preaching peace and non-violence at a time when the Government met our peaceful demands with force' (1965: 179).

Before talking about Afrikaans literature it is of absolute importance to note that at this time of almost total repression, an upsurge of black writing was consciously and purposely banned: '. . . the lively and important group of black writers who burst into South African literature in the fifties and early sixties disappeared . . . as if through a trap door' (Gordimer, 1976: 100). 'Black South African literature had gone into exile' (Barnett, 1983: 25). There was almost total silence on that literary front.

But there was an economic boom: 'After Sharpeville, when it was apparent that African resistance would be crushed (at least for the moment), foreign capital (American, British, West German, and Japanese most prominently) began to pour into manufacturing, helping to inflame and sustain the prolonged boom' (Saul and Gelb, 1981: 20).

In Afrikaans literature there was a renewal. According to the literary historians the renewal in poetry was introduced in 1955 by Peter Blum; while there was an anxious endeavour for a radical renewal in prose, with Van Wyk Louw heading the search.[5]

A crisis, the consolidation of white hegemonic power, repression, the banning of the literature of the oppressed, an economic boom, a renewal in Afrikaans literature. These are the contradictory facts one has to take into account in noting what was happening in Afrikaans literature at this time.

The time of the 'Sestigers' (the writers of the sixties) has become known as the decade of prose-writing. Here 'modern Afrikaans literature' began, and it found its sources in Europe and America, in modernist prose and drama: Joyce, Faulkner, Beckett, Sartre, the Theatre of the Absurd, the Dutch writers Hermans and Wolkers, and later the French, such as Alain Robbe-Grillet; and the psychology of Jung. The umbilical cord still led to Europe, although the domicile was Africa. Ironically Peter Blum — a European who for a short while wrote in Afrikaans — was the first white writer to state clearly in poetry the European connections, but also to sense with foreboding the presence of Africa:

> Maar as die bergwind so rukkerig waai
> . . .
> ruik ons droogte en brand, en gerug
> van sprinkaan, aardbewing en oproer
> op daardie skroeiende binnelandse lug
> – dan, dan
> weet ons op watter vasteland ons boer.
> ('Nuus uit die binneland', 1956: 8)

> (But when the berg wind gusts, / we smell drought and fire, and rumours / of locusts, earthquakes and unrest / on that scorching air from the interior / — then, then / we know on which continent we farm.)

Apart from writing poetry in a modern European idiom, Blum also adapted poetic forms such as the sonnet to South African conditions — in the tradition of the Italian Guiseppe Belli's *Sonetti Romaneschi* (1791-1863). In his 'Kaapse sonnette', written mostly in the Cape 'dialect' of Afrikaans, he satirizes white, bourgeois values — but is also the first modern Afrikaans poet writing from an awareness of class and in the language of a proletariat.

Peter Blum is the precursor of the Sestigers, and although the poets of the previous decades still produce verse in this time, in the tradition of 'excellent poetry' (Van Heerden, Eybers, Pretorius, Opperman, Rousseau, Toerien, Cussons), the time from the early sixties, often late into the eighties, belongs to Ingrid Jonker (1933-1965), Adam Small (1936-), Anna M. Louw (1913-), Elsa Joubert (1922-), Jan Rabie (1920-), Etienne Leroux (1922-1989), Dolf van Niekerk (1929-), André P. Brink (1935-), Chris Barnard (1939-), Bartho Smit (1924-1987), Abraham de Vries (1937-), Hennie Aucamp (1934-), Breyten Breytenbach (1939-). Of these only Jonker, Small and Breytenbach are predominantly poets.

Concerning the 'ideology' of most of these writers J.C. Kannemeyer talks of a 'polarisation in the sixties and seventies between writers on the one hand and the authorities, the church and the literary ''establishment'' on the other. This makes for the fact that the renewal of Sixty is not limited to literature only, but has an influence on the whole social system in South Africa, breaks down many of the taboos and prejudices of society and adjusts the literary, moral, religious and political conventions of the Afrikaner.' (1983: 229)

Kannemeyer, typical of the average Afrikaans literary critic, dramatizes the effect of the 'superstructural' on 'the whole social system in South Africa', because in characteristic apartheid-conditioned thinking the only society that exists is that of the Afrikaner. In the light of the beginning of a major South African crisis in the sixties the effect of the polarization of the Afrikaans writer is minimal and probably had no influence on the advance of the state's engine of destruction. The dilemma faced by Afrikaans writers was, of course, that it was their state which had been achieved by the invention of nationalism and tradition; and the hegemony was jealous of its producers of culture: it was actively appropriating culture by means of prizes, bursaries and scholarships.

The powers of oppression did, however, become aware of the potential dangers of the written word, as the fate of black writers indicates. Along with the host of laws of all kinds the fifties also saw the beginning of censorship. In 1963 the Law on Publications and Entertainment was promulgated. At the same time the first two novels of the 'renewal' were published: *Lobola vir die lewe* (Lobola for life) by André P. Brink and *Sewe dae by die Silbersteins* (Seven days at the Silbersteins) by Etienne Leroux. The fear that work of 'literary merit' could be banned led Afrikaans writers, especially N.P. van Wyk Louw, into making a fatal compromise with censorship. They protested vehemently but eventually accepted the law, on condition that they could have people of their choice on the Council for Publications. In this manner they became part of the state apparatus. Even today established Afrikaans writers cannot really succeed in being radical opponents of the state, and this is underscored by their ready acceptance of the Hertzog Prize or the lucrative Rapport Prize; by the fact that most of their writing is published by state-supportive publishers (Tafelberg, Perskor, HAUM); or by their participation in the review industry of pro-Nationalist newspapers (*Beeld, Die Burger, Rapport*).

Although the Sestigers were innovative, daring, iconoclastic, rebellious they could not distance themselves from the white, oppressive, bourgeois culture — excepting Breytenbach, but then he left the country in 1960. It would only be a handful of writers of the late seventies and eighties who would break away and write towards a different culture.

Despite the created tradition, especially via N.P. van Wyk Louw and later D.J. Opperman, of the 'well-constructed poem', where the poem is important in itself, certain events in the history of South Africa did find their way through the sheen of aestheticism into modern Afrikaans poetry; initially in the work of Toerien, then with Ingrid Jonker (see 'Die kind', based on the unrest in Langa, in 1960), and totally in the poetry of the black poet Adam Small.

Afrikaans prose had its tradition of 'coloured' characters (in Malherbe and Mikro), the poetry had its share of folk-verse in the colourful language of the coloured peasant (the expressions and images appropriated by Van Wyk Louw and Boerneef). But the first black and politicized poet writing from 'their world' was Small, where the political consciousness created the poetry, where poetry and politics were not separated. The language is the material language of the people, the poems (in *Kitaar my kruis*, 1961, and *Sê sjibbolet*, 1963) are about the people, from the people, on the liberation of the people, and the plays (especially *Kanna hy kô hystoe*, 1965, Kanna comes home) are about poverty, suffering and class distinctions. It has been for *literary* reasons that Small has not been considered part of the aesthetic cult of Afrikaans literature. His obsession with his people has been seen as a 'danger' in that it 'can reduce the work of art to a weapon in the struggle and give precedence to the extra-literary purpose above intrinsic literary values' (Kannemeyer, 1983: 297).

The 'realism' of Small, his 'popular' literature, stood apart from the development of mainstream literature, which was moving away from the traditional, the romantic and nostalgic, and the realistic mode towards experimentation.[6] If one keeps in mind Bertolt Brecht's statement on the realistic ('Realistic means: discovering the causal complexes of society / unmasking the prevailing view of things as the view of those who are in power / writing from the standpoint of the class which offers the broadest solutions for the pressing difficulties in which human society is caught up / emphasizing the element of development / making possible the concrete, and making possible abstraction from it' (1977: 82)), then the question is why should prose — the best vehicle for 'reflection' and 'depiction' — begin moving away from the realistic, particularly in these times of oppression. An easy answer cannot be given, but in terms of the development in Afrikaans poetry towards creating the monologic, the canonization of a literary genre, it is a fact that in the minds of the inventors of that tradition prose had not yet attained the status of 'Literature'. Or the Afrikaner had at this point closeted himself to such an extent within his own achievement that there was now no outside anymore, and no other reality, no history.

In the sixties the bourgeoisie was picking the fruits of 'racialised super-exploitation' (Johnstone, 1982: 21) and literature — experimental and modernist — had time to thrive on the boom. But by the seventies the options were becoming clearer: continued exploitation through racialism, or the possibilities of a socialist revolution. Afrikaner intellectuals were beginning to realize that the original apartheid ideology was too narrow and orthodox; they had to 'universalise the scope of hegemony' (Marks and Trapido, 1987: 391). Towards the end of the seventies there were reform proposals which practically amounted to a capitalist constitution, as suggested in the following revisionist phrases from the introduction to the Wiehahn Commission on labour reform:

> The Republic of South Africa subscribes to the principles of a free market economy based on individual freedom in the market place ... (Marks and Trapido, 1987: 394).

The choice of direction regarding the state was therefore clear: towards capitalism rather than socialism. How did Afrikaans literature react, how did it contribute towards or attempt to solve these rather swift historical fluctuations from boom to economic crisis and eventually to organic crisis? As Black Consciousness was growing in the early 1970s new black writers were beginning to produce again (see Oswald Mtshali's *Sounds of a Cowhide Drum* in 1971) and an oral literature was developing — a strong anti-hegemonic literature.

A brief introduction to the texts of the time may give an indication of preoccupations, concerns and literary modes.

In her first prose texts — *20 Days That Autumn* (1961) and the historical novels about President Paul Kruger (1964, 1968) — Anna M. Louw is aware of history and of the manner of documenting it. She writes about post-Sharpeville 1960 and about President Kruger's exile in Europe at the end of his life. Here perceptions about history are traditional, but the literary mode of expression has shifted from the straightforwardly realistic towards a different technique, somewhere between diarizing events and philosophizing about them. The emphasis, however, remains on the literary.

At this time the appearance of a series of novels which I would like to call 'master narratives' is significant. Louw's *Kroniek van Perdepoort* (1975, Chronicle of Perdepoort) can be considered as the first of these monumental texts, a family saga enacted on the farm created by the patriarch. This tale of a micro-community typifying, symbolizing and eventually allegorizing a wider community is told as history, centering around the burial of the patriarch, and it almost literally illustrates what Walter Benjamin said about the storyteller: 'What draws the reader to the novel is the hope of warming his shivering life with a death he reads about' (1982: 101). This is a Faulknerian narrative of power, of good and evil; but it also restructures the ideologemes and ideological signs the older Afrikaans novel had known into a complex, modernist text.

Like Anna M. Louw, Elsa Joubert also began her writing career with travel journals (indicative of the new Afrikaner of the time — affluent, travelled, well-read, exploring the world; the liberated Afrikaans writer explores the world at the height of his/her government's repression!). But she took Africa and decolonization seriously (see *Ons wag op die Kaptein*, 1963, translated as *To Die at Sunset*, and *Bonga*, 1971), writing the first novels in Afrikaans about the individual within a changing Africa. Her position is contradictory, as she still then believed — in a colonial fashion — in the Western 'light of civilization'. The literary execution of these 'themes' in her texts also shows signs of the contradictions: a mixture of modernism and realism, sometimes a documentary realism (*Die swerfjare van Poppie Nongena*, 1978, The wanderings of Poppie Nongena) and sometimes a quite straightforward allegory (*Die laaste Sondag*, 1986, The last Sunday). Joubert's *Swerfjare* can also be characterized as a master narrative, but moving closer to the evils of apartheid — a positive attempt at exposing those evils through the documentation of a black woman, a domestic worker's journeys through the infernos of discrimination, suppression and humiliation. But although produced to illustrate the effects of an ideology, it could not break the fetters of that subtle, always present, though seemingly absent, greater ideology: that of the language, Afrikaans, of literature, of culture. Written in peasant 'black' Xhosa-Afrikaans, perhaps consciously to reach the Afrikaner and address him in his own language and literature, it may have had the opposite effect. Poppie, Afrikaans-speaking Xhosa woman, has become appropriated for Afrikaans, has become an Afrikaans 'Mutter Courage', and was praised and accepted by the hegemony, revered and canonized. Even after Soweto 1976 the hegemony was so powerful that no text could crack its solidarity.

The writing of Jan Rabie is particularly illustrative of the phases some of the Sestigers went through, especially their 'Europeanization' and their return to Africa (physically and regarding the content of their texts — here Breytenbach remained the exception). They began writing in the old realist tradition, they became modernized in Europe (through contact with the European, especially Parisian way of life, the culture of bistro, metro, Left Bank, expressionism, surrealism, experimentalism), and back home they ultimately had to return to a contesting, realistic mode of expression, aware of the growing repression of the late seventies, but still emotionally bound to Afrikaans; striving to be anti-hegemonic, but part of the literary hegemony of prizes, publishers, writers' organizations, and the cult of the 'writer as anarchist' or 'the writer as intellectual'.

After returning from Paris in 1954 Rabie produced a book of short texts called *21* (1956): allegorical, surrealist, symbolical, modernist and even tending towards an early postmodernist 'schizophrenism'. But the realities of apartheid South Africa led him away from the consciously literary to the historical: the Afrikaner and his origins, and his relationship throughout history with his 'coloured' compatriots. Rabie's work created serious rifts in the literary establishment. Critics saw his 'political commitment' as an impediment to the 'literary': the tradition of the aesthetic stood in danger of becoming polluted by politics. With great erudition right-wing literary critics such as Prof. A.P. Grové (who became head of the large Afrikaans Department at Pretoria University, and whose heritage, and that of his colleagues such as Prof. Elize Botha and Prof. T.T. Cloete, is still alive at most Afrikaans universities) quoted Robert Liddell against Rabie: 'But he may not have an angry conviction. He must be able to understand and to sympathise with views he does not share. . . .' (1962: 172)

The division between cultural leaders, educational authorities, the church (or perhaps only individuals within the Dutch Reformed Church) and a striving-to-be-progressive group of Afrikaans writers was quite severe, and a marked division between 'left' (but still within the hegemony) and right (Nationalist, racist and fascist) was developing. Just as the growing divisions among Afrikaners since the sixties — with first the HNP, then the KP, and finally the blatantly Nazi-orientated AWB — may eventually destroy the concept of a homogeneous 'Afrikanerdom', so Afrikaans literature may divide, with a black, strongly anti-hegemonic, uncanonized literature beginning to develop, which is not part of a created culture and aesthetic.

Rabie's master narrative is his *Bolandia* series: the history of the birth of the Afrikaner, but also, simultaneously, of the birth of the 'coloured' people. Perhaps *Ark* (1977) could be read as such a narrative, having certain characteristics of the somehow similar, historical, carefully structured and 'monumental' texts being produced during the time of crisis, before and after 1976. There have to be definite socio-political and historical reasons for the production of these texts, as well as similarities regarding their use of ideologemes, omniscient authors, or the relationship between author and central characters, the Lukácsian type, the family and its parallel to class relationships, the individual positioned within a social totality, and finally a somewhat different dialectic in the narratives since the time of militarization. But this would, obviously, entail quite a major study on the effects of ideology.

The work of Etienne Leroux, from *Die eerste lewe van Colet* (1955, The first life of Colet) up to *Magersfontein, O Magersfontein* (1976) can be characterized as a consistent modernism, although the realistic mode of the late seventies does emerge, for the first time in his work, in *Magersfontein*. Here he moves into the historical and political, whereas in the earlier texts his concern is with the restructuring of myth and the Jungian archetypes of the collective unconscious. The grotesque, the macabre, Walpurgisnacht, vampires, Greek tragedy, detective story are the intertext, the building blocks of his novels for mythologizing modern realities. One reads Leroux along with Robert Graves, a knowledge of Jung's archetypes, and the canon of literary allegory.

His first major work, *Sewe dae by die Silbersteins*, should be read as a modernization and universalization of a concept present in the first Afrikaans novels: that of initiation. But it is not only the initiation of Henry van Eeden (of Eden) into the high capitalist world of the Silberstein estate, but also the beginning of a process of individuation, of the development of the individual, and the outsider, alienated from society, moving on the edge of chaos. Later on the world of the Silbersteins, the Welgevonden estate, breaks down in a way reminiscent of Edgar Allan Poe's *The Fall of the House of Usher*: a murder is committed, a scapegoat has to be found, a sacrifice has to be made.[7]

Leroux's idealist constructs have still to be integrated within the apartheid boom and the repression of the sixties and early seventies, and especially within the growth of capitalism. Why is he concerned with the process of individuation? Why does a community seek a sacrificial lamb? Why does Welgevonden become degenerate and fall apart? Can the initiation into Welgevonden simply be seen as a parallel to the Afrikaner becoming part of the modern world of capital, and being led into it by the writer, the interpreter, meturgeman, 'guide of dreams'? These questions cannot be answered unambiguously. There are many factors one will have to take into account, among which are the reactions his *Silbersteins* had with the people when it was awarded the Hertzog Prize in 1964. One also has to take into account that Leroux was consciously producing 'literature' and writing about 'universal' matters. One may in fact find that Leroux's texts were not attempts at symbolic solutions to the South African contradictions of the sixties and seventies at all.

The fact that the dialectics of the power struggle did not pass him by is, however, illustrated in his parody of a master narrative: his satire, in realistic mode, of the historical Anglo-Boer War battle at Magersfontein. The novel is a reconstruction of the battle (on 11 December 1899) at which Major-General Andrew Wauchope lost his life, and the Scottish Highland Brigade of 4 000 men was defeated by the Boers who had — for the first time in history — dug trenches to fire upon the marching Scots. A television team wishes to recreate the event, but an unexpected flood destroys everything. In this parody of history Leroux comes closer to South African actualities than he did in any of his previous works. And although he still plays the 'myth game' — now making of an event in history a new myth — and 'distances' himself from the events through parody, the book was nevertheless banned in 1977. However, it was then unbanned and later awarded the Hertzog Prize, thereby being canonized as a master narrative.

Experiments with chronology and space, the existential, the idealistic and the universal, and a consistent emphasis on 'literariness', characterize the work of the novelists and playwrights Dolf van Niekerk and Chris Barnard. Van Niekerk is concerned with the role of the past in its influence on life in the present, and it is significant that to him the past is a negative force with adverse influence on the present; and the 'past' is not history — it is the private past. In the texts we have been looking at there has not been much of an indication of a definite philosophy or approach to the past. It seems that the Afrikaans writer at this stage is still uncertain about 'history', and there is definitely no realization of the material forces of history. Barnard, who had memorable success with his adaptation of Beckett into Afrikaans (though not into South African settings), came the closest to a modernist rendering of Africa almost as a material force. But in his work Africa eventually becomes metaphor and universal. Africa is a waiting-room (but what is being waited for is never clear). Although one can sense that he knows the materiality of the bush and of the bushveld, Barnard's Africa is still that of the colonist, that is, Africa defined in terms of another world.

The most prolific writer, most erudite critic and most vociferous protestor against apartheid since the early sixties is André P. Brink, whose contact with Europe (Paris in 1959-1961, and again in 1968) immensely influenced his work during the sixties, when he seems to have been unaware of the repression in South Africa: 'I was born on a bench in the Luxembourg Gardens in Paris, in the early spring of 1960' (1983: 29). After writing several novels in the realist tradition his first 'modern' work, which heralded the 'renewal' of the sixties, was particularly European in execution (stream of consciousness, existential Angst, the 'new woman', the literary allusion): *Lobola vir die lewe*.

Like Van Wyk Louw, Brink was an apostle of renewal, of introducing new kinds of writing into Afrikaans. Where Leroux worked intertextually, Brink appropriated the technique of the literary allusion: a literary writer, who eventually brought literature into politics, but with the retention of 'literariness', and especially aesthetic self-consciousness. This self-reflexiveness, drawing attention to the process of creation, accentuating the materials with which he works, will remain the common denominator of his texts. Right into the eighties Brink will remain pre-eminently a Writer. After discovering the new sexuality, existentialism, Paris, the Inferno, Dante, Durell, Camus, Henry Miller; after experimenting with montage, multiple narrators, the bourgeois love triangle and the unashamed description of the sexual act; and after also writing plays in the Absurd idiom and in allegory, Brink eventually finds his roots in history.

But the heroic deeds of the past are idealized, such as in his plays on the Slagtersnek rebellion of 1815. History to him is where one begins looking for mythical truths, and all he really does is to 'anxiously conjure up the spirits of the past . . . and borrow from them names, battle cries and costumes in order to present the new scene of world history in this time-honoured disguise and this borrowed language' (Marx, 1984: 221).

Forsaking most of his modernisms for realism (excepting the varying role of the narrator, and the obsession with writing as signifier) Brink produces the first direct, oppositional political novel in Afrikaans in 1973, *Kennis van die aand* (*Looking on Darkness*). Rich in ideologeme, the oedipal, the family relationship, the individual within society, history and the heroic — this is Brink's master narrative, but with a carefully worded disclaimer at the beginning:

> The climate and history and circumstances where this story has its origin may look like recognizable reality, but within the new context of the novel everything is fiction. (1973: Preface)

The book was banned in 1974, the first Afrikaans book of 'literary merit' to be banned in terms of the 1963 legislation.

The banning of this text, Brink's disclaimer in his preface, and the weight the 'literary aesthetic' had attained in Afrikaans literature since the thirties, brought on a significant debate within the Afrikaans literary establishment regarding 'politics' and 'literature' and their supposed separate autonomies. To antagonistic critics it was clear that Brink wanted to use the 'sanctuary of literature' to say his say politically; but because to them his book did not succeed as literary text it could therefore be banned! Apart from the absurdity of the argument, the opposite would then also hold: there is a 'textual' protection, the 'literary', against which the hegemony will not act. This points to an important cultural-ideological 'achievement' of the Afrikaans writer: literature (and art) has a sovereign, independent, untouchable status; and that will explain why 'literariness', the conscious use of literary techniques, has thus far been part of even the most political Afrikaans prose. It does also often happen — and even Brink cannot always be exculpated — that the political reality, or atrocity, will be exploited for the sake of the literary.

The story of *Kennis* is told by a 'coloured' central character, and it begins with the discrimination against his family and their consequent suffering. Later the focus falls on his life as an actor and his love-affair with a white woman. Traditional criticism argued that he '. . . as character — who by virtue of the suffering of and injustice against his ancestors is "predestined" par excellence to become prototype — is not strong enough to bear the social suffering of his group' (Kannemeyer, 1983: 410). This may point to certain silences in the texts of modern Afrikaans writers: they may have the ability to create black characters, but they cannot create a class-oppressed character because they have not yet seen racial discrimination as part of class conflict. The deeper significance of class, rather than colour, still remains untouched in the bourgeois prose of the seventies. This deficiency in historical consciousness can possibly be attributed to the fact that alternative views of the social formation, and particularly the Marxist, have for so long been forbidden in South Africa; and it has only really been since the beginning of the eighties that a discourse on these matters has started among Afrikaner intellectuals.[8]

Although the novel was the central prose genre of the Sestigers, the short story developed in this period into an art form, especially in the hands of Abraham H. de Vries (1937-) and Hennie Aucamp (1934-), where the structure of narrative and the subtleties of understatement were finely developed. Also the plays of Bartho Smit

indicate a concern for structure, as well as a certain historical awareness of the South African situation.

The Sestiger who never returned permanently to South Africa (except for a few brief visits and a seven-year prison sojourn for 'terrorism'), wrote the most notable poetry of the time — but never fit-
ted into any Afrikaans literary tradition. When Breyten Breytenbach
left in 1960 his writing became part of his new environment: Paris,
with its artistic, literary and other cultural contexts. Breytenbach's
poetry broke with the tradition of the autonomous poem without
any possible biographical or social link to its producer, or of the poet
as the creator apart, and of the meticulously structured Opperman-
type poem. His consistent involvement in politics — which led to
his physical sacrifices — also broke the tradition of the writer as
revolutionary in his writing alone. He stopped writing and took part
in the struggle for liberation. In prison he did write again, but not
only about prison. He spent much energy considering the manner
of producing a text, and if writing has any purpose when there is
oppression.

His poetry is not popular poetry: it is poetry about poetry, and
even when he does write direct political verse the poem intrudes
as signifier, forcing the reader to regard the words, metaphors,
descriptions (often seen with the eye of a painter) and innovations.
J. Hillis Miller's comment about Shelley's poetry is also applicable
to Breytenbach's:

> The language which tries to efface itself as language to give way to
> an unmediated union beyond language is itself the barrier which re-
> mains as the woe of an ineffaceable trace. (1979: 246)

Breytenbach's condemnation of the South African state did,
however, in the case of some more overtly political poems, force
words into a more conventional signifier-signified relationship; and
these poems are probably the most memorable documents of political protest in Afrikaans writing. These include: 'Bruin reisbrief'
(Brown travel letter), 'Nie met die pen nie maar met die masjien-
geweer' (Not with the pen, but with the machine-gun), 'Please don't
feed the animals', 'Die beloofde land' (The promised land), 'Die lewe
in die grond' (Life in the ground), 'Brief uit die vreemde aan slag-
ter' (Letter to butcher from abroad — dedicated to Prime Minister
John Vorster, on the occasion of the many deaths in detention), and
'Vlerkbrand' (Burning wings) with its morbid apocalyptic images:

wanneer jy dink aan jou land
sien jy

vlegsels en 'n bril; 'n ou hond vol bloed;
en 'n perd versuip in die rivier; 'n berg met vuur;
'n ruimte met twee mense sonder tande in die bed;
donker vyge teen die sand; 'n pad, populiere,
huis, blou, wolkskepe;
riete; 'n telefoon;
sien jy

(when you think of your land / you see / plaits and spectacles; an
old dog covered in blood; / a horse drowned in the river; a mountain
with fire; / a space with two people, toothless, in bed; / dark vygies
against the sand; a road, poplars, / house, blue, ships of cloud; / reeds;
a telephone; / you see.) (1972: 30)

At the time of the master narratives of Louw, Joubert, Leroux and
Brink, with their awareness of power, heroism, the legendary, and
with their histories of family relationships; at the time when political repression was developing towards the crisis of 1976, there was
also another type of narrative. Particularly in his novels *Na die geliefde
land* (1972, *Promised Land*) and *Om te sterwe* (1976, To die) Karel Schoeman (1939-) presents apocalyptic scenarios for the whites in South
Africa. Both are written within the ideological codes of the farm novel, i.e. within a realistic mode and dealing with family relationships,
the role of nature, servants, and cultural events. In *Om te sterwe* (politically the forerunner of *Na die geliefde land,* although appearing after it) there is fighting on the border, servants are being removed
from the farms, and one of the sons of a farmer — conspicuous by
his absence in the novel — is fighting on the side of an unnamed
'them'. Eventually the idyll disintegrates. Although there is a sus-
picion in the text that the contradictions of the class relationship between owner and worker could be the cause of the destruction of
the idyll, it is still a vague idealist construct making a reconciliation
with a materialist view of reality impossible. The rural society in *Na
die geliefde land* has apparently lost its previous state of grace, affluence and power because of some kind of 'revolution' and the people now exist like those *bywoners* in the first Afrikaans farm novels
by authors like Van Bruggen. Although this novel has become very
popular — also in English — its silences and its indetermination may
actually amount to a denial of history. It has a strong suggestion
of class, but because of the conventional view of history, the eleva-
tion of the idealistic above the materialistic, and the apparent
privileging of the individual, it is possible to conclude that there is
not a post-revolutionary milieu in this text at all; and as a future
text one would perhaps have to read it as a negative scenario concerning change in South Africa — and therefore counter-

revolutionary? The necessity of reading a text within a literature and a socio-political context, of seeing it within its ideological frame of reference, within its field of interpellation (Althusser, 1977: 163), is well illustrated in the case of *Na die geliefde land*. The absences and silences of this text — i.e. the material facts of the political interregnum and the literary, even the stylistic, tradition of the idyll in Afrikaans — are necessary for a full understanding of the text. But when these matters are interpellated it may be found that Schoeman's silences are also evasions.

5 After 1976

Stephen Clingman's comment about Nadine Gordimer's *July's People* (1981) could apply equally well to Schoeman's *Na die geliefde land*: 'The novel, arrived at a dead-end of history, searches for the only way out' (1986: 193). Although Schoeman, Gordimer and to a certain extent John Miles (1938-) have felt this period to be the time for grimly looking ahead, it was Gordimer who gave this time a name: the interregnum. The epigraph to *July's People* comes from Antonio Gramsci. In full it reads: 'The crisis consists precisely in the fact that the old is dying and the new cannot be born; in this interregnum a great variety of morbid symptoms appear' (1978: 276).

The various crises — 1922, 1948, 1961, 1976 — may now have developed into the transition between two social formations. There seems to be acceptance that 1976 was a dividing date (Swilling, 1987: 408), and that the ruling class is losing its consensus, '. . . is no longer "leading" but only "dominant", exercising coercive force alone' (Gramsci, 1978: 275-276). Nevertheless a 'revolutionary rupture' is at present unlikely: 'For a revolutionary rupture to occur the security forces need to collapse, the state's social base must disintegrate and reformist attempts to reconstitute the goals of structural change must be an unmitigated failure' (Swilling, 1987: 426).

It appears that where in the case of previous crises one could have spoken of the forces of opposition organizing on the terrain of the conjunctural, one may now have to redefine — again from the Gramscian analysis: 'A common error in historico-political analysis consists in an inability to find the correct relation between what is organic and what is conjunctural. . . . The distinction between organic "movements" and facts and "conjunctural" or occasional ones must be applied to all types of situation.' (1978: 178) And with specific reference to the post-Soweto situation: 'Of course, the impact of Soweto was much broader, deepening the economic crisis into organic crisis and indicating to some sectors of capital that the system's very existence was in jeopardy' (Saul and Gelb, 1981: 24).

Disillusionment with apartheid, a more 'organic' opposition, as well as a decline in the economic boom can be related in part to widening cracks in Afrikaner hegemony: in 1982 the newspaper *Rapport* spoke of 'the year of the Afrikaner . . . and especially at conference time when the Afrikaner's identity . . . is . . . laid out on the dissection table' (Posel, quoted by Marks and Trapido, 1987: 435). At the same time the FAK, ASB (Afrikaanse Studentebond) and the Broederbond were similarly preoccupied with questions concerning Afrikaner identity. In 1985 students from Stellenbosch University were forbidden to meet the ANC Youth League in Lusaka. At the same time the Freedom Charter was translated for the first time into Afrikaans (Olivier, 1985: 96-99). In 1986 the right-wing Conservative Party ousted the liberal PFP as the official opposition in Parliament; and in 1987 a group of 'liberal' and 'radical' Afrikaners sneaked out of South Africa to meet ANC executives in Dakar.

On the side of the opposing majority it is necessary to note the rising radicalization of black people after the achievement of independence in Mozambique and Angola (after 1975). This increasing degree of radicalization can also be linked to the legalization of trade unions (1979), the emergence of community organizations in the major centres, the growth of radical student organizations at the beginning of the eighties, and the launch of the UDF (1983). May Day demands were drawn up by political organizations and trade unions in May 1985 (Swilling, 1987: 409), and the Freedom Charter received considerable public attention. On the cultural terrain there was a re-emergence of black literature from the beginning of the seventies. In 1973, for instance, Nadine Gordimer said:

> Three individual collections [of poetry] have been published within eighteen months. I know of at least two more that are to come this year. An anthology representative of the work of eleven poets has recently been compiled. Poems signed with as yet unknown names crop up in the little magazines: there are readings at universities and in private houses. (1973: 1)

It is also particularly important to note that the state had also begun to change its language, to begin defending itself in a new language of legitimation, yet still of domination. There is a tendency to move away from 'ideology' as a conscious concept; orthodox apartheid ideology is discredited, and there is the start of 'continuous consultation' with the business community (Marks and Trapido, 1987: 427). New phrases appear: 'apartheid is dead', 'constitutional reforms', 'free enterprise', 'total onslaught', 'total strategy'.

But arguably the most significant development — which has become a site of conflict in Afrikaans prose literature (the 'literary' as well as the 'popular') of the eighties — is the growth of the military, militarization, and a weakening of the boundaries between the civil and the military. This has led to the creation of what is known as a 'garrison state'. A liaison between the military and capital has developed, and the military is now also the champion and guardian of capitalism. The concept 'total strategy' is a counter-revolutionary one. Frankel comments: 'Firstly, and above all, South Africa's total strategy is an instrument of counter-revolution designed by the political and security apparatus of a beleaguered racial elite . . .' (1984: 62). In the final analysis a new form of consent especially among white people, a new hegemony, has arisen:

> Total strategy, and its related concepts of total onslaught and total involvement, is basically part of an exercise to construct a language of images with which the military and its small but influential group of civil sympathizers can communicate with the remainder of the elite on a persuasive basis. (1984: 135)

On the literary front, the prose texts of this period offer the most conscious attempt to present symbolic solutions to the contradictions caused by repression, the crisis of capitalism, and militarization. In this respect the following writers have to be taken into consideration: Wilma Stockenström, André P. Brink, Karel Schoeman, Elsa Joubert, John Miles, Etienne van Heerden, Alexander Strachan and Koos Prinsloo. The poetry remains sophisticated and competent, but in the established aesthetic and monologic tradition, and without significant awareness of the interregnum, except in the case of Antjie Krog, and in some of the poetry of Breytenbach (who was released from prison in 1982, where he wrote quite a considerable amount of poetry, mostly within a Zen Buddhist tradition).

The novel *Uitdraai* (1976, Turn-off), Wilma Stockenström's first prose production, is written in the tradition of the farm novel of previous generations, but with a contemporary awareness of race. The central character is pregnant, and the man who could be the father may have come from a racially mixed background. A central event is the abortion, which then releases her to marry within her own race. A recent re-reading of this text gives it much more significance than previous analyses: '. . . committing the abortion can be read as the restoration of the power base of the Afrikaner. The abortion . . . sees to it that the central character remains an Afrikaner woman . . . that the Afrikaner group keeps control of her as means of production and ensures therefore that one of the corner stones on which the present social formation is reproduced remains untouched.' (John, 1988) But the text also holds insoluble contradictions and evasions: it could be a radical analysis of the ruling class and the strategy whereby they retain power. Or it could be the unscrewing of the screw ('uitdraai' can also mean unscrew), which will result in the collapse of the rulers' structures. At the same time it could also be read as antagonistic to the interests of the working class.

The complex short text *Die Kremetartekspedisie* (1981, *The Expedition to the Baobab Tree*) is about an expedition during the time of slavery to a lost city, to collect spoils, to accumulate property. But the end is an inversion, with the narrator in a baobab tree — an upsidedown tree — and without any property. While it tells the story of a slave woman, and it may be an indictment of capitalism, it is also a post-modernist story of a text, of writing, écriture. The writing is eventually all that remains. This is the complex fusion of novel and poetry, of the word in its relationship of signifier to signified, but also as signifier of signifier.

Soweto 1976, Bram Fischer of the SACP, Afrikaner capitalism and the Afrikaner tycoon are the interrelated stimuli for Brink's *Gerugte van reën* (1978, *Rumours of Rain*). During disturbed times in his country the central character, a rich mining magnate, searches his past to find his identity, only to realize that he has lost contact with the future realities of South Africa, as explained to him by his friend, a communist. The tycoon's son becomes the bearer of the future. This is the first novel in Afrikaans about capitalism and revolution, but these conflicting forces are background to characters who are merely types. Here Brink had the elements for an historical materialist intervention in the Afrikaans novel. But because there is no awareness of ideology — of the ideology from which he himself is writing — this could not happen.

Deaths in detention (like that of Steve Biko in 1977) were the impetus for Brink's *'n Droë wit seisoen* (1979, *A Dry White Season*), which was not published by the establishment Afrikaans publishers and was banned for a while. A white Afrikaner schoolteacher clashes with the security police when two black people of his acquaintance die mysteriously in detention. He becomes involved in 'politics', realizes that he will have to sacrifice Afrikaner values, and is eventually exterminated. It is of ideological interest that the story is told by a middle-aged writer of popular fiction, the story editor of a women's magazine; the text is, self-consciously, a text showing all the markings of its structuring. This strategy obviously has a double purpose: it gives the appearance of authenticity. As stated at the end: it is a writer's task to record, so that no one can say they did not know. But we are nevertheless also left with the clear impression that this is a *novel*, written within a canonized literary mode, thereby emphasizing the literary. The question may then arise: which is the most important, the deaths in detention or the novel? The self-centredness of the text remains a preoccupation for the Afrikaans writer — whereas this is not the case with contemporary black prose writers writing about similar matters, for instance, Mongane Wally Serote, Sipho Sepamla, Mtutuzeli Matshoba. With *Houd-den-Bek* (1982, a place name, meaning more or less Shut-the-mouth), Brink produces his second master narrative, and not totally dissimilar to *Kennis van die aand*. As in *Kennis* the black-white apartheid relationship historically originates in the white master-slave, and therefore class, relationship. The novel — related by means of thirty narrators, or points of view — has a historical base in a slave uprising in 1825. It is the story of the revolt of slaves against their masters, and is a testimony of discrimination and cruelty; but again literary structure overrides the political discourses of the text.

The concern with text and the literary does, however, emphasize the singularity and 'role' of the writer in his/her society; and since Van Wyk Louw the writer has been pre-eminently the intellectual as well. The literary product is therefore also an intellectual product, through which the Afrikaans writer wants to interpret, reflect, solve contradictions; but as Afrikaner he/she is part of Afrikanerdom, the apartheid-order and the 'new' capitalism whether he/she likes it or not. In a study of the position of the Afrikaans writer/intellectual in the late seventies, Hein Willemse writes about Brink's utilization of the concept: '*A Dry White Season* is a view of the organic intellectual . . . an intellectual who wants to show the way for the future and time and again reconfirms his concern with being an Afrikaner' (1985: 7). The position of the traditional intellectual (in Gramsci's well-known terminology) is novelized by Karel Schoeman in *Die hemeltuin* (1979, The garden of heaven), where an ageing (Afrikaans) academic reminisces about a holiday forty years ago on a rich and gracious English estate, replete with Victorian values, while the Second World War was threatening that kind of society. Of his South African present very little is said concerning social upheaval. Where Brink's schoolteacher became something of an organic intellectual the central character here is alienated and wants to be on the outside: 'I want to withdraw and hope that the storms will pass me by — I don't know what else a person can do' (1979: 19). This condition is well described by Afrikaans political scientists:

Because of a lack of identifiable alternatives the great temptation of . . . alienated Afrikaner intellectuals will be to withdraw from political battlefields in search of an internal and apolitical domain of pure and/or cultural interest. (Du Toit, 1983: 7)

That is undoubtedly the position of most Afrikaans poets and literary critics of the seventies and eighties. Willemse compares Brink and Schoeman's positions in this way:

Die hemeltuin like the novels of Brink . . . signifies the search for solutions in the present South African juncture. The memory of a once paradisic order is passively experienced and the intellectual's experience of his present leads to no real action, but abstinence. But abstinence is a clear political choice. For the sake of survival. Here not survival of the group, but of the individual. (1985: 9)

John Miles's central character in *Blaaskans* (1983, Breathing space, half-time, but also: a time for blowing-up) — the first novel using the military and militarization as a basic 'premise'[9] — is also a schoolteacher, as in Brink's *A Dry White Season*, and also an intellectual, as in Schoeman's novel, but he goes much further than in these earlier productions: he blows up an army base after becoming politicized. In this text militarization is being defined: men are called up, people's privacies are destroyed; their space is bulldozed (bulldozers have become ideological signs); there is a levelling, a visible obliteration of all signs of political protest and a repression of resistance whether it be from the left or the right. In terms of consent or coercion Miles's text is a discourse on the loss of hegemony and the escalation of repression.

From the beginning of the novel the central character is continuously, consciously identifying with his surroundings. He then begins to identify with the material conditions of existence as determined by the socio-political realities of people, especially those living in the 'independent homelands'. He also attempts to determine what actions took place before the text existed, by implication — actions that have now made of the text a historical moment. That then brings one to History and its value as recollection.

In various places in the text there are cynical references to History: History is the Great Purpose, the future is determined by the past, the power of the past can never be forgotten, the Afrikaner shall not forget his history. But the text shows that history is no more than defective memory — for that reason it has always to be reinterpreted afresh. A reinterpretation of the Slagtersnek rebellion, on which part of the text is based, brings the central character to the conclusion: 'People who find meaningful patterns in history inevitably reach them by looking back, you cannot know in advance how history is going to look' (1983: 249). In terms of historical materialism one would be tempted to say: the material conditions of existence in the present determine how the past is read.

Miles's text is to a large extent an inversion of the Slagtersnek history. One can ask: is it an awareness of the material conditions of others that has caused a modern, white Afrikaans writer to negatively reinterpret his history? Or is it an attempt at the de-idealization of the Afrikaner's Past?

Blaaskans could perhaps also be considered as one of the master narratives: it has the historical base, elements of the legendary and the heroic, and the concern for textuality. But everything is inverted; and *Blaaskans* may even have indicated a reversal of this kind of narrative, with the growing uncertainty among Afrikaner intellectuals regarding apartheid, nationalism, even capitalism, were it not for the fact that the resistance against military power in this text is not strongly confirmed by later writers — and the old type of master narrative again resurfaces with Etienne van Heerden's *Toorberg* (1986, Magic mountain). The reason for this 'reversion' is not yet certain; one has to await the future.

Where Brink, Miles and the writers after them have persisted in writing in a textually aware, highly stylized, yet mainly realistic literary mode, Elsa Joubert's recent 'border novel', *Die laaste Sondag* (1983), tends to be symbolic, even allegorical. She tells of a border community, their symbols, their tattered culture, their hatreds and their evil thoughts of revenge. Plekhanov's words have a particular resonance when applied to Joubert's novel:

> The history of literature shows that man has always used one or other of these means (symbolism or realism) to transcend a particular reality. He employs the first (i.e. symbols) when he is unable to grasp the meaning of that particular reality, or when he cannot accept the conclusion to which the development of that reality leads. He resorts to symbols when he cannot solve the difficult, sometimes insoluble problems. (Jameson, 1971: 337)

The Afrikaner throughout his history has always, it seems, been at some kind of border, or he has been making boundaries, dividing people. Borders, the apocalyptic and militarization have become part of Afrikaans prose literature since the seventies. A recent development has been the prose text written 'from within', where a soldier is the narrator, and where the author is a soldier. One such author comments:

Where previous generations of writers struggled intellectually with social and political questions, the younger writers are physically experiencing the dispensation in the sense that everyone is compelled to do military service. (Strachan, 1985: 15)

Two diverging, but also similar, texts from within are *'n Wêreld sonder grense* (1984, A world without borders) by Alexander Strachan and *Om te Awol* (1984, To Awol) by Etienne van Heerden. The one book is a book about fighting, the other is a book about fleeing; but both have one factor in common: 'I'm tired of war' (*Grense*: 48) and 'I have had enough' (*Awol*: 22). The alternatives are: fighting and becoming part of a warring, family structure or fleeing and eventually fleeing from everything.

The choice Strachan makes is the more frightening, but also the one closest to the South African reality. His text, a succession of interconnected short stories, brings out the ideology of combat. It tells of a young man who leaves his home on a South African farm to join the recces (a tough reconnaissance commando, the heart of the SADF's repressive power) and then to mutilate SWAPO guerillas. He becomes alienated from civilian life, has disturbed relationships with women, and finally has to execute a friend in order to take control of a band of South African soldiers who have defied the SADF. The last episode can be read as a symbolic oedipal transformation, when he becomes reunited with a new 'family', the military. The writer of a recent study of this text comes to the conclusion:

This narrative, produced under capitalism, ends up refusing the contradictions inherent in its own social formation. It then . . . move[s] the ideological space into the feudal mode of production. It is in this sense that *'n Wêreld sonder grense* is a reactionary text. (Munnik, 1987: 64)

Military and police violence, greater oppression, bannings, censorship of the press, an unhealthy economy, the perpetuation of states of emergency are the facts of life of the late eighties in South Africa. Where does Afrikaans, as a site of struggle, stand in these troubled times, and what will become of its literature if it remains a literature written from within a created tradition, either by white intellectuals for white intellectual readers, or by soldiers for ideologically prepared readers? An answer may perhaps be read in a short story by Koos Prinsloo[10] in which the act of writing in Afrikaans can be seen to have become jeopardized by history, in which the history of the whitish Afrikaans-speaking pioneers and colonizers of the southern part of Africa can be seen as a threat to writing because of ideological accretion.[11]

There are signs that Afrikaner intellectuals are seriously reviewing the past and reconsidering the future. Whether they have the
power to bring about meaningful change is doubtful, but they do
still create texts, such as the following:

> Where does one have to look for political developments that can point
> towards a new and more democratic South Africa? Until recently, to
> most people, especially in white politics, it was obvious that it is the
> government that has to decide how reform can take place and where
> it will lead to. . . . Today the situation has changed very much. The
> government's constitutional and other political initiatives . . . create
> less interest than before. No one really becomes very excited about
> it. Few people expect that it will break through the political deadlock.
> . . . It has recently become clear that the problems of the South Afri-
> can economy are of a serious structural nature. Before new driving
> power can be found for the economy any constitutional plan will have
> difficulty in getting off the ground . . . there is a growing realisation
> that political progress can only be made when parliamentary and extra-
> parliamentary politics can begin to influence each other meaningful-
> ly. The days of one-sided white initiatives have irrevocably passed.
> . . . (*Die Suid-Afrikaan*, 1988)

Notes

1. The most recent and most authoritative history is J.C. Kannemeyer,
   Geskiedenis van die Afrikaanse Literatuur, I and II. 1978 and 1983. Pretoria
   and Cape Town: Academica.
2. *The Retreat from Class*. 1986. London: Verso.
3. Cf. the article by Frederick Johnstone, '''Most painful to our hearts'':
   South Africa through the eyes of the new school'. *Revue canadienne des
   études africaines/Canadian Journal of African Studies*, 16(1), 1982, 5-26.
4. Also the article by Deborah Posel, 'Rethinking the Race-Class Debate
   in South African Historiography'. *Social Dynamics*, 9(1), June 1983, 50-66.
5. Of special importance is his book of essays, *Vernuwing in die prosa, grepe
   uit ons Afrikaanse ervaring*. 1961. Cape Town: Human en Rousseau.
6. 'Realistiese kuns op pad na die eksperimentele' (Realistic art on the road
   to the experimental), Kannemeyer, II, 1983: 307.
7. *Een vir Azazel*, 1964. The three Welgevonden novels were published in
   Penguin in 1972 under the title *To a Dubious Salvation*.
8. Cf. J.J. Degenaar, 'Ideologie, vervreemding en woordkuns'. *Standpunte*,
   34(1), 1983. Parow: Nasionale Boekhandel.
9. Published by Taurus, Johannesburg. The following prose texts have used
   the military and/or militarization as background or theme or basis of
   contradiction. They have also been named 'border texts': J.C. Steyn,
   Op pad na die grens (Tafelberg, 1976); Welma Odendaal, *Keerkring* (Perskor, 1977); P.J. Haasbroek, *Heupvuur* (Human en Rousseau, 1974); P.J.
   Haasbroek, *Roofvis* (Human en Rousseau, 1975); Dan Roodt, *Sonneskyn
   en Chevrolet* (Taurus, 1980); George Weideman, *Tuin van klip en vuur*

(Tafelberg, 1983); Etienne van Heerden, *My Kubaan* (Tafelberg, 1984);
Louis Krüger, *'n Basis oorkant die grens* (Tafelberg, 1984); Koos Prinsloo,
Die hemel help ons (Taurus, 1987); Victor Munnik, *Oog van die Nyl* (Tau-
rus, 1987); Hans Pienaar, *Die lewe ondergronds* (Taurus, 1987); *Forces
Favourites* (Taurus, 1987).
10. *Jonkmanskas* (Tafelberg, Cape Town, 1982). The story 'Jonkmanskas'.
11. This matter was discussed in a paper titled 'The Ideological Burden of
Afrikaans' delivered at the University of the Witwatersrand, at a Col-
loquium on 'Emerging Literatures', June 1986. To be published by Berne
(New York).

References

Barnett, Ursula. 1983. *A Vision of Order*. London: Sinclair Browne.
Benjamin, Walter. 1982. 'Theses on the Philosophy of History'. *Illumina-
tions*. London: Jonathan Cape.
Blum, Peter. 1956. 'Nuus uit die Binneland'. *Steenbok tot Poolsee*. Cape Town:
Nasionale Boekhandel.
Brecht, Bertolt. 1977. *Aesthetics and Politics*. London: NLB.
Breytenbach, Breyten. 1972. *Skryt*. Meulenhoff, Nederland: Poetry
International.
Brink, André P. 1973. *Kennis van die aand*. Cape Town: Buren.
Brink, André P. 1983. 'Introduction: A Background to Dissidence'. *Map-
makers: Writing in a State of Siege*. London: Faber and Faber.
Clingman, Stephen. 1986. *The Novels of Nadine Gordimer: History from the
Inside*. Johannesburg: Ravan Press.
Dowling, William C. 1984. *Jameson, Althusser, Marx. An Introduction to the
Political Unconscious*. London: Methuen.
Du Toit, André. 1983. *Die sondes van die vaders*. Cape Town: Rubicon.
Frankel, Phillip H. 1984. *Pretoria's Praetorians: Civil-Military Relations in South
Africa*. London: Cambridge U.P.
Gerwel, G.J. 1983. *Literatuur en Apartheid*. Genadendal: Kampen.
Gordimer, Nadine. 1976. In Heywood, Christopher (ed.). *Aspects of South
African Literature*. London: Heinemann.
Gordimer, Nadine. 1973. *The Black Interpreters*. Johannesburg: Spro-cas.
Gramsci, Antonio. 1978. *Selections from Prison Notebooks*. Edited and trans-
lated by Quintin Hoare and Geoffrey Nowell Smith. London: Lawrence
and Wishart.
Grové, A.P. 1965. 'Die Afrikaanse prosa — diagnose en voorskrif?'. *Oor-
deel en Vooroordeel: Letterkundige opstelle en kritiek*. Cape Town: Nasou.
Hofmeyr, Isabel. 1987. 'Building a Nation from Words: Afrikaans Language,
Literature and Ethnic Identity, 1902-1924'. In Marks, Shula and Stanley
Trapido (eds). *The Politics of Race, Class and Nationalism*. New York:
Longman.
Jameson, Fredric. 1971. *Marxism and Form*. New Jersey: Princeton.
Jameson, Fredric. 1981. *The Political Unconscious*. London: Methuen.
John, Philip. 1988. 'Ideologiese patrone in die roman ''Uitdraai'' van Wil-
ma Stockenström'. University of the Witwatersrand: unpublished thesis.

366   *Ampie Coetzee*

Johnstone, Frederick. 1982. '''Most painful to our hearts'': South Africa through the eyes of the new school'. *Revue canadienne des études africaines*, 16(1).

Kannemeyer, J.C. 1978 & 1983. *Geskiedenis van die Afrikaanse Literatuur, I & II*. Pretoria: Academica.

Karis, Thomas and Gwendolen Carter (eds). 1973. *From Protest to Challenge: A Documentary History of South Africa, 1882-1964*. Stanford: Hoover Institute Press.

Louw, N.P. van Wyk. 1962. *Tristia, en ander verse, voorspele en vlugte, 1950-1957*. Cape Town: Human en Rousseau.

Macherey, Pierre. 1978. *A Theory of Literary Production*. London: Routledge and Kegan Paul.

Mandela, Nelson. 1965. *No Easy Walk to Freedom. Articles, Speeches and Trial Addresses of Nelson R. Mandela*. Edited by Ruth First. London: Heinemann.

Marais, Eugéne. 1941. *Versamelde gedigte*. Pretoria: J.L. van Schaik.

Marks, Shula and Stanley Trapido (eds). 1987. *The Politics of Race, Class and Nationalism in Twentieth Century South Africa*. New York: Longman.

Marx, Karl. 1984. *Selected Writings*. Edited by David McLellan. Oxford: Oxford U.P.

Miles, John. 1983. *Blaaskans*. Johannesburg: Taurus.

Miller, J. Hillis. 1979. *Deconstruction and Criticism. Harold Bloom, Paul de Man, Jacques Derrida, Geoffrey H. Hartman*. New York: Continuum.

Mphahlele, Es'kia. 1982. 'Fireflames: Mtshali's Strident Voice of Self-assertion'. In Chapman, M. (ed.). *Soweto Poetry*. Johannesburg: McGraw-Hill.

Munnik, Victor. 1987. 'Confined to Base: A Psycho-political Reading of '''n Wêreld sonder grense'''. University of the Witwatersrand: unpublished thesis.

Ngubane, J.K. 1987. '40 Years of Black Writing'. In Mutloatse, Mothobi (ed.). *Umhlaba Wethu*. Johannesburg: Skotaville.

Olivier, Gerrit (ed.). 1985. *Praat met die ANC*. Johannesburg: Taurus.

O'Meara, Dan. 1983. *Volkskapitalisme: Class, Capital and Ideology in the Development of Afrikaner Nationalism, 1934-1948*. Johannesburg: Ravan Press.

Plaatje, Sol T. 1982. *Native Life in South Africa*. Johannesburg: Ravan Press.

Posel, Deborah. 1983. 'Rethinking the Race-Class Debate in South African Historiography'. *Social Dynamics*, 9(1).

Saul, John S. and Stephen Gelb. 1981. 'The Crisis in South Africa: Class Defence, Class Revolution'. *Monthly Review Press*, 33(3).

Schoeman, Karel. 1979. *Die hemeltuin*. Cape Town: Human en Rousseau.

Sole, Kelwyn. 1979. 'Class, Continuity and Change in Black South African Literature, 1948-1960'. In Bozzoli, Belinda (ed.). *Labour, Townships and Protest*. Johannesburg: Ravan Press.

Strachan, Alexander. 1984. *'n Wêreld sonder grense*. Cape Town: Tafelberg.

Strachan, Alexander. 1985. *Rapport*, 21 July 1985.

Swilling, Mark. 1987. 'Living in the Interregnum: Crisis, Reform and the Socialist Alternative in South Africa'. *Third World Quarterly*, 9(2).

Toerien, Barend J. 1983. *Aanvange. Verskeuse, 1938-1962*. Cape Town: Tafelberg.

Van Heerden, Etienne. 1984. *My Kubaan*. Cape Town: Tafelberg.

Willemse, Hein. 1985. 'Ter wille van oorlewing'. *Stet*, June 1985.

Die Skrille Sonbesies: Emergent Black Afrikaans Poets in Search of Authority

Hein Willemse

The affirmation of nonhegemonic cultural voices remains ineffective if it is limited to the merely 'sociological' perspective of the pluralistic rediscovery of other isolated groups: only an ultimate rewriting of these utterances in terms of their essentially polemic and subversive strategies restores them to their proper place in the dialogical system of social classes.

— *Fredric Jameson: The Political Unconscious*

Since the mid-seventies more black Afrikaans writers have committed themselves to publication than in the preceding four decades. For a variety of reasons, not least the perceived biases against the Afrikaans language, this upsurge in black Afrikaans writing is noteworthy. In the popular mind Afrikaans has been firmly associated with Afrikaner Nationalism and its political expression, the Nationalist Party. The rejection of Afrikaner Nationalism and particularly the educational policies of the Nationalist government was demonstrated most cogently in the June 1976 Soweto uprising. It is generally accepted that the introduction of the teaching of science subjects through the medium of Afrikaans was the motorial cause for that extensive period of revolt (see Hirson, 1979: 175-180; Lodge, 1983: 331; Magubane, 1979: 323).

My appreciation to Ampie Coetzee, Julian Smith and Martin Trump who read earlier drafts of this essay and made valuable suggestions.

I am responsible for the translations from the Afrikaans primary and secondary sources of reference. In the translation of the poetry communicative accuracy rather than poetic nuance took precedence.

368   *Hein Willemse*

The rejection of Afrikaans, that intimate symbol of Afrikaner Nationalism, reverberated through Afrikanerdom and not long thereafter some Afrikaner academics were predicting the language's conceivable end. Since 1976 a genre of writing on the survival of the Afrikaner and by logical extension also the survival of Afrikaans has developed (see Steyn, 1980; Prinsloo and Van Rensburg, 1984; and Du Plessis and Du Plessis, 1987). André Brink (1984: 36) in his contribution to that debate posits that '[i]f the language remains identified with the present establishment and its ideology, clearly its fate is sealed. And the more ferociously the Extreme Right calls forth crusades to battle for the purity and the preservation of *volk en taal*, the more surely such a movement will itself become the guarantee and the agent for the annihilation of Afrikaans.'

It is in the face of these predictions of the possible annihilation of Afrikaans that the number of black Afrikaans writers has steadily increased. Writing by black Afrikaans writers has always been sparse and their participation within Afrikaans literature limited.[1] This essay is an attempt at exploring and interpreting the apparently contradictory increased productivity among black Afrikaans writers, with particular reference to poetry. Their poetry, it is suggested, seeks to define their political and cultural experience in an authoritative manner.

An important consideration in this study is the necessity of a critical approach which can determine the historical and ideological preconditions and functions of emergent literary activity within institutionalized cultural contexts. These texts by black Afrikaans poets are situated in a very particular cultural, economic and political setting and furthermore form part of a dialogical relationship between ruler and dominated. The emergence of black Afrikaans writing is not an isolated happening but determined by real socio-political struggle.

A political reading of the Afrikaans literary tradition makes it possible to identify the terrain of Afrikaans literature as a site of struggle. This assertion may appear to be axiomatic but in contemporary Afrikaans literary criticism only a few serious attempts have been made to uncover or deepen the existing fissures and contradictions within Afrikaans literature. In reviewing contemporary black Afrikaans poetry some of these fissures may be revealed.

This essay will explore the emergence of a more relaxed attitude towards Afrikaans in left political activism, especially in the Western Cape region; the relationship between younger black Afrikaans writers and the Afrikaans literary establishment and some current preoccupations and priorities of these writers.

Afrikaans in the Western Cape

Afrikaans has been firmly connected to Afrikaner Nationalism, and the 1976 uprising tended to mythologize and reinforce that perception. The objective in this section is to reveal the materiality of Afrikaans and provide a background for the development of black Afrikaans writing in the Western Cape.

Eagleton (1979: 63) in a perceptive essay draws a distinction between the 'emotive and cognitive structure of ideological discourse'. Ideology cannot be merely 'reduced to miscognition, but [can also] be seen as a signifying set of practical relations with the "real"'. Eagleton (1979: 64) argues further that ideological propositions are only *apparently* propositions about the real: 'What differentiates ideological "propositions" from genuinely referential enunciations is that the former may be "decoded" into "emotive" (subject-oriented) discourse.'

This notion of ideological discourse may be employed fruitfully to disaggregate the proposition 'Afrikaans is the language of the oppressor', implying that 'Afrikaans is *solely* the language of the oppressor'. Viewed simply this could be considered a referential proposition: the Afrikaner speaks Afrikaans; the Afrikaner is the political oppressor; thus: Afrikaans is the language of the oppressor. Considering the large number of black Afrikaans speakers — in the 1980 official census 47% of all Afrikaans speakers were black (see Ponelis, 1987: 10) — this is obviously not a completely referential proposition, and could, in Eagleton's terminology, be decoded into 'emotive ideological discourse': we hate the Nationalist government for denying us unfettered economic, political and social participation; therefore we reject the Nationalist government — the Afrikaner — its institutions and symbols, including the Afrikaans language.

The following quotation illustrates compellingly the perception of that causal relationship between language and repression:

> [T]he Afrikaners spoke Afrikaans, which is a mongrel Dutch with some German. Afrikaans has a guttural and ugly sound. It would later be very effective to use when the authorities ordered native families from our homes or commanded soldiers to fire into unarmed crowds. It is the language of genocide, and, in fact, it sounds like the German the Nazis speak in Hollywood movies. (Makeba, 1988: 5)

Afrikaner ideologues generated, for the purpose of ethnic mobilization, a premise perceiving themselves to be the 'proprietors' of the language. Their political opponents on the other hand uncritically accepted that false premise in determining consciously their own relationship to the language.

However, deconstructing this discourse does not imply depreciation of a harsh political experience: what is at stake in the last analysis is not whether the proposition is true or false, but whether it defines a person's experience in the real world. 'What *is* important to recognize is that the cognitive structure of an ideological discourse is subordinated to its emotive structure' (Eagleton, 1979: 64).

The rejection of Afrikaans in 1976 thus served as a symbolic rejection of Afrikaner Nationalism and the educational policies of the Nationalist government. Moreover, it also assisted to obscure all other relationships between Afrikaans and other, primarily black speakers of the language. It is only in recent years that attempts have been made to redeem the place of black Afrikaans speakers in the history of Afrikaans (see Belcher, 1987; Davids, 1987; and Du Plessis, 1986).

For the current study the political and socio-cultural background of Afrikaans and its relationship to black people with reference to the Western Cape region is particularly pertinent as the majority of black poets are living there. The relationship of black people to Afrikaans in other regions of the country may be markedly different from that in the Western Cape and warrants its own in-depth treatment.

The predominance of Afrikaans in the Western Cape, the region where it originated, is obviously not a miracle, but a part and a product of history. Besides the original development of Afrikaans in this region, in the proximity of various African, Asian and European languages, its position has further been maintained or strengthened by a series of historical processes: the pivotal role of the language in the development of Afrikaner Nationalism, the existence of a large Afrikaans-speaking working class and more recently the social engineering legislation on the settling and movement of Africans (see also Goldin, 1987) ensured that the population composition and consequently the language ratio remained relatively stable and homogeneous over a long period of time.

The city, Cape Town, has a tradition of bilingualism — Afrikaans and English — with a bias towards English in commerce and politics, whereas in the surrounding rural areas Afrikaans is dominant. A class breakdown of the spoken languages among the urban black population suggests that working class people speak primarily Afrikaans and Xhosa and the middle classes English. In the adjacent rural areas, especially among the 'coloured' population, Afrikaans is the major language cutting across class divides. The majority of black Afrikaans writers are either living in the surrounding rural areas, or are new arrivals to the city, or live in the (predominantly Afrikaans) northern suburbs or working class areas of the city. This phenomenon is material in understanding the presence of the black Afrikaans writer.

With the onset of Afrikaner Nationalism and the formative role Afrikaans played in its invention (see Hofmeyr, 1987) the relationship of Afrikaans to Afrikaner Nationalism has dominated discussion on the language, to the point that analyses into the class origins and nature of the language have been virtually non-existent. A similar dearth exists in the historiography of the Afrikaans language in revealing subaltern history and cultural life.[2] A major task in reclaiming history recommends itself in this regard.

Since its early beginnings Afrikaans was not only an indicator of class differences among whites (Hofmeyr, 1987: 96-97) but also among the black population. Dr Abdullah Abduraghman, an important political figure in the African People's Organization (APO) in the early years of this century, was reported to have renounced Afrikaans audaciously as

'barbarous Cape Dutch', and the APO [a journal] described it as a 'vulgar patois, fit only for the kitchen'. . . . The APO conducted all its proceedings in English, associating Afrikaans with Afrikaner racism and 'lower-class' Coloureds. [This position] no doubt . . . served to reinforce the organisation's elitism since the vast majority of those categorised as Coloureds, especially rural and urban workers, spoke Afrikaans as their first language. (Lewis, 1987: 71)

Major shifts, during the late 1970s and early 1980s, in the practice of political and cultural activism, the prominence of trade union campaigns and the upshot of educational and political struggles resulted in the rethinking of set ways of political and trade union organization. A sensitivity developed in political and trade union activist discourses towards the material composition of particular groups and classes. This is pre-eminently reflected in terms of language.

A shift from *ex cathedra* political engagement to greater grass-roots activity sensitized political activists to the expediency of Afrikaans. In certain political quarters this conscious use of Afrikaans is said to have taken place well before 1976: 'Long before 1976 . . . Afrikaans was used regularly, at political meetings as a vehicle of liberation' (Benson, 1988: 9). During the 1988 May Day celebrations in the Western Cape 'some of the speeches were in Xhosa, translated into Afrikaans — "because these are the languages of the working class", a Cosatu organiser said' (quoted in *South*,

4-11 May 1988, p.11). In the working class townships of the Cape Peninsula pupils protest in Afrikaans as well as in Xhosa and English (see Willemse, 1987: 244); similarly, convicted ANC cadres have on occasion delivered their evidence in mitigation, usually considered as the last public political act for the guerilla, in Afrikaans (Michels, 1987: 2; Wescott, 1988: 57).

In many areas of the Cape Peninsula, the Karoo, the Northwestern Cape and the Eastern Cape Afrikaans has been used in grass-roots campaigns. Whereas Afrikaans was previously limited to pamphlets, especially in rural communities, greater attention has now been paid to the production of Afrikaans 'alternative' newspapers, e.g. *Saamstaan* in the Southern Cape and *Alternatief* on the Atlantic west coast.

In related developments, especially in the area of artistic production, a recognition of the potential for the development of a 'people's culture' has also influenced the attitude towards the Afrikaans Cape patois. In an interview in *New Era*, a publication sympathetic to the UDF, a Cape Town 'cultural worker' described 'people's culture' as an emerging cultural activity

> that is firstly patriotic and national — *dié land is onse land die*. But for a whole community this doesn't mean absorbing itself into 'African' culture and losing all sense of its own specific features. Rather, it says *nooit* — our Kaaps way of speaking Afrikaans, the Goema-Goema beat, tamatiesous and kerrie kos . . . those things are as 'African' as the Xhosa language, the Mbaqanga beat and pap. It's almost as if a 'brown African' is emerging. (Williams, 1987: 13)[3]

Within democratic political and cultural organizations previously accepted notions of 'Afrikaans as the Afrikaner's language' have been challenged. Jonathan de Vries (1988), a young English-speaking cultural activist, expresses himself as follows on this issue:

> The people who have done the greatest disservice to the sustenance and development of Afrikaans are the Nationalists and their cultural organs. They hijacked Afrikaans for the purpose of Afrikaner nationalism and formalised it into a framework that is presently dying. A living Afrikaans is now (sic) developing in the townships — an enriched form of Afrikaans, one that will stand eventually as another patois of Africa.

For other cultural activists the use of Afrikaans is justified in terms of the exigency of communication:

> On leaving high school I decided never to speak Afrikaans unnecessarily. This was my protest against the Afrikaner government, the

Volk and the system in this country. Later in my development I came to realise that workers on the farms speak Afrikaans. I became aware of the fact that if I wanted to identify with the struggle of the working class I had to speak, understand and write the language we all know. (Jansen, 1986: 80-81)

In the process of inserting Afrikaans into progressive political and social discourse the first ripples on the educational level can be seen. A case in point is the appearance of 'alternative Afrikaans' educational publications, e.g. Randall van den Heever's *Treë na vryheid* (1987) and *Afrikaans en bevryding* (1988). Within progressive teachers' organizations some energy has been spent on attempts at changing the syllabi and at least one Afrikaans project, taking as its focus the whole of the Afrikaans language community, is underway (Botha, 1987). In the related sphere of literacy the publication of Afrikaans texts has also taken a liberating turn: students' own stories are published and used for literacy exercises, thus valuing their experiences as worthy.[4]

Although no one-to-one correspondences may necessarily be found between black Afrikaans writers and specific politico-cultural developments the general cultural environment has in no uncertain way impacted on their writing: the conscious manner of producing writing in Afrikaans and inserting it within the broader democratic political and cultural movement could otherwise not have taken place. This present niche for Afrikaans was forged in the furnace of the contemporary national liberation and workers' struggle in the Western Cape.

The Politics of the Afrikaans Literary Canon

The poetry of black Afrikaans poets is produced as a consequence of particular socio-political conditions. As such, the work is embedded within a broader system of opposing political and social orders (Jameson, 1981: 84). This dialogical relationship is intrinsically antagonistic. In the present case this relationship exists within the shared code of Afrikaans literature.

Recently a reviewer discerningly grasped this dialogical relationship in terms of language:

Afrikaans — the language of Botha, the police sergeant, the bantustan bureaucrat — is not normally associated with resistance. Yet the poet Breyten Breytenbach . . . once sought to distinguish between 'Apartaans', the idiom of apartheid, and Afrikaans, one of Africa's many tongues. The case for that split becomes dramatically strengthened when one considers the lot of the black Afrikaans writer. (Nixon, 1987: 453)

Far from being an uncontested whole, Afrikaans literature experiences various ruptures and contradictions. There is, however, a semblance of unity and wholeness largely cultivated through Afrikaans literary criticism.

The underlying socio-political criteria of selection to the Afrikaans literary canon are largely determined by the aesthetic and cultural demands of Afrikaner Nationalism and the university-educated Afrikaner middle class. Earlier in the history of Afrikaans literature the central criteria were the maintenance and strengthening of Afrikanerdom across class divisions whilst of late, since the mid-1950s, the dominant voice has effectively been that of the aesthete and the intellectual.

Traditionally other forms of literary expression — e.g. Afrikaans orature or folklore — have been relegated to the 'invisible' fringes of Afrikaans literature. Little or no research within Afrikaans Literature departments focusses on this kind of expression. Consequently its historical meaning has been suppressed 'in ways designed precisely to make its political and ideological significance invisible' (Jameson and Kavanagh, 1984: 5). Although not completely ignored, black writers in general have suffered a similar fate of exclusion and marginalization; I will return to this point in the next section of this essay.

Black Afrikaans poets are quite conversant with establishment Afrikaans literature, having being schooled in its aesthetic requirements and worth. In their work there are frequent references to corresponding themes, genres or stylistic experiments in establishment literature. In general they evince a tendency to follow Afrikaans literary trends closely and some even declare definite influences from Afrikaner writers. Vincent Oliphant (1986: 82), for example, directly attributes his coming to a non-racial consciousness to André Brink's earlier novels: growing up in a rural area conditioned him to view white people as superior; however, through the reading of Brink's earlier, non-political novels he was freed of this stereotypical image of white people.[5]

Fuelled with a critical evaluation of their relationship to the Afrikaans literary canon and their limited power within Afrikaans publishing, black editors have initiated little magazines such as *Praat*, *Skryf* and *Akuut*. Prog Publishers, a publishing house concentrating exclusively on black Afrikaans writing, has recently been established in rural St Helena Bay on the Atlantic coast. According to Patrick Petersen (1988: 7), it was established because 'most Afrikaans publishing houses are extensions of Nationalist Party ideology, and that causes our work never to see the light of day'.

The growth in black Afrikaans writing can be ascribed to a series of multifarious conditions, among others the influence of the Black Consciousness Movement in the early seventies; the general political and cultural developments in the late 1970s and early 1980s outlined earlier; the insertion of black Afrikaans writers in the rural areas and, in the case of exiled writers, the need to recreate in exile something genuinely South African.

The contemporary growth in black Afrikaans writing takes place in the wake of the Soweto revolt. It is not unexpected that in the aftermath of the revolt some aspirant writers experienced a schism and negation of their relationship with Afrikaans: 'Although I grew up in an Afrikaans house, at one stage my friends and I spoke only English,' says Patrick Petersen. He concludes that: 'Those days are gone. Today we have a free association with the language, because it is also my language.' This rediscovery of the self ties in with earlier expressions of Black Consciousness. Gerwel (1986: 18) suggests that,

> Just as Soweto 1976 was a culmination of the Black Consciousness movement, so the revival of black writing was a product of that same politico-cultural movement. Black Consciousness, in spite of reactionary political tendencies which may be identified by critics, as an intellectual and cultural movement fundamentally challenged the definitions of the rulers and restored to black people the sociopsychological confidence to define themselves. It is out of this, I suspect, that the willingness to write in the mother tongue medium of Afrikaans arises.

A factor contributing to the development of black Afrikaans writers is their insertion into mostly rural areas. It is generally only at a relatively late stage in their lives — with employment or post-matric education — that they are introduced to city life and its language conventions.

The Afrikaans language and literature are uniquely South African. Exiled poets Julian de Wette, Vernie February and Jan Wiltshire evoke a former existence. The lonesome, elegiac individual experiencing a foreign country and recalling the joyful moments of a previous South African life is the outstanding trait of the poetry of De Wette (*Koning in die buiteland*, King in Exile, 1977; *Verban: Verbinne*, Banned: Internalized, 1980). February's poetry (*O, Snotverdriet*, Oh, Snotty Sorrow, 1979) abounds with Afrikaans folksongs, expressions and recollections of history, and richly uses the peculiarities of the working class Afrikaans spoken in the Western Cape. Wiltshire's collection (*Die verkeerde land / Das Verkehrte land*, The Wrong Land, 1985), with accompanying German translations, functions primarily as a first-hand report of 'life under apartheid'.

Preoccupations and Priorities

Besides the central thrust of the dialogical relationship between black Afrikaans writing and the Afrikaans literary tradition, it is also suggested that black Afrikaans writers are in search of the authority to define their socio-political experience. Erica Jong comments as follows on a similar search by women writers: 'She must . . . . have the authority to say "I am important, and what I have to say is important". If the writer's voice lacks authenticity, readers will dismiss the work as failing to express universal experience. If it lacks authority, readers will dismiss it as trivial or peripheral.' (Quoted in Schulz, 1984: 206)

An important choice for a writer in the competing discourses of power is the choice of language. In the case of black Afrikaans writers the usefulness of Afrikaans patois has been a highly emotive issue. Let us consider this more fully.

1

For writers participating in the discourses of power a central issue is that of the voice in which to speak: determining an audience, the nature of linguistic expression and the process of literary production. That choice unavoidably situates the writer within the domain of contending discourses.

In the case of Afrikaans a comparable debate simmers. Afrikaans's association with the oppressor and its political legacy raise questions as to its usefulness in a changing political environment. The majority of poets express themselves on their choice of language and its suitability in the present political environment. The poet Leonard Koza states a rather common view among younger black Afrikaans writers: 'We are primarily Afrikaans speaking. . . . We still love the language, in spite of what the system did to us. This is our mother tongue. Through our feeling for the language, we show that we promote the language. The language is a bridge between people.' (Koza, 1984)

This ambivalent relationship — the language both as a sign of violent oppression and as mother tongue ('moerstaal') — is also brought to bear on their poetry. Vernie February (1979: 29) in his 'Moerstaal' alludes to this dichotomy, where the obscene exclamation — *moer* — in its connotations of physical violence and verbal abuse is read simultaneously with the obsolete Afrikaans word, *moer*, indicating womb, motherhood, breastfeeding and fertility:

jou moerstaal
is meer moer dan taal
so skop hom in sy maaifoerie,
en die aap val vannie balie,
tot die strot uithang,
want die taal van jou moer
lê tussen têt en jou moer,
so skryf ma ou pêllie,
want die taal van jou moer
lê tussen têt en jou moer

(your mother tongue / is more feud than language / so kick his arse, / and the ape falls from the pail, / until the throat hangs out, / because the language of your mother / lies between her tit and 'you motherfucker', / so write on, pal, / because the language of your mother / lies between her tit and 'you motherfucker'.)

This relationship of some black writers to Afrikaans extends to the conservation of the language, a topic which has become pronounced among Afrikaner literary academics in particular. In 'Skryfwerk' (Writing) Marius F. Titus (1988: 69) relates a similar concern and recommends a solution:

Soe die beste manier
omme taal te bewaar is:
Liesit, praatit, skryffit,
ontginnit en bedryffit.
net soelank jy my verstaan,
stap ek en taal 'n lang pad saam.

(So the best way / to conserve a language is: / to read it, speak it, write it, / explore it and practise it. / as long as you understand me, / the language and I shall go a long way.)

A highly controversial subject among black Afrikaans writers is the use of patois. The Cape Afrikaans patois, 'Kaaps' as it has been dubbed by Adam Small (1973: 9), refers essentially to a working class and proletarian variety of Afrikaans; this has popularly, mainly pejoratively, been typified as *kleurling-Afrikaans*. Afrikaans literary studies and linguistics in turn have sanctioned this prejudice.[6]

Kaaps in written form has a long history in Afrikaans literature. Its first known appearance in literature was around the 1820s when Bain lampooned the slaves' speech in his *Kaatje Kekkelbek*.[7] Intermittently over the next century and a half the patois has become, through a process of co-optation and appropriation, an accepted element of Afrikaans literature. It gained currency, literary acceptability and stereotypical value through the writings of Bain, the 'language movement' generations, Von Wielligh, I.D. du Plessis, Uys Krige, Van Wyk Louw, Boerneef, Peter Blum and especially Adam Small. With Small, classified as a 'coloured' poet, the correspondence between 'the coloured people' and the patois became virtually uncontested in Afrikaans literature. To a limited degree Small employed satire through proletarian speech to uncover accepted truths.[8] Following in the wake of Small, some contemporary black Afrikaans poets have taken the Cape Afrikaans patois as the distinctive trait of their writing.

Recently several writers have advocated the use of patois in literature (see Willemse, 1986: 70-72). Peter Snyders (1987: 5) sees the distinct possibility of Afrikaans patois developing into a language embracing 'all those using the linguistic and scientific rules of neo-Afrikaans':

> I want to give this particular language a new name, namely neo-Afrikaans. By neo-Afrikaans I mean all the working classes, the urban youth, the residents of Vyfster [prison], the fans of Goosen and Kramer, *tsotsi's*, the men on the border and all those using to a degree the linguistic and scientific rules of neo-Afrikaans. I see Afrikaans as the indigenous parent language of the post-apartheid period. But she must rid herself of her so-called cultured [image] and become more in tune with more universal linguistic approaches to language.

Afrikaans as 'the indigenous parent language of the post-apartheid era', proclaimed by Snyders in his fervour for a new Afrikaans, is at best suspect. His formulation tells us more about his emotional attachment to the language and his authorial intentions than his professed scientific or linguistic accuracy. Snyders perceives as his task 'to give voice to the voiceless, to uplift the underdog, to give status to insignificant people and to create a pride that would lead to the further upliftment of my people' (Snyders, 1984).

The determined ideology of individual poems by Snyders, February and Titus is clearly expressed through identical formulaic strategies in exploring 'the "coloured" working class': the poems are populated with working class and proletarian characters — invariably men — who witness or experience an incident or narrate a past happening on which they pass a witty concluding comment. The effect is comic relief no matter how gloomy the described situation. Through orthography a distance is created, marking the patois as different and setting it apart from regular Afrikaans spelling, with the added effect of emphasizing the described experience for the reader or listener.

Here as a representative illustration of these poems is Titus's (1988: 74) 'Seblief' (Please):

Master, omlat ek partime christian is,
het ek sieke 'n policy van
lifetime insurance by jou.

Ek's opgefok en innie gutter,
deergeroes; my engine splutter,
quote virrie djop seblief.

Die Dywel was ees my mechanic,
hy't opgefok en my lat panic,
doen Jy die djop seblief.

Laaswiek het hy weer gesê
laat hyrrie djoppie oek wil hê,
ek trust hommie my Lord.

Master, ek's 'n scrap djaloppie,
fix my op, doe Jyrrie djoppie:
Help my Lord! seblief.

Dan Master, asse final plea,
gie my 'n lifetime guarantee:
Soelat ek Hiemal toe kan ry.

(Master, because I'm a part-time christian / I probably have a policy
/ of lifetime insurance from you. // I'm fucked up and in the gutter,
/ rusted through, my engine splutters, / please quote for the job. //
Earlier the devil was my mechanic, / he fucked me up and let me panic,
/ You must do the job, please. // Last week he again said / that he
also wanted the job, / I don't trust him my Lord. // Master, I'm a jalo-
py, / fix me, You must do the job: / Help me, Lord! Please. // Then
Master, as a final plea, / give me a lifetime guarantee: / so that I can
ride to heaven.)

The 'cognitive ideological intention' of this poem lies clearly in the
introduction of township and working class people to the reader
or listener: in a moment of desperation a person calling on his God
for redemption. The poem denotes a witty (drunken?) hedonism,
and on the 'emotive ideological level' accepts entrenched stereotypes. The 'boss' or 'master' in the labour relationship is carried
through to the religious realm. The laughter employed here is the
laughter of submission and not of subversion or criticism.[10]

A criticism levelled by Bannerji (1984: 134) against 'progressive'
Bengali playwrights is applicable in this instance: 'the "slice-of-life"
approach to reality left unanswered and unposed some major questions regarding analytical and explorative ways of uncovering social relations that structured those lives. It took "reality" for granted, blocked questions regarding the methods of realism and equated a real portrayal with a naturalistic mode of depiction.'[11]

In a situation of heightened language consciousness the development of 'contrastive self-identification' (Fishman, as quoted by
Fasold, 1984: 3) can be expected. This is the feeling of 'the members of a nationality that they are united and identified with others
who speak the same language, and contrast with and are separated
from those who do not' (Fasold, 1984: 3-4). A similar development
in South Africa bears an intrinsic dilemma. Whereas it is not con-
tentious to be 'Afrikaans-speaking' or 'a writer in Afrikaans', any
indication that the conscious literary use of 'Kaaps' panders to
apartheid-spawned and enforced notions of 'ethnic groups' will
meet with fierce criticism. The potential for this exists exactly in the
emphasis on 'alternative' Afrikaans as a formal and exclusive expression, on 'Kaaps' or 'neo-Afrikaans' as a thing in itself — a third
language — as opposed to emphasizing the contesting values expressed through the Afrikaans language.

Critical rejection of the notion of Kaaps as 'the language of a special group of people . . . [with] a right to a special, ethnic, literary
existence' is exemplified by Rive (1986: 68):

> One could see Kaaps as propounding the acceptance of a brand of
> Colouredism in the face of strong anti-racism. It is difficult to see it
> as serving any other purpose. It is easy to counter its claims that it
> is the language of a special group of people (or a section of it) and
> thus has a right to a special, ethnic, literary existence. It is easy to
> counter its claim that it adds an extra dimension of authenticity.
> Authenticity should be inherent more in content than style, more in
> what is said than in how it is said. It is also debatable whether Kaaps
> as it is written is Kaaps as it is spoken. A genuine poem does not
> rely on a dialect for its continued existence. Genuine poetry will last
> regardless of the medium it employs as long as its use is a genuine
> blending of content and style. The use of dialect in any creative work
> in South Africa only has relevance insofar as that dialect is used to
> show up the pseudo-ethnicity that brought about its creation. The
> Nigerian writers used English and not Pidgin in order to attack Brit-
> ish imperialism, and the Negritudinists used immaculate French and
> not Creole in order to attack their suffocation by French culture. Kaaps
> can be used to expose the legalised socio-political deprivation that
> has created it. And to the extent that it does so, its legitimacy will
> be tested.

The questions Rive raises are numerous and controversial: genuine
poetry vs. non-genuine poetry; content vs. style; real experience
(Kaaps as it is spoken) vs. the artistic reproduction (Kaaps as it is
written); dialect vs. immaculate ('standard'?) language; language
as indicator of acceptance of ethnicity; authenticity and authority.
Rive's position on literature and language in this passage is informed

by a conservative view of literariness, Literature, literary production and transhistorical literary standards. The passage is however representative of a widely-held attitude, mainly amongst the middle class, towards 'Kaaps': it is the language of the 'coloured people', it signifies a separate 'coloured' culture and the stereotype of working class people who are lazy, drunk, hedonistic and stupid.

Rive, paradoxically, in terms of his own view, suggests in the last two sentences a second position: that the language may be used 'to expose the legalised socio-political deprivation that has created it'. For the creative writer participating in discourses where the hegemonic 'truth' in cultural and political spheres is challenged the writing act may indeed be more complex than employing a mere naturalistic mode of language to encode 'the voiceless'. It is in developing a literary use of language, including the patois, which uncovers and interprets the inscribed traces of conflict in social relations that he or she may subvert the language of dominance.

2

In significant ways black poets are constant interlocutors with the dominant Afrikaans poetic tradition. Unlike their English counterparts who grew up with a non-South African poetic tradition, black Afrikaans poets have been nurtured at school with South African, primarily Afrikaans, poetry. Their immediate role models are normally Afrikaans poets. Through the rigid control over the syllabus at schools or teacher training colleges these role models are frequently the older poets, canonized within the framework of Afrikaner Nationalism and Christian National Education.

The broader historical place and literary education of black Afrikaans poets have a crucial impact on the extent to which their poetry contests the dominant culture. These factors also influence the breadth of technical exploration and the level of polemical engagement available to emergent black poets within the limits of the Afrikaans poetic tradition. This is often evident in the nature of versification and frequent references to older Afrikaans poetry.

Given the experience of their own historical space it is no wonder that black Afrikaans writers are conscious of their relationship to Afrikaans Literature. Faced with the dominant version of history through Afrikaans poetry younger black poets enter into a dialogue with the older Afrikaans literary tradition.

The reaction against Afrikanerdom involves developing alternative symbols and expressions. André Boezak in his poem 'Julle kamma sing' (You ostensibly sing, 1988: 26) uses lines from 'Die Stem van Suid-Afrika', the official national anthem of South Africa, to challenge dominant cultural perceptions. The following lines from the anthem are incorporated into Boezak's poem:

Uit die blou van onse hemel, uit die diepte van ons see,
Oor ons ewige gebergtes waar die kranse antwoord gee,
Deur ons ver verlate vlaktes met die kreun van ossewa -
Ruis die stem van ons geliefde, van ons land Suid-Afrika.

(Ringing out from our blue heavens, from our deep seas breaking round, / Over everlasting mountains where the echoing crags resound, / From our plains where creaking wagons, cut their trails into the earth — / Calls the spirit of our Country, of the land that gave us birth. (Official translation.))

Boezak undermines the lyrical pastoral imagery, the comfort and political control signified by the official anthem, by ironically juxtaposing them with the daily experiences of black people: vigilantes, teargas, and dispossession. In opposition to the image of Afrikaner nationalist achievement Boezak portrays the 'tearful' enmity and resistance of black people:

Julle kamma sing
    witdoeke
vannie bloutes vannie hiemel
    vol teargas
vannie ewige gebêgtes
    hoeg soes ôs afsin in jou
vannie dieptes vannie sie
    ôs trane makkit vol
vannie vê velate vlaktes
    wattie joune issie
hulle erwe bly hul kinners in
    ôs sin hettie law gevat.

(You ostensibly sing / witdoeke (vigilantes) / of the blue of the heavens / full of teargas / of the everlasting mountains / high as our aversion to you / of the depths of the sea / our tears fill it up / of the far forlorn plains / which aren't yours / their heritage remains their children's /ours the law took away.)

The ox-wagon is a central symbol of Afrikaner nationalism and recurs frequently in earlier Afrikaans poetry. The prototype of this nationalist poetry is Jan F.E. Cilliers's 'Die Ossewa' (The ox-wagon) (see Van den Heever and Nienaber, 1949: 91), a eulogy to the ever-willing, patient, dumb oxen, the primary method of transport for the Voortrekkers:

Die osse stap aan deur die stowwe,
geduldig, gedienstig, gedwee;
die jukke, al drukkend hul skowwe -
hul dra dit getroos en tevree.
. . .
So, stom tot die stond van hul sterwe,
bly ieder 'n held van die daad . . .
Hul bene, na swoee en swerwe,
lê ver op die velde verlaat.

(The oxen plod on through the dust, / enduring, subservient, meek;
/ the yoke presses against their humps — /docile and content they
bear it / . . . // So, mute until the time of their death, / each one remains a hero of action . . . / their bones, after toiling and wander-
ing, / lie far off, abandoned on the veld.)

Wiltshire (1985: 58) is conscious of the canonized elements of the
Afrikaans literary tradition. In a few lines he challenges an entire
history of literature and education within the confines of Afrikaner
nationalism:

die osse stap aan deur die stowwe
geduldig gedienstig gedwee
ek is al moeg vir die vers
wat hulle uit jou wil pers
die heldedade van voortrekkers
wat die zoeloes uitmerg.

(The oxen plod on through the dust, / enduring, subservient, meek
/ I'm tired of this verse / which they squeeze out of us / heroic deeds
of voortrekkers / who massacred the zulus.)

Black writers also frequently express their relationship with the
Afrikaans folk tradition. The writing of Vernie February, in particular, evokes Afrikaner and African folklore. Among his poems which
consciously draw on these traditions are 'Jannie met die hoepelbeen'
(Bow-legged Jannie), 'Vat jou goed en trek Ferreira' (Take your
things and leave Ferreira), 'Abelungu Ngodem' (White man go to
hell) and recollections of historical occurrences as in 'Bloedrivier'
(Blood River).
   Redefining 'official history' and a demand for 'a historicity of their
own and a claim to an autonomous, self-determining role on the
contemporary staging grounds of history' (Harlow, 1987: 33) are
strong undercurrents in the writing of black South Africans generally. The struggle of the Afrikaners for liberation from British rule
is juxtaposed with the liberation struggle of black people in South
Africa. In February's 'Met ekskusies aan oom Gert vertel' (With apo-

logies to uncle Gert's story) the narrator recounts the experiences
of black people serving under white masters, juxtaposing these experiences with C. Louis Leipoldt's 'Oom Gert vertel' (Uncle Gert
narrates). Leipoldt's poem has been characterized as 'a cry of hor-
ror and terror over all the grief inflicted by the British on the Boers'
(Dekker, n.d.: 86-87). February's narrator asserts that Oom Gert's
story, compared with black people's grief, sounds like a 'third-rate
funeral'.

> ek vrees die magte wat my lewe skik,
> meer dan die ou kapel se pik,
> my teringopgevrete long kan ek weerstaan,
> van huidsmania sal ons almal vrek.
> 'Ja, neef, die storie van ons lyding',
> sal Oom Gert vertel se ou relasie
> van hul stryd om hul bevryding
> laat klink soos 'n derderangse lykstasie.

> (I fear the powers which control my life, / more than the cobra's bite,
> / my phthisis-infested lung I can resist, / we'll all die from skin ma-
> nia. / 'Yes, my friend, the story of our grief' / will make the story
> told in 'Oom Gert vertel' / about their struggle for freedom / sound
> like a third-rate funeral.)

Jameson (1971: 377) suggests in general that 'the work is precisely
not complete in itself but is handed down to us as a kind of gesture
or verbal thrust incomprehensible unless we understand the situation in which the gesture was first made, and the interlocutors to
whom it was a reply'. Within the shared code of Afrikaans literature the writings of emergent black Afrikaans writers constitute an
important way of wresting 'that expropriated historicity back, reap-
propriat[ing] it for themselves in order to reconstruct a new world-
historical order' (Harlow, 1987: 33).

3

Striking a rather independent note within the overtly socio-political,
public domain of black Afrikaans poetry are those poets accentuating primarily personal and private matters. The individual experience is a central code in the poetry of Julian de Wette, Vincent
Oliphant and Clinton V. du Plessis. The first-person narrator is often
a lonesome, elegiac, pensive, sometimes cynical individual.

The title of Oliphant's collection *Bloed vloei in stilte* (Blood Flows
in Silence, 1983), suggests socio-political concerns; but the poem 'In
stilte' (In Silence), which contains the collection's title, expresses
the narrator's agony as a decidedly private one:

Jy laat nou die tinteling
oor my
jou gesonde gladde jongeling
en jy is bly

Maar weet ook
my vel is bloot die geluk
waaragter die sluimerende droefheid skuil

En as ek eendag seer sou kry
en jy sien hoe my liggaam vlek van bloed
moenie huil nie
    onthou
        die bloed is altyd daar
        die bloed vloei in stilte

(Now you sparkle / over me / you, healthy, smooth youngster / and you are happy // But also know / my skin is only the bliss / behind which the slumbering gloominess hides // And if one day I should get hurt / and you see my body stained with blood / don't cry / remember / the blood is always there / the blood flows in silence).

The melancholy in this poem, expressive of what is perceived as an inherently miserable human condition — 'my skin is only the bliss / behind which the slumbering gloominess hides' — is the hallmark of Oliphant's poetry. In this his work is reminiscent of Arthur Nortje and the Afrikaans poet Wilhelm Knobel.

De Wette's poetry reveals an urbane, contemplative individual writing primarily about personal matters. The essence of his work is an attentiveness to established notions about the craft of poetry and aesthetic value linking it more directly than most of the other black poets to the Afrikaans literary tradition. In this extract from the title poem of his second collection, *Verban: Verbinne*, the narrator concludes instructively on his 'bloodthirsty struggle: I, the defamer of blood — white and black, apart, blackened':

Kan ek uithou teen die magskelkie wat my verlei?
Nee, want die sweet verblind, verbinne die ervaring
van bruin-en-wit wees
in stede van swart
en my stryd is verloor, verlore ekself.

(Can I resist the chalice of power which entices me? / No, because sweat blinds, internalize the experience / of being brown and white / instead of black, / and my battle is lost, myself lost.)

In De Wette's work then whatever conflict is generated in social experience is 'privatized', internalized.

The narrators in Du Plessis's poems (1984) are generally reclusive, lonesome, artistic, cynical figures, looking disdainfully upon a consumerist society. Here the individual braces himself against public issues in favour of his private self, as in 'my verweer teen die sosialisme' (my defence against socialism):

> die welsyn van die volk
> gaan my nie aan nie:
> ek stel slegs belang in die bekamping
> van die verspreiding van my skilfers
> die gewelddadige uitroei van my oorblywende aknee
> en die beswering van my ingroeitoonnaels
>
> (the welfare of the nation / does not concern me: / I am only interested in combating / the spread of my dandruff / the violent extermination of my remaining acne / and the exorcism of my ingrown toenails).

The reception of the Afrikaans literary text is guided by received notions of 'literature', 'aesthetics' and 'universality' and these serve as the fine sieve through which emergent literary expressions are filtered. Afrikaans texts with overt public concerns have often met with indignant critical response. It seems that overtly personal work can have the same effect. Oliphant (1986: 81) remarks on the reception of his poetry: 'The collection [*Bloed vloei in stilte*] probably received more attention than it merited, because it is a rare phenomenon: literary writing by a black man which cannot be recognized as such.'

In the case of black Afrikaans poetry of the 'private ache' one tends to look for idiosyncratic explications, when the attention should be directed at the nature of the environment giving rise to this poetry. Eagleton (1978: 75) suggests that: 'Our mistake was to search [the writer's] environment for an object to correlate with his gesture, rather than to grasp his gesturing as a relationship to the environment itself.' These poetic 'gestures' — as objects — are closely related to the dominant notions of aesthetics and the poetic art. Besides reflecting individual inclinations and preferences (deeply social phenomena in themselves), these 'gestures' can also be viewed as ways of negotiating the discourses of power, the dialogic interaction in Afrikaans literature and language. The poetry interlocks with traditional and current tendencies in Afrikaans poetry and satisfies dominant aesthetic value judgements in Afrikaans literary criticism. For black poets this may in part overcome the limitations of the publishers' market, and bring about a greater potential of insertion into the dominant Afrikaans literary canon. In this context it is then not coincidental that the collections of De Wette, Du Plessis and Oliphant were published by establishment Afrikaans publishers.

4

In relationships of power the dominated often find their reality interpreted for them by the dominant power. The first literary publication of a black Afrikaans poet, S.V. Petersen in 1944, was followed by an attempt to marginalize the concerns of his poetry, a response exemplified in the magisterial, Olympian judgement of Dekker (n.d.: 292):

> In the chorus of the recent poetry *the voice of the Coloured is also heard, as yet understandably untrained.* S.V. Petersen's (born 1914) *Die Enkeling* (The Loner) (1944) grabs our attention, because *for the first time in our language* the dreadful grief is articulated of those who are the victims of the sins of the fathers. *It is not yet true poetry.* Petersen *did not yet penetrate to the essence of art*: aesthetic embodiment of the emotion. These are *raw shrieks of revolt* against the 'curse of a dark skin' *in impotent rhetoric and conventional phrases in formless verse.* Also the endeavours to depict stormy nature scenes *remain too shrill* (my emphasis).

This evaluation of Petersen's work represents a strategy of exclusion under the guise of an aesthetic judgement. Similar strategies will be used against the writers who follow Petersen.

In the face of such strategies emerging black Afrikaans writers are engaged in attempts at defining their reality authoritatively *in Afrikaans*. Patrick Petersen in the foreword to his collection *Amandla Ngawethu* (c. 1985) affirms the role of a distinctive black Afrikaans poetry sprouting from the repressive political experience of black people: 'the black man's life in south africa is a never ending succession of humour with the world laughing along, of bitterness, fanatical hatred, colour apartheid in own quarters, endless love, hope, despair and finally death, a struggle for survival.' In this situation, according to Petersen, poetry has a very specific authoritative function: it is a 'mighty weapon, a messenger of the fighting voice, where the black (experience) cannot be a clone of the white (experience); through this black Afrikaans poetry becomes a force out of Africa for liberation; in this sense black Afrikaans poets have power'. As with their black English counterparts, a major part of that power consists in descriptive documentation of the apartheid experience, the marginalization of people, the greed of white people, the countless tales of terror and suffering.

Kenneth de Bruin in his 'swart kind' (black child) (*Skryf*, December 1987) depicts the essence of a black child's life and his momentary revolutionary desires shaped in a repressive environment:

in jou bors
swart kind
brand die begeerte vurig
en binne jou worstel
jy met jouself
'n AK
of 'n skermutseling
om jou persoonlike lewe
daar buite is 'n township
wat brand
daar buite is mense wat sterf
en net 'n dun lagie
van sy vel
dit is wat jou lewe werd is
swart kind
'n doodskoot uit die vuurwapen

(in your chest / black child / desire burns fiercely / and inside you're wrestling / with yourself / an AK / or a skirmish / for your personal life / outside the township / is burning / outside people die / and just a thin layer / of his skin / that is what your life is worth / black child / a deadly shot from a firearm).

The loss of a child is likened to the 'decayed foetus in the belly of the state' by Shawn Minnies (*Skryf*, December 1987):

treur nie o donker mamma
oor die verlies van jou kind
huil oor die verrotte fetus
in die pens van die staat

(don't mourn oh dark mama / over the loss of your child / wail for the decayed foetus / in the belly of the state).

The overpowering presence of the South African Defence Force in the townships is portrayed, in 'terreur' (terror), a poem by De Bruin (*Skryf*, December 1987), as an amorphous menace:

terreur kom stadig aangedreun
moeg van die gejag op die grens
tussen krale en vlugtende vrouens met honger kinders.

terreur kom dreigend nader
nader aan die protesterende township kinders,
gewalg deur leuens van die stelsel.

terreur neul al tergend,
vretend aan die siele en klippe wek ritme.
strate brand. skote knal. die township treur.

terreur glip terug na die grens.
protesterende kinders is dood.
terreur sal net 'n lagie verf makeer.

(terror drones slowly closer / tired of hunting on the border / between
the kraals and the fleeing women with hungry children. // terror closes
in threateningly / closer to the protesting township children, / sick-
ened by the lies of the system. // terror jeers tauntingly / gorging the
souls and stones trigger a rhythm. / streets are burning. shots ring
out. the township mourns. // terror slips back to the border. / protesting children are dead. / terror will only need a layer of paint.)

Even Clinton V. du Plessis whose *metier* is more nihilistic on occasion writes overtly political poems. In 'communique' (*Skryf*, December 1987) he depicts an Orwellian world of tyranny:

die dekreet is uitgevaardig:
in triplikaat versprei -
in die vrye volksrepubliek
gaan almal
voortaan donkergebril
blanko blaaie
in die koerante lees
doofstom luister na die nuus:
dat die son skyn,
dat daar sewe dae in 'n week is:
voortaan verkondig slegs die minister
die waarheid
streng volgens die vyfde
evangelie van
mickey mouse.

(the decree has been issued: / distributed in triplicate — / in the free
people's republic / everybody will / from now on wear dark glasses
/ read blank pages / in newspapers / listen deaf-mutely to the news:
/ that the sun shines / that there are seven days in a week: / from
now on only the minister will announce / the truth / strictly according to the fifth / gospel of / mickey mouse.)

Frank Anthony's *Robbeneiland my kruis my huis* (1983) is a poetic
report of his incarceration on Robben Island and brings, according
to Gerwel (1986: 20) 'an authentic black experience to Afrikaans writing'. The long title poem centres on the experience of the 'terrorist-
prisoner' on the Island:

o robbeneiland
my kruis
my huis
ek herstel
van eensame
opsluiting
ek voel
nie die gruwel
van die grasmat
nog ruik
ek die priemende
stank
van die balie
ek hou
my honger hande
oor die warm vlam
van die mensestem

(oh robben island / my affliction / my house / I'm recuperating / from
solitary / confinement / I do not feel / the evil / of the grass mat / or
smell / the piercing / stench / of the pail / I hold / my hungry hands
/ over the warm flame / of the human voice).

In response to state-sponsored violence there are indications of retri-
bution. Bertram Adams (*Skryf*, December 1987) rewrites Psalm 23
into ''n psalm vir die revolusie' (a psalm for the revolution):

p.w. is my herder
o alles ontbreek my
hy laat my opsluit in grysgroen selle;
na townships met onrus lei hy my heen
hy vermink my siel
hy lei my in die dooie spore van apartheid
om sy mags ontwil;
al gaan ek ook deur 'n kordon van polisiegeweld
ek sal geen caspir vrees nie,
want mandela is met my
sy pyn en sy straf, die verwek my
hy berei die Revolusie voor vir my
opstand teen die Staat;
p.w. is alweer besig met 'n Nuwe Bedeling
my gemoed loop oor;
net onmenslikheid en dood volg my
al die dae van my lewe
en ek sal in die huis van die dowe woon
tot in die aanvang van die revolusie . . .
AMANDLA!

(p.w. is my shepherd / oh, I want for everything / he causes me to
be locked up in grey-green cells; / he leads me to townships with un-

rest / he maims my soul / he leads me in the dead tracks of apartheid
/ for the sake of his power / though I go through a cordon of police
violence / I will fear no casspir, / for mandela is with me / his pain
and his punishment they spur me on / he prepares the Revolution
for me, for my / revolt against the State; / p.w. is busy again with
a New Dispensation / my heart runs over; / only inhumanity and death
follow me / all the days of my life / and I will dwell in the house of
the deaf / until the beginning of the revolution . . . / AMANDLA!)

Writing about the workplace among black Afrikaans poets is generally quite scarce. Snyders (1987: 4) is the one writer who constantly
asserts the necessity of writing about 'working class experience':
'Our relevance, as the youngest group of writers in the country,
lies firstly in a small beginning, similar to that of Afrikaner writers.
We are writing from our own working class experience.' He distances himself from the Afrikaans literary establishment and asserts
that

> I'm not trying to be a Van Wyk Louw or Opperman. I am in the serv-
> ice of ordinary people — not the literary establishment. If the lives
> of ordinary people are banal, or if I present their state as banal, then
> my writing is probably banal. But sometimes flowers do grow in the
> mud. And our appreciation of the flower depends on our experience
> of flowers. (Snyders, 1987: 4)

Snyders's collection, *'n Ordinary mens* (1982), consonant with his intention 'to give voice to the voiceless and to uplift the underdog',
is typified by the prominence of the ordinary person: the labourer,
workers as bus or train commuters, the gang-leader Kanna Groot-
vark, the rape victim, the street-cleaner and the disabled. Here is
an example: 'Dis-ability' (Snyders, 1982: 24).

Ek sit hiesa elke dag
onder die boem
met my doppie,
ek henner niemand nie.

Elke end van die maand
trek ek disability — nei,
war veterans —
dit betaal meerderer.

Ma kry nog maintenance grant vir Kettie,
sy's mos nog altyd onder Valkenberg,
maar ek is specially bly
dat Ma oek nou Old Age trek —
dis darem 'n ietsie meerder.

Ja, ek is heeltemal heppie
hier tussen die groente;
die goewerment sorg:
hy moet.

(I sit here every day / under the tree / with my shot (of wine), / I bother
no one. // At the end of every month / I draw my disability — no,
/ war veteran's — / it pays more. // Mom still gets the maintenance
grant for Kettie, / she's still at Valkenberg, / but I'm especially happy
/ that Mom's drawing Old Age as well now — / at least that's a bit
more. // Yes, I'm completely happy / here amongst the vegetables;
/ the government provides: / it has to.)

Despite the sympathetic intentions of the poet, his work in the end
describes a comfortless, unalterable environment which these disabled or working people cannot change or escape from. In the case
of John Fredericks ('Ek word vasgepen tussen die mure', I am
pinned between the walls, *Akuut*, September 1987) the worker expresses a desire to escape from his situation. He does not, as expected, long for a change in working conditions, but a flight to an
idyllic, romantic paradise:

Ek word vasgepen tussen die mure
die stof verwurg en bedek my hare

Ek wil wegkom
Ek wil wegbreek
van die gejaag
en opdragte van mense.

ek verlang na die koel
helder water van 'n bergstroom
wat kibbel oor die rotse.
ek verlang na lang gras
en groot bome langs riviere
vir kaalvoet loop sonder sorge.

Ja! ek verlang na vryheid
Ek, die fabrieksgevangene.

(I am pinned between the walls / the dust chokes and cloaks my hair
// I want to get away / I want to break loose / from the hustle / and
orders of people. // I long for the cool / clear water of a mountain
stream / lapping over rocks. / I yearn for long grass / and big trees
along rivers / for walking barefoot without problems. // Yes! I long
for freedom / I, the factory convict.)

The unemployed speaker in the poem 'Oop gemoed' (Open Mind)
by Marius F. Titus (1988: 75) is faced with a dishearteningly bleak

future. This frank and unaffected narrator — an alcoholic beggar —
is depicted not only in his poverty, but also as morally degenerate.
Addressing a middle-class listener — 'die hoës' — he says:

> Soe gie jou maar yt, en hou jou hoeg,
> ek vra nette vyfsent want my liewer is droeg.
>
> Hier lieg ekkie meer virrie Hylige Gies:
> Soe . . . dis bieter om openlik sleg te wies.
>
> (So you are pretending, and you're putting on airs / I only ask for
> five cents, because my liver is dry // Here I no longer lie to the Holy
> Spirit: / So . . . it is better to be openly sinful.)

The temptation is great for writers from the South African oppressed
community — more often than not middle-class writers from that
community — to depict their political experience and social life 'truth-
fully', without the pretences associated with 'die hoës'. However,
what this conveys to the middle-class reader is a stereotypical setting of poverty, neglect and moral decay. It would not be imprecise
to suggest that such a stereotypical view is in fact the dominant racial and class version of the black unemployed and worker's reality. This understanding of 'the reality' is determined by the poets'
class position, the Afrikaans literary tradition and the socially
dominant view of society.

Most of these poets are inserted within a middle-class environment, as teachers, priests or in other white-collar occupations, and
they tend to express their central socio-political concerns not in terms
of their relationship to the labour market but to the symbols of their
worth as human beings: 'to define yourself as human is to define
yourself in terms of the rights that are denied you' (Zulu, 1987: 34).
This desire for acknowledgement is most evidently expressed in
Leonard Koza's poem, 'Ag wanneer' (Oh, when, *Akuut*, March
1987):

> Wanneer gaan die vaal mis weg sak
> Wat my uitsig verhinder en gees beknop
> Wanneer gaan die son opkom
> Sodat ek kan sien waar ware gedagtes sweef
> Wat diep denkende wesens verstandelik laat leef
> Wanneer word ek verlos van die drukkende bande
> Wat my permanent beperk tot eiesoortige leed en skande
> Ag wanneer gaan ek ook langs die ronde tafel
> Sit en bepeins om daaglikse probleme te ontrafel
> Ag wanneer gaan ek ook saam wette maak
> Na my geestelike skikking en kulturele smaak
> Wanneer, wanneer, ag wanneer

(When will the grey fog settle / which obstructs my view and throt-
tles my mind / when will the sun rise / so that I can see where true
ideas float / allowing deep-thinking beings to live in a cerebral way
/ when will I be delivered from these pressing bonds / which permanently restrict me to a suffering and shame all my own / oh when
will I also sit at the round table / and ponder how to unravel daily
problems / oh when will I co-legislate laws / according to my mental
needs and cultural tastes / when, when, oh when.)

In asserting the 'power of the poets' black Afrikaans writers have
generally attempted to depict their environment, thus contributing
towards a body of South African literature documenting and high-
lighting the plight of the oppressed; and, by making this contribution in Afrikaans, they have sought to express the apartheid experience authoritatively from within. This does not imply that the
experience of apartheid is alike for all black people. Different class
and racial positions, unequal access to education, the rural-urban
divide and varying political orientations among other factors prevent the 'black experience of apartheid' from being uniform. Most
black Afrikaans poets have been relatively well-educated individuals. They may not be representative of all black Afrikaans speakers,
and the black working class in particular. But they do derive a degree
of authority in a situation where, in the words of Patrick Petersen,
'the black experience cannot be a clone of the white experience'.

But as Schulz (1984: 211) suggests 'authority — like any form of
power — requires the consent of another'. In this power relationship an establishment Afrikaans publisher remarked in a telling reference to black Afrikaans poetry that

> poetry of the struggle is necessary. But most of the poetry of this type
> that I have seen made a monotonous impression. It is written in the
> same shrill, protest tone. That is why it is called *sonbesie-poësie* (cica-
> da poetry). . . . It is a noise that you are conscious of; but you do
> not pay close attention to it. (Fryer, 1988)

At base in this evaluation, despite the presumed aesthetic criteria,
is the dominant-dominated discourse: the dominant seeking to define the dominated's experience. The same strategies of exclusion
we noted earlier are operative here. An attempt is being made to
short-circuit the black Afrikaans poets' authority to express their experience of apartheid from within. Instructively Schulz (1984: 211)
further notes that

> Writers redefining their experience often become enraged at the cul-
> tural model they are renouncing, and their writing is likely to be

characterized negatively as being shrill — said of the feminists — or strident — said of Blacks. However it is characterized, the tone sets such writing apart from that of the established writers.

Conclusion

This essay has demonstrated the dialogical relationship between the established Afrikaans literary tradition and emergent black Afrikaans poets. The emergence of these poets over the last decade cannot be seen outside the context of the confident and vociferous upsurge of the broadly defined democratic forces against the established political and economic system. Whereas the ruling order is engaged in various efforts to legitimate its continued hegemony and control, an oppositional political culture is burgeoning, essentially undermining the established value system.

The nascent notions of people's culture and people's education, the intensification of a sanguine oppositional political culture and the development of a strong working class movement are all indications of the deep and fundamental shifts that are taking place in South Africa. The formerly muffled, marginalized voices of black people are increasingly raised as a confident counterhegemonic voice. Black Afrikaans writers are very much part of these broader attempts to redefine, reappropriate and control South African political and social life.

Moreover, within the dialogical relationship of the established Afrikaans literary tradition and emergent black Afrikaans poets the existing discourses of power play a significant role in determining the degree of penetration of emergent literary activity. Subtle strategies of exclusion could lead on the one hand to marginalization and 'invisibility', or on the other to appropriation by 'an enfeebled and asphyxiating "high culture"' (Jameson, 1981: 87). In both instances the polemic and subversive potential of these creative utterances may be severely curtailed.

Black Afrikaans writers, sustained in their literary activity by received notions and traditions of established Afrikaans literature, have not fully explored literary influences outside the realm of Afrikaans literature. Their efforts to define their own position in relation to the dominant cultural and political powers can only benefit from greater involvement in a larger, more comprehensive South African literature, drawing on and contributing to the struggles waged in other areas of culture.

Notes

1. This does not imply that this situation is the result of a natural process. Writing is influenced by material conditions such as access to education, access to publication and broadly the politico-ideological criteria determining the scope and nature of 'literature'. Consequently this situation is influenced by fluctuations and changes within these variables.
2. Brink (1988: 28) comments as follows on the official version of history and the silences on the role and place of black people in the history of Afrikaans: 'An aspect of Afrikanerskap and Afrikaans . . . is simply the fact that in all officially recorded statistics on the Great Trek etc. only whites are accounted for: this became the "official" history. But constantly there was also an unofficial history, based on the basic fact that on the Great Trek and similar historical adventures, a very large percentage of non-white Afrikaans speakers were present. . . . All along they also contributed in co-shaping the language: forging it to what it has become, fathoming its potential, exploring its horizons. As regards *language* they were not the "servants" to which the official history damned them: they were worthy — and in many cases probably decisive — co-creators and co-formulators.'

    Research into the non-Germanic, African and Asian origins, linguistic structure and influences of Afrikaans as well as the manipulative process of 'Dutchification' of the language (see Uys, 1983) has been neglected. The re-evaluation and rewriting of the essentially Afrikaner-centred history of Afrikaans should however prompt new interest in these disregarded areas.
3. Countering a possible charge that this position represents an updated, reified form of apartheid identities Williams (1987: 13) asserts that 'I am not upholding "coloured chauvinism" or "colouredism" encouraged by the enemy. Nor am I suggesting that the various national groups exist in isolated watertight compartments. Of course, they interact, they mix, they influence each other. In language, music, acceptance of common leadership etc., a unified South African culture is emerging. But, we as activists and cultural workers, we cannot force the process and isolate ourselves from the masses.'
4. See the publications, e.g. 'Ons leer mekaar', of the Samewerkingsgroep vir Afrikaanse Geletterdheid, Rondebosch.
5. Oliphant (1986: 82) states that, 'The first Afrikaans writer I read of my own volition is André P. Brink. I am not referring here to Brink's later "committed" work, but his earlier novels such as *Die Ambassadeur* (*File of a Diplomat/The Ambassador*). Brink's influence on me was considerable, particularly because of the way in which I grew up in my rural town. There you lived only in a boss/boy relationship to white people. You were conditioned through this lifestyle to a perception of whites as superior. Through reading Brink's books I realized for the first time that white people are people like ourselves: there are not weaknesses to which they, because of their skin colour, are not inclined. In other words, I was liberated in this way of a stereotyped perception of my fellow human beings.'
6. Compare Rademeyer (1938: 11-12): 'The coloured language of our country has as yet not enjoyed [our] attention and all along served one pur-

pose only: to amuse! That the coloured sometimes expresses his thoughts in a very comical manner, that his descriptions leave nothing to be desired in terms of originality, that he frequently uses expressions and turns of phrase which may be strange to the white man and are *thus* calculated to raise laughs [om die lagspiere te prikkel], almost every white inhabitant of the country knows.' Rademeyer's (1938: 22-23) racist prejudices and patronizing proclivities surface clearly when he attempts an 'ethnographic' description of the speakers of his subject matter: 'The ongoing misfortunes and changes in fate of this group of creatures [klompie wesens] need not be recounted much further. Suffice to say that they are today a wretched and degenerate group of human beings ['n rampsalige en ontaarde groepie mensekinders], whose laziness, lewdness and tendency to waste seem to be innate. Co-operation towards a common goal they do not understand: they are recalcitrant and always argue among themselves; reliability and honesty are virtues which one would seek in vain among them; because they lost their land through their own ignorance and thoughtlessness, they have a thousand and one grievances against the white people; hard liquor is their idol and jeremiads their greatest consolation in this vale of tears of unrighteousness. In short, the impression one gets is that they are doomed, sooner or later, to total extinction.'

Half a century later the eminent Afrikaans literary historian, Kannemeyer (1983: 292) accepts uncritically similar racial prejudices, e.g. 'the *piquant use of language of the coloured* suggested through "phonetic" spelling' (my italics). For more examples see Kannemeyer (1983: 19, 276-277, 432). Van de Rheede (1986: 34) argues that Kaaps should be described in terms of socio-economic indexes instead of ethnic ones: language is acquired within a specific socio-political context and 'colouredness' is not a prerequisite for a specific variant of Afrikaans. For further linguistic opposition to the concept of *kleurling-Afrikaans* see De Klerk (1968).

7. At about the same time the *Ashrakal*, a praise poem to the prophet Mohammed, in the self-same proletarian speech was reputed to have been recited in the mosques of Cape Town (see Coetzee, 1988: 50-51).

8. Small is obviously aware of the class nature of Kaaps in his poetry collections and *Kanna hy kô hystoe*. Virtually all his overtly political poems are written in patois, whereas the more personal and private lyrical poems are written in the 'standard' variant of Afrikaans, signalling the implied class position of the different narrators. The main character in his drama *Kanna hy kô hystoe* uses both the patois and the 'standard' variant. The patois serves as token of identification with his poor family members whilst the 'standard' variant indicates class and social distance.

9. Analogous to the 'emotive and cognitive structures' in ideological discourse, according to Eagleton, are those of literary discourse. The cognitive structure of a text's ideological discourse could be defined as the conscious textual objective to describe a particular world or theme. The emotive structure could be defined as the unconscious decision or closure according to which the described world is organized. The emotive structure could be seen as a product of will or desire to impose relative coherence on the position of the individual or his class (see Eagleton, 1979: 63-68 and JanMohamed, 1983: 266-267).

10. Laughter as a device can be a powerful means of criticism in cultural expression. In this poem, and in poems of this sub-genre, laughter more often than not serves to conform to ruling class perceptions. Instructively Horn (1987: 10-11) remarks that 'the most superficial acquaintance with the way in which the workers of all ages created their own cultural forms will show that the central element of any people's culture is laughter, and thus criticism and subversion. From the ancient carnivals to the most modern forms of people's culture this laughter, in which all rules of the church, or morals and standards of the ruling class are revoked, was the one thing which made bourgeois intellectuals most uncomfortable. This culture of laughter is no less great culture than the culture of tragedy and blood: it is serious in its rejection and criticism.'

11. In fairness: Titus and Snyders are not totally oblivious of the implications of written patois. In 'Of hoe?' ('What do you say?') Snyders (1982: 3) grasps the potential for satirizing and subverting stereotypes: 'Moetie rai gammat-taal gebrykie; / dit issie mooi nie: / dit dieghreid die coloured mense — / of hoe? // wat traai djy / om 'n coloured culture te create? / of dink djy is snaaks / om soe te skryf? / of hoe? // Traai om ons liewerste op te lig; / os praat mossie soe nie . . .? / of hoe?' (Don't use that gammat lingo; / it's not nice: / it degrades the coloured people — / what do you say? // are you trying / to create a coloured culture / or do you think it's funny / to write like that? / or what? // rather try to uplift us; / we don't talk like that . . .? what do you say?)

In 'Potjiekos' (Stew in a three-legged pot on an open fire) Titus (1988: 73) exploits ironically the incidence of poorer people cooking their food (usually a stew) in three-legged iron pots on open fires, a practice which recently found its way to the patios of plush suburban homes. This poem juxtaposes the two lifestyles: 'Dan . . . assie vrouens innie potte roer, / dan maak ôs kos, / potjiekos my broer. / Nou hoor ek die whaities maak oek soe, / sieke by ôs gesien wat en hoe: // shame, dan keer hille oek maar sieke / tienie koud ennie starvation.' (Then . . . when the women are stirring the pots, / then we're making food, / potjiekos, my pal. / Now I hear the whites are doing the same, / probably got it from us — saw how and what to do: // shame, then they're probably also shielding / against the cold and starvation.)

However, these poems are exceptions and the bulk of their work veers towards the formulaic and naturalistic depiction of 'reality'.

References

Anthony, Frank. 1983. *Robbeneiland my kruis my huis*. Kasselsvlei: Kampen.

Bannerji, Himani. 1984. 'Language and Liberation: A Study of Political Theatre in West Bengal'. *Ariel*, 15(4), 131-144.

Belcher, Ronnie. 1987. 'Afrikaans en kommunikasie oor die kleurgrens'. In Du Plessis, Hans and Theo du Plessis (eds). *Afrikaans en Taalpolitiek*. Pretoria: HAUM, 17-34.

Benson, N. 1988. 'Tree na Vryheid'. *The Educational Journal*, October-November, 9-10, 14.

Boezak, André. 1988. *Aankoms uit die skemer*. St Helena Bay: Prog.

Botha, Keriesa. 1987. 'A learner-centred Afrikaans course'. *Language Projects Review*, 2. Observatory: National Language Project, 18-19.

Brink, André. 1984. 'The Future of Afrikaans'. *Leadership*, 3(2), 28-36.

Brink, André. 1988. 'Afrikaans en bevryding'. In Van den Heever, Randall. *Afrikaans en bevryding*. Kasselsvlei: CTPA, 23-39.

Coetzee, Ampie. 1988. 'Afrikaans — dit is ons erns'. In Erasmus, G.F. *Afrikaans: Horisonne en Ideale*. Paarl: Afrikaanse Taalfonds, 47-52.

Davids, Achmat. 1987. 'The Role of Afrikaans in the History of the Cape Muslim Community'. In Du Plessis, Hans and Theo du Plessis (eds). *Afrikaans en Taalpolitiek*. Pretoria: HAUM, 37-59.

Dekker, G. n.d. *Afrikaanse Literatuurgeskiedenis*. Cape Town: Nasou.

De Klerk, W.J. 1968. 'Die aard van dialektiese verskeidenheid in Afrikaans'. University of Pretoria: unpublished Ph.D. dissertation.

De Vries, Jonathan. 1988. 'Defining people's culture'. *South*, 22-28 September.

De Wette, Julian. 1980. *Verban: Verbinne*. Johannesburg: Perskor.

Du Plessis, Clinton V. 1984. *Geloofbelydenis van 'n kluisenaar*. Cape Town: Perskor.

Du Plessis, L.T. 1986. *Afrikaans in beweging*. Bloemfontein: Patmos.

Du Plessis, Hans and Theo du Plessis (eds). 1987. *Afrikaans en Taalpolitiek*. Pretoria: HAUM.

Eagleton, Terry. 1978. *Criticism and Ideology*. London: Verso.

Eagleton, Terry. 1979. 'Ideology, Fiction, Narrative'. *Social Text*, 2, 62-80.

Fasold, Ralph. 1984. *The Sociolinguistics of Society*. London: Basil Blackwell.

February, Vernie. 1979. *O, Snotverdriet*. Haarlem: In de Knipscheer.

Fryer, Charles. 1988. 'Digters nie op kleur getakseer'. *Die Burger*, 30 September.

Gerwel, G.J. 1986. 'Van Petersen tot die hede: 'n kritiese bestekopname'. In Smith, Julian F. *et al.* (eds). *Swart Afrikaanse Skrywers*. Bellville: University of the Western Cape, 11-22.

Goldin, Ian. 1987. *Making Race: The Politics of Coloured Identity in South Africa*. Cape Town: Maskew Miller-Longman.

Harlow, Barbara. 1987. *Resistance Literature*. New York: Methuen.

Hirson, Baruch. 1979. *Year of Fire, Year of Ash*. London: Zed.

Hofmeyr, Isabel. 1987. 'Building a nation from words: Afrikaans language, literature and ethnic identity, 1902-1924'. In Marks, Shula and Stanley Trapido (eds). *The Politics of Race, Class and Nationalism in Twentieth Century South Africa*. London: Longman, 95-123.

Horn, Peter. 1987. 'Art is like breathing freely: the necessity of a people's culture'. Mimeo.

Jameson, Fredric. 1971. *Marxism and Form*. Princeton: Princeton University Press.

Jameson, Fredric. 1981. *The Political Unconscious*. London: Methuen.

Jameson, Fredric and James Kavanagh. 1984. 'The Weakest Link: Marxism in Literary Studies'. In Ollman, Bretell and Edward Vernoff. *The Left Academy: Marxist Scholarship on American campuses*. New York: McGraw-Hill, 1-23.

JanMohamed, Abdul. 1983. *Manichean Aesthetics. The Politics of Literature in Colonial Africa*. Amherst: University of Massachusetts Press.

Jansen, Beverley. 1986. 'Swart Afrikaanse skrywers en hulle ambag'. In Smith, Julian F. *et al.* (eds). *Swart Afrikaanse Skrywers*. Bellville: University of the Western Cape, 79-81.

Kannemeyer, J.C. 1983. *Geskiedenis van die Afrikaanse Literatuur*. Pretoria: Academica.

Koza, Leonard. 1984. 'Ontmoet vir Leonard Koza'. *Die Burger-ekstra*, 13 June.

Lewis, Gavin. 1987. *Between the Wire and the Wall: A History of South African 'Coloured' Politics*. Cape Town: David Philip.

Lodge, Tom. 1983. *Black Politics in South Africa since 1945*. Johannesburg: Ravan.

Magubane, Bernard Makhosezwe. 1979. *The Political Economy of Race and Class in South Africa*. New York: Monthly Review Press.

Makeba, Miriam. 1988. (with James Hall) *Makeba: my story*. Johannesburg: Skotaville.

Michels, Quentin. 1987. Untitled. *UWC News*. Bellville: UWC.

Ndebele, Njabulo. 1985. 'Noma Award — Acceptance Speech'. *Staffrider*, 6(2), 39-40.

Nixon, Rob. 1987. 'Optimistic Tragedies'. *The Nation*, New York, 24 October, 453-454.

Oliphant, Vincent. 1983. *Bloed vloei in stilte*. Cape Town: Tafelberg.

Oliphant, Vincent. 1986. 'Swart Afrikaanse skrywers en hulle ambag'. In Smith, Julian F. *et al.* (eds). *Swart Afrikaanse Skrywers*. Bellville: University of the Western Cape, 81-83.

Petersen, Patrick. c. 1985. *Amandla Ngawethu*. Genadendal: Morawiese Boekhandel.

Petersen, Patrick. 1988. 'Digbundel vertel wat hul mense beleef'. *Die Burger*, 16 July.

Ponelis, F.A. 1987. 'Die eenheid van die Afrikaanse taalgemeenskap'. In Du Plessis, Hans and Theo du Plessis (eds). *Afrikaans en Taalpolitiek*. Pretoria: HAUM, 3-15.

Prinsloo, K.P. and M.C.J. van Rensburg. 1984. *Afrikaans: stand, taak en toekoms*. Pretoria: HAUM.

Rademeyer, J.H. 1938. *Kleurling-Afrikaans — Die taal van die Griekwas en Rehoboth-Basters*. Amsterdam: N.V. Swets & Zeitlinger.

Rive, Richard. 1986. 'Culture, Colouredism, Kaaps'. In Smith, Julian F. *et al.* (eds). *Swart Afrikaanse Skrywers*. Bellville: University of the Western Cape, 60-68.

Schulz, Muriel. 1984. 'Minority writers: the Struggle for Authenticity and Authority'. In Kramarae, Cheris; Muriel Schulz and William O'Barr (eds). *Language and Power*. Beverley Hills: Sage Publications, 206-217.

Small, Adam. 1973. *Kitaar my kruis*. Cape Town: HAUM.

Smith, Julian; Alwyn van Gensen and Hein Willemse (eds). 1986. *Swart Afrikaanse Skrywers*. Bellville: University of the Western Cape.

Snyders, Peter. 1982. *'n Ordinary mens*. Cape Town: Tafelberg.

Snyders, Peter. 1984. 'Die rol van die skrywer vandag'. *Die Burger*, 29 February.

Snyders, Peter. 1987. 'Mening'. *Akuut*, 1(4), 4-5.

Steyn, J.C. 1980. *Tuiste in eie taal: die behoud en bestaan van Afrikaans*. Cape Town: Tafelberg.

Titus, Marius F. 1988. In *Aankoms uit die skemer*. St Helena Bay: Prog.

Uys, Mariette D. 1983. *Die vernederlandsing van Afrikaans*. University of Pretoria: unpublished D. Litt. dissertation.

Van den Heever, C.M. and P.J. Nienaber. 1949. *Bloemlesing Uit Die Gedigte Van Jan F.E. Cilliers*. Johannesburg: Afrikaanse Pers-Boekhandel.

Van den Heever, Randall. 1987. *Treë na Vryheid*. Kasselsvlei: CTPA.
Van den Heever, Randall. 1988. *Afrikaans en bevryding*. Kasselsvlei: CTPA.
Van de Rheede, I. 1986. 'Kaapse Afrikaans: 'n sosio-politieke perspektief'. In Smith, Julian F. *et al.* (eds). *Swart Afrikaanse Skrywers*. Bellville: University of the Western Cape, 34-39.
Wescott, Shauna. 1988. *The Trial of the Thirteen*. Mowbray: Black Sash.
Willemse, Hein. 1986. 'Neigings en opvattinge by jonger swart Afrikaanse skrywers — 'n voorlopige verkenning'. In Smith, Julian F. *et al.* (eds). *Swart Afrikaanse Skrywers*. Bellville: University of the Western Cape, 69-76.
Willemse, Hein. 1987. 'The Black Afrikaans Writer: A Continuing Dichotomy'. *TriQuarterly*, 69, 236-246.
Willemse, Hein. 1988. ''n Kritiese bestekopname van huidige swart Afrikaanse digwerk'. In Wiehahn, Rialette and P.H. Roodt. *Teks en Tendens*. Durban: Owen Burgess, 81-94.
Williams, Alex. 1987. 'Toyi-Toyi to the goema-goema beat'. *New Era*, 2(2).
Wiltshire, Jan. 1985. *Die verkeerde land/Das Verkehrte Land*. Erfstadt: Lukassen.
Zulu, Paul. 1987. 'Black youth — a profile'. *Die Suid-Afrikaan*, 10.